Problem-Driven Political Economy Analysis

DIRECTIONS IN DEVELOPMENT
Public Sector Governance

Problem-Driven Political Economy Analysis

The World Bank's Experience

Verena Fritz, Brian Levy, and Rachel Ort, Editors

THE WORLD BANK
Washington, D.C.

ISBN (paper): 978-1-4648-0121-1
ISBN (electronic): 978-1-4648-0122-8
DOI: 10.1596/978-1-4648-0121-1

Cover photo: © "One Out of the Crowd" (1993) by El Anatsui, Ghana/World Bank Art Program. Used with permission from El Anatsui; further permission required for reuse.

Cover design: Debra Naylor, Naylor Design, Inc.

Library of Congress Cataloging-in-Publication Data

Problem-driven political economy analysis : the World Bank's experience / Verena Fritz, Brian Levy, and Rachel Ort, editors.
        pages cm. — (Directions in development)
    Includes bibliographical references.
ISBN 978-1-4648-0121-1 (alk. paper) — ISBN 978-1-4648-0122-8
    1. Developing countries—Economic policy—Case studies. 2. Infrastructure (Economics)—Developing countries—Management—Case studies. I. Fritz, Verena, editor of compilation. II. Levy, Brian, 1954- editor of compilation. III. Ort, Rachel, editor of compilation.
    HC59.7.P72127 2014
    338.9109172′4—dc23   2013043834

Contents

Boxes

Figures

Foreword

I welcome this volume as a valuable contribution to an ongoing effort among development practitioners to adapt our operations and engagement strategies to the context in which we work. This volume addresses the dual challenge of identifying the binding constraints to improved development outcomes and finding politically feasible ways to address those constraints.

Attention to the political and economic incentives that drive policy making and development outcomes has increased among donors over the past 10 years. Significant exploration of a more politically informed approach to development has occurred both within the World Bank and among other donor agencies. This effort began in the early 2000s with the United Kingdom's Department for International Development's *Drivers of Change*. It gained significant momentum at the World Bank after the adoption of the Governance and Anticorruption Strategy in 2007.

Why did reforms in Papua New Guinea fail to strengthen the ability of communities to gain access to funds? Chapter 8 shows that the allocation of project funding continued to depend on (a) the community's relationship with its representative in the national parliament; (b) from an analysis of the incentives, the proposed grants targeted directly to the ward level rather than the district level; and (c) the public information provided on local infrastructure allocation decisions. Why were new investments in commercial agriculture in Ghana limited, even though national political commitments and economic policies were favorable to large-scale investments in the sector? Chapter 6 illuminates how the absence of formal property rights in land at the local level can leave multiple stakeholders with veto power over new investments. Rather than investors acquiring large tracts of land, the analysis recommends that they take advantage of existing ownership patterns through contract farming, a model in which investors supply inputs and, in return, farmers grow and resell crops to the investors.

Through these and other selected cases, this volume brings together examples of operationally oriented political economy analysis conducted under the umbrella of the World Bank. The analyses included in the volume all begin with a very specific development challenge or opportunity and use this circumstance to guide the focus of their analytic work. They seek to identify the incentives and constraints that shape the behavior of the key governmental and nongovernmental actors associated with the challenge, and they seek to locate these incentives in the broader political economy environment—giving attention to formal and informal dimensions. Critically, rather than asserting that constraints are insurmountable, these analyses suggest practical approaches to adapting policy dialogue and operations.

Nick P. Manning
Head
Governance & Public Sector Management Practice
The World Bank

Acknowledgments

This volume grew out of an April 2012 conference in Washington, D.C., on the impact of political economy analysis on World Bank operations. We would like to thank all who participated in the conference. Their insightful comments and enthusiasm for developing good practice examples of this type of analytic work convinced us to put together the present volume.

The Governance Partnership Facility (GPF) and its donors—the United Kingdom, the Netherlands, Australia, and Norway—provided generous financial support for this effort, including the April 2012 conference, several of the studies included in this volume, and the development of the volume itself. We are very grateful for the GPF's contributions that made the development and publication of this volume possible, as well as to Piet Hein van Heesewijk and others from the GPF secretariat.

We would also like to express our appreciation for the guidance provided by Nick Manning and Linda van Gelder, directors of the World Bank's Poverty Reduction and Economic Management Governance & Public Sector Management Practice at various stages of the project. In addition, Bob Beschel, governance cluster leader, offered helpful advice. Aditi Hate supported the conference and the initial stages of the work on this volume. Furthermore, we would like to thank Laryssa Chiu for her continuous excellent administrative support and Stephen McGroarty, editor in the World Bank's Publishing and Knowledge Division, for shepherding the volume to the publication stage.

Our motivation for this volume has greatly benefited from the enthusiasm of many World Bank staff members as well as from many experts elsewhere to strengthen the ability of international aid organizations to become more aware of how the incentives and constraints grounded in political economy dynamics affect development efforts and to engage productively with such dynamics. In particular, we are grateful to the external reviewers, Tim Kelsall, Tom Carothers, and Diane de Gramont for their feedback. The volume is much improved thanks to their insightful advice. As usual, all remaining errors are those of the authors and editors.

Finally, we would like to thank the more than 300 staff members who, since 2009, have been part of the World Bank's Political Economy Community of Practice and have helped build momentum for the work that led to the conference and this volume.

Abbreviations

£	pound (Ghana)
₱	peso (the Philippines)
AEIH	Asociación de Empresas Industriales de Herrera
APC	All People's Congress
CAS	Country Assistance Strategy
CAZ	Communications Authority of Zambia
CDEEE	Corporación Dominicana de Empresas Eléctricas Estatales (Dominican Corporation of State Electricity Companies)
CEC	Copperbelt Energy Corporation
CMP	Child Money Program
CMU	country management unit
CNE	National Energy Commission
COMECON	Council for Mutual Economic Assistance
CONEP	the Dominican Republic's national business council
CPP	Convention People's Party (Ghana)
CSO	civil society organizations
CT	Country Team
DBM	Development Bank of Mongolia
DFID	U.K. Department for International Development
DH	dirham (Morocco)
DILG	Department of Interior and Local Governments
DOH	Department of Health
DP/MDC	Democratic Party/Motherland Democratic Coalition
DPWH	Department of Public Works and Highways (the Philippines)
DU	Democratic Union (Mongolia)
ECD	early childhood development
EDE	electricity distribution entity
ENIGH	Encuesta Nacional de Ingresos y Gastos de los Hogares, or National Income and Expenditure Household Survey
ERI	Economic Research Institute

ERP	Economic Recovery Program (Ghana)
ESW	Economic and Sector Work (Sierra Leone)
EU	European Union
FY	fiscal year
GDP	gross domestic product
HDF	Human Development Fund
IADB	Inter-American Development Bank
IBRD	International Bank for Reconstruction and Development (maps)
IDSS	the Dominican Republic's social security institute
IMF	International Monetary Fund
IPAC	Participative Anti-Corruption Initiative
IRA	Internal Revenue Allotment (the Philippines)
JDPBPC	Joint District Planning and Budget Priorities Committee
K	kina (Papua New Guinea)
K	kwacha (Zambia)
km	kilometer
kWh	kilowatt-hour
LAC	Latin America and the Caribbean
LC	local council
LCE	local chief executive
LGC	Local Government Code (the Philippines)
LGU	local government unit (the Philippines)
LHB	local health board
LLG	Local-level Government
LPV	Limited Preferential Voting
MCA	multicorrespondence analysis
MDC	Motherland Democratic Coalition (Mongolia)
MED	Ministry of Economic Development
MENA	Middle East and North Africa
MEPD	Ministry of Economy, Planning, and Development
MMD	Movement for Multi-party Democracy (Zambia)
MNDP	Mongolian (National) Democratic Party
MoEWR	Ministry of Energy and Water Resources (Sierra Leone)
MP	member of parliament
MPRP	Mongolian Peoples' Revolutionary Party
MSDP	Mongolian Social Democratic Party
MW	megawatt
NDC	National Democratic Congress (Ghana)
NDIC	National Development and Innovation Committee

NGA	national government agency
NGO	nongovernmental organization
NPA	National Power Authority (Sierra Leone)
NPC	National Power Company (Sierra Leone)
NPP	New Patriotic Party (Ghana)
OC	Coordination Entity
ODA	official development assistance
OPPPI	Office for Promoting Private Power Investment (Zambia)
PAD	project assessment document
PC	Paramount Chief
PCN	Project Concept Note
PDAF	Priority Development Assistance Fund (the Philippines)
PEA	political economy analysis
PIN	Pre-Identification Note
PLD	Dominican Liberation Party
PRA	Programa de Reducción de Apagones
PRD	Dominican Revolutionary Party
RAMED	Regime d'Assistance Médicale pour les Economiquement
RD$	pesos (the Dominican Republic)
RMFA	Road Maintenance Fund Administration (Sierra Leone)
RUF	Revolutionary United Front
SADA	Savannah Accelerated Development Authority (Ghana)
SAP	structural adjustment program
SENASA	the Dominican Republic's national health insurance program
SERCE	Second Regional Comparative and Explanatory Study
SIE	Superintendence of Electricity
SLPP	Sierra Leone People's Party
SLRA	Sierra Leone Roads Authority
Tog	togrog (Mongolia)
UGCC	United Gold Coast Convention
UNIP	United National Independence Party (Zambia)
WDC	Ward Development Committee
WPT	Windfall Profits Tax
ZESCO	Zambia Electricity Supply Corporation

CHAPTER 1

Problem-Driven Political Economy in Action: Overview and Synthesis of the Case Studies

Verena Fritz and Brian Levy

The fox knows many things, but the hedgehog knows one big thing.

—Isaiah Berlin

Introduction

Why does development progress in some places but not others? Very often, the distinguishing factor is not a lack of financial resources or of knowledge about the *right* technical solution. Rather, a crucial distinguishing factor for whether and where progress happens is how incentives and constraints shape the willingness and ability of national or local elites to act in pursuit of development goals.

Governments may decide to allocate agricultural services to their core supporters or to key swing voters and to deny them to others, thereby reducing the incentive for farmers to seek increases in productivity. Social health insurance benefits may be extended ahead of elections, but removed once elections have taken place. Procurement decisions may be skewed for the private benefit of those involved or for the financing of ever more costly electoral campaigns. At the same time, political incentives play a powerful role not only in frustrating development efforts, but also in shaping opportunities for change. Often, there are various stakeholders—within government, in the private sector, and in civil society—who want to change what government does for the better. However, in many situations, advice based on technically optimal solutions is not that helpful for potential reformers because such solutions may not be politically feasible

The findings, interpretations, and conclusions contained in this synthesis report are entirely those of the authors. They do not necessarily represent the view of the World Bank, its executive directors, or the countries they represent. The World Bank is not responsible for the contents of this research.

or may even backfire and have unintended negative consequences. Applied political economy analysis (PEA) therefore holds considerable promise to help identify what policy responses and strategies are most likely to work for addressing difficult and persistent development challenges.

The general problem that political incentives are frequently at odds with a technocratic approach to development has long been recognized. Politicians prefer policies and seek institutional changes that support their current needs, including exigencies such as horse trading when negotiating over policies with other powerful stakeholders or designing intergovernmental relations with a view to maintaining some form of centralized control, rather than optimizing service delivery.

At the same time, the interests of politicians can also broadly converge with development objectives, such as seeking to deliver growth, jobs, or social protection benefits as a way to secure legitimacy or reelection. But even when politicians seek development progress, they may struggle to pursue these goals effectively because of the need to maintain the support of vested interests, including pressures for favor from family members or close allies; to lead difficult-to-manage coalition governments; or to navigate a difficult mix of fiscal problems and public discontent.

The rediscovery of the importance of political economy has been part of a broader movement of rethinking development. In the 1970s, donor agencies and other development practitioners sought to sidestep politics as much as possible and focus advice on technical questions and solutions, both because political incentives appeared so frequently incompatible with development in the public interest and because politics had become so deeply entangled with foreign policy considerations at the time. In the 1980s, structural adjustment considerations dominated (especially, but not only, in the World Bank) as a policy paradigm for countries seeking broad-based development, including a strong focus on the need to roll back the state. Furthermore, neoclassical economics aimed at *constraining* political decision-making powers through mechanisms such as independent regulation, "getting the prices right," and so on as the best solution for many policy areas. Although such a perspective has merits, in many instances the underlying political drivers are too strong for technical constraints on politics to have their intended effects.

Over the past quarter century, recognition has grown that institutions—the rules of the game—matter. Institutions underpin markets and provide the framework within which the bureaucracy acts and political contestation plays out. Good governance moved to center stage in the development discourse as part of an extended ("structural adjustment plus") Washington Consensus. Initially, the hope was that governance represented a new development magic bullet. However, it became increasingly evident that using a technically strong design combined with importing the proper legal and regulatory rules were not sufficient to develop good institutions. Behind institutions lie politics: effective institutional (and policy) reform requires coming to grips with the political underpinnings and the drivers that shape how institutions develop and how decisions are made as well as how de jure institutions are used de facto.

Given this challenge, there has been an increasing effort to better understand stakeholder incentives and the way they shape institutions. Why do good policies and effective institutions emerge in some places, even though these changes typically entail some powerful losers? What is blocking reforms in other places, and what could be done about it? Such questions are at the heart of a political economy perspective on development. The premise of PEA for development effectiveness is that it is important to understand how such political incentives shape decisions and to build an awareness of political constraints—as well as opportunities—into the provision of advice and development engagement.

These insights have triggered a search for how political economy challenges can be included more explicitly in the operational approaches of development agencies. There has been cumulative learning over time on these issues, and this process is continuing (see also Desai 2011; Carothers and de Gramont 2013; Harris and Booth 2013).[1] In the early to mid-2000s, the U.K. Department for International Development's (DFID) Drivers of Change analytic work constituted the first time that a major development agency invested seriously in PEA. In parallel, the World Bank undertook a number of initial Institutional and Governance Reviews, the Swedish International Development Cooperation Agency undertook its power analysis, and, a few years later, the Netherlands initiated its Strategic Governance and Corruption Analysis. The learning process has also included substantial cross-fertilization between academics and development practitioners (although even more could still happen in this regard).[2]

In the late 2000s, the World Bank made a major effort to raise its game in incorporating political economy considerations into its work, as part of the implementation of the Bank's Governance and Anticorruption strategy. PEA moved from being a rare activity commissioned occasionally by an adventurous team within the organization to becoming more widely used and considered. As part of this effort, there was sustained interaction between staff members from the World Bank and from other donor agencies working to mainstream political economy. Indeed, a significant share of the World Bank's effort was financed by a special-purpose grant made available by DFID, the Netherlands, Norway, and, more recently, the Australian Agency for International Development.[3]

This book results from a systematic effort at taking stock of what the World Bank has learned from its efforts to mainstream PEA. The effort included an open invitation to staff members active in the area to submit their work for presentation and discussion at a 2012 review conference. The goal was to identify work that was strong analytically and that provided practical recommendations that resulted in action. The eight cases presented in this book comprise good practice examples that emerged from the stocktaking effort.[4] The book is thus intended to illustrate (and reflect on) what the Bank has been able to achieve in this area so far and to help others learn more about how PEA perspectives can be effectively integrated into development approaches.

This chapter provides an overview and comparative synthesis of the lessons that emerge from the individual cases. The first section outlines the problem-driven approach, which has broadly guided much of the work over the past six years, and summarizes the problems that were addressed by each of the case studies. The second section compares the diagnoses undertaken in each case; the focus is on similarities and differences in both the methodologies that were used and the explanatory variables that were highlighted in each case. The third section addresses options and lessons about evidencing PEA. The fourth section reviews the policy implications that were derived from the PEAs. The fifth section focuses on the extent to which the analyses and their policy implications indeed influenced operational practice in the World Bank. The final section highlights some overall lessons that emerge and concludes the chapter with some reflections on how to effectively address the difficult challenges that taking politics seriously can pose for development practice.

A Problem-Driven Approach

At the outset of the current wave of World Bank work on political economy, a team of in-house specialists laid out a problem-driven approach to governance and PEA.[5] Its guiding principle was that to be concretely useful for practitioners, PEA—whether applied at the country or sector level or used to inform a specific operation—should start with a diagnosis of a specific problem, that is, a specific unresolved development challenge or an opportunity that a team seeks to seize. The presumption, the validity of which the reader can judge from the cases in this volume, was that a problem-driven approach was more likely to lead to specific findings and actionable recommendations than would approaches that have a broad emphasis on "understanding the context" or a focus on testing existing theories.[6]

As figure 1.1 illustrates, the problem-driven approach broadly comprises three steps. The first step is to identify a specific development challenge, often one where technical analysis and engagement on their own have failed to gain operational traction. The challenge could be narrowly focused: for example, what to do about continued teacher absenteeism or about stalled efforts to improve electricity provision. It could also be framed more broadly, such as how best to pursue further health sector reform, how to promote a more level playing field for businesses, or how to help a country deal with fundamental shocks.

The second step consists of analyzing *why* the observed, dysfunctional patterns are present, that is, the political economy drivers. This step should cover three dimensions: (a) relevant structural factors that influence stakeholder positions; (b) existing institutions, including institutional dysfunctions that channel behavior, as well as ongoing institutional change; and, finally, (c) stakeholder interests and constellations.

As the arrows on the right-hand side in figure 1.1 illustrate, structural factors, stakeholders, and institutions are interdependent.

Figure 1.1 Layers and Key Aspects of Problem-Driven Political Economy Analysis

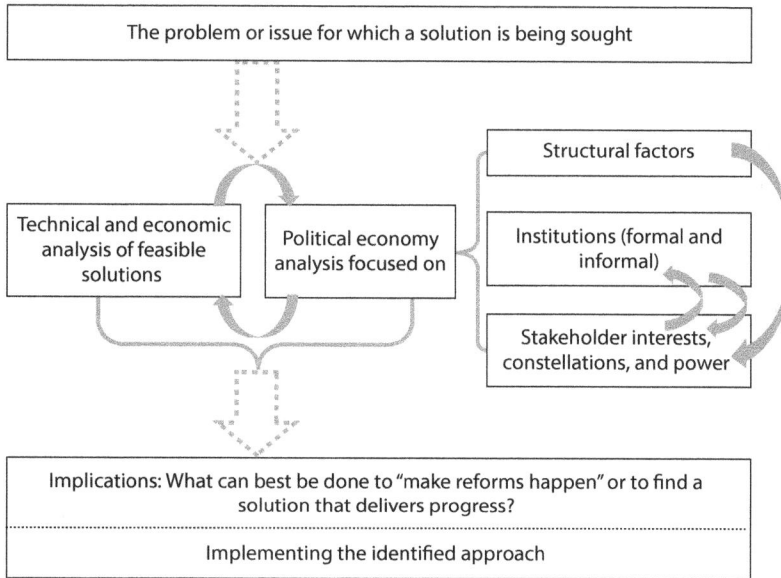

Source: Based on Fritz, Kaiser, and Levy 2009.
Note: This figure is an amended version of the three-layer approach proposed in their 2009 Good Practice Framework (see Fritz, Kaiser, and Levy 2009, 7).

Structural factors influence stakeholder incentives and opportunities. Relevant structural factors can include a country's geography, resource endowments, or demographic dynamics. These factors may also include elements that may be subject to change but that are outside the control of stakeholders, such as shifts and swings in commodity prices that can have significant effects on stakeholder incentives and opportunities (for example, by increasing rents or, conversely, by contributing to growing fiscal pressures).

Formal and informal institutions channel what stakeholders can do positively as well as negatively. Institutional strengths or weaknesses influence opportunities for collective action and can reinforce or mitigate social cleavages.

Stakeholders also often have opportunities to shape the design of formal institutions (such as laws, regulatory bodies and their powers, and so on) and the degree to which informal institutions support or diverge from formal ones.

The third and final step is to identify ways forward, including how to initiate change. These are analytical recommendations intended to offer a road map for operational engagement for potential entry points and ways to engage. As will be discussed further in the fourth section, such recommendations must be clear about risks (including unintended consequences of first-best policy reforms) and offer options and positive ways of engaging with political economy drivers. These options may include how to identify the areas with the greatest potential overlap between political incentives and policies that foster development progress, how and with whom to engage to expand opportunities for progress, or how to increase the prominence of certain policies on a government's agenda.

Below the dotted line in figure 1.1 stands the implementation of the identified approach. The line is where analysis ends and implementation picks up. The fifth section discusses the post-assessment efforts for the eight cases in greater detail. The section examines the cases' dependence on the responsiveness of the operational staff members and their managers and the cumulative momentum of subsequent events.

Each of the eight cases presented in this volume has been broadly consistent with a problem-driven approach. As table 1.1 summarizes, each case focused on a specific development challenge. These challenges can be organized into three broad groups:

- The Mongolia and Morocco cases explore political drivers of different aspects of resource allocation by the central government such as the use of mineral rents and energy subsidies.
- The Dominican Republic and Zambia cases address the performance of national infrastructural agencies—electricity supply in both cases and Zambia's telecommunications sector.
- The Ghana and Sierra Leone cases analyze sectoral development challenges at the interface between national and subnational political drivers, the former

Table 1.1 Problem-Driven Political Economy—Eight Development Challenges

Country	Focus area	The development problem
Resource allocation		
Mongolia	Mining resource boom	Risk of rising natural resource rents contributing to populist pressure and potential misuse of public funds
Morocco	Subsidy reforms	Government facing fiscal pressure to reform existing subsidies, yet having concerns about backlash against reforms
National infrastructure		
Dominican Republic	Electricity	Unreliable electricity provision and failed past efforts to improve the system
Zambia	Electricity and telecommunications	Inefficient sectors; failure to implement restructuring despite repeated government plans to do so
National, sectoral, and local interactions		
Ghana	Commercial agriculture	Lack of credible commitment for private investors, including establishment of reliable purchasing arrangements with smallholder farmers
Sierra Leone	Service provision at subnational levels	Challenging interplay of incentives between the national government and subnational ethnic and voter divisions for enabling decentralization in a way that would more effectively enhance service provision at subnational levels
Papua New Guinea	Local infrastructure	Unclear whether institutional reforms meant to empower communities have their intended effects
Philippines	Local and health	Allocation of national funds to subnational units for roads and health services highly uneven and not explained by development criteria

through the lens of commercialized agriculture and the latter with a focus on the roads and power sectors. For Papua New Guinea and the Philippines, the focus is principally at the decentralized level—the provision of small-scale infrastructure in Papua New Guinea and health services and (again) roads in the Philippines.

Diagnosing the Political Drivers of Decision Making

The eight examples of PEA vividly illustrate how to move from general attention to political influences on development to specific problem-focused diagnoses. This section will highlight some emerging comparative lessons from the cases.

One common way to think about the interactions between politics and development is to focus on regime types—whether a country has a democratic, authoritarian, or hybrid regime (Bogaards 2009; Levitsky and Way 2010; Norris 2011; Przeworski et al. 2000). Among the sample of countries discussed here, four are considered to be democratic (the Dominican Republic, Ghana, Mongolia, and Zambia), three are hybrids leaning toward democracy (Papua New Guinea, the Philippines, and Sierra Leone), and one is a hybrid leaning toward an authoritarian regime (Morocco).[7]

However, understanding the opportunities and constraints to reform calls for a much more nuanced analysis than is provided by a regime-type focus. In some democratic countries, political elites care about social welfare; but there are also countries with democratic or hybrid regimes where that is not the case. Conversely, whereas a significant number of authoritarian regimes are solely focused on maintaining a fragile stability and economic rents for narrow insider groups, some also seek to deliver services to the public at large. As each of the case studies illustrates, a more useful way forward is to focus on the specific constellation of incentives that shape the actions of key decision makers.

Understanding Incentives

As the cases underscore, careful attention to the *interaction* of economics and politics is crucial to understanding the actual incentives that prevail for stakeholders associated with a specific problem in a specific setting. Policies and their development effects are shaped by incentives that derive from the political as well as the economic realm. Moreover, understanding the way in which political and economic interests intersect can be much more revealing about fundamental drivers than just looking at politics and day-to-day political maneuvers in isolation.[8]

Learning about these incentives is not easy. This difficulty is particularly true of ownership patterns in the economy that are often important for analyzing certain interest structures (see the following section). Other economic factors can be more readily observed: for example, fiscal pressures (such as spiraling costs of food or fuel subsidies) create strains on governments and may compel action in a variety of policy areas. Natural resource booms frequently create new economic interests and power holders in countries that previously had fewer sources of wealth.

The primary purpose of PEA for development effectiveness is not to "name names", that is, not to identify who are the "good guys" and the "bad guys" in a specific situation. Rather, it is to understand the underlying drivers that shape the incentives of decision makers. As the case studies reveal, much can be learned about these underlying drivers without delving into a detailed account of who did what to whom and when. Such actor-specific analysis can also create a misleading sense that particular individuals are the problem, whereas in many cases, the incentive structures are embedded and changes in individuals often have limited impact. That said, knowing about potential allies and opponents can be helpful in facilitating subsequent engagement if the knowledge is used in a nuanced way and avoids caricatures. Most individuals are not pure champions or opponents of reform, but rather respond to a variety of incentives and challenges, including the need to reach compromises, to balance interests, to be selective about spending political capital, and so on.

Understanding the Mechanisms Used to Manage Political Support

Strikingly, for all of the diversity of the country settings and the problems being considered, one common theme emerged across all the case studies: the role of clientelism and the importance of incentives related to managing political support. At the most general level, clientelism means the discretionary targeting of public resources and favor by influential political actors to specific constituencies in exchange for political support.[9] In each case study, discretionary control over public resources was used to promote elites' chances of maintaining power or being reelected. However, how this played out in practice varied from country to country. In some countries, regional or ethnic considerations dominated; in others, the alliances were more personalized; and in yet others, the focus was more on general populist appeals.

In Sierra Leone, the targeting of resources to build networks of support had a predominantly regional or ethnic dimension. The two major parties had their principal bases of support in different regions whose ethnic configurations are distinct from one another. The party in power directed resources disproportionately to its ethnic and regional base and, within that, targeted resources to politically connected allies.

Center-regional dynamics played out in a more fragmented way in the Philippines and Papua New Guinea. In these countries, many national-level politicians have sought to target resources to subnational levels in ways that secure the allegiance of powerful allies and promote the chances of being reelected, primarily to national parliaments. In contrast to Sierra Leone, ethnicity has not been a dominant political dividing line in the Philippines. Rather, much of the spoils flowed through family clans that spanned national and local levels and that used targeted intergovernmental transfers and discretionary local allocation to consolidate control. The Papua New Guinea case study provides less information on the dynamics of national-level politics, but it highlights the influence of elected members of the national parliament who maintained high levels of influence over how resources were allocated within districts despite initial donor-supported efforts to change institutions in ways that would allocate such decision-making powers to local communities.

In the Dominican Republic and Zambia, clientelism was less regional. Both countries were characterized by the relative absence of a programmatic, ideological (or ethno-regional) basis for politics. In Zambia, the spoils system was centralized in the president who used his discretionary authority to cultivate alliances within the elite. In the Dominican Republic, subsidized power tariffs and the tolerance of nonpayment for electricity by various groups have been used by successive presidents to shore up political support. In addition, jobs and contracts related to the sector have been used for rewarding supporters. The practices have created powerful obstacles to reforming the sector and to attracting investment funds to expand generation and distribution capacity.

The Dominican Republic, Mongolia, Morocco, and Zambia further illustrate how intraelite arrangements and rent allocations can be intertwined with a populist political discourse and policies that complement the search for political support. For example, the low power tariffs in the Dominican Republic and in Zambia or the energy subsidies in Morocco benefit many groups in society. This wide-reaching benefit in turn means that reforms face broad-based popular opposition. At the same time, the prevailing arrangements also benefit elites and entrenched insiders: wealthier citizens consume most of the subsidized and underpriced energy in the Dominican Republic and Morocco, and insiders within state-owned power companies in the Dominican Republic and in Zambia benefit from the status quo and the preferential access it offers to job and contracting opportunities. There are further significant opportunities for insider gains, for example, for those who are licensed to import diesel fuels while the networked power sector remains underdeveloped or for those who deal directly in the mining sector in a resource-rich country such as Mongolia.

Moreover, through populist discourse, elites and insiders can sponsor public opposition to reforms, even when the principal beneficiaries of the status quo are the elite insiders. It is important to note that combinations of elite settlements and populist policies may do better at broad-based development than a settlement where allocation of rents takes place exclusively among elites (as observable in some highly exclusive and repressive resource-rich countries). However, these combinations often lead to policies that are fiscally unsustainable. For example, energy subsidies in Morocco have come to consume more than 5 percent of gross domestic product per annum, and in Mongolia, the increase in social transfers has contributed to sizable fiscal deficits despite record-high commodity prices and to an inability to maintain transfers during downturns in commodity prices, when social protection measures are most needed.

Ghana and Mongolia appear to be cases where national-level electoral politics revolve around policy issues and (potentially) government performance and where politicians cannot simply rely on ethnic or regional loyalties to win elections. For Ghana's national-level politicians, who operate in a relatively competitive electoral environment, the potential of developing new types of commercial agriculture in new geographic areas offers an opportunity to show progress and, ultimately, to bolster their prospects to win votes if the development succeeds. However, in rural areas, institutions governing property rights are ambiguous and fluid. This institutional uncertainty contributes to the risk of opportunistic behavior as new, commercial entrants come onto the scene and to the concerns among some stakeholders that they could end up being losers. The case study argues that, because of the way in which Ghana's national politics works, the national-level actors are more likely to be supporters than hindrances to the effort at agricultural reform. In Mongolia, politicians motivated by winning and maintaining electoral support have negotiated a better deal for the country from foreign mining sector investors than many countries elsewhere, in terms of securing significant revenue from the projects. At the same time, the pursuit of electoral advantage has made it difficult for politicians to collectively commit to sustainable fiscal management and to move from a rapid succession of different cash handouts and social welfare payments to a more consistent approach.

Between "One Size Fits All" and "Every Country Is Unique"

Overall, the wave of recent PEA points to an evolution in thinking about contexts. Economic and technical approaches have tended toward recommending similar approaches across a broad range of (very) different environments based on the assumption that best practices—once identified—should be replicated. At the other end of the spectrum, advocates of social, political, and historical analysis have at times gone beyond pointing to the importance of understanding specific contexts and have argued that every country and every society is highly particular and that solutions therefore have to be unique, with few opportunities for learning from elsewhere.

The insights from PEAs highlighted in the case studies suggest a more intermediate possibility. As outlined above, there is considerable resemblance among the political economy challenges encountered across a range of countries and sectors. The allocation of road projects to specific localities and the allocation of funding to building new roads versus investing in maintenance are affected by political economy calculations in surprisingly similar ways in countries as different as postconflict Sierra Leone and the middle-income Philippines. Governments are reluctant to increase power sector tariffs out of concern about a popular backlash on the one hand and insider resistance on the other hand in countries as different as the Dominican Republic and Zambia. In each case, the particular dynamics are specific to how different drivers—such as the regime type and the space for civil society, the presence of reformers within government, and the effect of economic cycles—interact, but the type of challenges encountered in many policy areas and sectors are remarkably common. Correspondingly, as discussed in the section below, titled "Policy Implications of Political Economy Assessments," the recommendations derived from PEA also share certain features across countries.

"Evidencing" Political Economy Analysis

Complementing the learning about diagnostic approaches that can help to understand the political economy obstacles to development progress is the learning about the specific evidence that can provide the empirical underpinnings for PEA. Wariness of PEA stems in part from a concern that its focus is on issues that can be difficult to evidence sufficiently. However, the examples in this book demonstrate that the evidencing can, in fact, be relatively robust.[10] Connecting data about decisions (such as fiscal allocations) and information such as the de jure design of institutions and the de facto use of institutions can be used as the basis for analytic narratives that drill into specific development challenges and for identifying constraints and opportunities for progressive change. Crucial information for deciding how to engage with the stakeholders can be developed by identifying, through formal surveys as well as informal interviews, the stakeholders that are relevant for a sector, their policy positions, and their mutual influence on one another.

The traditional approach has been to assemble such information informally as part of the tacit understanding of various agency staff members. Whereas such knowledge is very important, it is too unsystematic to be relied on as the *only* source of analysis for incentives and interests. Moreover, tacit knowledge accumulated by individual staff members tends to remain disconnected. For example, insights on a particular sector and into the broader political drivers of intergovernmental relations in a country and, in turn, the links of these to other sectors or policy aspects are rarely connected when analysis stays entirely informal.[11]

Experience is accumulating about the type of evidence that is both useful and accessible for problem-driven PEA. As the examples in this volume illustrate, more is being learned about the specific ways in which rents are reaped and distributed within different sectors as well as about the types of information that can be used: such as fiscal, price, and household survey data; analysis of electoral systems and mapping of election results; qualitative evidence about stakeholder interests; positions, incentives, and opportunities for exercising accountability; careful mapping of institutional rules and their implications; and historical legacies and the way they influence current views and expectations.

As table 1.2 reflects, the chapters brought together in this volume have taken a range of methodological and evidencing approaches. The table also reflects the tremendous opportunities for bringing both qualitative and quantitative information to bear in order to explore and corroborate political economy drivers and opportunities for change. The increasing availability of indicators of sector-specific and overall development progress as well as of information about budget allocations or utility pricing offers opportunities to more precisely pinpoint the nature of problems and whether progress is being made as expected. Existing public opinion surveys such as Latinobarómetro and Afrobarometer can be useful sources on political views and trends (for example, see chapter 4 on the Dominican Republic). At the same time, process tracing from a growing range of public sources and well-selected interviews continue to be important

Table 1.2 Types of Evidencing Used in the Eight Country Chapters

Country	Focus area	Specific issues addressed and evidencing
Resource allocation		
Mongolia	Risks and management of a mining sector boom and use of emerging fiscal space	Fiscal and commodity price dynamics, historical legacies (primary and secondary sources), analysis of electoral dynamics and resulting political incentives, process tracing of policy decisions, motivations (including interviews and public election programs) and results, constitutional and other institutional provisions, and compliance with formal institutions
Morocco	Subsidy reforms	Citizen survey focused on knowledge about the subsidy system, including survey questions about likely reactions to various degrees of price increases
National infrastructure		
Dominican Republic	Electricity reforms	Country-level collective action dynamics and elections (including survey evidence and secondary sources), analysis of opting-out strategies (based on household survey data), analysis of utility pricing and tolerance of nonpayments, process tracing of past policy reform decisions and of current stakeholder positions, and interests based on interviews and publicly accessible information
Zambia	Electricity and telecommunications reforms	Analytic narrative and process tracing of decision making in relation to sectoral restructuring and pricing, based on interviews and insider understanding
National, sectoral, and local interactions		
Ghana	Potential and challenges for developing commercialized agriculture in new areas	Narrative tracing current investment and development opportunities as well as reasons for recent failed attempts linked with in-depth historical perspective based on team expert; assessment of stakeholder interests at local, regional, and national levels through interviews; and analysis of resulting opportunities
Sierra Leone	National-level accountability challenges and implications for government efforts at subnational service provision	Tracing of country historical trajectory using various sources of information; electoral patterns in an ethno-regionally divided setting (based on data on geographic distribution of electoral support) and resulting incentives; analysis of institutional arrangements for subnational service delivery; sector and survey data on current status, budget, and aid allocations; and tracing of progress with rehabilitation and expansion
Papua New Guinea	Challenges of effective institutional reforms and participatory approaches for channeling infrastructure projects to local communities	Detailed analysis of institutional provisions, and electoral rules and incentives Commissioned survey of about 1,100 households across 49 wards in 9 districts of the country, focusing on how communities used reformed institutional arrangements; analysis of community characteristics and projects obtained (using regression analysis); and comparison with stated policy intentions
Philippines	Challenges and opportunities for strengthening local infrastructure delivery	Summary of unexplained challenges from technical analysis (budget and sector data), country-level dynamics based on expert understanding and secondary sources, commissioned survey of 1,200 households in 30 municipalities in Isabela province, regression analysis of electoral characteristics, and relative service delivery benefits received by localities

to fully understand country and issue-specific dynamics and to be clearer about motivations and perceptions of stakeholders and decision makers. Also, history—in the sense of how things have evolved over time—matters. For example, in Mongolia, current attitudes about mining sector policies are rooted in the experience with the country's first major mining operation.

Some of the key economic dynamics and realities of a country and their links with politics can be opaque and tend to be little documented—often despite the availability of a large body of general economic analysis—while sometimes being covered in existing academic work.[12] Depending on the problem being analyzed, it can be relevant at a minimum to outline the degree to which an economy is competitive versus being controlled by a narrow set of insiders. Such an exercise can often be done using publicly available sources, including interviews and official records. Similarly, the extent to which corrupt practices affect a sector or policy area can remain difficult to pinpoint in the absence of an official investigation; but comparative indicators, such as those compiled by Transparency International, as well as perception surveys can help highlight to what extent stakeholders perceive problems. These data can be used alongside other information to analyze prevailing incentives and the likely obstacles and opportunities for engagement.

For the road sector, analyzed in the Sierra Leone and the Philippines chapters, it was important to be attentive to how funding for the sector was being controlled as well as whether actual construction and maintenance kept pace with resource allocations made. For power sector reforms, as illustrated by the Dominican Republic and the Zambia examples, considering the current set of winners and losers from existing power tariffs was important, as well as thinking about which actors could gain the most from changing the status quo. In a resource-rich country, such as Mongolia, the nature and timing of contracts with major investors was a key policy issue, and the specific electoral incentives and the way they shaped the programs used in political competition also played an important role. For decentralization, and for subnational service delivery and infrastructure development, the role played by national-level politicians in directing the allocation of resources emerges as an issue to be analyzed and is particularly important in the Papua New Guinea, the Philippines, and Sierra Leone cases.

To understand political drivers of decision makers, evidencing can take a number of approaches. A closer look at the governance structure of state-owned enterprises and their political connections is part of the analysis in the Dominican Republic and Zambia. In different ways, the Morocco and Papua New Guinea chapters indicate the important contributions that surveys can make. Surveys help to corroborate and nuance, but in some instances they also contradict prior assumptions about citizens' preferences and their views and familiarity with policy issues and processes (in the case of Papua New Guinea). Greater attention to vote buying, the specific forms it takes, and the consequences it has for the way public funds are allocated to particular localities informs the Papua New Guinea and the Philippines chapters.

Some streams of recent PEA include experiments and other quantitative techniques that have only recently been applied to developing country settings (see, for example, Keefer and Khemani 2012; Vincente and Wantchekon 2009). Such efforts deliver interesting new data, such as data on patterns of vote buying or the allocation of service delivery across local units of government, and can help drill into the relationship between political strategies and the allocation of development efforts (as used in the Papua New Guinea and the Philippines chapters).

Inevitably, trade-offs need to be considered. Typically, within the resources and time available, trade-offs have to be made between the breadth and depth of the analysis, as well as on what to focus in depth. Generating primary data through a survey or tracing in detail how and to what extent fiscal resource allocations are influenced by political rather than technical considerations takes time and resources, as does an analysis that seeks to carefully dissect the role of particular stakeholders around state-owned utilities and their management. Given that the overall purpose of the analysis is to inform development interventions, trade-offs should be made with a view to issues and questions that are most critical for the operational design or approach. Furthermore, because the incentives of actors in regards to specific policy issues and sectors are frequently derived from broader political economy dynamics, the analytical net should not be cast too narrowly.

However, such trade-offs are less sharp if different pieces of analytic work are considered not in isolation but rather as contributing to a body of knowledge about a particular country, sector, or set of issues. The design and implementation of a lending operation typically stretches over two to five years and even more when there is a long-term engagement in a certain sector. So in principle, teams often have an opportunity to incorporate political economy perspectives into multiple pieces of analytic work over time.

Policy Implications of Political Economy Assessments

Consistent with the discussion in the introduction of this chapter of the limitations of technocratic approaches, each of the eight cases shows in detail how political economy drivers undercut "best practice" policy recommendations. One way or the other, technocratic recommendations were at variance with the incentives and constraints confronting politically powerful actors. In response to this challenge, broadly speaking, two sets of options are available. As figure 1.2 illustrates, these options can be considered as a spectrum that includes various intermediate points. At one end of the spectrum is the option to accept the existing set of political economy incentives as given and to seek out feasible options for reform within that context. At the other end of the spectrum are pro-active efforts to expand the available reform space through actions such as multistakeholder engagement, with the aim of altering the relative influence of different stakeholders and hence expand reform possibilities.[13]

In settings where most influential stakeholders are opposed to far-reaching reforms and where repeated efforts to adopt far-reaching governance or policy

Figure 1.2 The Spectrum of Reform Space

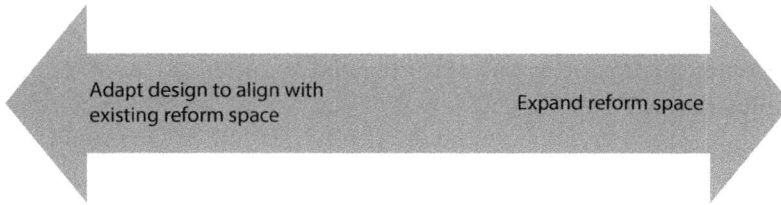

Adapt design to align with
existing reform space

Expand reform space

reforms have failed, the focus might usefully be on the left-hand side of the spectrum. In other situations, there may be opportunities as well as a need to consider engagement more toward the right-hand side of the spectrum. When the development value added of engaging in modest, incremental progress is very small, the only useful alternative to exit might be to engage proactively to expand the reform space, with an understanding that such an approach implies working against the grain and that progress is uncertain. Opportunities may still exist to combine this approach with a continued search for entry points that are more consistent with the incentives of key stakeholders. For example, even politicians who are focused on controlling power often need to demonstrate some development results, or there may be opportunities to foster a consensus among stakeholders that allows progress in a specific domain even while the broader political situation remains fluid and contested.

Approaches from across the spectrum can also be used in complementary ways. For example, adapting reform design to political economy constraints can be combined with encouraging greater engagement of hitherto excluded stakeholders. More toward the left-hand side of "adaptation," but adding a more deliberate engagement, are approaches that seek to take into account political cycles as well as windows of opportunity and that seek to time engagement and reform proposals accordingly. More toward the side of proactive engagement are efforts to enhance transparency and to stimulate or deepen domestic debates about policy issues.

A second dimension on which PEA can provide insights is whether a proposed policy solution is likely to be robust given continuing political economy challenges. In the case of Zambia, the resulting strategic advice was to back away from far-reaching efforts to restructure the power sector as a whole that included sector-wide tariff rebalancing. Instead, the Zambia reformers focused more narrowly on agreeing on private provision and increased tariffs for electricity supplied to the mining sector; broader tariff reforms came later. In Papua New Guinea, changes were made in formal institutional arrangements for transferring resources to local levels, with the intention of getting more money to the poorest communities. But the PEA found that the changes were not robust and did little in practice to alter the incentives and the resource flows. The analysis suggested that reforms that strengthened transparency and feedback mechanisms between members of parliament and local citizens and that targeted funds directly to the lowest levels of local government would be more effective in addressing the underlying political economy incentives.

Table 1.3 summarizes the policy recommendations made in the case studies. The recommendations generally incorporated a combination of options for politically informed responses.

Table 1.3 From Diagnosis to Recommendation: What the Assessments Proposed

| | Proposed, politically informed response | | |
Country and focus	Politically responsive policy design (second best)	Enhanced information on policies and options	Multistakeholder engagement
Mongolia: mining resource boom	Consider engaging in reform options preferred by local stakeholders even if these contravene perceived best practices.	Develop domestic capacity for policy analysis on mining sector–related policy areas.	Intensify outreach to the public and civil society, as well as to decision makers in parliament on policy options and risks for resource boom–related policy areas.
Morocco	Create innovative social programs to support poorest to be introduced in parallel to subsidy reforms.	Initiate communication campaign to ensure that citizens understand costs and benefits better in advance of implementing subsidy reforms.	
Dominican Republic: electricity	Prioritize professionalization of electricity distribution companies over price adjustments.	Engage middle class via participatory anticorruption initiative, including enhanced monitoring of public expenditures.	
Zambia: electricity and telecommunications	Narrow the sectoral reform agenda; focus on those reforms that enjoy support of influential stakeholders.		Engage service users around the benefits of reform.
Ghana: commercial agriculture	Enhance mutual confidence around rules of the game for access to land via multistakeholder consensus-building process around local benefits of incoming commercial agriculture investment.		
Sierra Leone: local levels: roads	Redirect resources toward local levels given greater opportunities for accountability for both general funds and roads.		Support democratically accountable local governments; include road users in governance.
Papua New Guinea: local infrastructure	Target grants directly to ward level rather than to district level.	Provide citizen-friendly information on local infrastructure allocation decisions.	
Philippines: local roads and health	*Roads:* target allocations based on precise criteria. *Health:* provide comparable public information on health delivery performance across localities.		*Both:* link allocations to performance directly comparing participation and transparency benchmarks.

Considering first the politically responsive policy design options, two broad approaches are evident:

- A focus on incremental policy reforms that add value developmentally and are likely to enjoy the support (or at least not the active opposition) of politically powerful constituencies. This option is exemplified by the proposal to reach an accord with Zambia's copper mining companies to increase the prices they pay for electricity to a level sufficient to support new investment in electricity generation capacity.

- A focus narrowly on actions that can be implemented straightforwardly within or by the government rather than seeking major structural changes. This approach is exemplified by the proposal to invest in capacity building of the Dominican Corporation of State Electricity Companies. These recommendations are underpinned by careful analyses of why key stakeholders might be willing to support these particular improvements.

In both cases, the proposed approaches combine considerations about feasibility with considerations about finding solutions that are robust and meaningful.

Turning to efforts to expand reform space, a common thread in almost all the cases is a call to use demand-side approaches to empower stakeholders who have an incentive to seek better development performance. As table 1.3 underscores, this approach can be done through a combination of information strategies and engagements to strengthen stakeholder participation. In doing so, it is important to recognize that a number of easy assumptions about how greater access to information would translate into better governance have been shown to be inconsistent with real-world experience (Khemani 2007; see also Booth 2012). Further research into these causal links is ongoing. From a political economy perspective, better information should be an important asset for fostering political incentives in favor of development objectives. However, rather than as a complete solution on its own, better information needs to be seen as complementing the other key implications: identifying second-best policy solutions that are more compatible with prevailing incentives and capabilities within government and, wherever possible, leveraging development-compatible interests of other stakeholders.

Specific approaches suggested by the cases assembled in this volume include the following:

- Provide user-friendly information that can better enable citizens to assess the performance of local political and bureaucratic leaders in areas of their concern. Examples include comparative information across locales on the quality of health services (in the Philippines); information about which localities are provided resources for community-level infrastructure and about institutional opportunities to request projects (in Papua New Guinea); and, more broadly, information to citizens about the benefits and costs of different policy choices and the effectiveness with which public resources are being used (in the

Dominican Republic, Mongolia, and Morocco). Furthermore, in the Mongolia case, the proposal targeted expanding domestic capacities for policy analysis to establish a more continuous and more locally credible source of relevant policy assessments and information for political as well as technical debates.

- Engage affected citizens in participatory processes on sectoral reform by, for example, building consensus for the benefits of new commercial agricultural investment and at the same time strengthening participatory processes for including local stakeholders with the ability to veto or disrupt investments in commercial agriculture (in Ghana) and sensitizing users of electricity and telecommunications services to the costs of the status quo and creating new avenues for them to participate in dialogue on reforms (in Zambia).

- Strengthen the capacity, accountability, and authority of democratically elected local governments. The Philippines case proposes to link resource transfers from the center to performance through the use of greater participation and transparency benchmarks. The Sierra Leone case argues that gains in government capacity are more likely at local levels, where populations are more homogenous, with correspondingly fewer distortions from regional and ethnically based political contestation.

These approaches can be complemented by "supply-side" initiatives that would constrain the channeling of resources predominantly for short-term political gains by defining more precisely the possible uses of the resources transferred from the center. For example, the supply-side initiative would target community infrastructure financing in Papua New Guinea by sending it directly toward the lowest level of government rather than the more encompassing district level. And in the Philippines, the suggested approach is to set very precise criteria for allocations of funding for road construction and maintenance.

The mix of recommendations combines strategic nuancing of what policies and institutional changes are likely to be feasible and deliver development results as well as where, when, and how broader stakeholder engagement can make significant contributions. The mix brings to the forefront a search for viable second-best or out-of-the-box options that are aligned with country and sectoral realities, and it modulates general ideas like transparency and multistakeholder engagement for a specific context, highlighting what it would take for these approaches to work. For example, although transparency is being widely advocated, much of the information that becomes available to citizens goes unused. What matters is that the information is sufficiently focused to generate traction on policy issues. This need for usable information is why the Mongolian assessment complemented its call for better policy analysis with a strong focus on building the capacity of nongovernmental actors to generate and use such analysis and why the Moroccan and Zambian analyses—each in different ways— advocated putting information on the actual costs of the status quo into the public domain as a way of facilitating greater demand for reforms to emerge.

From Recommendation to Action

Any analysis only affects what happens on the ground if key actors are aware of the findings and implications and are able and willing to act on them. To get from diagnosis and recommendation to action with problem-driven PEA, each of the following three links in a causal chain needs to work:

- First, and as discussed in the previous sections, the PEAs need to meet a benchmark of quality. They need to have diagnoses that are credible, and they need to suggest recommendations that are feasible to implement.
- Second, as also mentioned above, assessments need to be available to practitioners and stakeholders and incorporated into dialogue on policy formulation and implementation.
- Third, the recommendations need to be taken up as part of the actions that follow and to be used in a way that actually influences the design of projects or the nature of the policy dialogue rather than just broaden awareness about politics.

Meeting the Quality Benchmark

To begin with the first link, as discussed in the second section of this chapter, not all PEAs over the past 5–10 years have adequately met the necessary quality benchmark. Sometimes they have been overly general. Sometimes they have been strong from a research perspective, but lacked practical policy recommendations. Sometimes their conclusions have been overly negative; they have shown why political constraints are likely to block the implementation of desired policies but have not suggested ways to influence and change this situation. Doubtless, these shortfalls are a continuing challenge, at times because of mismatches between the expected scope and available budgets for analytic work and at other times because of the difficulty in identifying the right skills and expertise for problem-driven analysis. Doubtless, the case studies included in this volume are hardly perfect. That said, as table 1.3 summarized, all of the cases assembled in this volume made a serious effort to propose credible and feasible recommendations for action. As argued in this chapter, learning how to meet the criteria for quality analysis and operational relevance is accumulating and is leading to better results. This learning includes a significant emphasis on identifying opportunities for constructive engagement—both directly with decision makers and the goals they care about and with a wider range of stakeholders.

What has been the follow-up on the recommendations made in the eight case studies? Answering this question takes us to the next two links in the chain: availability and uptake. To understand how these links played out, some background is needed on the organizational setting within which the case studies were embedded—the World Bank.[14]

The World Bank has an extraordinarily diverse mandate. It is often still perceived to be staffed principally by economists and engineers who are preoccupied only with economic growth. In fact, it has evolved into an institution with global expertise covering a wide range of sectors and issues relevant to development: education, health, governance, the environment and climate change, and a range of others have all become part of the Bank's diverse areas of activity. In response to this diversity, the Bank has been organized in a decentralized way. Within broad parameters set by the organization's management, both the design of new initiatives and their implementation were delegated. The effort to mainstream political economy was no different.

Management provided a signal that this mainstreaming was desired, including incorporating support for political economy diagnostic work into the Bank's high profile Governance and Anticorruption strategy.[15] Follow-through on undertaking political economy work, along with its dissemination and uptake, was left to staff. Specifically, deciding whether and how to disseminate the findings and to implement recommendations arising from PEA has been left to country management teams and sectoral staff. Country teams have been tasked with developing the Bank's strategic priorities in its country program and the overall dialogue with the government, and sectoral staff members have been tasked with the design and implementation of sector-level operational programs.

Making Political Economy Work Available

For any study to have an influence, it must traverse the second link in the causal chain. The study needs to become part of a conversation involving those responsible for designing and implementing development operations. But the choices for how broadly to disseminate PEAs are not straightforward, even for those studies that meet the benchmark of quality.

Frequently, PEA is treated as sensitive and confidential. In a number of instances after reviewing the analysis, governments themselves have been highly reluctant to put any critical analysis into the public domain. One intermediate option agreed to by World Bank staff members and relevant government counterparts in some cases has been the distribution of a limited, largely informal version of a PEA study. Other work has been shared more broadly, sometimes after removing some of the content that was considered particularly sensitive. Sometimes sensitivity has been less, and applied PEA work has been published as chapters in World Bank Country Economic Memoranda and Public Expenditure Reviews, as well as in notes and working papers by academics who carried out the analysis and occasionally by World Bank staff members.

Reports can raise sensitive issues, such as (a) the way in which a few individuals or groups control large swaths of economic activity in a country or a certain sector, (b) the fact that politicians use public funds and channel public contracts to pay back those supporters who funded their election campaigns, or (c) the fact that politicians have limited incentives to pursue improvements in service provision because they rely on ethnic loyalties as their main electoral strategy. World Bank country teams in turn face a strong incentive to maintain a good relationship with the government of the day; without such a relationship, programs may become stalled and funds may be difficult to disburse.

At the same time, concerns about the sensitivity of PEAs can be exaggerated. As discussed earlier, many analyses focus on systemic incentives rather than particular "bad individuals." The PEAs seek to identify policy recommendations oriented toward suggesting pragmatic ways forward. Importantly, findings can also be helpful for governments if they are interested in making reforms happen. In some instances, recently elected governments have been happy to embrace PEA findings, considering these helpful for moving forward on their new agendas. Also, as a number of cases in this volume show, including Mongolia, Morocco, Zambia, and others, PEAs can help World Bank teams better understand the constraints that governments face and, in turn, can help to devise policy approaches that are better adapted to engage with these constraints.

Full publication has some advantages over more informal circulation. In particular, findings are more continuously accessible to a wider range of stakeholders, which can promote greater uptake over time. It also makes studies more accessible to other agencies and researchers interested in building on what has been done. Hence, formal publication promotes learning, accumulation of knowledge about the specific development challenge addressed, and improvements in quality. Among the eight cases assembled in this volume, a few have been made public previously, including findings for the Dominican Republic and some related work on Mongolia and on Sierra Leone. Most other studies in this volume have been circulated informally among World Bank teams, government counterparts, and various other stakeholders.

Overall, there are clear challenges related to traversing the second link, but these are surmountable in most instances and perhaps more so than has been past practice. Depending on the context, potential sensitivity can be defused in many ways, ranging from the language used, to publication by the consultant team rather than the development agency (thereby reducing concern about an agency report's official status), to sharing of key insights and messages in briefings with a range of stakeholders rather than sharing of all the underlying detail. Defusing sensitivity is important, so that the issues raised can be put on the table. At a minimum, the results of PEAs need to be made available to those involved in decision making, including the staff of a development agency as well as other stakeholders (reformers within government, citizens interested in seeking better public services, and others). Circulation of the study thereby allows the stakeholders to use the results to explore how better development outcomes can be achieved even in the face of political economy constraints.

Ensuring Uptake

Only when the quality and availability links have been adequately addressed can the crucial test for PEAs come into focus: are their recommendations incorporated into operational programs? The case study narratives of what happened subsequent to the analytical work can be grouped into three broad categories: (a) those where uptake was relatively comprehensive and affected the Bank's engagement with the country as well as with specific sectors (Mongolia and Zambia); (b) those with evidence of at least some uptake (the Dominican Republic,

Ghana, Morocco, and Sierra Leone); and (c) those where the effect has, at least so far, been more limited (Papua New Guinea and the Philippines).

Consider, first, the more comprehensive Zambia and Mongolia cases. In Zambia, as chapter 5 details, the analysis had a substantial effect on both country and sectoral strategies. At the country level, the political economy diagnosis contributed to a far-reaching reformulation of strategy with a focus on less ambitious but more achievable goals. The approach to engagement shifted in a similar way in both the electricity and the telecommunications sectors. As per the recommendations summarized in table 1.3, sectoral reforms backed away from dialogue around far-reaching efforts at restructuring. Instead, there was an enhanced focus on partial reforms prioritizing enhanced engagement with potentially influential stakeholders. In both sectors, the result was to unlock a previously stalemated sectoral engagement (for example, by facilitating new investment in electricity generation to supply Zambia's mining sector). However, as a controversial privatization of the telecommunications parastatal signals, sometimes there were unintended consequences.

In the face of an imminent mining sector boom in Mongolia, the analysis supported the reorientation of the country team's engagement. It helped the team take advantage of a window of opportunity during the 2008–09 worldwide financial crisis to promote the adoption of legal constraints on fiscal management aimed at reducing volatility. The analysis contributed to a mining sector specialist being based in the country office (the first time the Bank had ever done so anywhere) to come to grips with key trends, stakeholder interests, and other concerns affecting the development of the mining sector. Perhaps most important, it laid the foundation of the Bank's greater engagement with nongovernment stakeholders. The analysis led to the crucial decision to support the development of a local think tank dedicated to policy issues about managing a resource-rich economy and about engaging with civil society on the monitoring of procurement processes. However, a key limitation has been the fact that although the World Bank's engagement and outreach built on findings from the analysis, the policy solution that was supported—the Fiscal Stability Law adopted in July 2010—remained rather grounded in a first-best approach. This approach proved not to be robust in the face of continuing stakeholder incentives to spend increasing fiscal resources and to incur deficits and risks from government guarantees.[16]

In five countries, the political economy diagnostics made valuable contributions to operational design and engagement at the sectoral level:

- In the Dominican Republic, the political economy work led to a refocusing of the approach to electricity sector reform, which somewhat paralleled the shift in Zambia: the focus moved from a broad effort at sectoral restructuring to a narrower effort to strengthen the management and capabilities of the electricity parastatal and to seek to build reform constituencies at the national level.
- In Ghana, the sectoral team responsible for designing a new commercial agriculture operation was enthusiastic from the outset about the potential

value added of the political economy work. It was supportive of the recommendations of the sector analysis and drew on them to foster dialogue among stakeholders on the benefits and costs of different design options for a US$64.5 million loan to Ghana for a commercial agriculture project.
- In Morocco, the analysis was conducted with an explicit demand from the government to support efforts to facilitate subsidy reforms and findings fed into the government's communications campaign.
- In Sierra Leone, the principal consequence of the political economy diagnostic was a reintensification of efforts to support decentralized levels of government, primarily focusing on roads.

In the third group, in the Philippines PEAs were undertaken across a range of activities, including the way health and road services were allocated at local levels. Some of this work was directly commissioned by the country team to inform not only debates within sector teams but also a range of local stakeholders about which development challenges were amenable to reforms and how these could best be approached. The specific piece of analysis included in this volume was more experimental and intended to stimulate a discussion, which is still ongoing, about the challenges related to supporting improvements in service delivery at subnational levels of government. Similarly, the Papua New Guinea analysis has provided an important corrective to the assumption that new formal procedures would empower communities to decide which infrastructure projects were priorities. At the same time, development agencies and local stakeholders have yet to decide and agree on how best to pursue and provide support for further reforms.

Some Wider Lessons

Supporting development through external public funds, policy discussions, analysis, and projects has been a challenging and, at times, frustrating endeavor ever since development aid emerged on a larger scale in the 1950s and 1960s. As argued at the outset of this chapter, the initial reaction to the particular challenges posed by "messy politics" had been to strongly emphasize economic and technical analysis and advice. However, political economy drivers continuously influence where and how development progress becomes possible and therefore also influence the effectiveness of external support.

Recent political economy assessments have begun to open up a new understanding of such dynamics in developing countries and the implications these dynamics have for development prospects. The recent PEA work brings a stronger focus on how politics and economics interact to shape particular development issues, such as whether and how a society copes with sudden mining wealth, what it takes to develop new commercial agriculture, or how likely it is that funding for roads leads to improved infrastructure. But it remains challenging to combine these insights from PEA with a more immediate usefulness to influence actual operational design and the policy dialogue on specific issues.

An overarching contribution of PEA is that it has begun to change the mind-set of development practitioners. Indeed, in discussions within the World Bank about proposed operations, management now routinely questions whether the hoped-for results have taken political economy realities into account. The eight case studies in this volume suggest that questions about feasibility and about whether specific interventions are likely to be effective at achieving progress are amenable to systematic analysis. But the case studies also suggest that there is a long road to travel before the new approach can decisively take hold.

Seven key lessons emerge from this overview of experiences assembled here.

Lesson 1

To be operationally useful, PEAs need to focus on specific development problems. PEA can only influence how development efforts are carried out if it directly engages with the specific and practical challenges that emerge—be they related to improving a country's roads, providing better delivery of health services, developing a mining sector that promotes a society's long-run welfare, or fostering equitable service delivery within an evolving intergovernmental system. The aim is to provide practical advice for the design and management of development engagement and interventions and to set out findings and recommendations that are relevant and specific as well as clearly grounded in the findings of the analysis.

Lesson 2

PEAs need to be anchored in a substantial understanding of the country-level drivers of decision making. Many political economy incentives are ultimately linked to the pursuit of political support: for example, to win or maintain political positions and power; to control lucrative parts of a country's economy, balanced by the need to maintain or win popular support among groups of citizens; and to strike deals with other power holders. Thus, country-level political economy drivers affect each and every sector and policy issue in some form. As almost all of the eight case studies underscore, the incentives of front-line decision makers are shaped by the broader political and institutional environment in which they operate.

Lesson 3

Therefore, a third lesson emerges from the combination of lessons one and two. PEAs should connect the dots, that is, they should link the specific analysis of a development problem with the systemic analysis of the broader country-level dynamics. To be sure, the balance between the overarching and the specific analysis can vary depending on the purpose at hand. If the aim is to offer broad guidance to the development of a country strategy, the problem can be defined in broad terms, for example, the challenge of governing Mongolia's natural resource boom. Conversely, if the aim is to help find a way forward on a very specific operational problem, such as the provision of local health services in the Philippines or of community infrastructure in Papua New Guinea, then the country-level part of the diagnostic can be much lighter, and often primarily drawn from secondary sources. But without both some anchoring from the bottom up and support from the top down, a PEA almost certainly falls short of its potential.

Lesson 4

A political economy perspective and the way it is used must contend with the evolution of realities on the ground. To be sure, in some settings fundamental drivers remain stable for extended periods even if noisy day-to-day politics create a facade of constant change. But in most settings and for most issues, political economy constellations continually evolve—sometimes gradually, sometimes at a faster pace, or sometimes in the form of decisive turning points—rather than being stable. In Mongolia, increased revenues from the mining sector are gushing in. Across developing countries, the boom in natural resources that has taken place since the early 2000s, as well as trends such as urbanization, demographic shifts, and the arrival of affordable mobile communications, are generating important changes in the political and economic drivers, with numerous other changes being triggered by these wider trends. Other changes may result from more specific events, such as the sudden death of a leader (for example, Meles Zenawi of Ethiopia) or the emergence of new political players. Such constant evolution does not render PEA a futile endeavor. Rather, it implies that PEAs need to be situated in a specific time period and need to incorporate a sense of dynamics and likely trajectories or scenarios when providing advice. For teams seeking to have PEA inform their approach, this lesson implies a need to revisit earlier analyses when a new situation arises and often a need to update the information and the implications derived from the analysis.

Lesson 5

The fifth, sixth, and seventh lessons focus on process. Lesson five suggests that for PEAs to have an impact, they need to be done in close coordination with the country and the sectoral teams responsible for addressing the problem being considered. Among the eight case studies, the assessments for which the collaboration was closest (the Dominican Republic, Ghana, Mongolia, and Zambia) were also the ones that had the most significant effect. Collaboration is greatly facilitated when the analytic team, the country, and the sector team jointly discuss and clarify expectations ex ante and then consider findings and implications as to what might be done differently after the analytic work has been carried out.[17]

Lesson 6

PEA needs flexibility with regard to the accessibility and the involvement of a wider range of stakeholders. Some governments support this type of analytic work as assisting a constructive dialogue among stakeholders. Among donors, some staff members argue strongly that PEAs should be joint initiatives, especially insofar as these assessments comprise the basis for changes in operational approach. But others argue that for donor staff members to be effective partners, they may need opportunities for learning about the environment in which they are working and a safe setting in their organizations in which to explore questions that might previously have been perceived to be taboo.

Lesson 7

PEAs are worth doing only if they affect how donors act, and this is an ongoing challenge. Effective engagement on the ground may require donor agencies to reorient organizational skills and resources. Many of the policy proposals laid out in table 1.3 are not ones that country and sector teams can readily implement, given time and budget constraints and existing skill mixes. Key actions highlighted in table 1.3 include (a) seeking greater outreach through a country's public media to explain the benefits of particular reforms and to debate alternatives; (b) integrating social accountability actions into an operation, for example, by helping to develop the capacity of civil society organizations for monitoring public contracts; and (c) intensifying discussions with multiple factions in parliament to build a greater understanding of policy choices and to better understand parliamentarians' incentives and concerns. These actions may require dedicating staff time to implement them as well as integrating new skills into sector teams and country offices in ways that keep technical experts closely involved but better leveraged in their ability to be part of stakeholder engagement and outreach.

Also, it can be challenging for sector teams to adopt suggestions that point to nonorthodox approaches. Giving up on the idea of "independent" regulatory agencies, which tend not to be truly independent given political economy constraints, or accepting that there is a broad stakeholder consensus in favor of government ownership in certain sectors can be challenging for technical specialists—and all the more so if the suggestions are made by a team of political economy experts rather than by leading experts in a particular field. Consequently, building greater knowledge about how PEA perspectives have helped more effectively address similar problems in other countries will be crucial to developing suggestions and solutions that find more ready acceptance.

Looking Forward

Looking forward, as PEA matures as an analytic perspective, it is important to consider how it can be productively combined with other efforts to rethink and reshape development approaches to achieve better solutions. For example, the growing interest in impact assessments can be helpful in identifying missing links that are related to political economy drivers. On the action side, PEAs can contribute to efforts to identify and implement agendas for change that use "rapid results" methodologies.[18] Political windows of opportunity for reforms, such as the honeymoon periods of newly elected governments, the presence and relative influence of a reformer in government, or even a fiscal crisis, are typically of limited duration. Therefore, a politically smart engagement will frequently involve ways of gaining traction quickly, followed by more long-term efforts to develop a sensible policy agenda or to strengthen the public dialogue about necessary improvements.

In a broader lens, a political economy perspective is crucially important for some of the emerging frontier issues to achieve inclusive and sustainable growth and development. Within many countries, socioeconomic inequality has increased in recent years, and the collective risks from environmental degradation are rising. Political economy perspectives are an essential ingredient to any efforts at mitigating and reversing such trends. More broadly, politics—and the way it interacts with economic interests and incentives—is a key ingredient in how societies function, how they allocate and use resources, and whether and how they enable citizens to prosper both individually and collectively.

Notes

1. In addition, the World Bank's Africa region is in the process of undertaking a meta-review of PEA done in the region over the past five years, and the contributing donors of the Governance Partnership Facility have commissioned a review of PEA work funded from the facility.

2. A number of studies have sought to take stock of these efforts, including DFID (2005), Dahl-Østergaard et al. (2005), NMFA (2010), and OECD DAC (2008). Further reviews are currently being developed. Other agencies such as AusAID are newly developing political economy frameworks—building on existing experiences— for use within their agencies.

3. In 2008, following the adoption of the Bank's Governance and Anticorruption strategy, these donors came together to establish a major trust fund at the World Bank, the Governance Partnership Facility.

4. The process to select what would be presented at the conference was robust, with the decisions unanimously agreed by panels of four to five experts from the Bank staff. Not all studies presented at the conference are included here. One study (commercialization of agriculture in Ghana), not originally presented at the conference, is additionally included in this volume.

5. See Fritz, Kaiser, and Levy (2009). A summary is contained in the 2010 How-to Note (World Bank 2010). There have also been two other World Bank publications: *The Political Economy of Policy Reform: Issues and Implications for Policy Dialogue and Development Operations* (2008), summarizing the experience of social development teams with PEA, and *Understanding Policy Change: How to Apply Political Economy Concepts in Practice* (Corduneanu-Huci, Hamilton, and Ferrer 2013). The latter provides an overview of key political economy concepts (with a primary focus on those developed under the auspices of game theory).

6. A problem-solving approach is not unique to this type of analysis, but it has been used in a variety of disciplines. This approach built on the earlier experience by DFID, Sida, and the World Bank with applying broader, more open-ended tools that often were thought to result in too little concrete guidance for action.

7. These categorizations are based on the U.S. nongovernmental organization Freedom House and Polity IV Project assessments, the two most widely used comparative assessments of regime types. The two sources differ somewhat for several of the cases.

8. The focus on this link between politics and economics also distinguishes the PEA carried out by development agencies from the political monitoring typically done for foreign policy purposes.

9. For some important analyses of clientelism, see Robinson and Verdier (2013) and Roniger (2004).

10. It is important to note that applied PEA *can* have the express purpose to capture, systematize, and set out issues and information that are important, but for some, hard evidence cannot be obtained within the frame of analytic work. For example, in the absence of a court case, allegations about illicit activity frequently cannot be proven. Depending on the issue at hand, the alleged actions may be part of a syndrome of reform bottlenecks that should not be ignored, but rather, if plausible, the presence of allegations should be noted, with due recognition that they are unproven.

11. In addition, new staff members have typically been left to re-accumulate these insights over a period of time that can easily be equivalent to about half the time spent in a given position.

12. In particular, in many places it is challenging to track who holds interests in which companies or who owns what tracts of land and how, in turn, these stakeholders relate to political decision makers. In some situations, important interests may be illicit and therefore intentionally hidden, such as the role of drug cartels in Central America or the globally widespread practice of kickbacks paid as part of public contracts and used to fund political campaigns or to line private pockets.

13. See also Albert Hirschman's earlier distinction between projects that are "trait taking" versus those that seek to be "trait making," that is, fitting easily into an existing social and cultural structure versus seeking to change aspects of the existing structure. See Hirschman ([1967] 1995, chapter 4).

14. The organizational arrangements described here are the ones that prevailed when the cases were written—before an internal reorganization that was launched in late 2013.

15. The Bank's Governance and Anticorruption strategy was adopted in 2007, and an update was issued in 2012.

16. The issue that this policy solution might not be effective was also flagged in the original analysis, but there was no subsequent exploration of alternatives or adjustments.

17. This collaboration also entails the need to find the right mix of skills and experience for the analytic team. For example, experts on a particular country often lack knowledge of specific sector problems.

18. Many of these ideas originate in the business literature and some even in military thinking. Whether these ideas can be applied to development problems involving a different range of stakeholders and institutions given political economy realities needs to be considered in each case.

Bibliography

Bogaards, Matthijs. 2009. "How to Classify Hybrid Regimes? Defective Democracy and Electoral Authoritarianism." *Democratization* 16 (2): 399–423.

Booth, David. 2012. *Development as a Collective Action Problem. Addressing the Real Challenges of African Governance.* Africa Power and Politics Programme, London, U.K.: Overseas Development Institute.

Carothers, Thomas, and Diane de Gramont. 2013. *Development Aid Confronts Politics: The Almost Revolution.* Washington, DC: Carnegie Endowment.

Corduneanu-Huci, Cristina, Alexander Hamilton, and Issel Masses Ferrer. 2013. *Understanding Policy Change: How to Apply Political Economy Concepts in Practice.* Washington, DC: World Bank.

Dahl-Østergaard, Tom, Sue Unsworth, Mark Robinson, and Rikke Ingrid Jensen. 2005. *Lessons Learned on the Use of Power and Drivers of Change Analyses in Development Co-Operation.* Organisation for Economic Co-Operation and Development, Development Assistance Committee Network on Governance, Paris.

Desai, Raj. 2011. "An Evaluation of Political-Economic Analysis in Support of the World Bank's Governance and Anticorruption Strategy." IEG Working Paper 2011/4, Independent Evaluation Group, World Bank, Washington, DC.

DFID (Department for International Development). 2005. "How-To Note: Lessons Learned—Planning and Undertaking a Drivers of Change Study." DFID Practice Paper, DFID, London, U.K.

Fritz, Verena, Kai Kaiser, and Brian Levy. 2009. *Problem-Driven Governance and Political Economy Analysis: Good Practice Framework.* Washington, DC: World Bank.

Harris, Daniel, and David Booth. 2013. *Applied Political Economy Analysis: Five Practical Issues.* London, U.K.: Overseas Development Institute.

Hirschman, Albert O. (1967) 1995. *Development Projects Observed.* Washington, DC: Brookings Institution.

Keefer, Philip, and Stuti Khemani. 2012. "Do Informed Citizens Receive More ... Or Pay More? The Impact of Radio on the Government Distribution of Public Health Benefits." Policy Research Working Paper 5952, World Bank, Washington, DC.

Khemani, Stuti. 2007. "Can Information Campaigns Overcome Political Obstacles to Serving the Poor?" In *The Politics of Service Delivery in Democracies: Better Access for the Poor*, edited by Shanta Devarajan and Ingrid Widlund, 56–69. Stockholm: Expert Group on Development Issues, Ministry for Foreign Affairs.

Levitsky, Steven, and Lucan Way. 2010. *Competitive Authoritarianism: Hybrid Regimes after the Cold War.* Cambridge, U.K.: Cambridge University Press.

NMFA (Netherlands Ministry of Foreign Affairs). 2010. "Political Analyses and Development Cooperation: Draft Synthesis of the Power and Change Analyses 2007–2009." NMFA, The Hague, the Netherlands.

Norris, Pippa. 2011. "Making Democratic-Governance Work: The Consequences for Prosperity." Harvard Kennedy School Faculty Research Working Paper RWP11-035, Harvard University, Cambridge, MA.

OECD DAC (Organisation for Economic Co-operation and Development, Development Assistance Committee). 2008. *Survey of Donor Approaches to Governance Assessment.* Final survey report, OECD DAC Network on Governance, Paris.

Przeworski, Adam, Michael Alvarez, José A. Cheibub, and Fenando Limongi. 2000. *Democracy and Development: Political Institutions and Well-Being in the World, 1950–1990.* Cambridge, U.K.: Cambridge University Press.

Robinson, James A., and Thierry Verdier. 2013. "The Political Economy of Clientelism." *Scandinavian Journal of Economics* 115 (2): 260–91.

Roniger, Luis. 2004. "Political Clientelism, Democracy, and Market Economy." *Comparative Politics* 36 (3): 353–75.

Vincente, Pedro, and Leonard Wantchekon. 2009. "Clientelism and Vote Buying: Lessons from Field Experiments in African Elections." *Oxford Review of Economic Policy* 25 (2): 292–305.

World Bank. 2008. *The Political Economy of Policy Reform: Issues and Implications for Policy Dialogue and Development Operations.* Washington, DC: World Bank.

———. 2010. "Political Economy Assessments at Sector and Project Levels." GAC-In -Projects How-To Notes, World Bank, Washington, DC.

PART 1

The Political Economy of Resource Allocation

Dealing with a Resource Shock: Political Economy Analysis and Its Impacts in Mongolia

Verena Fritz

Introduction

Mongolia saw a takeoff of investments in its natural resource sector starting in the mid-2000s. One of the largest unexploited copper deposits in the world, at Oyu Tolgoi, is located in Mongolia. In addition, the country is richly endowed with a range of other minerals, including gold, coking-grade coal, uranium, and others. As the development in the Oyu Tolgoi mine got under way, growth reached 17.1 percent in 2011, making Mongolia one of the fastest-growing economies in the world. Given the small population of 2.5 million, the size of the natural resource boom relative to the country's economy is very large (EBRD 2012). The resource boom has a significant effect on per capita incomes, whereas the distributional impacts are still evolving. Furthermore, growth has been very volatile in recent years, accelerating in the mid-2000s, going negative in 2009 in the wake of the global crisis, and then recovering and reaching double-digit levels in 2011 and 2012 (figure 2.1).

As the mining sector began its rapid acceleration around 2006, there was a growing concern—within the World Bank team itself as well as among many domestic and external stakeholders—whether the coming resource windfall could be well managed. This concern was based on historical experiences with natural resource booms in low-income countries, which had often ended in calamity rather than sustainable development. Resource-dependent economies are susceptible to external shocks, and windfalls reaped for some years can easily

This chapter provides a summary of work that involved a team consisting of Genevieve Boyreau (task team leader), Naazneen Barma, Chris Finch, Zahid Hasnain, and others.

The findings, interpretations, and conclusions contained in this synthesis report are entirely those of the authors. They do not necessarily represent the view of the World Bank, its executive directors, or the countries they represent. The World Bank is not responsible for the contents of this research.

Figure 2.1 GDP Growth and Volatility

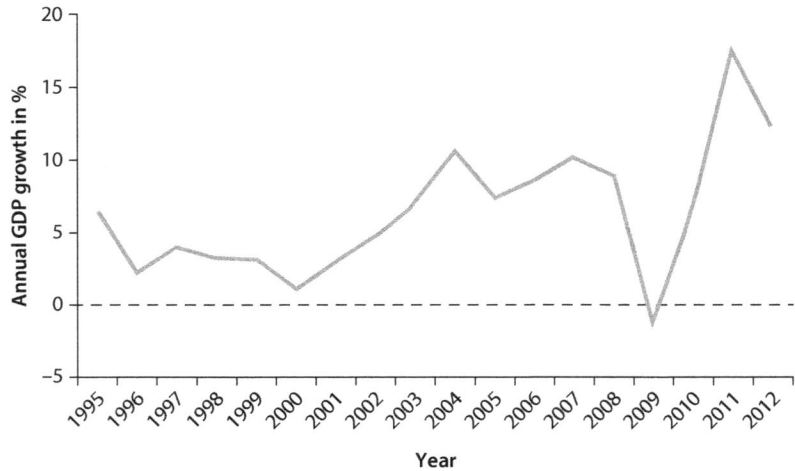

Source: World Bank, World Development Indicators.
Note: GDP = gross domestic product.

be wasted, rather than being invested in projects that enable long-run sustainable growth (Auty 1993, 2001). In addition, there were some immediate concerns about policy choices and trends, including the emergence of pro-cyclical fiscal policies, greater volatility in decision making, and licensing practices in the resource sector that were not well regulated.

In addition, from an operational point of view, the World Bank's country team had been repeatedly surprised in 2006 and 2007 by government policy decisions. One of the most notable surprises was the fact that after an intensive and extended dialogue on the targeting of social benefits, the government unexpectedly decided to create a universal benefit to be received by all children and to finance this from a newly introduced windfalls profit tax imposed on copper and gold production. Against this background, the Country Management Unit decided to commission several interlinked pieces of governance and political economy analysis (PEA) under the broad umbrella of a Governance Assessment on how best to counter the risks of a resource curse in the country. The PEA consisted of a country background note, as well as eight more focused notes covering specific aspects of the "mining sector value chain"—from the upstream areas of allocating mining rights, through revenues and fiscal management, to downstream areas of how money is being spent on public investments on the one hand and social transfers on the other.

Three key issues explored by the PEA are highlighted in this chapter. The first issue is the overall incentives and challenges for the country's elites in seeking sufficiently good management of the resource boom, including in reaction to public expectations. The other two issues relate to how newly accruing resources were being spent: the rapidly expanding volume of public investments on the one hand and the implementation of new social transfers on the other. Spending decisions in both of these areas were significantly influenced by political considerations and incentives. Although political considerations underpin spending decisions in any country, risks of problematic decisions are particularly great when fiscal resources increase very rapidly and when political competition becomes highly opportunistic rather than programmatic (Keefer and Vlaicu 2008). The challenge was to identify what would constitute good-enough management in each of these areas and, related to this, to consider opportunities for World Bank engagement.

This chapter reflects the initial analytic work, its findings, and its implications. In addition, it traces what happened subsequently and how different efforts are evolving. This approach enables one to check for plausible connections between the analytic work done, and its more direct effects and efforts at "doing things differently," with a view to maximizing the World Bank's developmental impact with limited resources.

Mongolia illustrates how PEA can assist a country team in reshaping its engagement in a rapidly evolving environment. Initial analytic work was started in 2007 in response to the emerging natural resource boom. Over a five-year period, the World Bank's country team built an innovative engagement and achieved a number of successes. At the same time, the challenges posed by the resource boom remained substantial, including powerful incentives against sufficiently good management of resources, as well as the sheer challenge of developing the capabilities to manage a very rapid economic expansion. Also, with rapid economic growth, the financial importance of the World Bank and that of other aid agencies declined. Overall, how significantly this reorientation of the Bank's engagement will contribute to helping Mongolians manage their resource boom in a better way is still evolving.

Country-Level PEA

The first part of the Governance Assessment consisted of a country-level background note. This captured key historical legacies influencing the current situation, as well as the emerging dynamics and trends related to the resource boom. Such country-level analysis is typically not directly operationally relevant. However, it is important to capture the fundamental incentives and dynamics of the political leadership and decision making in a country, and clearly so when the challenge is to understand how a society is likely to cope with a large-scale natural resource boom relative to the existing size of the economy and the country's population.

As is the case with many newly resource-rich countries, Mongolia's development and political economy dynamics have been strongly affected by (global) structural factors and shifts, that is, changes that are well beyond the control of any individual or group of citizens, but that deeply affect the position and incentives of many stakeholders. Two crucial structural shifts included the price fluctuations of copper on the one hand, and the rise of China on the other.

Problem-Driven Political Economy Analysis · http://dx.doi.org/10.1596/978-1-4648-0121-1

Historical Legacies and Structural Drivers of Mongolia's Development

Mongolia's resource endowments were initially explored during the country's 70-year communist period (1921–92). However, only one major deposit—the Erdenet open pit copper mine—was developed during this time, in the very north of the country, in 1974 (see map 2.1). The Erdenet mine's development was completed just as a 30-year phase of low commodity prices set in (figure 2.2). As a result of the Chinese-Soviet split and China's own relative economic backwardness during this period, Mongolia's minerals exports were oriented almost entirely toward the Soviet Union and other Council for Mutual Economic Assistance (COMECON) countries. Although some knowledge about other significant deposits was gathered during this period, there was no interest in developing these at the time in the context of low prices, unclear access to export markets, and a trade orientation away from China.

With the collapse of the Soviet Union, Mongolia lost previous trading relationships as well as significant external assistance that had been provided by a range of COMECON countries. Furthermore, the transition period coincided with a period of further falling prices for copper (figure 2.2). The country experienced a deep transition recession and substantial social dislocation.

Map 2.1 Mongolia

Source: Map number: IBRD 40242, August 2013.

Figure 2.2 Key Commodity Prices and Political Economy Events and Turning Points

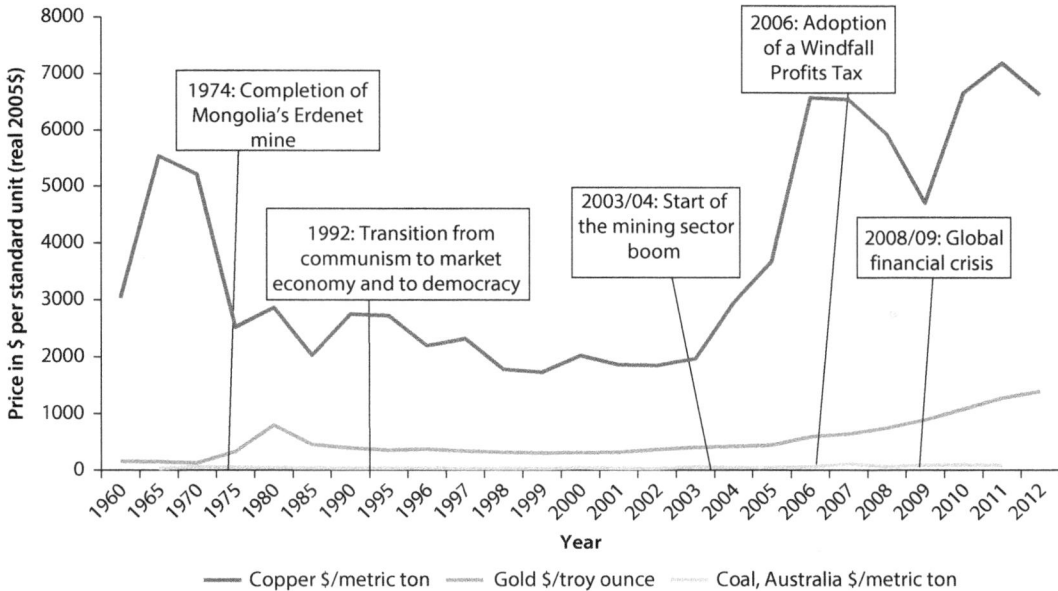

Source: Based on World Bank, Commodities Price Indices (database).
Note: 1960–95 is shown in 5-year and 1995 onwards is shown in 1-year increments. mt = metric tons; toz = troy ounce.

On the positive side, despite these economic challenges and other factors, such as geographic distance from established democracies and a lack of prior experience with a democratic system, political and civil freedom emerged and was maintained, in contrast to the reversal to more authoritarian forms of government that occurred in many former Soviet countries (Fish 1998; Fritz 2002, 2008). Furthermore, relative openness to the outside world also translated into a number of economic and public sector reform efforts during this period (Laking 1999).

In contrast to some resource-rich countries, the risk of violent conflict has been small in Mongolia. The country is ethnically homogenous on the whole, with ethnic Mongolians accounting for 95 percent of the population. Internal religious cleavages have been largely absent, with a revival of Buddhism taking place during the post-communist period. A defining structural feature of the country is its geographic location between two far bigger neighbors, the Russian Federation and China, imparting a degree of external threat, which, as Leftwich (2001) has argued, can strengthen internal coherence.

A key social cleavage is that between the urban population mainly based in the capital, Ulaanbaatar, and the rural population, as well as increasingly that between wealthier and poorer groups.[1] Poverty rose during the transition and still remained at close to 40 percent until the late 2000s, with a significant spread between urban (lower) and rural (higher) poverty but also with substantial deprivation in rapidly expanding periurban areas.[2]

Figure 2.3 The Rapid Rise of per Capita GDP since the Late 1990s

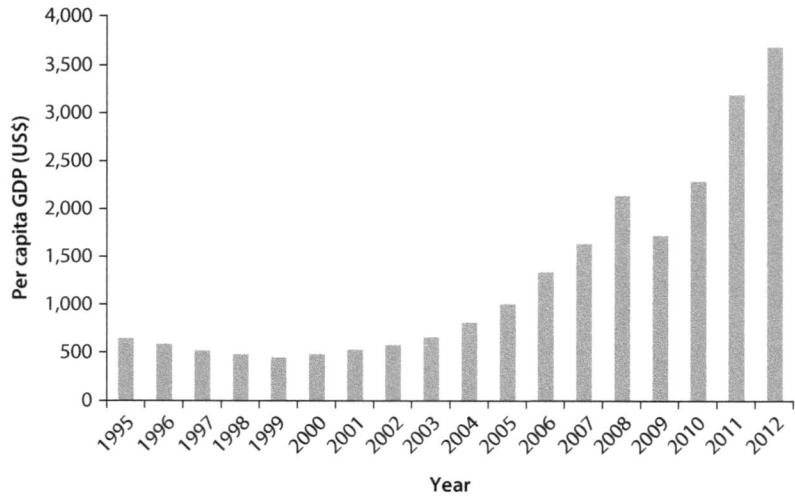

Source: World Bank, World Development Indicators (database).
Note: GDP = gross domestic product.

The post-communist crisis of the 1990s was followed by a second transition: from an impoverished economy recovering from a severe post-communist recession to one experiencing very rapid expansion and double-digit growth (see figure 2.1). This transition was driven by the coincidence of a sharp rebound in prices for copper and the discovery and confirmation of the size of additional deposits. Moreover, it coincided with the rise of China as a major importer of natural resources—thus opening up a huge market for Mongolia's resources in close proximity.[3] The resource boom transformed the economy and moved Mongolia from the ranks of low-income countries to lower-middle-income countries, with (average) per capita incomes rising sixfold within a decade (see figure 2.3).

The background note summarized political economy dynamics and pointed to a set of trends and political economy drivers that shaped the risks as well as potential entry points for engaging in support of sufficiently good management of the resource boom.

The Evolution of Political Competition during the Post-communist Period

Political competition in the post-communist period has been marked by several major swings, in particular in 1996 and in 2000, as well as by the way in which the initial electoral rules of the game provided some advantages to the communist legacy party. The experience of successive elections informed how political parties sought to appeal to voters as fiscal space began to grow with the emerging resource boom.

During the initial post-communist decade (1992–2002), three main parties emerged: the Mongolian Peoples' Revolutionary Party (MPRP), the Mongolian

(National) Democratic Party (MNDP), and the Mongolian Social Democratic Party (MSDP), as well as several smaller parties. The MPRP was the communist legacy party (and had governed as the sole legal party from 1921 to 1990), while the MSDP and the MNDP were founded by a younger generation of urban intellectuals, many of whom had studied in and were inspired by the transitions in Central Eastern Europe.[4] A new Constitution was adopted in 1992, establishing a mixed parliamentary-presidential system. The unicameral parliament and the government based on a majority in parliament dominate the system of government, while the Constitution also stipulates a directly elected president. Generally, rural voters remained the stronghold of the MPRP, while urban voters have been more likely to vote for the various newly founded parties. Initial electoral rules and districting were adopted in 1992, allocating 25 seats to urban districts and 51 seats to rural districts, thereby locking in an electoral advantage for the MPRP. In addition, a majoritarian electoral system was adopted that tended to magnify the gains in parliamentary seats of the winning party.

The initial election in 1992 was won by the MPRP. The post-communist party then had to preside over a deep transition recession as prior trade and funding arrangements with the Soviet bloc dissolved, with strong negative repercussions for Mongolia's economy. During this period, the country's existing copper mine at Erdenet played an important role in keeping the country and the government's budget afloat. The 1996 election then resulted in the first change in government. The Democratic Union (DU), an electoral bloc uniting a number of the parties formed since the early 1990s, won 47 percent of the popular vote and just under two-thirds of the seats in parliament. During this initial stint in government, the DU alliance pursued social and economic policies broadly aligned with the liberalization and austerity agenda of the Washington Consensus, including a major scaling back of the pension system. Predictably, the alliance lost the following elections in 2000, when the majority swung back to the MPRP, which gained a super-majority in parliament with 72 of 76 seats—based on winning 52 percent of the popular vote.

The 2004 election campaign was the first during which the prospect of a mining boom emerged as copper prices began to rise (see figure 2.2) and the prospect of major new investments in mining appeared. The Oyu Tolgoi deposit had been confirmed in 2001, and by 2003, intensive exploration activity was under way. A number of the parties that had united as the DU in 1996 now formed as the Motherland Democratic Coalition (MDC) electoral bloc. In a sharp departure from policies implemented in the late 1990s, the alliance this time proposed the introduction of a new social benefit—the Child Money Program (CMP)—in the bloc's election program. This proposal helped the MDC to pull nearly even with the MPRP, winning 34–36 seats in the elections, and forced the formation of a first coalition government (with three different prime ministers serving between 2004 and the following elections in 2008).

The 2008 elections were hotly contested between the two main blocs, in the context of rapidly accelerating copper prices (see figure 2.2) and amidst initial negotiations about an investment agreement with the consortium of companies that had been formed to develop the Oyu Tolgoi deposit. The MPRP again gained a majority, winning nearly 53 percent of the vote and (as a result of changes in the electoral system) about 60 percent of the seats in parliament. For the first time, the losing party raised strong allegations of voting fraud, and postelection violence erupted. Eventually, a coalition government was formed that brought all major parties into the government, and hence to the negotiating table over contracts concerning the development of major deposits.

Summary of the Country-Level PEA of 2008

Each of these shifts in the political and economic currents had important repercussions for the World Bank team's engagement. In the late 1990s, the team undertook some initial engagement in the mining sector, advising on a law that was adopted in 1997 in the context of low commodity prices and the premise that Mongolia would need to provide a very favorable climate to attract investments to its mining sector, in light of the country's remote location and high transport costs. In the early 2000s, the MPRP enjoyed a supermajority in parliament, resulting in a coherent and relatively predictable government, but also giving rise to some concerns that the party might seek to steer toward greater authoritarianism and state control over the economy. Since 2003/04, dynamics fundamentally changed: the prospect of a mining sector boom emerged, while politics again became not only more competitive, but also more fragmented and unpredictable. Accelerating resource prices and electoral calculations gave rise to new spending pressures and opportunities and the overarching concern of how the boom could be well managed in the long-term interest of society as a whole.

When the country team began preparing its 2008–12 Country Assistance Strategy (CAS),[5] it sought to develop a better understanding of the country and the mining sector value chain from the allocation of contracts through to the way resulting additional resources would be used. The governance and PEA pointed to the following trends and resulting risks and opportunities for engagement.

Rapidly Rising Mineral Revenues, Weak Institutional Constraints in Key Areas, and Public and Political Pressure to Spend and Distribute Mining Revenues

Rapidly rising mineral revenues raised the expectations of citizens in terms of the economic benefits to be received. The rising mining revenues and the increased expectations for distribution were particularly powerful given weak institutional constraints on government spending. The existing fiscal framework did not have provisions for mandatory savings during booms (and for avoiding pro-cyclical spending) or restrictions on the levels of debt or annual deficits. This enabled populist electoral campaign promises to be made on the basis of growing fiscal resources—especially because these pressures coincided with a period of increasing political competition and fragmentation.

Figure 2.4 Inflation, 2001–12

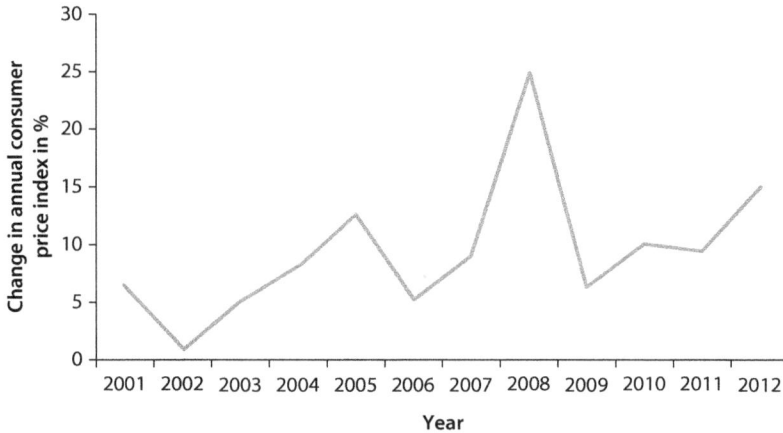

Source: World Bank, World Development Indicators.

The acceleration in spending also raised inflation (see figure 2.4), which hurt especially poorer groups.

Political Institutions, Electoral System, and Populism

The closely contested parliamentary election in 2004, with the two major parties winning near-equal shares of seats, led to three fragile coalition governments between 2004 and 2008. The succession of coalition governments contributed to a short-term horizon for policy makers, which promoted unpredictability and reversals in policies. During this period, parliament gained a significant role in policy formulation and decision making, adopting populist policy measures and overruling policy proposals from the executive. The evenly distributed parliament gave greater power to individual members of parliament (MPs) compared with the previous legislative cycles when successive governments had been able to rely on large or super large majorities in parliament. Moreover, parliament's increasing influence over policy decisions was initially not matched by increased capacity for policy analysis or by institutionalized mechanisms for consultations on draft legislation with the wider public.

In particular, parliamentarians had a growing influence over spending decisions. On the one hand, incumbent MPs sought to allocate more public investments to their constituencies. The selection of investments became more strongly influenced by electoral considerations, and therefore also by the rural bias in the electoral system that gave rural districts overrepresentation. On the other hand, candidates for those parties that were less entrenched in rural areas sought to strengthen their appeal through proposing further social benefits. Thus, electoral strategies on all sides rested on promises to significantly expand spending going into the 2008 elections.

Overall, the combination of a political system that provided significant power to parliament and to individual MPs as government majorities declined, with political fragmentation, and with electoral incentives, provided the incentives for many of the policy changes that took place during the emerging boom period. These included changes in the mining code, amendments to the procurement law (facilitating more direct contracting), the allocation of a large number of small investment projects, and the adoption of universalized benefits rather than more targeted support to the country's poor.

Limited Policy and Institutional Mechanisms to Ensure Accountability and Transparency

Despite the relatively successful establishment of a democratic regime, there were still vestiges of the old, more closed and secretive system. The policy-making process remained nontransparent in several important areas. For example, a Law on State Secrets restricted public access to government documents. There were no legal rules for making information on draft laws or the budget public. The voting record of MPs was not accessible for public scrutiny. For the mining sector specifically, the lack of a detailed regulatory framework enabling the implementation of the Mineral Law resulted in a high level of discretion in the allocation of mining licenses.

Patronage Networks and Unregulated Conflict of Interest

Patronage links have been strong and embedded not only in political parties, but also in regional networks and business conglomerates—and the latter two also cut across party lines. Politics and economic opportunities were closely linked and became more strongly so in the course of the 2000s.[6] Opportunities for conflicts of interest in the public sector were substantial and were not regulated. For example, there was no regulation of conflict of interest in mining licensing. Similarly, many politicians either had or developed interests in the construction sector, while the scale of public contracts rapidly accelerated. At the same time, and in contrast to a number of other resource-rich countries, no single player was able to monopolize power.

Concerns over Sovereignty and National Interests

With rising commodity prices and an increased presence of foreign companies, sovereignty and foreign policy concerns were widely held up as a key political justification for many proposed policy changes and decisions. These have included proposals to increase state participation in the mining sector and to raise taxes on mining companies and foreign investors, as well as to carry out public investments in remote locations, argued as important to secure a large and very sparsely populated territory.[7] In this context, the Erdenet mine—in operation since 1974 and in which government has held a 51 percent share—was taken as a good example of a company that contributed to government revenues and local development. This general perception overlooked, however, important aspects of how investments in the mine had been made during the Soviet period, which would not be replicable in an era in which Mongolia had to attract major private sector investments to develop its large-scale deposits.

Mongolian policy makers publicly advocated repeating a 51 percent stake in future major mining projects. Among citizens, it was felt that higher state ownership would translate into greater revenue, and there was a fear that if the state did not control shares, then companies could be sold to investors with lower standards for transparency, environment management, and corporate responsibility.[8] However, these positions did not confront the facts of the relative riskiness of direct government involvement—with regard to economic aspects and the governance of a large state-owned share, as well as the government's ability to make such investments and reach agreements with private sector investments.

Limited Awareness of the Costs and Benefits of Policy Options Related to Managing a Mineral-Based Economy

There was public interest in knowing how government obtains and manages resources from mining. Yet the level of information available to citizens was limited, and the sector was publicly perceived as affected by rent-seeking and clientelism. This lack of information was typical of a country that experiences a sudden growth in the mining sector. Limited public information and understanding of mining-related policy issues also meant that citizens found it difficult to tell which political arguments to trust or how to hold politicians and public servants to account.

These dimensions interacted in various ways: for example, the great game of allocating property rights was feeding back into the fragmentation of the political party system, which had been rather clearly structured and programmatic during the initial post-communist period (Fish 1998).[9] Looking forward, the analysis suggested that the complexity of networks and the emerging fragmentation of the political and institutional system would make politics and policy making more unpredictable and that the main focus of policy makers would be on distributing lucrative rights over natural resources—while keeping an eye on competitors.

At the same time, the political economy situation was also marked by some advantages relative to other low-income, resource-rich countries. A small and relatively homogenous population, mainly divided by a significant urban-rural cleavage and increasingly by diverging income levels, meant that natural resources entailed little risk of armed conflict—the worst form that a natural resource curse can take (Collier and Hoeffler 2005). The country had made some significant investments in improving public financial management systems during the late 1990s and early 2000s, although these had also left a number of institutional issues unresolved, especially with regard to public investment management, that had been less pertinent during lean times.

In contrast to a number of other resource-rich countries, a basic democratic system of government had emerged about a decade prior to the onset of the resource boom. In addition, Mongolia had a fully literate society as part of its Soviet legacy.[10] Given that a constitution that dispersed rather than concentrated power had been in place since 1992, the capture of natural resource wealth by an over-powerful president or a very narrow clique of insiders was less of a risk than elsewhere.[11] There were significant drivers toward a more inclusive development and use of natural resources, alongside incentives toward individual rent-seeking that have also been powerful and influential.[12] Political fragmentation has gone hand-in-hand with the rising power of the legislature, and consequently, key policy decisions have to be agreed upon by at least half of the 76 MPs, rather than the fiat of an individual strongman.

Implications from the Country-Level Analysis

Based on the country-level analysis, the Governance Assessment arrived at the following recommendations for World Bank engagement in Mongolia. These sought to focus on positive aspects of the country and to identify ways in which progressive policy developments could be supported and enabled.

- Strengthen domestic capabilities for policy analysis, with stronger dissemination and outreach, to facilitate a more informed and transparent public policy debate, highlighting policy trade-offs. For example, initiate regular policy forums on mining and economic performance that reach not only policy makers but also other key stakeholders, journalists, and the public; seek to strengthen the capacity for policy analysis by local think tanks, and the research and analytical capability available to the executive branch as well as to parliament.

- Engage more with parliament and political parties, and strengthen parliament's capacity for policy making. Given the importance of parliament in decision making, the World Bank should engage in dialogue with parliamentarians and find ways to improve their knowledge of policy choices and likely impacts.

- Strengthen social accountability by supporting community-driven initiatives in monitoring mining and public resources management, for example, in monitoring allocations of licenses, especially when these involve subnational governments; and in monitoring the impact of the CMP or other social transfers.

- Engage in institutional and policy options that fit policy makers' concerns and visions as opposed to first-best options. For example, given the widely shared preference for a significant government share in new mining projects, it would make sense to help analyze such options, rather than dismiss them as overly risky and unlikely to work from the outset. Some "best policy practices" proposed by the World Bank were not being taken up by decision makers who preferred different models (for example, with regards to public investment management and mining sector legislation) for various reasons. This posed a challenge in terms of adapting the engagement.

- Sustain assistance to the development of strong institutions for public financial management, building on successful past experiences. The Bank should build on its excellent record in public financial management reform, in particular with the implementation of a Government Financial Management and Information System, which had contributed to reducing opportunities for leakages from the budget. Assistance should be provided in strengthening horizontal accountability (for example, audits) and effectiveness in the use of public monies at service delivery (with monitoring from civil society).

The fourth recommendation, especially, targeted a shift from a first-best approach to one focused more on feasibility. The other recommendations targeted how to shape an emerging engagement in a challenging environment—in ways that would both help to mitigate risks of such an engagement and enable the team to play a role in proactively expanding the reform space in ways that were feasible for the Bank.

There was significant uptake of the study's findings and recommendations. From 2008 onward, the country team built a strong public outreach engagement. In doing so, the team benefited from converging factors. Among these, Mongolia was the first country to have a senior mining sector specialist based in country. A further key factor was that shortly after the conclusion of the analytic work, the World Bank team was able to attract some additional funding that allowed it to deepen its multistakeholder engagement. At the same time, and as will be discussed in the following section, there have also been some important limitations in particular with regard to the robustness of the solutions adopted.

Impact on Country-Level Engagement: Macro-Fiscal Management and Investments in Domestic Capacity for Policy Analysis

A key area to which the findings and implications were applied was macro-fiscal management. From 2004 onward, governments had adopted strongly pro-cyclical policies, rapidly accelerating spending as more resources became available. The rapid increases in expenditures were contributing to rising inflation (figure 2.4). Little attention was given to saving funds to help smooth a potential downturn, and concerns emerged over whether additional expenditures were well allocated. As outlined above, there was a strong political logic favoring these spending increases on social transfers as well as on public investments.

Shortly after the country-level analysis was completed in early 2008, the next parliamentary elections were held in the summer. Building on the 2004 experience, the two main political camps outbid each other with electoral promises of new cash handouts to citizens. This time, the MPRP promised a higher payout of new benefits to citizens and won a majority of seats. However, a number of seats had been tightly contested, and a leader of the opposition raised an accusation of electoral fraud, triggering a wave of violent protests—a first in Mongolia's post-communist history. Eventually, a truce emerged, and the main political camps formed a coalition government in September 2008.

While the fallout from the election was still playing out, the global financial crisis struck, affecting Mongolia by way of a sudden, significant decline in copper prices (see figure 2.2). This fed through to lower budget revenues than expected for 2009, and the government was forced to cut back its ambitious spending plans.

The need for a fiscal stabilization rule or mechanism had been discussed among policy makers and donors providing policy advice for some years, but it had not yet seriously entered the political agenda. The 2008–09 fiscal shock focused attention on how to achieve greater fiscal stabilization as one central pillar for managing a resource boom. It reinforced the need to find a way to tie the hands of policy makers in a situation of increasing political fragmentation and electoral competition involving significant new spending promises. However, doing so was likely to be challenging given political incentives and as political fragmentation made it more difficult than in the past to pass major reforms.

Members of the executive branch of government increasingly agreed that a Fiscal Stability Law would provide an important pillar of improving fiscal management and reducing the tendency toward strongly pro-cyclical policies. However, based on the country-level analysis that had been done, it was clear that technical dialogue on this issue with the Ministry of Finance was necessary and useful, but insufficient to get such a measure passed. Because the ministry itself wanted the measure to be adopted, the government was supportive of the Bank engaging in strong outreach to individual MPs and parliamentary factions, as well as the wider public via television and other media.

Increasing Outreach

The country team engaged in a variety of ways that included workshops, conferences, and study tours to other resource-rich countries with experts and MPs. For the general public, the team gave presentations in the media, seeking to develop a better understanding of macro-fiscal relationships and to highlight that a tying of hands was indeed a good choice for the country. It sought to address an initial perception that such a policy of relative fiscal constraint would be detrimental to the interests of citizens. This strategy of greater outreach was also agreed upon with the International Monetary Fund (IMF)—which had been called in for an 18-month standby agreement in April 2009. It should be noted, however, that while the PEA strongly informed the engagement process, the likely robustness of the policy solution—that is, the adoption of legal provisions to mandate a degree of fiscal savings during high-revenue years—was not further reviewed from a political economy perspective.

As noted above, the intensified outreach was enabled by additional resources that had been received as part of a Governance Partnership Facility trust fund.[13] Some activities focused on engagement with a range of stakeholders would most likely have been undertaken in any case, but the availability of additional and relatively flexible funds was an important facilitating factor for moving from analytic work to innovative engagement.

An initial payoff of the engagement was achieved in July 2010 when parliament passed a Fiscal Stability Law. The law imposed the following constraints: (a) it limits the structural fiscal deficit to 2 percent of gross domestic product (GDP), stipulates that excess revenue is to be saved in a stabilization fund, and limits the growth of expenditures to the nonmineral GDP growth rate; (b) a debt rule creates an overall ceiling on borrowing at 40 percent of GDP; and (c) annual budget and budget amendments must abide by the Medium-Term Fiscal Framework (which in turn must follow the fiscal rules).

An important caveat, however, was that the decision-making MPs left themselves considerable flexibility: key provisions of the law were to come into effect only in 2013, that is, after the subsequent elections in 2012 and by the time a new governing coalition would have been formed. Over the following two years, politicians made ample use of the flexibility: in 2011, government spending expanded by 61 percent and the fiscal balance again worsened (see figure 2.5) despite the return of high rates of growth and rapidly growing government revenue. In 2012, in the six months leading up to the end-of-June elections, government spending rose by a further 57 percent (year on year) as civil servants' wages were raised by more than 50 percent, cash handouts were stepped up, and capital expenditures were brought forward.[14]

As noted above, the 2012 elections yielded a parliament with no single party holding a clear majority. The Democratic Party (which now combined several of the parties that in 2008 had formed the MDC into a single party) emerged as the largest party and formed a coalition with several smaller parties. The Government's Action Plan for 2012–16 (equivalent to a coalition agreement) endorsed adherence to fiscal stability, as did the proposed budget for 2013. However, various other policies, such as moving some spending—via a newly

Figure 2.5 Overall Fiscal Balance, 2000–12

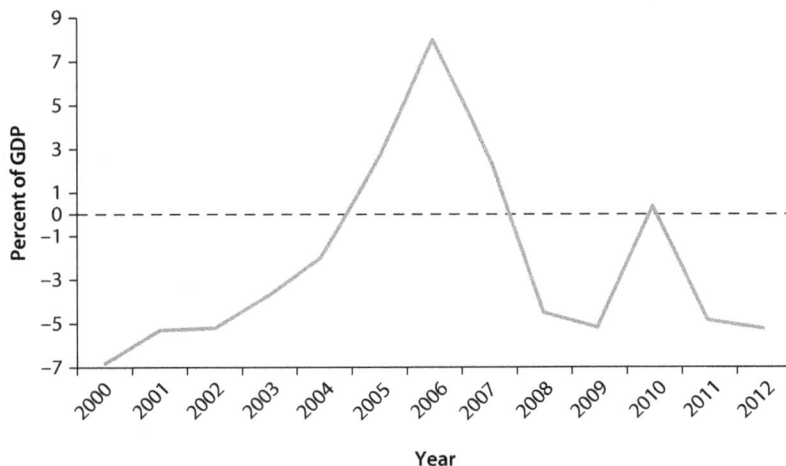

Source: IMF Mongolia Country Reports, various years.
Note: GDP = gross domestic product.

founded Development Bank of Mongolia (DBM)—off-budget and adopting a budget with optimistic revenue estimates, nonetheless contradicted full adherence de facto. This reflects the continuing struggle that successive governments face in truly limiting spending demands in the context of political fragmentation, considerable spending needs, and electoral incentives to spend in ways that are seen as bolstering electoral opportunities.

Strengthening Domestic Capabilities for Policy Analysis

A related engagement, but one with a longer-term perspective—suggested by the PEA and subsequently supported by the World Bank—was support for the establishment of the Economic Research Institute (ERI). After preparations were pursued in 2009 and early 2010, the institute was formally established in October 2010.[15] The rationale for supporting such a think tank was that it would be important for Mongolia to develop capacity for analyzing policy options related to managing a resource-rich economy. Internally generated advice brings important strengths: domestic knowledge can be accessed on a continuous basis by policy makers as well as by other stakeholders, such as civil society organizations (CSOs) and the media, and it also helps to establish trust that the research is aimed at identifying what is in the country's best interest in both the short and the long term.[16] As with any such effort, developing such an institute into an organization able to achieve high-quality research and policy analysis, as well as effective outreach, has taken time. As of 2012, ERI had begun to stimulate research on issues such as fiscal stability and the existence and role of a middle class in Mongolia. Through seminars and conferences, it seeks to inform public debate on key policy issues, thus beginning to fill crucial gaps in stimulating informed public debate.

Political Economy Aspects of Key Spending Areas: Public Investments and Cash Transfers

This section looks more deeply at two areas that have driven spending in Mongolia, public investments and social transfers. Both are links in the sector chain, reaching from the upstream management of the mining sector to the downstream management of spending that was analyzed as part of the set of political economy notes developed in 2008. The overarching question was how the expanding fiscal resources were being used and why. The PEA showed how both public investment and social cash transfer spending were influenced by electoral strategies, which in turn had implications for the specific design of these policies. For public investments, the political calculations revolve around the allocation to particular localities in the expectation of electoral advantage—an issue that appears to be shared across a number of countries as reflected in other chapters in this volume (for example, the Philippines and Papua New Guinea). The evolution of social transfers in Mongolia has also been targeted at winning votes, in this case from voters across constituencies. Moreover, these transfers were subject to a high degree of volatility both in terms of policies and in terms of actual payments made—given political exigencies to identify new policy promises for each election on the one hand and volatility in available fiscal resources on the other (prior to stabilization efforts becoming more effective). Findings from the analysis have been an important part of the country team's deeper understanding of sectoral dynamics, while the concrete uptake in operational engagement has been stronger on the public investment side.

Public Investments and Procurement

Public investment spending was identified as a critical issue. From an economic management perspective, it is a key hinge for translating the revenues from a resource boom into sustainable growth (World Bank forthcoming). Good public investments can allow a country to build a stronger and more modern economy and to invest in economic diversification. This is crucial to ensuring that a resource boom results in shared prosperity, sustainable beyond the resource boom itself. At the same time, public investments are prone to political influencing on the one hand and to governance and integrity challenges on the other.

Capital expenditures began to expand rapidly in the mid-2000s (figure 2.6). This expansion started from a low base as few domestic resources had been available for investments during the extended transition recession of the 1990s. By 2007, domestically funded public investments overtook those made by donors. After a brief decline in the wake of the global financial crisis, public investments continued their sharp upward trend from 2010 onward.

Figure 2.6 Rapidly Rising Capital Expenditures, 2003–11

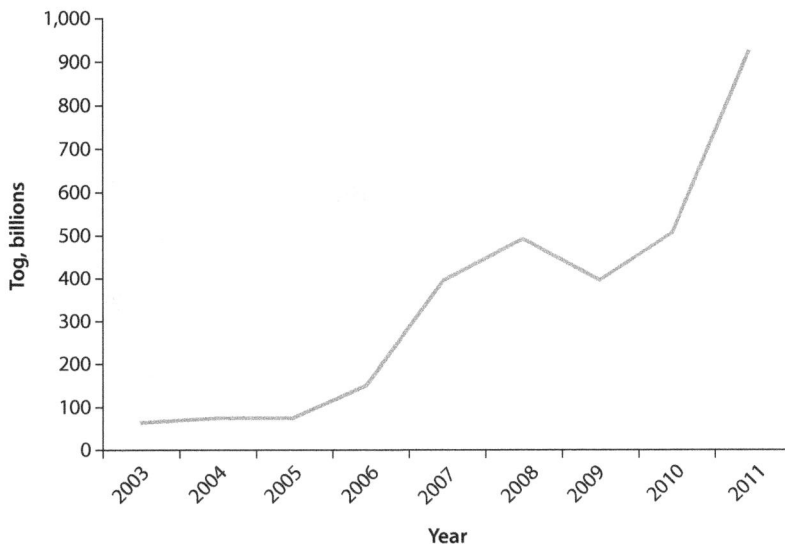

Source: Hasnain et al. 2013 based on Ministry of Finance data.
Note: Tog = togrog.

Prioritizing public investments inevitably poses a challenge. From an economic point of view, investments should be selected that yield the greatest medium- and long-term economic and social benefits. In Mongolia, choices are particularly challenging given a low population density on the one hand and a harsh climate that increases the cost of most infrastructure investments on the other.

Demands included the need to invest in infrastructure directly related to (a) developing mining deposits and facilitating exports; (b) increasing spending on maintenance and rehabilitation of existing infrastructure—from roads to power-lines to school buildings, much of which had been neglected for the past 15 years; and (c) finding the right balance between investing in infrastructure in Mongolia's few but significant urban centers, in its far-flung and very sparsely populated regions, and in major transport links. At the same time, there was a growing concern among the country and economic teams working on Mongolia that public investments were not well prioritized and that their planning and execution were not well managed (World Bank 2009a).

The political economy note identified the following set of drivers. First, existing institutional and legal capabilities were weak and overwhelmed by the rapid rise in investment volumes. During the extended transition period, Mongolia had dismantled its earlier planning institutions and had merged public investment planning into the Ministry of Finance, but as a relatively small and subordinate division. In addition, the organic budget legislation that had been adopted in 2002[17] barely mentioned capital spending as a specific category of expenditures. Procurement legislation had been reformed, with new provisions adopted in 2006, but the new institutional arrangements had yet to take root.[18]

Second, this relatively thin legal and institutional setup coincided with the strengthening of political incentives to utilize public investments for political gain. One significant incentive in this regard was the channeling of investment resources to electoral districts, which in turn favored shifting funds to rural areas. In 1996, Mongolia had adopted a system of single-member electoral districts, with a total of 76 districts and a corresponding number of seats in parliament. As a consequence, each MP had to seek reelection from a group of about 10,000–40,000 voting-age citizens living in a particular area. As discussed above, the distribution of districts had been fixed prior to significant internal migration toward the capital city and had not been revised,[19] and as a consequence, relatively more seats were being allocated from rural areas. When more resources became available, and at the same time individual MPs gained greater political weight, the MPs actively sought to channel money to their constituencies. MPs' incentives were not well balanced by mechanisms to vet public investment proposals for their social and economic benefits for the country as a whole. This rural bias, furthermore, favored the communist legacy party, the MPRP, which as outlined previously, retained its strongest support in rural areas and benefited from much deeper organizational roots across remote locations than did the more recently founded parties.

As a consequence of these incentives combined with weak institutional gatekeeping, decisions on investments were suboptimal. A large number of public investment projects were targeting rural areas, and capital expenditures were highly fragmented—66 percent of all projects included in the 2008 capital budget had a value of US$400,000 or less (with a total of 758 projects, equivalent to approximately one project per 3,000 citizens). Moreover, many public investment projects were rather poorly planned in terms of technical feasibility, analysis of economic and social benefits, and costings. Some of the politically motivated investments were integrated late into the budget with minimal or no proper project preparation. At the same time, the surge in demand for public investments crowded out other objective priorities, such as improving maintenance spending and repairs or setting funds aside to finance projects of strategic importance.

In addition, there were also growing concerns about procurement practices. Despite the reform in procurement rules in 2006 that broadly followed international standards, problems grew with the rapid expansion of expenditures. Companies were being awarded contracts on the basis of political connections rather than technical competency (see also Hasnain 2011). Because of a lack of guidance and oversight ex ante with regard to costing and prices set in tenders, many challenges with cost and time overruns emerged. Interviews with public officials as well as with private sector representatives suggested that excessive unit costs and similar mechanisms served to accommodate the cost of kickback payments. According to one official from the capital city's administration, "everyone wants to sit on tender boards." The transparency measures stipulated in a reformed 2006 public procurement law were not fully implemented for a number of years. At the same time, improper actions and real difficulties were not always easy to disentangle, as the cost for many construction inputs accelerated rapidly during the initial boom years.

The analysis indicated that these informal practices around public contracting were linked to trends in the political realm. On the one hand, the cost of running election campaigns had rapidly accelerated during the post-communist period. On the other hand, incentives for direct participation in politics increased with the onset of the great game of distributing rights to natural resources. Furthermore, the declining coherence of the traditional parties opened up opportunities for new players to seek a parliamentary seat. According to official figures alone, election-related spending jumped more than threefold (in nominal terms) between the 1996 and 2000 parliamentary elections. According to unofficial estimates, spending per district reached the equivalent of US$150,000 in 2004 (for all 76 districts combined, this would be equivalent to 0.6 percent of national GDP at the time[20]) and continued to rise further in 2008. One way for elected MPs to recoup such costs, which available evidence suggests is widely used across many countries (see IDEA 2003), is via kickbacks paid as part of public sector contracts.

On the "demand side," that is, among citizens and organized social groups, nongovernmental organizations (NGOs) paid as yet little attention to issues around public investments and procurement by the mid- to late 2000s. When the World Bank team began to focus more on the actual implementation of the

2006 procurement legislation, NGO attention to and experience with procurement was only nascent. However, public discontent with the quality of public infrastructure gradually emerged. Public attitudes were beginning to change, especially with regard to the poor condition of the road network. Whereas in previous years citizens had accepted the fact that the government simply did not have money to improve infrastructure, with rising government revenues and investment activity, citizen expectations increased. Meanwhile, economic expansion was also leading to much heavier traffic, thus accelerating the deterioration of roads and bridges.

For the area of public investments and procurement, the initial analysis suggested three important potential drivers of change:

1. The tangible sense of frustration and concern among some politicians and senior civil servants regarding the situation
2. The likely continuing expansion of the scale of public investments
3. Public expectations that the funds generated by the mining boom would be used to improve current infrastructure

And it suggested three recommendations:

1. The World Bank should support local stakeholders to pursue a strengthening of institutions, including legal and organizational aspects. At the same time, it would have to strike a balance between advising only on "international best practices" and following the preferred institutional solutions of local stakeholders with regard to creating stronger institutions responsible for public investments. Furthermore, any solution would need to be designed to be sufficiently robust given likely continuing incentives for political influencing.[21]
2. Complementing this approach with fostering emerging attention among citizens toward how public investment funds were being allocated and used and how this could be improved because politicians facing more informed voters would have greater incentives to increase the development benefits of public investment projects.
3. Balancing the reform agenda over time between upstream and downstream aspects of public investment management (that is, combine attention to macro-fiscal management and upstream project selection with attention to downstream procurement and project execution as both influence whether resources are well used).

The recommendations highlight the issue of feasibility and local effectiveness versus preferred first-best solutions, while trying to find entry points for tugging existing dynamics into a direction likely to yield better development outcomes. As became visible at the time of the analysis in 2008, a variety of stakeholders within government pursued institutional changes to develop a stronger capacity for managing public investments.

The World Bank team continued its analytic engagement on the evolving agenda on how to move toward good-enough management of public investments. Subsequent analytic work (Hasnain 2011; World Bank 2013) further deepened earlier findings while capturing the evolving situation. The World Bank also provided advice and was invited to provide some prodding on several key pieces of legislation and on emerging institutional changes.

In reaction to the recognition that public investments were undermanaged relative to fast-growing resources, the government began to introduce new institutional "rails," both legally and organizationally. However, in particular with regard to new organizational structures, the choices made contradicted technically defined international best practices. First, a National Development and Innovation Committee (NDIC) was created in 2009 (subsequently transformed into a Ministry of Economic Development [MED] in 2012). Furthermore, the DBM was set up in early 2011. On the legal side, amendments to the Procurement Law were adopted in mid-2011 and an Integrated Budget Law was passed by parliament in late 2011, which replaced existing organic budget legislation.[22] An important emphasis of the new Integrated Budget Law was public investment planning, financing, and monitoring. The law also sought to clarify intergovernmental transfers and the allocation of locally targeted public investments (Local Development Funds), and it significantly strengthened fiscal transparency and opportunities for citizens' participation, in particular with regard to proposing and planning local public investment projects.

The NDIC/MED and the DBM are loosely modeled on institutions found in China and other developing countries, including other rapid developers such as Brazil.[23] However, both institutions are at odds with more orthodox notions on the optimal design of public finance institutions, which posits that responsibilities on financing and planning should be under one roof rather than separate. And with regard to the DBM, existing thinking highlights the risk related to state-owned development banks, because they raise funds on capital markets that are ultimately government liabilities. Thus, a development bank can add to the risk of excessive borrowing during resource boom years as happened in a number of resource-rich countries during the 1970s, contributing to the subsequent debt crisis. By creating the DBM, therefore, Mongolian stakeholders also created a new source of risk. Since its creation, the DBM has in fact been used to circumvent some of the restrictions imposed by the Fiscal Stability Law (discussed previously), by opening a new route for off-budget expenditures (IMF 2012).

The PEA had suggested that the Bank team should engage with reform-oriented senior bureaucrats and policy makers, as well as other stakeholders, on the development of institutions aimed at strengthening public investment management—even if some of these ran counter to perceived international best practice. While the World Bank engaged with the NDIC/MED and the DBM, in-depth engagement predominantly focused on the Fiscal Stability Law and the Integrated Budget Law, that is, institutional components more aligned with prevailing notions of good fiscal management. This reflects some of the dilemmas involved in engaging on the design of institutions that are considered as problematic from the outset.

In parallel, the continuing analytic work revealed in particular the close links between MPs and the construction sector—with a number of the largest construction companies directly owned by MPs. It also provided more in-depth information on some of the problematic impacts of ad hoc decision making on the quality, timeliness, and cost overruns in public infrastructure projects, and it confirmed the considerable bias in investment programs in favor of rural areas and in favor of new construction over maintenance and capital repair outlays. For example, although Ulaanbaatar represented 45 percent of the population, it received only about 20 percent of total investment allocations for energy and about 30 percent for roads. In particular, although the periurban population had grown rapidly as the result of internal migration, there had been little effort to expand urban infrastructure to these areas despite the rapid growth in government revenue. Leaving people in periurban areas disconnected contributed in turn to very serious environmental problems in the city (see World Bank 2009b, 2011a).

The World Bank team continued to engage with the government and a wider range of stakeholders on procurement reform.[24] This approach involved advice on how to strengthen central agencies and mechanisms for overseeing procurement processes.[25] Furthermore, some of the Bank's advice and prodding contributed to the decision by the government and parliament to amend the Public Procurement Law to include specific provisions for CSOs and professional associations to become involved in bid evaluations and contract monitoring. This in turn created a window of opportunity, which the team used to intensify its work with CSOs and associations to develop their capacity to fulfill a watchdog role. Hence, the recommendations to focus on a strengthening of public demand and to ensure sufficient attention to downstream aspects of how public investments are actually implemented have come to be reflected in the actual engagement.

Social Spending Policies: Sharing the Pie and the Electoral Calculus

In addition to rapid increases in capital expenditures, social programs have been a key issue related to Mongolia's natural resource boom. From 2005 onward, successive governments created a variety of new social benefits and general payments to citizens (see table 2.1). These programs reflect the tension and incentives in the relationship between citizens at large and political and economic elites in the transition to a resource-rich country, as well as some of the challenges of a policy dialogue when technical economic insights and political incentives are at odds. From a technical "best practice" perspective, social benefits should seek to maximize poverty-reduction effects in a way that is fiscally sustainable. From a political, vote-seeking perspective, in contrast, benefits should be promised so as to maximize electoral gains, with longer-term affordability being secondary.

On the one hand, the introduction of social programs signals two positive characteristics of the country: (a) elites perceive an incentive to share (some)

Table 2.1 Evolution of Key Social Transfers, 2003–12

2003	Throughout 2004	May–July 2004	January 2005	July 2005	July 2006	January 2007	January 2008
Adoption of the Social Sector Master Plan, envisaging a system of targeted benefits for the poor	Development of targeting methodology at the technical level	Inclusion of a CMP proposal in election platform of the DP/MDC; inclusion of other benefits in MPRP election platform Elections result in split parliament Inclusion of the CMP in the coalition government Plan of Action	First introduction of the CMP Tog 3,000 (US$2.70) per month, conditional and targeted at families below the poverty line with 3+ children	Requirement that a family has 3+ children dropped	WPT approved by parliament in May CMP becomes universal (all children are eligible) and targeting dropped Addition of new benefits: newborn children and newly married couples added, retroactively from January 2006 Two conditions (living with family and being in school) remain	CMP payments increased by Tog 100,000 (US$85) per child per year, to be paid from DF	Adoption of the MDG-based Comprehensive National Development Strategy by parliament with strong social, family protection, and poverty reduction elements

Summer 2008	October–November 2009	2010	2011	January 2012	June–July 2012	October 2012
Election campaign promises: "Motherland bounty" (Tog 1.5 million [~US$1,300]) payment promised by the MPRP and "Share of Treasure" promised by the Democratic Party (Tog 1 million [~US$900]) MPRP wins the legislative elections; postelection violence takes place Late 2008: falling commodity prices reduce government revenues	October: Oyu Tolgoi Investment Agreement signed Ivanhoe mine agreement to prepay royalties to fund social payouts in 2010 (given economic downturn) November: approval of the HDF law (Mongolia's version of a Sovereign Wealth Fund); payments from the HDF to replace the CMP	HDF cash handouts of Tog 120,000 (~US$90) per citizen (paid in two tranches during the year) CMP stopped	HDF payments of Tog 252,000 (~US$190) per citizen for the year (in monthly installments of Tog 21,000 [~US$16])	Amendments to the Social Welfare Law passed—established targeted benefits for poor households Amendments to go into effect July 1, 2012 (that is, postelections) Payments of Tog 1 million (~US$900) to disabled and retirees, Tog 70,000/month (US$50/ month) to students	End of June: parliamentary elections July 1: amended Social Welfare Law goes into effect New coalition government decides not to implement poverty-targeted household benefits HDF payments stopped	Coalition government reintroduces universal CMP

Note: CMP = Child Money Program; DF = Development Fund; DP/MDC = Democratic Party/Motherland Democratic Coalition; HDF = Human Development Fund; MDG = Millennium Development Goal; MPRP = Mongolian Peoples' Revolutionary Party; Tog = togrog; WPT = Windfall Profits Tax.

benefits from the boom with citizens at large, in contrast to regimes that are predominantly exclusive and oppressive and where all benefits from resource rents accrue exclusively to a narrow circle of domestic and outside investors (see Barma et al. 2012, 12), and (b) the introduction of such programs reflects the fact that Mongolia has been comparatively successful at capturing a significant share of natural resource rents for the national purse.[26] On the other hand, the design of the social programs has been far from following technical best practice. The sudden jumps in fiscal space offered opportunities to the politicians of the day to score short-term political advantages. The consequences included ratcheting effects, as more or new transfers had to be promised with each election, as well as a high degree of year-to-year volatility in who received what levels of transfers, including a reduction rather than expansion of benefits during the downturn period in late 2008–09. That said, if the system eventually stabilizes, it may realize some of the potential of a "social contract" through cash transfers as suggested by Birdsall and others for resource-rich countries.[27]

Since the early 2000s, several donors, including the Asian Development Bank and the World Bank, had provided extended advice to the Mongolian government about best practices for targeted and conditional social programs to address the persistent level of poverty. In early 2005, the government and parliament initially introduced a targeted benefit, broadly aligned with the advice. However, in mid-2006, parliament suddenly adopted two measures: (a) a Windfalls Profit Tax to be levied on copper and gold production that sought to capture some of the additional profits from rapidly accelerating prices, and (b) based on this additional revenue, the introduction of a universal child benefit program (see table 2.1). Thus, the money to be paid to families became linked to the newly introduced and potentially highly volatile revenue source. The policy came as a surprise for the World Bank team at the time: it became possible as a result of the surge in commodity prices and the sudden decision to impose a windfall tax, and it was one of the first major policy decisions through which parliament asserted its expanded influence.

The PEA helped to bring into the discussion the way in which these policy decisions were linked to the evolution of electoral competition. The promise of a universal social benefit had been a key element in the election platform of the main opposition party (the Democratic Party/Motherland Democratic Coalition, or DP/MDC) going into the 2004 elections. Page 1 of the election platform proclaimed the following:

> It is in these circumstances that we, the political parties coalescing under "The Motherland-Democracy" Coalition and its thousands and thousands of members and supporters, shall implement radically new social policies. We are putting forward an agenda of improving the livelihood of households and providing support to families through children.
>
> We shall allocate and pay ten thousand tugrugs of "Money of Trust" every month to all children below the age of 18. We consider this method of supporting households

and families through their children, a policy implemented in many rich and poor countries, shall contribute to an equitable distribution of social wealth, alleviate the daily pressure of the majority of the people, and shall be an impetus for people to acquire hope for a bright future. (MDC 2004, 1).

Making social spending a key plank in its platform, the DP/MDC was able to achieve a decisive political comeback in the 2004 elections, winning 34 seats, as compared with just two seats four years earlier. Furthermore, the political block managed to shed its negative image as a party favoring neoliberal policies, which it had gained while governing in the late 1990s, when it sharply reduced pensions in the face of a challenging fiscal situation.[28]

Although the DP/MDC gained a large number of seats, it did not win a majority. Rather, as discussed previously, the 2004 elections ushered in a period of more evenly split parliaments. Holding a nearly equal number of seats, the two largest parties in the country—the DP/MDC and the post-communist MPRP—entered a grand coalition government for the period 2004–08. As part of the coalition agreement reached, the CMP was inserted into the Government Plan of Action. Thus, it became part of the government's proposed policy agenda, albeit not based on technical considerations and consultations carried out by the Ministry for Social Welfare and Labor, but rather based predominantly on a political rationale.

As reflected in the time line (table 2.1), the real move toward implementing this policy came mid-way through the legislative period, in 2006. It was enabled by the continuing steep rise in natural resource prices (see figure 2.2). As commodity prices rapidly accelerated, politicians decided to adopt a Windfall Profit Tax. This newly introduced tax contributed to a sharp and sudden expansion in government revenue and created the fiscal space needed to implement a large-scale new social program. Although the DP/MDC was the slightly smaller partner in the coalition government, the public appeal of the program made it hard for the MPRP to block the measure. Instead, moving into the 2008 elections, the two main parties tried to outdo each other with promises of additional payouts from the mining sector to citizens—with the Democratic Party promising Tog 1 million (~US$900) and the MPRP topping this with Tog 1.5 million (~US$1,300) to be paid to all citizens.

The analytic note completed in early 2008 suggested that there was little appetite among key decision makers to revisit or revise the adopted universal policy. Instead, it suggested the following:

- Encourage monitoring of the impact of the CMP, so as to build evidence of the program's achievements and engage in knowledge transfer about how to design monitoring systems.
- Encourage public debate on the social policies and transfers and their impacts and use the Bank's convening power to bring different stakeholders around the table, in parallel to building an evidence base.

- Engage in a dialogue with key policy shapers in the main political parties on the wider issue of how to preserve and rebuild social cohesion in the context of the continuing substantial dislocations, which result from rapid internal migration and changes in opportunities, as well as a widening income gap.
- Understand that a renewed crisis could open a window of opportunity.

The rationale for these suggestions was mainly twofold: first, because decisions about social programs were driven by political incentives and had shifted to parliament, a dialogue involving the public and politicians would be essential to complement more technical discussions with staff members in the responsible ministry. Second, once politicians decided to spend significant funds, it was important to encourage monitoring of the impacts on poverty and social cohesion. The experience with the initial targeted child support that existed between early 2005 and mid-2006 had been rather disappointing, but was too brief to really allow for an assessment of impact. During this period, the targeting in use had involved significant errors of exclusion as well as inclusion (that is, poor people being unable to access the benefit, apparently because of the bureaucratic requirements involved, as well as nonpoor families receiving the support).[29] In addition, it appeared important to focus public policy debates on issues that would not be addressed through the CMP (such as the need to expand employment opportunities, in particular for internal migrants).

In contrast to the work on overall fiscal and public investment management, the work on social programs was less closely linked to the relevant sector team because of a variety of factors.[30] This had some implications for the take-up of the work. On the one hand, although engagement on social benefits continued, inter alia as part of a development policy loan approved in 2010, the dialogue remained more focused on the technical design questions. On the other hand, efforts at outreach—similar to those made on fiscal policies discussed previously—remained constrained by the fact that the responsible Ministry for Social Welfare and Labor had more limited technical capacity and political and administrative clout compared with the Ministry of Finance. Hence, the former played less of a role in articulating and presenting policy options than the latter was able to do with regard to fiscal policies.

In terms of its implications and predictions, the PEA was broadly confirmed by subsequent events: social welfare policies remained closely influenced by electoral considerations, filtered by immediate fiscal conditions, and linked to efforts at increasing revenue from the mining sector.

In early 2008, a Millennium Development Goal–based Comprehensive National Development Strategy was adopted by parliament, setting out an ambitious agenda of poverty reduction and social protection, in particular for families. This was followed by the mid-2008 parliamentary election campaign, during which both main camps made major preelection promises of new cash payments to citizens (see table 2.1, column titled "Summer 2008"). As discussed earlier, the elections resulted in a win for the ex-communist MPRP, but after a tense period of contestation over the results, the two main parties/blocs decided to again form a grand coalition. However, in late 2008 and through 2009, the fiscal crisis then forced the newly formed coalition government to scale back on the combined political campaign promises. Given the sudden downturn and the fact that the government had not saved funds during the preceding growth period, Mongolia had to turn to the IMF for a standby agreement, which included the agreement to rescind untargeted social transfers.[31]

Nonetheless, the political maneuvers to increase mining revenues to fund greater social transfers continued. After years of negotiations, the investment agreement for the Oyu Tolgoi copper-gold mine was finally signed in October 2009 between the government and the consortium of Rio Tinto and Ivanhoe mines. An important aspect of the deal was that Ivanhoe agreed to prepay future mining royalties. Using these funds, parliament then passed the creation of a new Human Development Fund (HDF) in November 2009 and for 2010 allocated Tog 120,000 (~US$90) to be paid in cash handouts to every citizen.[32] However, at the same time, given the overall fiscal constraint and to satisfy the conditions of the IMF program, parliament decided to make zero allocations for the CMP (as well as the newlywed benefit and the newborn benefit) for the 2010 budget, essentially abolishing these recently introduced benefits.

The following year, 2011, fiscal space reexpanded with the return of rapid growth. In the budget, spending from the HDF was scaled up to Tog 21,000 (US$16) per person per month, or Tog 252,000 (US$190) for the year.[33]

In early 2012, parliament then reversed course again, adopting a Social Welfare Law that reintroduced more targeted social assistance. The law was to go into effect immediately after the 2012 parliamentary elections, on July 1, 2012. As noted, the 2012 elections resulted in a divided parliament and another coalition government, but with the relative majority and coalition leadership shifting to the Democratic Party. By October 2012, the recently formed government again reversed course: it decided not to implement targeted social benefits, to stop HDF payments, and to reintroduce universal (that is, untargeted) child allowances (see table 2.1). It also reopened discussions with the Oyu Tolgoi consortium to extract higher payments than had been agreed to in the 2009 Investment Agreement, leading to a tense relationship between the government and the country's largest investor.[34] Thus, a very unstable course over what social policy payments would be made, to whom, and in what amounts continued from year to year.

In terms of poverty trends, Mongolia recorded a decline in poverty levels, to about 27 percent living below the national poverty line by 2012, a decline by more than 10 percent from the 2010 level.[35] After nearly two decades of high and persistent poverty, this shows a clear trend in the right direction, albeit one that still needs to be confirmed to persist. It is also worth noting that poverty rates fell similarly in a number of countries in East Asia, with significantly lower average per capita GDP and relatively lower growth (such as Cambodia and the Lao People's Democratic Republic).

Overall, there is a close and tense relationship between the resource boom and social welfare policies in Mongolia. For politicians, initially proposing the

CMP was a way to win popularity and secure seats in parliament in the 2004 elections, as well as to respond to the trend of rising "resource nationalism" (as discussed previously). Subsequently, rising popular discontent over growing wealth disparity combined with political competition contributed not only to a ratcheting effect of further expanding these payments, but also to a rapid succession of changes, leaving families and citizens unable to plan with a more stable level of benefits, and to fueling inflation (see figure 2.4). Efforts to better target the subsidies on poor citizens were ultimately not effective, although they continue to be part of the public debate, and in particular of the continuing dialogue between donors and the government.

At the same time, the social transfer experience in Mongolia reflects that even problematic political and policy dynamics contain potential positives—in this case, the fact that politicians have perceived incentives to share resource wealth with citizens and have competed on this policy issue. The challenge for donor agencies is to find ways to engage constructively with such messy and tactically driven politics and resulting policy designs and changes, in ways that not only point to the risks and efficiency losses involved, but also leverage the positives, engage politicians and other stakeholders, and challenge stakeholders constructively to achieve more. The contrasting experience between the engagement on fiscal policies and the engagement on social policies also indicates that it is easier to pursue outreach and a broadened dialogue when there is a stakeholder within government who seeks to use the expertise and the contribution to public policy debates that donors can provide.

Conclusion: PEA and World Bank Engagement during a Resource Boom

PEA in Mongolia has focused on a number of critical policy issues, with the main analytic effort made in mid-2007 to early 2008. There are multiple indications that this effort made a positive contribution to the World Bank team's ability to engage in a rapidly evolving environment over the following years. The analysis was undertaken at a point when the team sought to identify options for approaching engagement on the mining boom, and the PEA fed effectively into these efforts.

Three main lessons emerge from the experience with applying PEA in the issue of managing a natural resource boom. First, in the case of Mongolia, the combination of country-level and issue-specific analysis addressing the three sets of drivers—structural drivers, institutions, and contingent choices made by stakeholders (see chapter 1 in this volume)—proved to work well for understanding how key policy choices emerged. Among structural drivers, the swings in commodity prices have had a crucial impact on the opportunities faced by political decision makers. At the same time, how these structural drivers have played out has been significantly influenced by key rules of the game (that is, institutions), including the absence of a presidential system found in many other resource-rich countries, as well as the set of electoral rules and resulting incentives. Successive governments, political parties, and individual politicians in turn responded to the incentives and opportunities with their ideas and initiatives—responding among other considerations to perceived demands from voters.

Second, overall, the PEA contributed to a strengthened relationship between the World Bank team and its Mongolian partners. Although sometimes the concern is voiced that PEA will result in advising against lending in countries facing governance challenges, this clearly was not the case: lending volumes increased from US$15.3 million in 2008 to US$65.7 million in 2011. This provides an illustration that use of PEA can very well be associated with an intensification of engagement, rather than with the advice to pull back in the face of constraints and obstacles. It is also worth noting that the perceptions of the effectiveness of the Bank's engagement on governance among country stakeholders—from within government and among civil society—strengthened between fiscal year (FY) 2007 and FY2011, from 6 to 7 on a scale of 1–10 (see World Bank 2011b, 33). Furthermore, stakeholders indicated the Bank's engagement on governance and government effectiveness as the most important area of work—surpassing an earlier emphasis on employment and economic growth.

Third, in terms of influencing engagement, the PEA had both benefits and limitations. The PEA influenced two generations of country strategies, the Interim Strategy Note developed in 2009 and the CAS adopted in 2012 (FY2013 to FY2017). A focus on incentives became embedded in subsequent mainstream analytic products such as the quarterly economic outlook notes and further work on public investment management. An important hinge between the PEA work and subsequent efforts was the allocation of a Governance Partnership Facility grant.[36] The grant provided significant resources to pursue recommendations emerging from the PEA, such as supporting domestic research and policy advice capacity and significantly strengthening the World Bank's multistakeholder engagement around crucial policies related to the resource boom. Overall, the PEA provided a key input for the team to identify how best to realize its overall intention to engage on a challenging set of policy issues.

There were also limitations, in two ways. First, the PEA did not effect a full-fledged shift to advice that would have deliberately deviated from international best practices and instead sought to identify potential alternatives from a perspective of robustness in the face of the diagnosed political economy constellations. Second, considering the overall causal chain, any changes in the World Bank's approach to policy advice in a country experiencing a large-scale natural resource boom are most likely to have a limited impact on the country's course—albeit potentially still significant in particular policy areas.

Regarding the first limitation, some of the cautions related to the strength of political incentives and dynamics (such as the challenges resulting from growing political fragmentation) could have been further heeded to realize that a de jure mechanism such as the fiscal stability law will not easily be effective at binding the hands of politicians. The need to search for nonstandard institutional solutions in such an environment could have been more fully internalized in the policy dialogue. However, for individual country teams to go such a route, it may first be necessary that nonstandard approaches become more widely recognized and specific alternative options identified among technical experts.

In terms of on-the-ground change, success with restraining government spending has clearly fallen short during recent boom years and in the run-up to another crucial election in mid-2012. Public investment spending has continued to increase in leaps and bounds, with limited regard for economic and social justification and proper due diligence on projects, and social transfers continue to be highly politicized. Some of the legal constraints that were created in the wake of the 2008–09 global crisis are likely to be reversed.

At the same time, though there is no directly available counterfactual, having initiated institutional constraints—on overall fiscal spending, as well as on the way public investments should be selected and implemented—may still prove better than not having done so. Public debate has intensified and has begun to benefit from better evidence and information about other countries' experiences. The environment and opportunities for social accountability is improving, especially in terms of strengthening fiscal transparency and the rights for CSOs to engage in public procurement and oversight of contracts. Mongolia's ranking in terms of budget transparency improved in recent years,[37] alongside greater transparency about key mining sector agreements. The PEA helped the World Bank to engage proactively with these efforts toward greater transparency and public debate and to contribute to the progress that has been made.

In sum, the example showcases that an engagement that ignores political economy drivers very easily risks growing stale. Using PEA and its findings has not been an easy endeavor and has not been a panacea. However, the PEA has contributed crucially to ensuring that the World Bank's engagement is relevant and significant for counterparts and stakeholders and that it is a knowledgeable and strategic partner for country stakeholders rather than just a technically competent external source of advice.

Notes

1. The picture is somewhat blurred by rapid rural-urban migration that has taken place since the late 1990s (following a prior period of urban-rural migration during livestock privatization in the early 1990s).

2. See UNDP (2011). Note that specific figures on poverty for the 1990s and early 2000s are subject to some uncertainty (see also note 35).

3. Given Mongolia's land-locked location, transport costs to destinations other than Russia and China are substantial. In contrast, the export distance to China is short, in particular from the new major deposits discovered in the south of Mongolia, and the demand for natural resources in Mongolia's southern neighbor has been growing rapidly.

4. Several additional small parties, such as a Green Party and a National Progress Party, were also founded, some of which subsequently formed electoral blocs.

5. The CAS was never adopted because of the onset of the financial crisis in 2008. Instead, an Interim Strategy Note was adopted, with a shorter time horizon for calendar years 2009 and 2010. A new CAS was then developed in 2012 for fiscal years

2013–17. Both the Interim Strategy Note and the eventual new CAS were informed by the governance and political economy analysis work.

6. During this period, the cost of election campaigns rose rapidly, and the overlap between owners of large businesses and the holding of parliamentary seats increased with each election.

7. In the case of Mongolia, this was not against a threat of internal unrest or conflict, but rather against a perceived risk related to a potentially growing influence from neighboring countries.

8. These public perceptions were confirmed by a 2008 public opinion survey.

9. An international database classifying whether a country's parties have a programmatic base covers Mongolia since 1999. It rates Mongolia as having had one main programmatic party up until 2004, and then none from 2005 onward.

10. As the experience of other countries in Central Asia and elsewhere indicates, literacy among citizens does not provide a strong impediment against authoritarian forms of rule in which a small circle enjoys most benefits from natural resources. However, literacy is nonetheless an asset when the political space is more competitive.

11. Several presidents have sought to expand the role of the office, but the effects of such efforts have remained limited.

12. Barma et al. (2012) more recently distinguish between different types of coalitions in resource-rich countries.

13. The Department for International Development of the United Kingdom provided this trust fund to the World Bank starting in FY 2008, and the bulk of funding was passed on to selected country teams that were proposing innovative engagement strategies on governance.

14. For more on the economic developments, see the International Monetary Fund website at http://www.imf.org/external/np/ms/2012/092512.htm.

15. ERI is based in the School of Economic Studies at Mongolia's National University. For more information, see the ERI website at http://www.eri.mn.

16. This does not mean that external analytic inputs—such as those delivered by the IMF and the World Bank—become irrelevant. However, domestic policy research capacity is an important complementary strength, especially as policy makers and citizens have to grapple with complex domestic issues and relationships with external investors.

17. That legislation was the Public Sector Management and Finance Law. It had been under consideration since the late 1990s and was inspired by new public management considerations.

18. See Public Procurement Law of Mongolia, February 1, 2006. A previous public procurement law dated from 2000.

19. The potential revision of district boundaries was subject to substantial political debate.

20. For comparison, the 2012 U.S. presidential elections cost an estimated US$2 billion, equivalent to 0.013 percent of GDP (US$15.7 trillion).

21. International best practices suggested that institutional responsibilities should remain within the Ministry of Finance, whereas the emerging preference among Mongolian senior officials and politicians—also based on their observation of the Chinese experience—was in favor of creating a separate planning institution.

22. The law went into full force on January 1, 2013.

23. The Chinese institutions are the National Development and Reform Commission, a successor to the former State Planning Commission, and the China Development Bank. In 2005, about 750 National Development Banks existed worldwide (see UN DESA 2006, 5).

24. The Bank did so as part of a Governance Assistance Project and funding from the Governance Partnership Facility Trust Fund.

25. This has included the establishment of a Procurement Management and Monitoring System and a strengthening of the Procurement Policy Department in the Ministry of Finance.

26. To illustrate, both Mongolia and Zambia are large exporters of copper, and in both countries copper exports account for more than 70 percent of total exports. However, in Zambia taxes and royalties from the sector account for only 4 percent of its total revenues, whereas in Mongolia, just under 30 percent of revenues come from its resource sector.

27. For more information on cash transfers, see the Center for Global Development website at http://www.cgdev.org/initiative/oil-cash-fighting-resource-curse-through -cash-transfers (accessed April 24, 2013); Birdsall and Subramanian (2004).

28. The DP/MDC as the more recently established party had always found it more challenging to connect with voters in rural areas, whereas the MPRP held significant advantages in terms of the strength of its grassroots organization. Therefore, powerful populist promises were particularly appealing as an electoral strategy for the DP/MDC.

29. According to an assessment by UNICEF (2007), the share of poor households remaining that were excluded from receiving the support was 20 percent.

30. The Governance Assessment closely involved economists, public sector governance specialists, and mining sector specialists, whereas engagement with other sector teams was less close.

31. An 18-month IMF program (Stand-By Agreement) was in place from April 2009 to October 2010.

32. Payments could be used for (a) pension and health insurance premiums, (b) purchase of housing, (c) cash benefits, and (d) payments for education and health services.

33. The European Bank for Reconstruction and Development (EBRD) paper discusses incentive impacts of unconditional transfers and finds that these need not be negative. Based on this assessment, the paper argues that the main concern should be to better link the payments to actual income from mining and also to encourage citizens to seek good management. See EBRD (2012).

34. As the *Wall Street Journal* (2013) commented: "The politics around that project [Oyu Tolgoi] are unlikely to ever be simple."

35. Poverty data based on household surveys are available only for 2002 and 2008; during this period, there was a very significant drop from 61 percent to 35.6 percent; and data for 2012 show a decline to about 27 percent. Specific data for 2006, the starting year of the universal benefit and the increase in the monetary value of the benefit, is not available. See also http://www.oecd.org/derec/undp/48341650.pdf; and World Bank Press release 2013/05/21, available at: http://www.worldbank.org/en/news /press-release/2013/05/21/poverty-rate-came-down-to-27-4-percent-in-2012.

36. The innovative approaches and the contributions made by the underlying analytic work were also positively assessed in the 2011 review of the 18 countries that received similar grants. See Governance Partnership Facility (2011, 19–20).

37. Mongolia's ranking improved from a rating of 36 (2008) to a rating of 51 (2012) on the Open Budget Index (which has a scale from 1 to 100, with higher numbers reflecting greater transparency). See the International Budget Partnership, http://internationalbudget.org/what-we-do/open-budget-survey/rankings-key -findings/rankings.

Bibliography

Auty, Richard. 1993. *Sustaining Development in Mineral Economies: The Resource Curse Thesis*. London: Routledge.

———. 2001. *Resource Abundance and Economic Development*. Oxford, U.K.: Oxford University Press.

Barma, Naazneen H., Kai Kaiser, Tuan Minh Le, and Lorena Viñuela. 2012. *Rents to Riches? The Political Economy of Natural Resource–Led Development*. Washington, DC: World Bank.

Birdsall, Nancy, and Arvind Subramanian. 2004. "Saving Iraq from Its Oil." *Foreign Affairs* 83 (4): 77–89.

Collier, Paul, and Anke Hoeffler. 2005. "Resource Rents, Governance and Conflict." *Journal of Conflict Resolution* 49 (4): 625–33.

EBRD (European Bank for Reconstruction and Development). 2012. "Managing Mongolia's Resource Boom." EBRD, London. http://www.ebrd.com/downloads /research/economics/workingpapers/wp0138.pdf.

Fish, M. Steven. 1998. "Mongolia: Democracy without Prerequisites." *Journal of Democracy* 9 (3): 27–41.

Fritz, Verena. 2002. "Mongolia: Dependent Democratization." *Journal of Communist Studies and Transition Politics* 18 (4): 75–100.

———. 2008. "The Rise and Travails of a Deviant Democracy." *Democratization* 15 (4): 766–88.

Governance Partnership Facility. 2011. "Implementing Country-Level Governance Programs: A Review of GPF Window 1 Country Programs." Governance Partnership Facility, World Bank, Washington, DC.

Hasnain, Zahid. 2011. "Incentive Compatible Reforms: The Political Economy of Public Investments in Mongolia." Policy Research Working Paper 5667, World Bank, Washington, DC.

Hasnain, Zahid, Munkhnasan Narmandakh, Audrey Sacks, and Marek Hanush. 2013. *Mongolia: Improving Public Investments to Meet the Challenge of Scaling Up Infrastructure.* Report 74944, World Bank, Washington, DC.

IDEA (International Institute for Democracy and Electoral Assistance). 2003. *Funding of Political Parties and Election Campaigns*. Stockholm: IDEA. http://www.idea.int /publications/funding_parties/funding_of_pp.pdf.

IMF (International Monetary Fund). 2012. "Mongolia: Second Post-Program Monitoring Discussions." IMF Country Report 12/52, IMF, Washington, DC.

Keefer, Philip, and Razvan Vlaicu. 2008. "Democracy, Credibility, and Clientelism." *Journal of Law, Economics, and Organization* 24 (2): 371–406.

Laking, Rob. 1999. "Don't Try This at Home? A New Zealand Approach to Public Management Reform in Mongolia." *International Public Management Journal* 2 (2): 217–35.

Leftwich, Adrian. 2001. *States of Development: On the Primacy of Politics in Development.* Cambridge, U.K.: Polity.

MDC (Motherland Democratic Coalition). 2004. "Election Manifesto." MDC, Mongolia.

Narangoa, Li. 2012. "Mongolia's 2012 Parliamentary Election." East Asia Forum, January 9. http://www.eastasiaforum.org/2012/07/10/mongolias-2012-parliamentary-election/.

Pomfret, Richard. 2000. "Transition and Democracy in Mongolia." *Europe-Asia Studies* 52 (1): 149–60.

UN DESA (United Nations Department of Economic and Social Affairs). 2006. "Rethinking the Role of National Development Banks." UN DESA, New York. http://www.un.org/esa/ffd/msc/ndb/NDBs-DOCUMENT-REV-E-151106.pdf.

UNDP (United Nations Development Programme). 2011. "Snapshot of the XacBank of Mongolia." UNDP, New York. http://www.undp.org/content/dam/undp/library/Poverty%20Reduction/Participatory%20Local%20Development/Mongolia_XacBank_web.pdf.

UNICEF (United Nations Children's Fund). 2007. *Child Benefits and Poverty Reduction: Evidence from Mongolia's Child Money Program.* New York: United Nations. http://www.unicef.org/socialpolicy/files/Child_Benefits_and_Poverty_Reduction_Evidence_from_Mongolia.pdf.

Wall Street Journal. 2013. "Rio Tinto Overhaul Will Be a Long Slog." August 9.

World Bank. 2009a. "Public Expenditure and Financial Management Review." World Bank, Washington, DC.

———. 2009b. "Air Pollution in Ulaanbaatar: Initial Assessment of Current Situation and Effects of Abatement Measure." Discussion Paper 52970, World Bank, Washington, DC.

———. 2011a. "Air Quality Analysis of Ulaanbaatar: Improving Air Quality to Reduce Health Impacts." Working Paper 66082, World Bank, Washington, DC.

———. 2011b. "Mongolia: The World Bank Country Survey FY2011—Report of Findings (September 2011)." Working Paper 66083, World Bank, Washington, DC. http://www-wds.worldbank.org/external/default/WDSContentServer/WDSP/IB/2011/12/20/000333037_20111220235126/Rendered/PDF/660830WP00PUBL0lia0CS0FY0110Report.pdf.

———. 2013. "Mongolia: Improving Public Investments to Meet the Challenge of Scaling Up Infrastructure." Poverty Reduction and Economic Management, East Asia and Pacific Region, World Bank, Washington, DC. http://www-wds.worldbank.org/external/default/WDSContentServer/WDSP/EAP/2013/01/31/090224b0818dfbaf/1_0/Rendered/PDF/Final0Report.pdf.

———. Forthcoming. *Investing to Invest.* Washington, DC: World Bank.

———. Commodities Price Indices (database). World Bank, Washington, DC. http://go.worldbank.org/4ROCCIEQ50.

———. World Development Indicators (database). World Bank, Washington, DC. http://data.worldbank.org/data-catalog/world-development-indicators.

CHAPTER 3

Assessing Public Opinion in the Political Economy of Reform: The Case of Energy Subsidy Reform in Morocco

Dorothée Chen, Andrea Liverani, and Judith Krauss

Introduction: Subsidy Reform in Morocco, More Than a Technical Issue

Over the past several years, the government of Morocco has engaged in a process to reform its subsidy regime. Subsidies' contribution to economic and political stability through price stabilization of key commodities has formed a key pillar of the social contract in place in the country since the 1940s. Although an important part of the country's social protection system, the subsidy regime presents a number of challenges for the country. These include the untargeted nature of the program, the fiscal pressures it puts on the country's budget, and its inefficiency. In a country marked by inequality and persisting pockets of poverty, universal subsidies stabilize prices for all strata of society but they benefit the wealthy more than those most in need of targeted support. Furthermore, the subsidy regime is unsustainable from a fiscal and macroeconomic perspective. With fiscal costs spiraling upward in the face of rising global prices, 17 percent of the total government budget and roughly 60 percent of the investment budget in 2011 were absorbed by subsidy expenditure, representing a considerable fiscal liability. Finally, the regime is inefficient, exempting the consumption of imported goods such as fuel from the influence of world market developments.

This chapter provides a summary of the work on the *Political Economy of Subsidy Reform* in Morocco. The work was conducted in 2010–11 by a team led by Andrea Liverani (MNSSO) in the context of a regional activity on the political economy of subsidies in the Middle East and North Africa managed by Sabine Beddies (MNSSO) and including Ruslam Yemstov (HDNSP). Dorothée Chen (MNSSP) was a key team member during the entire analysis and the main author of the final activity report. Judith Krauss contributed to the chapter as a GIZ Young Professional during a placement with the World Bank Morocco Office.

The findings, interpretations, and conclusions contained in this synthesis report are entirely those of the authors. They do not necessarily represent the view of the World Bank, its executive directors, or the countries they represent. The World Bank is not responsible for the contents of this research.

Because of the challenges the subsidy system presents in Morocco, the government has explored options for reform since the late 1990s. Expert groups from government and academia have proposed policy options for remedying the inequities of the present system and reducing its budgetary toll, including a proposal for capping subsidy expenditures and using part of the savings to provide targeted support to the poor and most vulnerable. Additionally, for over a decade, the World Bank has engaged in a dialogue with the government about the economic, budgetary, and distributional benefits of reform and has presented proposals for an integrated approach to social protection policy. However, this engagement has resulted in only partial and ultimately insubstantial modifications to the current system.

Recently, both the World Bank and the government began to recognize that the obstacles to reform go beyond identifying the right technical solution and derive from the political realm. Specifically, the popularity of the subsidy system emerged as a key bottleneck to the reform process. Historically, announcements of increases in the prices of basic commodities have resulted in large-scale demonstrations. Gaining a better understanding of the likely political reverberations of changes to the status quo, as well as finding options to broaden the room to maneuver toward reform, became a central priority for the government.

Given the delicate social and political dimensions of subsidy reform, the government of Morocco asked the World Bank to undertake a political economy assessment of the potential political impacts of reform. To determine whether there were any politically acceptable avenues for change, the Bank assessed the perceptions of stakeholders as well as the public at large. This political economy analysis focused on wheat flour and butane gas subsidies. However, for the sake of brevity and an in-depth discussion, this chapter highlights only the findings regarding butane gas.

The second section begins with a discussion of the technical challenges facing Morocco's subsidy regime. It continues with a brief discussion of the political economy drivers of national decision making and reviews how these have impacted previous attempts at reform. The third section describes the methods and approach used to assess public perceptions of the subsidy regime and their views about changes. It also lays out the key findings and recommendations from the analysis. In the final section, the chapter concludes with a discussion of the impact of the analysis on the prospects for subsidy reform in Morocco.

Morocco's Subsidy Regime: Technical Challenges, Political Economy Drivers of Decision Making, and a History of Partial Reform

This section lays out the technical challenges presented by the subsidy system, in particular the inequity of the system that provides significant benefits to the best-off groups in society, as well as the rising fiscal cost. It then summarizes some key features of the country context and national-level dynamics, as well as the reform discussions and efforts made over the past two decades. The section highlights both the growing urgency of reforming the subsidy regime and the reasons that the adoption of technically sensible solutions has remained blocked for an extended period of time.

The Problem: The Inequity of Benefits and the Rising Fiscal Cost of Subsidies

The subsidy system was established in the early 1940s. The main entity charged with its implementation is the Compensation Fund (Caisse de compensation). Designed to protect all consumers' purchasing power and foster economic development by protecting input prices in key sectors, the system stabilizes prices for staple food products such as sugar and flour, as well as energy products such as butane gas and different types of fuel. The subsidy regime is therefore an integral part of the wider Moroccan social protection system, which also comprises noncontributory social assistance programs benefiting disadvantaged, vulnerable, and poor individuals, as well as contributory social security schemes such as pensions and health insurance. Thus, Morocco's subsidy regime constitutes a mainstay of the relationship between the state and its citizens.

Morocco's subsidy regime faces three main challenges. First, the untargeted nature of the current subsidy regime makes it fundamentally unfair. Given a lack of consistent and coherent targeting, the universally administered support payments are profoundly regressive in nature. On the national level, the poorest quintile of households receives less than 10 percent of total subsidies, while over 40 percent of government subsidies benefit the wealthiest fifth of the population (Government of Morocco 2008b; see table 3.1). Even if one takes into account the second-most disadvantaged quintile, the poorest 40 percent of the population receives a mere 22 percent of the state's total subsidy payout. Regarding energy subsidies, the poorest quintile receives only 10 percent of subsidies for butane gas, compared with 32 percent of subsidies benefiting the wealthiest fifth of the population. The discrepancy is even more marked for liquid fuels, with the wealthiest quintile (Q5) pocketing 75 percent of all subsidies for diesel and gasoline, while the poorest quintile (Q1) receives only 1 percent of the funds. With the largest compensation item in the budget earmarked for petroleum products, it can be said that these public funds fail to further the government's social equity agenda.

Besides failing to address social inequities, the current subsidy system absorbs a substantial proportion of the government's budget. The past decade saw aggravating raw material shortages and soaring oil and food prices on international and

Table 3.1　Distribution of Subsidies among Income Quintiles
Percent

	Q1	Q2	Q3	Q4	Q5	Total
Butane gas	10	15	19	24	32	100
Diesel and gasoline	1	3	6	15	75	100
All products	**9**	**13**	**15**	**20**	**43**	**100**

Source: Government of Morocco 2008b.
Note: Q = quintile. Q1 is the lowest quintile, and Q5 is the highest.

national markets. As a result, the budget resources spent on subsidies expanded tenfold in eight years, from dirham (DH) 4.89 billion or 1 percent of gross domestic product (GDP) in 2003 to a substantial DH 48.8 billion in 2011, constituting 6.1 percent of GDP (figure 3.1). A vast portion of public spending on social assistance is thus dedicated to food and energy subsidies, accounting for 85 percent and 68 percent, respectively, in 2008 and 2009. Given the finite nature of government funds, the expenditure consumed by universal price supports is unavailable for public investments and social programs. Social protection initiatives addressing key risks for the most vulnerable (providing health care for children under four or dealing with unemployment) are therefore limited.

The subsidy system exacerbates budget and balance of payment deficits and constitutes a contingent liability affecting budgetary planning. Morocco has neither oil nor gas reserves. In a context of dependency on energy imports and rising crude oil prices, it is unsurprising that hydrocarbons account for the largest share of price subsidies—78 percent in 2008. The current subsidy system is thus driving up macroeconomic imbalances, while complicating budgetary planning by constituting a substantial item dependent on erratic exogenous factors. In 2009, DH 15.7 billion were saved unexpectedly as crude oil prices considerably lagged the predicted US$100 on the basis of which budgetary calculations had been made. The opposite situation presented itself in February 2011, when the government had to add DH 15 billion to the DH 17 billion previously earmarked for the Compensation Fund, tantamount to a near-doubling of its resources. The unexpected additional expense contributed to a further increase in the budget deficit, with subsidies as a proportion of GDP rising from 2.1 percent in 2009 to 6.1 percent in 2011 and DH 48.8 billion in total.

In addition to raising equity and budgetary issues, the subsidy system encourages inefficiencies and market distortions. The price distortions caused by the system encourage rent-seeking and fraudulent behavior. Fixed prices lower the

Figure 3.1 Development of Subsidy Payments, 2003–11

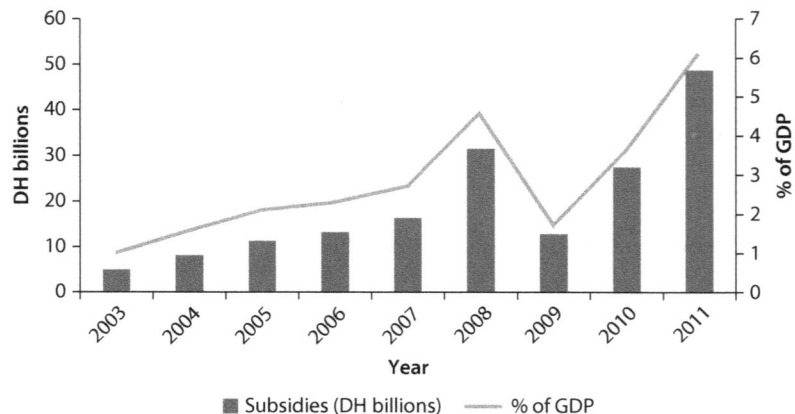

Source: Government of Morocco 2012a, 2012b.
Note: DH = dirham; GDP = gross domestic product.

incentives for consumers to adapt their consumption habits in light of world market developments, while value-chain stakeholders may forego opportunities to improve production and distribution methods in order to achieve price reductions and improved product quality. Equally, shortcomings in management and control systems lead to fraud and leakage.

Political Economy Drivers of National Decision Making and the Difficult History of Subsidy Reforms

Morocco's political economy shapes policy makers' room to maneuver toward reform. As in other countries in the Middle East and North Africa, the government is increasingly under pressure from its citizens to expand the inclusiveness of the political and economic system. Demands for accountability, transparency, and economic opportunity have led to unrest, political protests, and regime change throughout the region. For most of Morocco's independence period (since 1956), decision-making powers have been concentrated in the monarchy, in particular under King Hassan II, reigning for over 30 years from 1961 to 1999. A gradual shift in executive powers from the king, Mohammed VI, to the prime minister has taken place over the past two decades, culminating in constitutional reform in 2011. The new constitutional rules require the king to appoint a prime minister from the party that wins the most seats in the parliamentary elections. A range of appointment powers has been shifted toward the head of government.

As in much of the region, an uneven playing field for business has long constrained Morocco's economic development. A recent World Bank (2009) MENA (Middle East and North Africa) Development Report, *From Privilege to Competition: Unlocking Private-Led Growth in the Middle East and North Africa*, highlights the political barriers to increased economic opening in the region. Its "review of state-business relationships in seven MENA countries shows how alliances between privileged businessmen and governments are strong, exclusive, and often decades old" (World Bank 2009, 187). In Morocco, the constitutional reforms adopted in 2011 and successively implemented since then have begun to shift this equilibrium. However, the concentration of economic benefits within a narrow group for an extended period of time has also affected employment creation in the country. Thus, the importance of the subsidy system to average citizens in both economic and political terms has been particularly significant.

Consequently, by affecting the distribution of costs and benefits and reshaping a key element of the social contract, subsidy reform has proved to be a delicate subject prone to encouraging organized opposition over the past decades. Subsidy reform has caused civil unrest in Morocco (and similarly in a number of other Middle Eastern countries) in the past. Experiences in various countries have shown that reforming energy and food subsidies can entail considerable risks. In Morocco, strikes and violent protests particularly in urban environments met the announcement of price increases for staple products in 1980, 1981, and 1984. The so-called hunger riots evidenced the population's intense reaction, especially in cities, to attempts at cutting subsidies to food considered vital.

Consequently, reforming the subsidy system is regarded as a highly sensitive, controversial subject by the Moroccan authorities, who have proceeded with the utmost caution. In September 2007, riots again erupted in Séfrou in the Fès-Boulemane region after prices for staple foods were raised. As a result, the government rescinded the 30 percent increase in bread prices and has been particularly cautious regarding regions considered sensitive.

The government has been exploring options to reform the subsidy regime since the late 1990s. Against the backdrop of social, budgetary, and economic shortcomings, the government views the restructuring of the current system as vital to the wider reform of its social protection policy system. Since 2007, the government has emphasized the need to reform the compensation system to limit budgetary expenditure and render social protection more equitable, with several studies conducted to ascertain the status quo and identify reform avenues.[1] However, none of the various proposals to reform the energy subsidy system were implemented. Despite the launched initiatives unanimously calling for reform action, successive governments before 2012 have undertaken only partial and ultimately insubstantial modifications.

Past decisions introducing, extending, curtailing, or abolishing subsidies were customarily made in the face of not only economic pressures, financial bottlenecks, and consequential world market fluctuations, but also pressure exerted by adversely affected social groups and private stakeholders with marked vested interests. Stakeholders, public opinion, and decision makers appear separated by different viewpoints regarding the necessity and the method of reform, with some advocating progressive subsidy reductions up to the complete dismantling of the system in favor of support mechanisms benefiting the poor. Others champion support upholding the current structure, but improving it through measures ensuring proper targeting, price control, and optimization of the distribution channels.

In general, the precise manifestation of reform effects tends to be uncertain ex ante and therefore, bias in favor of the status quo can be widespread (Fernandez and Rodrik 1991), with opposition forming even in some of the very groups who should have been favorable to reform (Drazen 1996). Perceptions as to the future distribution of benefits and costs of the reform are likely to be affected by conflicts of interest (Alesina and Drazen 1991) among several sets of stakeholders. Another feature of subsidy reform has to do with its time dimension, with the immediate costs of reform being felt particularly keenly by certain groups, while the advantages tend to materialize only later and are frequently more diffuse, rendering beneficiaries difficult to predict.[2] Those negatively affected are generally more likely to mobilize themselves than those who gain, capitalizing on their political power and organizational, political, and financial resources. For instance, corporate actors may enlist the support of their representative bodies to oppose reform, as was the case in Morocco with subsidies for sugar for industrial use in April 1999. Equally, the middle and wealthy classes benefiting from universal subsidies may be well organized, particularly in urban areas. To prevent feelings of disenfranchisement and actors with political power blocking the process, the government may need to implement compensatory measures, but these ought to remain limited to avoid nullifying the reform's budgetary relief and undermining the coherence of reform.

Any reform of the current system is bound to face the dual challenge of efficiency and acceptability. The technical analysis that has been conducted over the past decade has identified many solutions to the efficiency question. Although reforming the current universal regime would seem inevitable in the face of its threefold shortcomings in budgetary, economic, and social terms, international experience has demonstrated that a sound technical conception of restructuring efforts is no guarantee that the desired outcome can be attained (OECD 2007, 2010). Thus, it is the question of acceptability that remains unsolved. However carefully the sequencing of interventions and accompanying social protection measures may have been planned, public reception is likely to make or break the success of a reform. Its anticipation therefore constitutes a key factor in the context of the wider political economy drivers of decision making given a reform's reception among key stakeholders and with the public at large. Ascertaining public perceptions of the present system, its shortcomings, and public attitudes to potential reform options would be crucial for moving forward, especially given the difficult history of subsidy reform in Morocco.

The World Bank has engaged the government in a broad dialogue on subsidy reform and social protection policy for over a decade. Over the 2000s, the Bank and the government of Morocco engaged in a dialogue on integrated social protection and the economic, budgetary, and distributional implications of the subsidy system, manifested in studies, technical assistance, and study trips. A Poverty and Social Impact Assessment for butane gas subsidies was conducted in 2007. The following year, the Bank organized a round table in Rabat presenting international experiences pertaining to more efficient and equitable social protection systems.

In 2008, the World Bank (2008b) published the paper "Reforming Energy Subsidy Prices and Reinforcing Social Protection: Some Design Issues." Its key recommendations included carefully analyzing subsidy reform impacts on poverty, health, and the environment and identifying target populations eligible for social assistance, while launching compensatory measures and mechanisms tailored to target populations. A crucial suggestion was implementing a multipronged communication initiative prior to and accompanying the reform process. In 2010, the World Bank (2010a) published a strategy paper on targeting and social protection, which not only offered suggestions on improving human development, poverty reduction, and growth, but also aimed to support the government in transitioning from a universal subsidy system toward targeted interventions benefiting those in need. With the Bank's principal interlocutor, the minister for economics and general affairs, also the champion of subsidy reform within the government, a new line of dialogue was opened in 2009 based on the awareness that politics rather than a technical issue may constitute the chief impediment to reform.

The Challenge of Acceptability: Capturing Public Views on a Potential Reform to Subsidies for Butane Gas

Methodology and Objectives

Aware of the social and political dimensions of subsidy reform, the Ministry for Economics and General Affairs asked the World Bank to conduct an investigation into both the political and the economic aspects of reform. It was clear that to move forward, the government needed to understand the political implications of a change to the status quo. The approach taken by the Bank aimed at testing political attitudes toward the sequencing, distributional impacts, and depth of subsidy reform. The study targeted two staple commodities, the typical 12-kilogram butane gas bottles (which are used in virtually every household for cooking, baking, and heating) and flour (as previously noted, only the former is discussed in this chapter). By exploring the views of various social groups and relevant influential actors, the analysis sought to test the acceptability of reform scenarios.

The analysis set itself three main objectives: understanding public reactions to reform options and price increases, identifying possible avenues for reform, and understanding what communication measures would be helpful to increase the acceptance of the reforms. The analysis comprised three key steps: (a) mapping stakeholders and social groups, (b) testing reform options and messages among stakeholders and the public, and (c) eliciting the position of different groups toward subsidy reductions for flour and butane gas to inform the development of a communication strategy.

The political economy analysis combined quantitative and qualitative elements in an innovative, practical, and flexible manner. The analysis used qualitative focus group interviews and conversations with stakeholders[3] to ascertain the preferences, expectations, and likely reactions to reform that were prevalent among the beneficiaries of the current system. The focus group interviews were conducted with members of Morocco's five socioprofessional categories in both urban and rural settings and included two especially sensitive regions. For stratification into socioprofessional categories, a multicriteria assessment was employed, placing the greatest weight on the household head's education, the type of residence, and the location, distinguishing among five categories from well-off (A) to most disadvantaged (E).[4] On the basis of these initial findings, the questionnaire for a nationally representative survey was elaborated and applied, with 1,375 households in 12 cities and towns between July and August 2010 included in the analysis.

The qualitative analysis investigated the perceptions held by beneficiaries of the current system, both stakeholders and general population. To comprehend prevalent opinions among value-chain stakeholders, semistructured interviews were organized with representatives professionally active in the butane gas sector.[5] First, conversations included discussions of stakeholders' roles within the existing value chains and compensation system, as well as their perceptions of and reactions to (a) the economic implications of the current system, (b) the potential impacts of compensation reductions on various stakeholder and consumer groups, and (c) the transitory measures needed to mitigate such impacts. Second, eight focus group interviews with members of the general population were conducted in different regions of Morocco, in rural and urban settings. Every focus group—some all male, some all female, and some mixed—comprised eight individuals.[5] The qualitative interviews reached members of all strata of society and all backgrounds by using different methods, including imaging, rating, and fictitious situations, to bring together perceptions of the state, the compensation system, envisaged social protection measures, and options for reform. The interviews also elicited information on participants' consumption habits and standards of living.

An opinion survey based on a representative sample of 1,375 households followed the qualitative analysis. The questionnaire used in the survey was informed by findings from the initial qualitative stage. The sample's representativeness was ensured through (a) a rural-urban division combined with a division between socioeconomic categories, (b) a rural-urban division combined with a division between zones benefiting from the national poverty reduction initiative and zones not included in the program, and (c) a rural-urban division combined with a division between zones targeted by the government's wheat flour support program and those outside the program. Two provinces considered to be sensitive were oversurveyed, with the stratification between disadvantaged and more privileged socioeconomic categories remaining representative. The survey collected information on the following:

- Media used as sources of information
- Consumption habits regarding wheat flour and butane gas
- Knowledge and perception of the compensation system
- Perception of social protection programs envisaged by the government (see table 3.2)
- Opinions on targeting mechanisms that the government aims to use (see table 3.2)
- Attitudes toward compensation reduction measures for flour and butane gas
- Preferences regarding scenarios combining subsidy-reducing measures and envisaged social protection measures

The survey aimed to test the population perceptions and attitudes vis-à-vis subsidy reductions. It then sought to identify whether such attitudes and perceptions corresponded to precise socioeconomic characteristics. Finally, it assessed whether there was any link between perceptions, sociodemographics, and the avenues by which different individuals and groups obtain information about the subsidy regime and avenues for reform (box 3.1).[6] The aim was to lay the

Table 3.2 Social Protection Reform Options Envisaged by the Government Used in a Quantitative Survey

Social protection program	
RAMED	Noncontributory scheme to cover public hospital treatment for poor and vulnerable populations
Tayssir	Cash transfer program conditional on school attendance
Unemployment insurance	Obligatory social insurance against unemployment risk for private-sector employees
Second-chance school	Program to (re)introduce school dropouts into school or work
National Promotion	Program for public utility work requiring high manual-labor input
Targeting mechanism	
Multidimensional eligibility test	Eligibility determined by living conditions (households do not know the details of these criteria)
Community targeting	Beneficiaries identified by a local representative of the state
Filtering	Exclusion of privileged population through information from fiscal authorities, social security, and so on
Geographical targeting	Eligibility determined by poverty rate at place of domicile

Source: Authors' compilation.
Note: RAMED = Regime d'Assistance Médicale pour les Economiquement (Noncontributory Health Insurance Scheme).

foundation for designing a communication strategy and to identify messages for particular segments of the population, the media channels to be used to roll out the communication, and timing and sequencing of the messages.

Key Findings

The analysis showed that in terms of attitudes toward subsidy reform, the Moroccan public can be divided according to three attitudinal profiles:

- moderate interventionists
- radical interventionists
- moderate liberals

At 63 percent, the moderate interventionists constitute the majority of the population. They generally favor gradual policy change and centrist policies. They advocate interventions by the state to benefit the most disadvantaged and tend to think that subsidies should not benefit the wealthy. While believing that the current system does not transfer enough from rich to poor, they are generally confident in the state's capacity for redistribution.

The 20 percent of the population that fall into the radical interventionists category tend to opt for more polar positions on issues. They strongly hold that benefits should not go to the wealthy and that the state should be responsible for ensuring solidarity in society, while also criticizing the current system's distributional capacity. Furthermore, they feel a majority of Moroccans are not living in an acceptable situation and believe that the majority of households would not be able to adapt to price increases.

Box 3.1 Choice Variables to Determine Profiles

Because the objective was to identify differentiated profiles, the variables generating mostly consensus in the sample were excluded from the exercise of multicorrespondence analysis (MCA) and segmentation.

Variables that seemed to have been misunderstood were also excluded, such as two variables regarding equity ("An equitable system is a system in which someone receives support to the degree they contribute," "An equitable system is a system in which someone receives support depending on their needs/on their poverty level"). Although the two variables contradict each other, paradoxically 30 percent of respondents answered both in the affirmative. Eight variables were thus used for MCA and the segmentation as follows:

"The subsidy should also benefit wealthy households as they pay for it through their taxes."
"The subsidy should not benefit wealthy households as they don't need it to live well."
"The current compensation system does not allow sufficient redistribution of funds toward the poor."
"I am confident that the state equitably redistributes the collected resources to those most in need."
"The majority of Moroccans live in a satisfactory human and social situation (education, health....)"
"It is part of the state's obligations to ensure solidarity in a society by transferring funds to the poor."
"If prices increase, most households will be able to adjust their consumption."
"If prices for staple products go up slightly, it would seem normal to me if protest movements were organized."

Five possible responses were given for each variable: "absolutely agree," "agree," "neither agree nor disagree," "disagree," and "absolutely disagree."

The moderate liberals represent 17 percent of the population. They express moderate views akin to the first category, yet generally oppose state intervention on behalf of poor households, believing that the state is not obligated to ensure redistribution and professing low confidence in its ability to do so. In general, this group does not believe that the current system is unfavorable to the poor. They oppose any protests that might be organized in reaction to price increases.

Attitudinal profiles cannot be easily attributed to socioeconomic factors, residence in urban or rural settings, or the information media principally used. Although there are slight tendencies visible, with radical interventionists more frequently based in rural settings and in lower socioprofessional categories, and moderate interventionists more often urban and of moderate income, all three attitudinal profiles were found across all socioprofessional categories and in rural and urban environments. Equally, the use of information media is virtually identical throughout all three groups, with television emerging as the consensus prime source.

The public demonstrates a general lack of knowledge regarding the subsidy system. When confronted with the question "Which public support programs for purchasing power do you know?" a mere 10 percent of the sampled population responded spontaneously by saying "the compensation system." Across all attitudinal profiles and socioprofessional categories, there is a low awareness of the system without prompting. Even after the system has been explained, still a large majority (79 percent) profess to never having heard of it, with awareness most limited in the disadvantaged socioprofessional categories (see figure 3.2). This generalized lack of knowledge of the system might also explain the lack of differentiation among different categories.

The scope and financial implications of the subsidy system are equally unfamiliar. When asked what products they think actually benefit from state subsidies, a limited majority of participants cites flour, sugar, and culinary oil, even though subsidies for oil were discontinued in 2000. Even fewer people are aware of the support for butane gas or fuels, which is still in place today. As a consequence of this limited awareness, the impact of the support measures is substantially underestimated. With the current butane gas price at DH 40 for a bottle containing 12 kilograms, the interviewees expected the real market price to stand at DH 55. In reality, however, removing all subsidies would cause the price to soar by 150 percent to DH 100, corresponding to an underestimation by 45 percent. As a result of this lack of awareness of the system's magnitude, there is also low awareness of the compensation regime's overall budgetary toll.

A large majority of the population regard the current compensation system as beneficial but in need of reform, primarily for reasons of equity. Seventy-six

Figure 3.2 Awareness of Subsidy System According to Socioprofessional Category

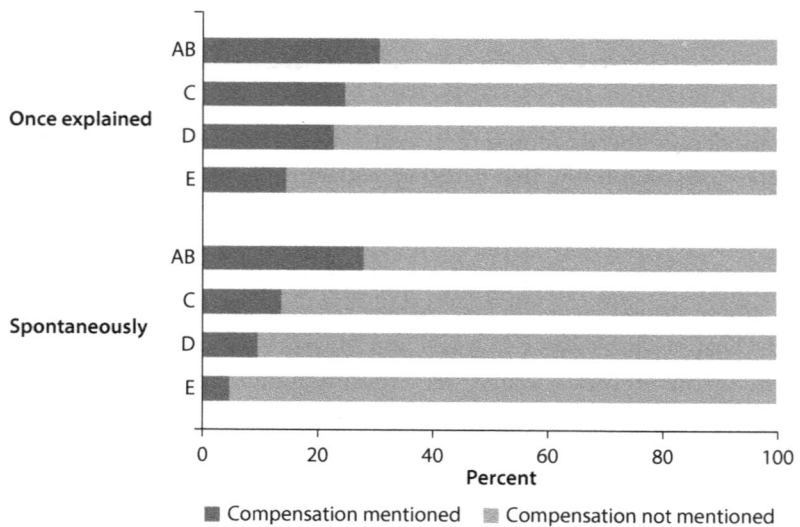

Source: Calculations based on survey results.
Note: See World Bank 2010d for a description of categories A–E.

percent of the survey participants throughout all socioprofessional categories and attitudinal profiles believe the system to be beneficial, with 91 percent considering subsidies to be an obligation of the state and 83 percent viewing the regime as maintaining the purchasing power of the poorest. Nevertheless, 76 percent believe the system ought to be reformed given grave dysfunctions, and 73 percent think controls should be tightened on producers and vendors who benefit more than consumers from the subsidy, while 71 percent agree that part of the compensation budget would be better spent on environmental protection. Furthermore, although a large majority of 84 percent believes that the entire population contributes to the financing of the system, it is "the rich" who are generally viewed—justifiably so—as benefiting the most, with only the most privileged socioprofessional categories disagreeing (figure 3.3).

The social protection programs that the government plans to implement are also hardly known but are viewed favorably, as are the related targeting mechanisms. The National Promotion initiative, comprising public utility works and existing since 1961 (see table 3.2), is just as poorly known as the innovative conditional cash transfer program (Tayssir) or the noncontributory health care program (RAMED [Regime d'Assistance Médicale pour les Economiquement, or Noncontributory Health Insurance Scheme]): only 11 percent of participants were aware of them. Once explained, all three schemes are viewed very favorably across all attitudinal profiles and socioprofessional categories. The main concern expressed regarding the usefulness of the schemes was that the programs may fail to target the needs of the most disadvantaged. In the same vein, targeting mechanisms were considered very useful in terms of equity, but concerns were raised regarding the risk of exclusion of eligible groups and individuals when using geographical targeting approaches, as well as risks of corruption for all three other approaches.

Positive attitudes toward social protection programs do not offset the marked opposition toward subsidy cuts. Large sectors of the population do not feel that

Figure 3.3 Perception of the Subsidy System: Who Benefits the Most?

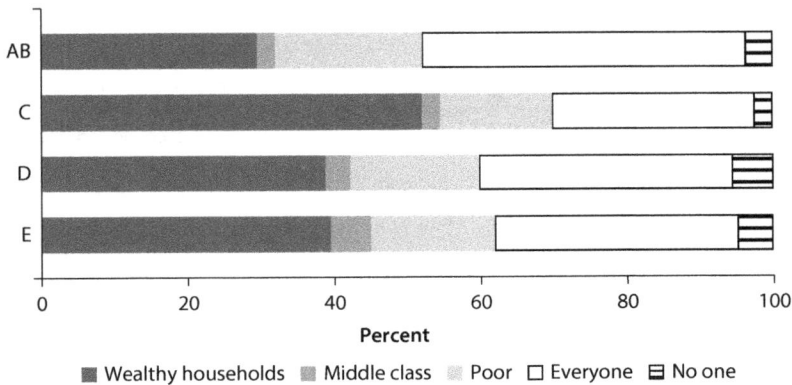

Source: Calculations based on survey results.
Note: See World Bank 2010d for a description of categories A–E.

a reduction in subsidies could be compensated for by the implementation of one of the government's planned social protection measures. In the focus groups, only a small part of the more privileged population considered such a coupling as making price increases more acceptable, with the majority opinion diverging: a lack of confidence in the effectiveness, the targeting, and the durability of such beneficiary schemes was voiced. A majority of participants across all socioprofessional backgrounds and attitudinal profiles objected to reducing price supports to increase funding for social programs targeting the poorest. The choice-based analysis showed that the perceived disutility of even limited price increases outweighed the perceived benefits of social protection programs (see figure 3.4).

Maintaining the status quo was viewed as the most favorable option. Over 80 percent of survey participants considered butane gas to be expensive or very expensive already, with the study also showing that consumers are keenly aware of the current price of butane gas (while being unaware of it being subsidized), offering no leeway for price increases. To ascertain the population's likely reaction to subsidy cuts, the survey raised the question as to what reaction a minimal increase in price, by DH 5 or 12.5 percent, would trigger. A considerable number of participants rated this as unacceptable.[7] Because of its stability over several years, the current price of butane gas is perceived as unchangeable. The price of the 12-kilogram butane gas bottle (DH 40) seems to be perceived as

Figure 3.4 Degree of Utility Attributed to Price Variations and Social Protection Programs
Index

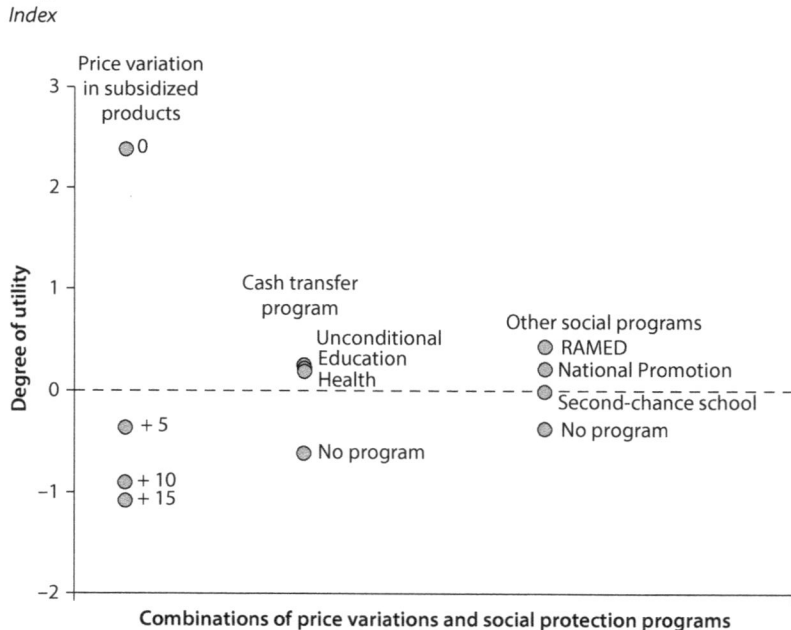

Combinations of price variations and social protection programs

Source: Calculations based on survey results.
Note: RAMED = Regime d'Assistance Médicale pour les Economiquement (Noncontributory Health Insurance Scheme).

an entitlement. Reactions to suggested price increases are not always in line with their actual impact on the respondent's overall budget, as the latter is very dissimilar across socioeconomic groups. This suggests the presence of a perception barrier to reform. Even a slight increase in bottle price aimed at breaking this psychological barrier could be useful to start a long-term reform dynamic. The second and third most common answers across attitudinal profiles and socioprofessional categories were that a price increase would cause consumption to diminish and force consumers to find substitutes to replace butane gas. Though they expressed dissatisfaction with the safety of the bottles and voiced concerns about leakage in filling levels, most survey participants advocated that the status quo be maintained (see below).

Reducing subsidies for butane gas is perceived as increasing energy poverty as well as environmental risks. A higher proportion of the energy consumption of disadvantaged households is covered by butane gas (between 30 and 34 percent), with a higher percentage of their monthly budgets (up to 6 percent) spent on the subsidized fuel. In the absence of viable alternatives, butane gas price increases would thus be likely to affect more disadvantaged households more strongly. As figure 3.5 illustrates, the two most common coping strategies stated when faced with a price increase would be reducing consumption or shifting to a different source of energy. However, the survey showed that the public does not see any obvious substitute for butane gas, while disadvantaged socioprofessional categories cite coal or wood. In the case of rural households with immediate access to forests, the latter option may risk deforestation.

In sum, the analysis found that a large share of the population consider subsidies to be an integral part of the social contract between the state and citizens. It furthermore showed that large parts of the population are entirely unaware of the magnitude and budget impact of price support measures. The majority of citizens and stakeholders express hostility toward any proposed price increase in butane gas. Moreover, the suggestion that the price support system might be replaced with new social programs that are better able to target the poor was not considered adequate compensation for subsidy reductions.

Figure 3.5 Reaction to DH 5 Increase in Price of Butane Gas

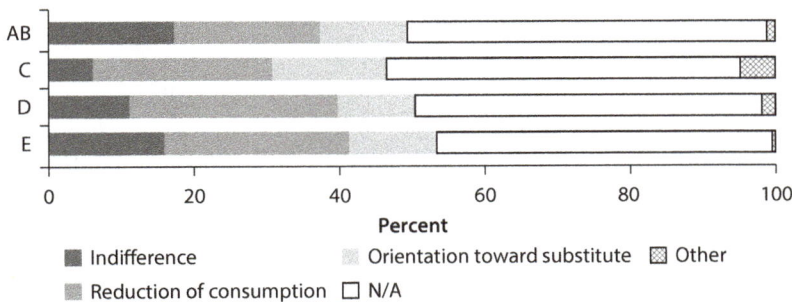

Source: Calculations based on survey results.
Note: N/A = Unacceptable. See World Bank 2010d for a description of categories A–E.

Implications for Reform Entry Points

Against the background of these findings, the team sought to identify some avenues toward energy subsidy reform that may nonetheless be feasible and that could gradually open up opportunities for further reform. The team sought in particular to identify foci that would make gradual changes and communications approaches acceptable. The key findings and implications for ways to approach subsidy reforms are summarized in box 3.2.

Concerns about security and leakage in the supply system suggest potential (imperfect) entry points for reform. The analysis showed that the vast majority of participants believed filling levels of the butane gas bottles have decreased recently, with a considerable majority also dissatisfied with the safety of the butane gas bottles. These perceptions may offer an entry point for reform by officially reducing filling levels and increasing safety while maintaining the same

---

Box 3.2 Key Conclusions

- Large parts of the population are unaware of the current price support measures, their magnitude, and budgetary impact, with implications for their understanding of the need and objectives of reform.
- Once informed of the existence and role of the subsidy system, a large share of the population considers subsidies to be part and parcel of the social contract between state and citizens.
- Despite minor differences, large majorities within the three attitudinal profiles react with marked hostility toward all price increase scenarios and agree on the fact that the subsidy system ought to be maintained.
- The various attitudinal profiles cannot be easily matched to socioeconomic features. The lack of opinion differentiation might be due to a general lack of knowledge or understanding of the overall subsidy system.
- Less privileged strata use comparatively more butane gas to cover their energy needs and spend a greater portion of their budget on it, with survey participants believing there was no obvious substitute for butane gas.
- The perception of a disproportionate impact on disadvantaged strata could affect the reform prospects.
- The introduction of new social programs based on better targeting mechanisms is not considered as compensating for subsidy reductions.
- Measures toward increased safety and control over filling levels of butane gas bottles might be used to justify moderate price increases.
- Without a targeted communication campaign, cuts can have delicate political and social implications.
- Communication should aim at informing the public about the existence and functioning of the system, as well as its implications.
- The lack of differentiation of public opinion groups provides an opportunity for shaping public opinion groups favorable to reform.

---

prices. Thus, in the short to medium term, price changes can be associated with measures such as making official the decrease in filling levels and improving the safety of butane gas bottles. The drawback of this option compared to a standard increase in prices is that reform would be predicated on a one-off renewal of the butane gas bottles nationwide and would not have clear follow-up steps to further reduce subsidies going forward. It is also likely to be resisted by bottle fillers as it would reduce margins. Nonetheless, this entry point would work toward breaking the psychological barrier.

Given the vast opposition to reform and the characteristics of public attitudes, any attempt at reform would need to be preceded and accompanied by substantive communication measures. The lack of socioeconomic differentiation among the various attitudinal profiles offers an opportunity to shape public attitudes. A targeted communication campaign would leverage latent perceptions of inequity to elicit support among most progressive constituencies.

The campaign would aim at informing the public of the current system and its functioning, its failures, and its drawbacks—notably its budgetary implications and largely regressive nature—with a view to opening a debate on options for reform. The introduction of innovative social programs supporting the poorest strata of society would be announced in parallel, not in conjunction, with subsidy reform measures, to convey the general direction of government policy without giving the impression of a retaliatory approach to buying consensus.

Moving toward Impact: Evolving Efforts at Subsidy Reforms

The results of the analysis were shared with representatives of the ministries of General Affairs, Economy and Finance, and Interior. A communication campaign informed by the study was launched in the fall of 2011, largely aimed at informing the public of the existence of the overall subsidy system and its costs and extent.

In the summer of 2012, the government then moved to reduce price support to diesel, gasoline, and industrial fuel through a sudden price increase effective June 2, 2012 (see table 3.3). A 2008 analysis by the Ministry of Economy and Finance (see table 3.1) had evidenced that although the wealthy benefited disproportionately more than the poorer strata from subsidies for all types of fuel, the balance in the case of diesel and gasoline subsidies was tipped even more in their favor than for butane gas. The World Bank's political economy analysis had found that butane gas was already considered to be expensive and used comparatively more by poorer households. A removal of butane gas subsidies as a first step could therefore have caused hardship among the poorest strata. Furthermore, the study had demonstrated that the current system was perceived to benefit wealthy households disproportionately. Therefore, reducing subsidies for liquid fuels offered an avenue for reform expected to be more widely accepted by the public.

A multipronged, large-scale communication campaign informed by the analysis involving senior government figures was launched to explain the

Table 3.3 Overview of Energy Subsidy Reform in Morocco, June 2012

Fuel subsidies				
Fuel type	Old price (DH)	New price (DH)	Absolute increase (DH)	Increase (%)
Diesel (per liter)	7.15	8.15	1.00	14.0
Gasoline (per liter)	10.18	12.18	2.00	19.6
Industrial fuel (per ton)	3,678.00	4,666.04	988.04	26.9

Communication campaign

Spearheaded by prime minister and senior government figures
Continuous communication and education on current system and subsidy reform
Highlights of system's inadequacies in three domains:

- budgetary implications
- unavailability of funds for other investment
- social inequities

Source: Based on political economy assessment and government of Morocco.

subsidy reductions for liquid fuels. The campaign was carried out through different channels, including television, radio, and printed press with a view to reaching all strata in society. The threefold narrative that was pursued reflected the key recommendations of the study. First, statements highlighted the backdrop of soaring world prices and the situation on world financial markets, as well as the sizable subsidies remaining in place for other fuels such as butane gas to protect purchasing power and competitiveness. Second, it was emphasized that the considerable volume of funds tied up in universal subsidies could not be used for crucial investments and growth promotion elsewhere. Finally, to reinforce the message of inequity in the system, the statements stressed that it was crucial to redirect funds toward those most in need of support. In line with recommendations, envisaged social compensation measures were communicated in parallel and without creating a direct connection to subsidy-reducing measures to avoid discrediting the planned programs.

In January 2013, the government began announcing further subsidy reductions to be undertaken during the year, with a view to limiting the deficit to 4.7 percent of GDP (from an actual deficit of 7.1 percent of GDP in 2012) and to reducing the total cost of subsidies to 3 percent of GDP by 2016. An annex pertaining to the reduction plan for subsidies was also included in the 2013 budget plan as a further signal of the government's intention and part of its communication effort. In parallel, the government has also continued with its efforts to strengthen its social safety net targeting the poorer strata in society. However, the continuing strains have also been evident. In early April, the government announced cut backs to the proposed public investment spending to reach its deficit target. In July 2013, it announced the introduction of automatic price adjustments for subsidized petroleum products based on international market prices, as well as a more comprehensive reform of the subsidy fund to be undertaken in late 2013.

Notes

1. See, for instance, Government of Morocco 2008a.

2. Williamson and Haggard (1994, 531) show that policy reforms "are like an investment that should ultimately benefit the majority by enough to make them happy they made it, but that in the short run will—like all investments—involve sacrifices. The distribution of these sacrifices over time and across groups is at the heart of the politics of economic reform."

3. For more details, see World Bank 2010b.

4. The polling institute entrusted with the study estimates the current distribution of socioprofessional categories in the overall population to be as follows: SPC A (well-off): 2 percent; B: 3 percent; C: 31 percent; D: 38 percent; and E (most disadvantaged): 26 percent. The estimate is based on studies conducted in four waves per year from 1989 to 2002, then in two waves per year after 2002.

5. For more details, see World Bank 2010d.

6. Attitudinal profiles were established through a multicorrespondence analysis (MCA) combined with segmentation. One part of the survey sought to identify awareness and opinions regarding the existing subsidy system. The findings of questions about perceptions were subjected to an MCA aiming to generate qualitative variables and a limited number of quantitative variables, the so-called principal factors (see box 3.2 later in this chapter; note that box 3.2 is about key findings). Through a classification combining hierarchical ascendant and dynamic cloud classification, three attitudinal profiles were identified and then analyzed to ascertain sociodemographic particularities and specific information habits. A choice-based correspondence analysis was used to evaluate reform alternatives and rank different combinations of measures. This method allows for an evaluation of the utility of alternatives for various attributes of a product. See, for instance, Liquet and Benavent (n.d.). In this instance, the product in question was a combination of measures, comprising three attributes: (a) a variation of the prices for subsidized products, (b) a cash transfer program, and (c) another social protection program. Four alternatives were assigned to each attribute: (a) the variation of prices was 0 percent, 5 percent, 10 percent, or 15 percent; (b) the cash transfer program could be conditional on school attendance or on visits to a health facility, unconditional, or nonexistent; and (c) the other social protection program could be a RAMED (Regime d'Assistance Médicale pour les Economiquement, or Noncontributory Health Insurance Scheme)–type of program financing hospital costs, a second-chance school, the public utility–work National Promotion scheme, or no program (see table 3.2 and figure 3.4). The joined analysis technique allows a relative evaluation of the utility of each alternative.

7. "Unacceptable" was not originally offered as an answer choice: it denotes the unwillingness to provide an answer among those foreseen in the questionnaire.

Bibliography

Alesina, Alberto, and Allan Drazen. 1991. "Why Are Stabilizations Delayed?" *American Economic Review* 81 (5): 1170–88.

Drazen, Allan. 1996. "The Political Economy of Delayed Reform." *Policy Reform* 1: 25–46.

Fernandez, Raquel, and Dani Rodrik. 1991. "Resistance to Reform: Status Quo Bias in the Presence of Individual-Specific Uncertainty." *American Economic Review* 81 (5): 1146–55.

Government of Morocco. 2007. "Rapport annuel de la cour des comptes." Government of Morocco, Rabat.

———. 2008a. "Fiche sur le système de compensation: Dysfonctionnements et pistes de réforme. [Overview of the compensation system: Dysfunctionalities and avenues for reform]." Government of Morocco, Rabat.

———. 2008b. "Etude du système de la compensation: Diagnostic et perspectives de réforme." Government of Morocco, Rabat.

———. 2009. "Rapport sur la réforme du système de compensation: Projet Takaâfoul pour une société de confiance dans un Maroc solidaire." Government of Morocco, Rabat.

———. 2012a. "Rapport economique et financier [Economic and Financial Report]." Government of Morocco, Rabat.

———. 2012b. "Notes de conjoncture: Notes de fin d'année couvrant la période 2003–2011 [State of Economy Reports: End-of-year memos covering 2003–2011]." Ministry of Economics and Finance, Government of Morocco, Rabat.

Labán, Raúl, and Federico Sturzenegger. 1994. "Distributional Conflict, Financial Adaptation and Delayed Stabilizations." *Economics and Politics* 6 (3): 257–76.

Liquet, Jean-Claude, and Christophe Benavent. n.d. "L'analyse conjointe et ses applications en marketing [Conjoint-based choice analysis and its application in marketing]." Institut d'Administration des Entreprises, Lille, France.

OECD (Organisation for Economic Co-operation and Development). 2007. *Subsidy Reform and Sustainable Development: Political Economy Aspects.* OECD Sustainable Development Studies. Paris: OECD.

———. 2010. "L'économie politique de la réforme: Retraites, emplois et déréglementation dans dix pays de l'OCDE." OECD, Paris.

Williamson, John, and Stephen Haggard. 1994. "The Political Conditions for Economic Reforms." In *The Political Economy of Policy Reform,* edited by John Williamson, 525–96. Washington, DC: Institute for International Economics.

World Bank. 2004a. "Royaume du Maroc–Rapport sur la pauvreté: Comprendre les dimensions géographiques de la pauvreté pour en améliorer l'appréhension à travers les politiques publiques." World Bank, Washington, DC.

———. 2004b. "Stakeholder Analysis on Moroccan Cereal Reform: Interactive Analysis prepared by Sentia." World Bank, Washington, DC.

———. 2005. "Royaume du Maroc: Réforme du système de compensation à la Farine Nationale de Blé Tendre." World Bank, Washington, DC.

———. 2008a. "Réformer les subventions au prix de l'énergie et renforcer la protection sociale: Quelques questions de conception." World Bank, Washington, DC.

———. 2008b. "Reforming Energy Subsidy Prices and Reinforcing Social Protection: Some Design Issues." ESMAP Paper 43173, Energy Sector Management Assistance Program, World Bank, Washington, DC.

———. 2009. *From Privilege to Competition: Unlocking Private-Led Growth in the Middle East and North Africa.* Middle East and North Africa Development Report. Washington, DC: World Bank.

———. 2010a. "Royaume du Maroc: Note stratégique sur le ciblage et la protection social [Kingdom of Morocco: Strategy paper on targeting and social protection]." World Bank, Rabat.

———. 2010b. "Analyse politique de la réforme du système de subventions au Maroc: Focus groups. [Political analysis of subsidy system reform in Morocco: Focus groups]." Power Point presentation, World Bank, Rabat, July 22.

———. 2010c. "Analyse politique de la réforme du système de subventions au Maroc: Focus groups." Paper, World Bank, Washington, DC.

———. 2010d. "Analyse politique de la réforme du système de subventions au Maroc: Synthèse des entretiens avec les parties prenantes. [Political analysis of subsidy system reform in Morocco: Synthesis of stakeholder interviews]." Power Point presentation, World Bank, Rabat, July 22.

———. 2010e. "Analyse politique de la réforme du système de subventions au Maroc: Synthèse des entretiens avec les parties prenantes." Paper, World Bank, Washington, DC.

———. 2012. "Ciblage et protection sociale au Maroc: Note d'orientation stratégique." World Bank, Washington, DC.

PART 2

Political Economy Drivers of National Infrastructure Reforms

The Dominican Republic: Moving from Exit to Voice—Shifting Incentives in the Power Sector

Carlos Rufín, Davide Zucchini, Roby Senderowitsch, and Miguel Eduardo Sánchez

High Growth, Limited Inclusiveness, and Poor Public Service Delivery in the Dominican Republic

Despite good economic performance, the Dominican Republic is marked by a lack of inclusive growth. During the period 1961–2007, per capita gross domestic product (GDP) in the Dominican Republic expanded at a pace of 3.0 percent, higher than the region's average (1.7 percent). However, the economic expansion has not been accompanied by a substantial reduction of poverty and inequality, nor has it produced significant improvements in social indicators. According to official poverty calculations, in recent years the Dominican Republic was able to reduce moderate poverty from approximately 50 percent of the population in 2004 to only 41 percent in 2011, whereas extreme poverty dropped from 16 percent to 10 percent in the same period. Although these reductions in poverty appear significant, they remain above the poverty levels observed a decade ago. in the aftermath of a banking crisis in 2003 that had severe macroeconomic consequences.[1]

Because the development pattern of the Dominican Republic has not often been inclusive, effective redistribution policies may be needed to achieve pro-poor growth. However, the Dominican Republic has traditionally presented low tax pressure (around 13 percent of GDP in 2012) and limited fiscal space (Sánchez and Victoria 2012), and ranked at the bottom of Latin America in public expenditure on health and education in 2012. Furthermore, a large electricity sector deficit crowds out public spending for social programs and capital investments. The challenge to expand revenue collection to increase welfare redistribution is not only fiscal; it has a governance dimension, because people are reluctant to pay taxes in a context of low institutional trust, of high perception of corruption, and of low quality of public services.

Persistent poor public service provision in the Dominican Republic is a roadblock to attaining more inclusive growth. The electricity sector is probably the paradigm of malfunctioning public goods in the Dominican Republic. As highlighted by Moya Pons (1998), over the past 40 years a combination of dependence on imported oil, a weak institutional environment, and in some cases fraud and theft led to poor service provision, frequent interruptions, and even complete system blackouts culminating in repeated crises (Rufin and Zucchini 2010). These authors argued that by 1986 the Dominican Electricity Corporation was unable to generate even 50 percent of the demand, which resulted in daily blackouts. By then, the average customer received only three hours of electricity a day. Service has not improved until recent years and still remains poor. According to World Bank–IFC Enterprise Surveys (2012), businesses suffer an average of 25.6 electrical outages a month or more than one blackout per working day.

In the case of education, over the past two decades, the Dominican Republic spent just about 2 percent of GDP, ranking at the bottom of Latin America.[2] The expansion of education infrastructure (for example, the number of classrooms) and human resources (for example, the number of teachers) has not kept pace with increased demand. As a consequence, there has been an increase in the number of children per classroom and a rise in the number of shifts (tandas) in schools. The quality of education is further hampered by teacher absenteeism, inadequate teacher supervision and training, and so forth. As a result, SERCE (Second Regional Comparative and Explanatory Study) scores suggest that the Dominican Republic is performing worse than countries at similar development levels (Luque, Hobbs, and Carlston 2010). The education system in the Dominican Republic is also characterized by high repetition rates and low completion because returns to secondary education are very low; only slightly above 10 percent of the total population has completed secondary school, which situates the Dominican Republic at the bottom of Latin America, right after República Bolivariana de Venezuela.[3] The case of public health care in the Dominican Republic is quite similar to that of education: coverage has expanded, especially over the past decade. But public expenditure to GDP remains at the bottom of Latin America, individual out-of-pocket expenditures constitute a burden for poorer households, and provision of quality services remains a challenge.

Though the Dominican Republic may be a middle-income country, the poor quality of public services poses a significant development challenge. Improving public service provision will be critical to achieve more inclusive growth and even to allow the Dominican Republic to remain on a high growth trajectory. Given this situation, the World Bank's local team in Santo Domingo started to question what hidden factors might be hampering the quality of public expenditure. Because the high growth, limited redistribution, and poor public service delivery puzzle is eminently rooted in governance problem, a political economy approach was adopted. Two studies were undertaken. The first found that the citizen-state link of the World Bank's service-delivery triangle was broken—in large part because of constraints on citizens' voice for better public service delivery, which originally emerged as a background paper for the World Bank flagship on the middle class in Latin America (Ferreira et al. 2013). The second study focused on the electricity sector specifically, assessing the feasibility of expert recommendations for getting the sector on a more stable footing and examining how stakeholders might react to specific reform initiatives.

Based on these political economy analyses, we argue that the Dominican Republic has fallen into an inefficient equilibrium characterized by a narrow tax base and limited redistributive policies, all reinforcing poor public service provision. Weak collective action, clientelism, a civil society with limited voice and fragmented interests, as well as the individual choice of private solutions to compensate for malfunctioning public goods (especially among the middle class) are some of the explanatory factors behind this equilibrium. The second and third sections of this chapter summarize the analysis and findings of the political economy studies undertaken by the World Bank's Dominican Republic team. These sections also present the recommendations that resulted from the analysis. The final section reviews the implications of this work for the World Bank's engagement in the country.

Service Delivery, Citizen Voice, and Opting Out

In general discussions on pending challenges, two factors are used to explain why the Dominican Republic has been unable to become a more developmental and inclusive state. The first is clientelism, defined by Stokes (2009) as an electoral strategy based on the nonprogrammatic exchange of votes for material resources. According to the World Bank (forthcoming), "(t)he pervasiveness of clientelism is a flip side of the lack of ideological or programmatic orientations in electoral contests." Over the past two decades, members of the Dominican Congress have perceived voters as increasingly motivated by party identification and person (leader) rather than by program or ideology. According to Jones (2010), political parties in the Dominican Republic have the lowest possible level of programmatic orientation in Latin America, along with those of six other countries in the region.[4] Around elections, vote-buying and patronage are a widespread manifestation of the prevalence of clientelism. During campaigns, especially for seats in parliament, it is quite common to see candidates promoting themselves as the "delegate who resolves," referring to their ability to solve people's problems.

Individual citizens are not the only ones who participate in clientelism; a series of well-organized commercial and industrial conglomerates use their political connections to preserve a series of privileges inherited from previous stages of economic development such as free trade zones, tax exemptions, and so forth (World Bank forthcoming). In fact, widespread clientelism may be one of the forces that is partially offsetting discontent with public goods and institutions and providing certain stability and continuity to a limited access order democracy, as defined by North et al. (2007). In this context, the developmental challenge in the Dominican Republic might be described as the struggle of a country to move from a clientelist mode of politics to one organized around programmatic competition between political parties, with the quality of public service delivery as a key basis for political competition.

The second factor that is used to explain why the Dominican Republic has been unable to become a more inclusive state is a history of weak labor organization. Labor union fragmentation in the Dominican Republic is explained historically by an economy dominated by sugar plantations dispersed over wide geographic areas, as well as the presence of illegal Haitian laborers, which reduces incentives to form a united front in defense of workers' collective rights and their capacity to mount effective collective action. Fragmented labor organization, or weak collective action more generally, might explain why citizens have not been able to make a stronger claim for social services such as education and health.

The World Bank team used these two perspectives as a starting point to explore more deeply the prospects for policy reform in the Dominican Republic. Sánchez and Senderowitsch (2012), building on the theoretical framework for public service delivery presented in the *World Development Report 2004: Making Services Work for Poor People* (World Bank 2003), argue that deficiencies in public service provision persist in part because there is weak citizen voice and limited collective action in the Dominican Republic,[5] especially among the middle class. In principle, the middle class can play an important role, in particular by demanding better quality public services. However, the middle class has few incentives to act collectively to demand higher state accountability, because this group has significantly opted out of the system, choosing to use individual solutions (private schools, private health insurance, owning an electricity generator, or private security) rather than public goods. Figure 4.1 identifies weakness on all three

Figure 4.1 Theoretical Framework for Public Service Delivery

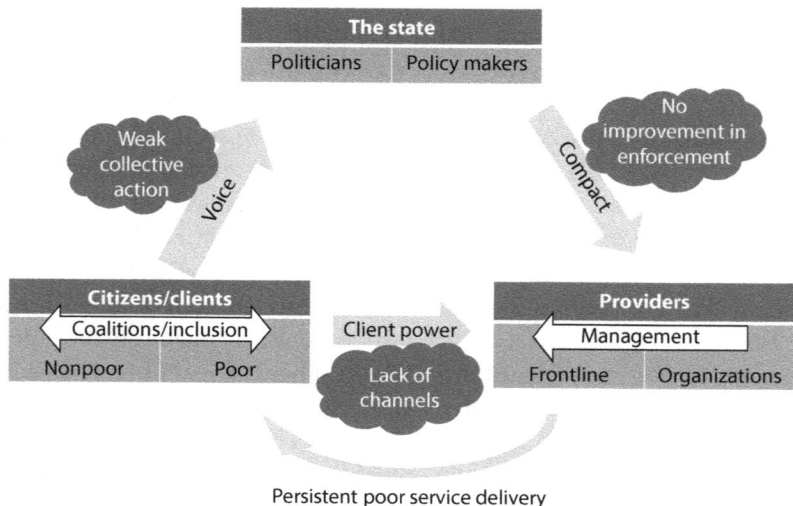

Persistent poor service delivery

Source: Adapted from World Bank 2003, 49.

sides of the service delivery triangle, whereas the following analysis focuses especially on the broken link between the citizen and the state. The analysis argues
that low levels of institutional trust and individualization of services can explain
in part the low collective action in the Dominican Republic, resulting in weak
accountability and persistent low-quality public goods.

The Context: Political Engagement, Citizen Voice, and Collective Action in the Dominican Republic

One finding of the Sánchez and Senderowitsch (2012) study is that the
Dominican Republic is characterized by high levels of membership in associa-
tions, but that citizens are not mobilized to protest or make claims on the state.
If one draws on public opinion surveys, it is possible to characterize the
Dominican Republic citizenship and to assess the perception that collective
action is weak. Looking at proxies for civil participation, one sees a striking fact
that, despite relatively low (and declining) levels of interpersonal trust, the
Dominicans participate in more associations than the citizens in any other Latin
American country. Dominicans are highly involved in committees for community improvement, religious groups, and parent associations, and, to a lesser
degree, in professional associations (locally known as *gremios*, or guilds).
Participation in religious groups is especially noticeable with 60 percent of survey
respondents reporting participation. However, the high tendency toward being
an association member does not necessarily mean that the organizations of civil
society are effectively coordinated and share common goals. Many organizations
may not be pursuing increased accountability of the government in public service delivery. Interestingly, protest participation levels in the Dominican Republic
are among the lowest in the region, which implies that the organizations are not
mobilizing the population to participate in public protests and claims. People
living in the north and the south of the country are more likely to participate in
protests than those living in Santo Domingo National District (Morgan, Espinal,
and Seligson 2010).

Interest in politics in the Dominican Republic is also high for regional
standards, although the levels of electoral participation and the percentage of
people involved in proselytizing are just slightly above regional averages. In contrast, the percentage of people who declare they have worked for political candidates is the highest in Latin America, almost double the average in any country.
This high number may reflect rent-seeking practices. In fact, the Dominican
Republic has the highest percentage of people who report receiving clientelist
offers during election campaigns (Morgan, Espinal, and Seligson 2010). According
to interviews with Dominican experts studying political parties and institutions,
expected benefits may be different across quintiles: from in-kind payments to
basic food products to special favors (tax exemptions, licenses, and subsidies) or
even a public office if the candidate is elected. Politically appointed positions
prevail over civil servants at the top of the administration. Thus, political activism
in the Dominican Republic may, in fact, be motivated by clientelism. This represents another feature of the broken link; where low institutional trust and

skepticism about improvements in governance exist, citizens often participate in politics to seek private benefits rather than hold political parties accountable for delivering quality public goods.

The poor responsiveness of public officials compounds the issue of weak collective action. At the municipal level, the Dominican Republic presents the highest level of participation in municipal meetings in the region. Few of the citizens surveyed (15.1 percent) declared to have made explicit requests for improvements to the local authorities, and just 27.8 percent of those considered that their demand was addressed, showing poor response by the municipality (Morgan, Espinal, and Seligson 2010). One of the implications of the lack of responsiveness is that more than 48 percent of the respondents were not satisfied with local government services, one of the largest shares of discontent in Latin America. This level of discontent illustrates limitations in a citizen's ability to exert demands and make local authorities accountable.

The existence of a broken link between the citizen and the state also seems to be manifest when the institutional trust dimension is assessed. According to Latinobarómetro 2010 figures, the Dominican Republic presents levels of institutional trust in its different dimensions that are below the Latin American average. Lack of institutional trust seems to be especially high in the Dominican middle class, as, according to Espinal, Hartlyn, and Kelly (2006), there is some evidence pointing to "a U-shaped relationship between socioeconomic status and institutional trust, with the poorest and wealthiest trusting government institutions more than middle-income sectors."

According to AmericasBarometer 2012, support for democracy in the Dominican Republic has decreased significantly from 2008 (74.9 percent) to 2012 (70.0 percent), and the country is now below the regional average. Similarly, only half of the population is satisfied with democracy, and support for the Dominican political system has significantly declined from 57.6 percent in 2008 to 48.8 percent in 2012. Thus, it is possible to talk about a relative deterioration in citizens' perceptions about democratic institutions in the country. Additionally, the perception of corruption remains high and also increased in 2012 (78.1 percent) relative to 2008 (74.5 percent). In 2010, 17.7 percent of the Dominicans in the survey justified the payment of bribes; they also showed high levels of tolerance for nepotism, as three out of four respondents believed that a politician's intervening to benefit his or her relative is not corruption.

To sum up, the Dominican society seems to be characterized by "strong 'associationalism' but not strong mobilization" (Morgan, Espinal, and Seligson 2010, xxxiii). In addition, an individual making demands to authorities is relatively ineffective, because citizen requests are not often addressed and satisfaction with public services remains low. Trust in redistributive policies is well below regional standards, and some institutions suffer from a credibility crisis, especially since the upsurge in the public sector deficit observed in 2012. Whereas strong political activism is observed in the Dominican Republic, it is likely linked to pursuing rent-seeking activities rather than to holding representatives accountable for delivering quality public goods.

As a part of the dynamics described above, the Dominican society, and especially the middle and upper classes,[6] is opting out and choosing private services. Faced with poor service delivery and limited ability to demand improvements, citizens seek private solutions. This opting out further constrains collective action. Thus, opting out feeds back on this vicious cycle of (a) poor public service provision, (b) private solutions, (c) lack of demand for state accountability and enhancement of public services, (d) lack of willingness to pay taxes, and (e) limited resources to improve public services. The next section addresses the causes and consequences of the middle class opting out in more detail.

The Choice: Opting Out

Besley and Coate (1991) argue that schemes for universal provision of public goods can redistribute income from the rich to the poor. They develop a model in which some individuals can afford to consume a higher-quality service in the private sector. When this occurs, the model shows that redistribution still takes place, but that it can involve an overall welfare loss to society. Concretely, if the quality of public goods supplied is low, both low-income and high-income individuals may be worse off. The poor receive a public service that is low in quality and thus not valued. The rich pay taxes for a service they do not use (opting for private solutions rather than public ones).

The Dominican Republic seems to have fallen into such an inefficient equilibrium for political economy reasons: it has been too costly to create the political and civil society coalitions that would be needed to achieve greater accountability and improvement in public services. Citizens' trust in institutions is low, and those who can afford to respond individually to the problems have already done so. In this section, we introduce some examples of sectors or activities in which the middle and upper classes in the Dominican Republic have opted for private solutions to substitute for or complement poor public service provision.

The choice of individual solutions to cope with low-quality public service provision is observed in the electricity case. The poor performance of the sector has encouraged wealthy-enough customers to substitute or to complement the service by looking for alternative sources of electricity, such as inverters[7] or off-grid diesel electricity generators for houses and enterprises. These backup systems allow upper- and middle-class households to insulate themselves against the shocks of frequent blackouts. In 2007, ONE (2007)[8] calculated that the monthly cost associated with a power inverter was RD$2,362.96 (US$60.00), far more than the average electricity bill of RD$896.09 (US$24.00). The scale of this behavior is both economically and socially notable. As pointed out by the Inter-American Development Bank (2010), which conducted a survey under the supervision of the National Energy Commission (CNE), "auto generation capacity (2,715 MW [megawatts] at the time) was already similar to installed power in the national interconnected system." Even if an important part of this auto generation capacity is installed in industrial facilities, the World Bank (2009, 3) estimated that "in 2005, US$400 million was spent to install and maintain self-generation for the

Figure 4.2 Percentage of Households That Have an Electrical Inverter or a Generator at Home, by Socioeconomic Class

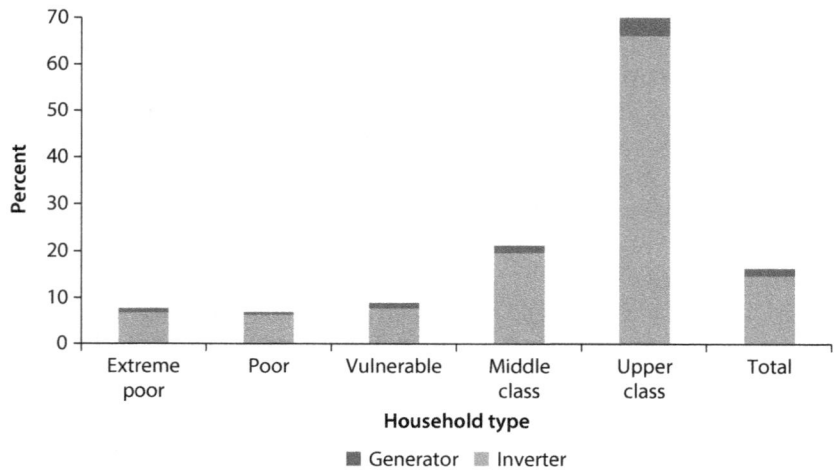

Source: World Bank staff calculations based on ONE 2007, http://enigh.one.gob.do.

commercial and industrial sector, and at least another US$150–200 million was spent on residential self-generation."

In a country where power blackouts are frequent, more than 20 percent of the middle-class households have an electricity inverter or generator in their buildings (figure 4.2). This percentage scales up to nearly 70 percent in upper-class households, showing a very high propensity to partially opt out. Beyond families, most businesses and companies have been forced to acquire private electricity generation devices to avoid disruptions in activity. In some extreme cases, large factories have chosen to directly buy industrial generators and disconnect from the national grid.

Despite clear diagnostics of the consequences of low quality and scarce provision of the electricity service and several proposals for improvement (see CONEP 2008; Inter-American Development Bank and World Bank 2009a; Maurer, Pereira, and Rosenblatt 2005), the sector has passed through recurring crises with just minor changes. Citizens appear to have adapted by providing their own backup systems such as inverters or even investing in generators. Most upper-middle-class apartments come with preinstalled inverters and generators. In addition to these collective action challenges, a number of key stakeholders have had a significant incentive to preserve the status quo rather than to seek reforms, as discussed further in this chapter's third section, titled "Poor Service Delivery in the Electricity Sector."

Private substitution and opting out also extends to other sectors, involving significant costs. In education, 43 percent of the household heads in the richest quintile were sending their children to private schools in 2010. Even among the poorest 20 percent of the population, almost 13 percent of households use private schools (a high percentage given that those families are living below the poverty threshold). Private out-of-pocket contributions to education in the Dominican Republic amounted to RD$17,147 million (~US$550) in 2005 (Dominican Republic Central Bank 2005), which represented 1.37 percent of the GDP that year. Overall, total private spending in education is thought to represent about 1.7 percent of GDP today, compared to public spending levels situated at 2.3 percent of GDP in 2011. Families contributed an average of 38 percent of total financing of education between 1995 and 2005, with enrollment in private schools amounting to two-thirds of expenditures in this field. Moreover, private substitution in education entails quality challenges. In most cases, private education does mean less crowded classrooms and better infrastructure but not better quality of services, because the majority of the teachers in the average private school do not possess the appropriate qualifications. A good public system would entail greater opportunities for investing in requisite teacher training and supervision.

In the health sector, private solutions are even more prevalent. The Dominican Republic Social Insurance System (Law 87-01) foresees three different modalities of social insurance: a fully subsidized regime, which is ultimately targeted at the total poor population of about 4 million people, but still reaches only about 2.3 million as of the end of 2011[9]; a contributory employer-employee regime, compulsory for public servants; and a voluntary, partially subsidized regime, originally aimed at covering the self-employed and professionals, but not yet under implementation. As a result of this structure, opting out behavior by the middle class in this case is even more pronounced than in education, as shown in figure 4.3. In a context of mediocre quality and limited health care coverage for beneficiaries of the contributory regime, most of the people in the middle and upper class choose private health insurance providers instead of SENASA, the national health insurance program.

It is also worth considering that budgeted public expenditure on health has averaged 1.5 percent of GDP between 2005 and 2011,[10] the lowest in Latin America. The state has been financing just about 36 percent of total health spending, whereas individual out-of-pocket expenditure amounts to 56 percent and private insurance covers just 8 percent. Out-of-pocket expenditure is clearly regressive, because the poorer households have to devote a larger share of income in relative terms, thus posing an important challenge for inclusive development (see Sánchez and Senderowitsch 2012).

In sum, the Dominican Republic seems to have evolved to an inefficient equilibrium with poor public service delivery. The preceding examples illustrate how part of the population, essentially the Dominican middle class and upper class, has internalized the costs derived from both state and market failures in the provision of public goods. As mentioned previously, the observed individualization of solutions and the choice of private alternatives appear to have further weakened the incentives for collective action that demands greater state accountability (see the "Voice" link in figure 4.1).

Figure 4.3 Health Insurance by Socioeconomic Class

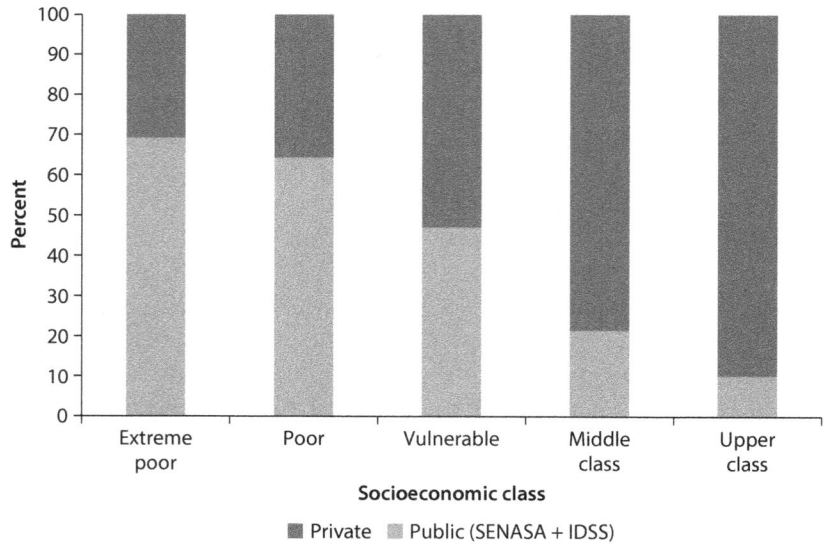

Source: World Bank staff calculations based on Instituto Nacional de Estadísticas y Geografía, ENIGH, 2007, http://www.inegi.org.mx/est/contenidos/Proyectos/Encuestas/Hogares/regulares/Enigh/Enigh2010/tradicional/.
Note: ENIGH's (Encuesta Nacional de Ingresos y Gastos de los Hogares, or National Income and Expenditure Household Survey) "total primary occupation income" figures are used for analysis. The population is classified according to the income bands selected in the latest Latin America and the Caribbean flagship report on the middle class (Ferreira et al. 2013): extreme poor, US$0.00– US$2.50 a day; poor, US$2.50– US$4.00; vulnerable, US$4.00– US$10.00; middle class, US$10.00– US$50.00; upper class, US$50.00+ (purchasing power parity). IDSS = Dominican Republic's social security institute; SENASA = Dominican Republic's national health insurance program.

The Policy Recommendations

How can the Dominican Republic enhance public accountability and improve the quality of services to restore the broken link between the citizens and the state? How can a country change a system where people adopt individual solutions, collective action is very limited, and sporadic protests do not create enough traction to change the status quo? The analysis by Sánchez and Senderowitsch (2012) presents three main courses of action to restore the broken channel for citizen voices in the Dominican Republic: (a) enhance capacity in civil society organizations to allow for more efficient and coordinated collective action; (b) introduce more redistributive policies and try to reduce informality levels to bring the interests of the middle class and the poor closer again; and (c) increase transparency mechanisms and move into e-government formulas.

Apart from empowering civil society and enhancing public accountability mechanisms, direct actions by the state or by the public service provision agencies can also be fostered to break inefficient equilibria. Improved services might encourage citizens to opt back in, giving them an increased stake in the sector. Direct action to improve service has been attempted in the electricity sector in the Dominican Republic. The next section details the political economy of that sector and of reform options.

Poor Service Delivery in the Electricity Sector

By the end of 2008 and the beginning of 2009, rising oil prices threatened to create a major economic crisis for the Dominican Republic. The difference between the electricity sector's revenues and the cost of electricity supply, which the government covered through the state-owned Dominican Corporation of State Electricity Companies (Corporación Dominicana de Empresas Eléctricas Estatales, or CDEEE), reached 3 percent of GDP, thereby draining public finances and leading to further arrears with private generators. In turn, this crisis forced the government to ration supply, thereby increasing the frequency and the duration of blackouts. These blackouts, along with the widespread perception of corruption among CDEEE holding and distribution companies, deepened the lack of trust in the sector and affirmed both opting out behavior and the social legitimacy of electricity theft.

In this situation, the government of the Dominican Republic asked for the support of international financial institutions such as the World Bank, the Inter-American Development Bank, and the International Monetary Fund. This support led to the formulation of an ambitious reform, the 2009 Electricity Sector Action Plan, designed to get the electricity sector back on its feet on the basis of the technical analyses and expert recommendations accumulated over several years (see box 4.1). Given the complexity of the governance issues and political

---

Box 4.1 Summary of the 2009 Electricity Sector Action Plan

The 2009 Electricity Sector Action Plan, created by a group of experts and outside consultants from the World Bank and the Inter-American Development Bank and supported by the International Monetary Fund, offered a diagnostic of the electricity sector's problems. The plan proposed seven recommendations to put the sector on a financially, technically, and socially sustainable footing:

1. Tariff adjustment to establish rates that reflect actual costs of service, simplify tariff structures, and focus cross-subsidies on the poorest consumers
2. Replacement of existing subsidies for the poorest families by a new subsidy system linked to the country's conditional cash transfer scheme for poor families
3. Investment in distribution networks to reduce technical losses, theft, and fraud
4. Full professionalization of the management of state-owned distribution companies to reduce losses, manage resources efficiently, and improve service quality
5. Creation of an escrow payment system for fuel subsidies to generators to increase transparency and predictability for such payments
6. Institutional reforms to improve the corporate governance of the public electricity holding company (CDEEE), strengthen the independence and capacity of the planning and regulatory agencies, and increase regulatory transparency
7. Preparation of a generation and transmission expansion plan and the development of appropriate incentives to meet plan targets through private investment

---

blockages in the sector, which created major concerns about the political viability of the plan, the World Bank commissioned a political economy analysis of the Dominican Republic electricity sector and the feasibility of the proposed reforms. The study paid particular attention to identifying entry points for reform, understanding stakeholders' preferences over policy choices for the structure of the sector (such as ownership, competition, and financing), and determining stakeholder power and influence. This last element focused on stakeholder influence over three key areas: (a) rate increases, (b) professionaliza- tion of senior management of the CDEEE and distribution companies, and (c) establishment of a new tariff benchmark based on cost of service. Some of the insights derived from the political economy analysis elaborated by Rufin and Zucchini (2010) are presented below.

Key Problems in the Power Sector

The electricity sector has been affected by several crises over the past decades. However, up until the second half of 2009, high losses, the high cost of energy generation, the weak regulatory environment, and other persistent challenges had been constant. As noted by Rufin and Zucchini (2010), "the persistence of these specific set of conditions in the sector over time makes it appropriate to use the concept of equilibrium, implying a certain stability or lack of change." The brief analysis of revenue generation, efficiency, and investment in the Dominican electricity sector in the following paragraphs helps explain the per- sistence of this low-level equilibrium. Major deficiencies in revenue collection from the sale of electricity to end users combined with gross inefficiency in the management of sector organizations have severely curtailed the financial self- sufficiency of the sector. This lack of self-sufficiency in turn distorts and under- mines private investment in the sector and increases direct government intervention over the sector, which has fed back into the issues of governance, management, and revenue generation.

In revenue generation, the two main elements limiting revenues from the sale of electricity to end users are (a) determination of rate levels, or prices, and (b) electricity theft, metering and billing fraud, and poor methods of electricity bill collection.

Rate levels bear little or no relationship to the actual costs of supplying elec- tricity to end users. First, the baseline electricity rates were not based on a cost of service study, but were adapted instead from Panamanian rates at the time of capitalization in 1998, under the assumption that similarities between Panama and the Dominican Republic extended to the cost of electricity supply. The rate structure based on actual cost of service—the so-called technical tariff—has not been fully implemented, despite being required by the country's Electricity Act and despite having a cost-of-service study completed in 2003. As a result, in December 2009, the electricity distribution entities' (EDEs) cost of purchased energy (that is, excluding capacity charges) ranged between US$0.125 and US$0.153 per kilowatt-hour (kWh); the average rate billed by EDEs was US$0.188/kWh, thereby leaving only a small margin to cover capacity charges, technical losses, and operating costs. Second, the adjustment of baseline levels over time to the factors that have a clear effect on the cost of supply—the cost of fuel and the exchange rates—has often been postponed. For instance, rates were frozen between November 2005 and June 2009 and again from July 2009 until the end of 2010.

In addition to the lack of a relationship between rates and costs, a great deal of electricity was supplied at an effective price of zero to end users by distributors that are supposed to collect revenues from them. This situation was due to the widespread theft of electricity, the alleged fraud in metering and billing, and the poor method of bill collection, plus the free, but rationed, supply of electricity to unmetered consumers in informal areas and some public housing areas (see *Diario Libre* 2009, 2013; *El Caribe* 2013). These conditions are reflected in persistently high levels of losses and receivables. In many cases, free electricity may have been explicitly or implicitly supplied in the past—for example, by providing housing units with unmetered connections, by enshrining certain types of consumers as "non-disconnectable" (*no cortables*), or even just by letting expectations of free electricity build over time. According to estimates from the ENIGH 2007 survey of household incomes and expenditures, of the 2.44 million households connected to the electricity grid in the country (about 94 percent of the total population),[11] only one-third had a meter, nearly 0.5 million households were being billed a fixed amount estimated by the distribution company because of the lack of a meter, and nearly 1.2 million households were not billed. In addition, there was a widespread perception of corruption in billing and collections, with allegations by numerous persons interviewed by Rufin and Zucchini (2010) for their study that distributor personnel or subcontractors were regularly bribed to underreport meter readings, to overlook fraudulent manipulation of meters and service lines, and to not collect outstanding debts.[12]

The problems in revenue generation and collection are indicative of major inefficiencies among the EDEs, as measured by losses of electricity in the EDEs and employment levels throughout CDEEE and its affiliates (see the international comparative evidence shown in Inter-American Development Bank and World Bank [2009b]). Inefficiencies of these kinds throughout the state-owned organizations in the sector have added to the financial losses experienced by these organizations by increasing their cost of service. The inefficiencies begin when appointments to a board of directors are based on political connections rather than knowledge about the electricity sector, and from there they flow to the rest of the organization, affecting not only its hiring practices but also its selection of subcontractors and of investment projects for political purposes.

Clientelism and the Electricity Sector

As discussed in World Bank (forthcoming), the political system in the Dominican Republic is characterized mainly by a bipartisan structure in which small parties may still potentially "have a large impact on the electoral outcome and accords it a disproportionate place in the governing coalition." "All parties in a coalition present to the leading party a registry of votes captured by the end of the elections," leading to a status quo in which vote-buying, exchange of favors, and nepotism are present (World Bank forthcoming). The perverse equilibrium in the electricity sector results from the strong dominance of the Executive in the institutional structure of the sector and the political system, and the nature of political competition in the country, as reflected in the interests and preferences of the two dominant parties. In other words, the perverse equilibrium in the electricity sector is the result of broader factors in the Dominican Republic's political system, not of specific conditions of the sector other than its attractiveness for clientelistic manipulation.

The Dominican political system has few veto points and no effective separation of powers to moderate the executive branch's freedom of action. As a result, there is substantial room for the executive branch to wield control over the electricity sector in the pursuit of electoral support. In a system where political competition revolves mainly around clientelistic bargains and pork barrel allocations, the electricity sector seems to be used as a means to strike such bargains and provide benefits to a variety of voters and political supporters. Clientelistic practices in the sector include all three forms of clientelistic exchange identified by Stokes (2009, 12–13): manipulation of public policies ("shifting of public programs away from their ostensible beneficiaries to other people in exchange for the latter's votes"), vote-buying ("exchange of goods for votes before elections"), and patronage ("exchange of public employment for electoral support"). These types of policies seem to be evident in the repeated rate freezes, the reluctance to increase rates, and the extremely high threshold for subsidizing residential electricity consumption. Set at 700 kWh/month, this threshold means that even some wealthy households receive a subsidy.

In a context of strong informal institutions, weak governance, and very limited accountability mechanisms, the electricity sector provides valuable resources for different types of bargains. The political manipulation of the electricity sector hinges on the government's power to appoint loyal persons to the sector's key positions in a centralized fashion and without scrutiny or confirmation by other actors. Public policies are manipulated mainly through the appointment of the lead regulator of the sector, who can then use this position to control electricity prices and requirements to provide free electricity to favored entities and constituencies. Vote-buying and patronage are largely conducted through appointment of the CDEEE's chief executive officer, who in turn has wide decision-making powers because the CDEEE, as a state-owned enterprise, is not subject to public sector employment and procurement rules. These appointments place at the hands of the government the unrestrained ability to engage in a variety of exchanges: patronage (jobs in exchange for votes or blocks of votes); contracts to supply services to CDEEE and its affiliates (for example, meter reading or local construction) in exchange for contributions that can be used to buy votes or fund local public goods; and local electrification or supply of free electricity (including tolerance for fraud and nonpayment), in this case most logically in exchange for the community's votes. According to officials who were familiar with CDEEE finances and who were interviewed by Rufin and Zucchini (2010), CDEEE has also included advertising for election candidates as part of its marketing budget. The importance of the CDEEE's resources is indicated by its large relative size: as of December 31, 2008, it employed 9,826 persons on a consolidated basis (including all three EDEs). Although this number represented only about 0.2 percent of the Dominican labor force, it made CDEEE the largest employer in the country outside the civil service. As a comparison, the second-largest company, Banco de Reservas, employed 7,401 persons, and the Santo Domingo water utility (Corporación de Acueducto y Alcantarillado de Santo Domingo) had 985 employees. In 2008, CDEEE holding billed approximately US$1,263 million (including amounts billed by its subsidiaries), or about 2.8 percent of the Dominican GDP at current prices, making it about the 12th-largest company in the country by sales volume (or asset value in the case of financial institutions).

Stakeholder Analysis

Given the evidence above, some stakeholders clearly benefit from the status quo and, consequently, have sought to preserve it despite the significant and rising fiscal cost and the negative development impacts of a dysfunctional power sector. Attempts at reform in 2001 and a capitalization in 2003, together with several other attempts to break the low-level equilibrium, have failed, were implemented for a limited time only, or were reversed. In part, this inability to bring about change is due to a failure to account for the political economy considerations that these reforms entail. Rufin and Zucchini's (2010) evaluation of the feasibility of reform sought to analyze the political economy context of the technical recommendations that were considered necessary to get the sector back on its feet. Their analysis called for the sector to (a) assess the main variables which might inhibit the effective implementation of the recommendations and (b) develop a proposal to overcome these obstacles.

The first step used by Rufin and Zucchini (2010) to explain the perverse equilibrium was to identify key stakeholders in the power sector. Following an institutional analysis and using a problem-driven framework, they identified organizations and influential groups with a stake in the Dominican Republic's electricity sector (table 4.1), that is, stakeholders with an interest, material or otherwise, in the policies, operations, and outcomes related to the sector. The objective of this analysis was to shed light on three main characteristics of stakeholders: (a) the degree of power or influence of each stakeholder; (b) their preferences for policies, operations, and outcomes for the electricity sector, and more specifically, their preferences for reform, understood as the 2009 Electricity Sector Action Plan; and (c) the logic they use to make specific choices when faced with several alternatives.

Then, for an understanding of the position, preferences, and incentives of these actors, an influence-interest matrix was created. Rufin and Zucchini used a combination of methods: first, they conducted a deep analysis of secondary source information (such as policy papers, reform proposals, and articles in the local press), and second, they then focused on interviews with key stakeholders to determine the stakeholders' position on selected issues.

Table 4.1 Stakeholders in the Dominican Republic Electricity Sector, as of 2010

Stakeholder	Description	Position on electricity sector reform
Dominican Corporation of State Electricity Companies (CDEEE)	CDEEE is a holding company charged with management and coordination of all strategy, policy, and projects related to all public utility companies (hydroelectric generation, transmission, and distribution).	CDEEE's position depends on government's position on reform. It was the most important opponent of reform in past years, but recent changes have reversed its position.
Coordination Entity (OC)	OC operates the interconnected electricity system, balances electricity demand and supply, and manages the electricity wholesale market. It is governed by a stakeholder board with a majority of seats controlled by CDEEE, but in practice is run by a professional staff recruited throughout Latin America with relatively good levels of transparency and credibility.	OC has strictly avoided any pronouncement on reform.
Superintendence of Electricity (SIE)	SIE is the regulatory body for the electricity sector. Its responsibility is to establish energy prices and ensure service quality. In practice, its autonomy is very limited—all superintendents are appointed and dismissed by the executive branch with absolute discretion, contradicting the spirit of the Electricity Act that had envisioned a more independent and autonomous regulatory body.	SIE's position depends on government's position on reform. It has been an opponent of reform in past years.
National Energy Commission (CNE)	CNE is tasked with the development of indicative plans for the electricity sector and the study and proposal of energy-related policies. It has very limited influence over the electricity sector in practice because the CDEEE holds the de facto power to establish policy and the CNE directors have been appointed at the government's discretion.	CNE's position depends on government's position on reform, but it has been supportive of reform in past years.
Ministry of Economy, Planning, and Development (MEPD)	The MEPD's responsibility is to coordinate the National Development Plan and to establish macroeconomic policy through the preparation of a medium- and long-term macroeconomic framework. Its power is limited given that the Ministry of Finance controls the budget.	MEPD is supportive of reform because it can increase efficiency and increase the resources available for other developmental goals
Ministry of Finance	The Ministry of Finance is in charge of the government's fiscal policy (including tax revenues and budget formulation). Because the energy sector recurrently needs fiscal resources, the ministry plays an important role in energy policy.	The ministry is supportive of reform to the extent that it reduces budgetary pressures.
Social Cabinet	The Social Cabinet is in charge of coordinating all social protection policies. The recent replacement of the Programa de Reducción de Apagones (PRA) (a geographically-based subsidy program) by Bonoluz (a program based on household incomes) has increased the cabinet's importance in the electricity sector.	The cabinet does not have a clear preference over policies in the electricity sector beyond the necessity to maintain the subsidy for poor families. Informally, the cabinet favors a reform to reduce fiscal deficits because this situation creates budgetary tension over social expenditure.

table continues next page

Table 4.1 Stakeholders in the Dominican Republic Electricity Sector, as of 2010 *(continued)*

Stakeholder	Description	Position on electricity sector reform
Legislature (Congress)	The Dominican Republic has a presidential system with a formally independent legislative assembly and an autonomous justice system. However, the Congress does not play a strong role in policy making or in supervision of the executive branch. Both the Upper and the Lower House have a committee for energy policy, but they systematically fail to propose solutions.	The position of Congress is unclear. Some members are said to have direct financial interests in the sector or have campaigned on giving away energy for free.
Political parties	The Dominican Republic is a de facto two-party system: two major parties, the Partido de la Liberación Dominicana (the current presidential incumbent and a strong majority in both houses) and the Partido Revolucionario Dominicano, attract more than 80 percent of the votes. One important attribute of the Dominican political system is its lack of ideological differentiation because both parties can occupy any position in the political spectrum depending on the issue. As a consequence of the ideological weakness, there is a bias toward personalism, and competition for party leadership does not rely on ideas or policy options, but on the ability to appoint party members to public office.	Emphasis on patronage and clientelism as key mechanisms for political competition predispose political parties against reform.
Civil society	For the electricity sector, civil society is represented primarily through the national business council (CONEP), which occupies a prominent role in shaping the debate over the energy sector, and through the activities of private electricity generators. Other civil society organizations do not play a significant role in the electricity sector.	Because the poor electricity supply negatively affects business activity (that is, raising production costs) there is a strong consensus on the urgency of reform, especially on the part of CONEP. Private generators and consumers of electricity in the private sector are equally supportive of reform because they share an agenda based on clear property rights, transparency, reliable service, and respect for contractual terms. Anecdotal evidence suggests that the rest of society broadly supports reform, as long as rate increases are accompanied by better service quality, transparent regulation, and equity in the sharing of cost burdens.
Media	The media has a strong influence in setting the political agenda. In the case of the energy sector, news on blackouts, new generation, and energy prices are well covered by the media.	Despite some differences between more pro-government and other independent media, there is mounting consensus over the urgency of reform.

Figure 4.4 Reform: Influence-Interest Matrix

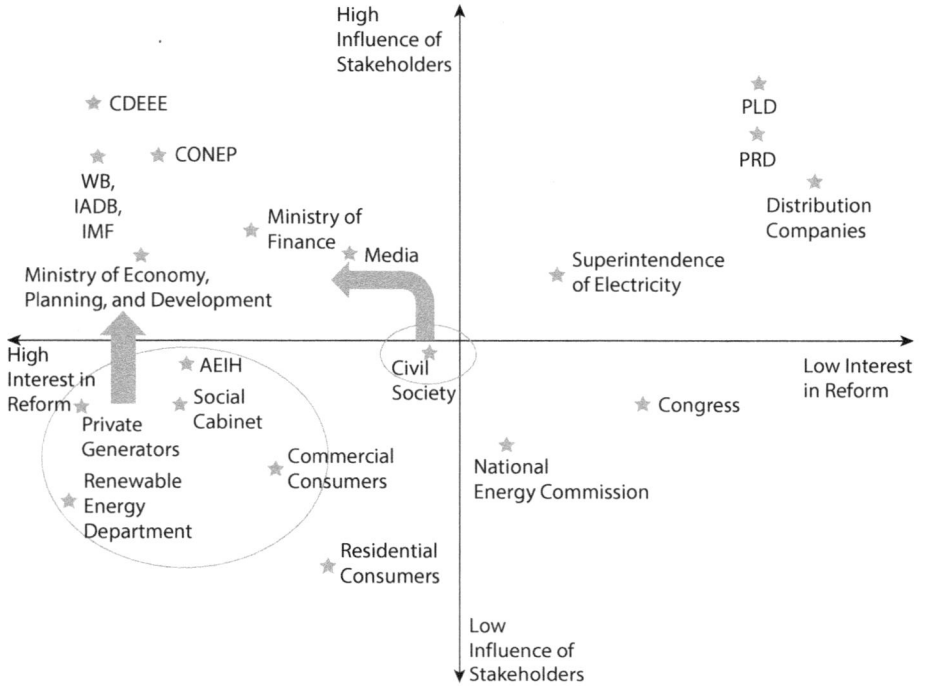

Source: Rufín and Zucchini 2010.
Note: AEIH = Asociación de Empresas Industriales de Herrera; CDEEE = Dominican Corporation of State Electricity Companies; CONEP = Dominican Republic's national business council; IADB = Inter-American Development Bank; IMF = International Monetary Fund; PLD = Dominican Liberation Party; PRD = Dominican Revolutionary Party; and WB = World Bank.

The analysis revealed the existence of an unstructured coalition broadly supporting the idea that reforms, like those reflected in the 2009 Electricity Sector Action Plan, would be needed to get the sector back on its feet. The coalition is represented in figure 4.4 by actors in the high influence–high interest quadrant of the matrix (upper left) and includes the CDEEE; the Ministry of Finance; the Ministry of Economy, Planning, and Development (MEPD); CONEP; and part of the media (see table 4.1). The analysis also identified a group of actors, including the Social Cabinet and private generators, who are just beginning to back the reform process (see table 4.1). A dynamic matrix would show these stakeholders moving from the high interest–low influence quadrant (bottom left) to the high interest–high influence quadrant (upper left), mainly through the articulation and publication of well-researched reports, above all on the part of CONEP. As one might expect, given the analysis of the electric sector, within the high influence–low interest quadrant (upper right) are political parties, distribution companies, and the Superintendence of Electricity. All of them are politically connected and systematically hamper any attempt at reform by claiming social costs and a risk to political stability. Indeed, they use the control over the sector as a tool for gaining and maintaining political power.

Policy Recommendations Based on the Stakeholder Analysis

The 2009 Electricity Sector Action Plan was based on seven policy priorities: tariff rates, subsidies, losses, management, escrow account, institutions, and investments (see box 4.1). Political economy analysis suggested it would be important to sequence the implementation of these policies in a way that would build trust with the public and strengthen the coalition for reform. Even if most of the stakeholders would agree on the necessity of reform in general, different coalitions might arise in reaction to the specific policy priority under discussion. It was, therefore, important to understand not only stakeholders' positions on the reform in general, but also their interests and incentives around particular policy priorities. To this end, the stakeholder analysis investigated the potential coalition dynamics for three specific policy alternatives: tariff rate adjustment, establishment of a new tariff benchmark based on cost of service, and professionalization of EDE management.

Tariff Rate Adjustments

One possible approach to reform (as suggested by the action plan) would be to increase tariff rates to market levels, hence reducing the fiscal gaps and the overall budget deficit. This policy option would, at least in the short term, find great opposition because of the perceived unfairness of increasing rates for those who already pay for electricity. The media and civil society would probably assume a very strong opposition. The government would also oppose the tariff adjustment, citing fear of social protests and political instability, and perhaps worry about losing control over the electricity sector as a tool for gaining and maintaining political power. Overall, a tariff rate adjustment would imply a major shift of stakeholders from the high influence–high interest quadrant to the high influence–low interest quadrant (figure 4.5). This collective opposition would represent a major blockages to reform.

Establishment of a New Tariff Benchmark Based on Cost of Service

In the short run, establishing a new tariff benchmark based on cost of service (the so-called technical tariff) could well be equivalent to an increase in rates. Similar to the scenario described above, this policy option would find, at least in the very short term, a strong opposition from the media, civil society, and most of the government. For coalitions, the situation would be similar to that shown in figure 4.5. However, in the long run, if the quality of management were to improve, and along with it the quality of service delivery, then distribution cost savings and reduction in losses would be reflected in lower tariffs. In this case, the tariff benchmark need not entail rate increases at all. Moreover, poor service delivery in the electricity sector has forced families and businesses to invest in small power plants and to assume high maintenance costs. As a described in this chapter's section titled "Opting Out," almost 50 percent of the generation capacity is autogenerated by private companies and individual consumers with small power plants and batteries. If the tariff would indeed lead to better provision of electricity in the long run, the supportive coalition would be larger and likely

Figure 4.5 Policy Alternative 1: Tariff Rate Adjustments

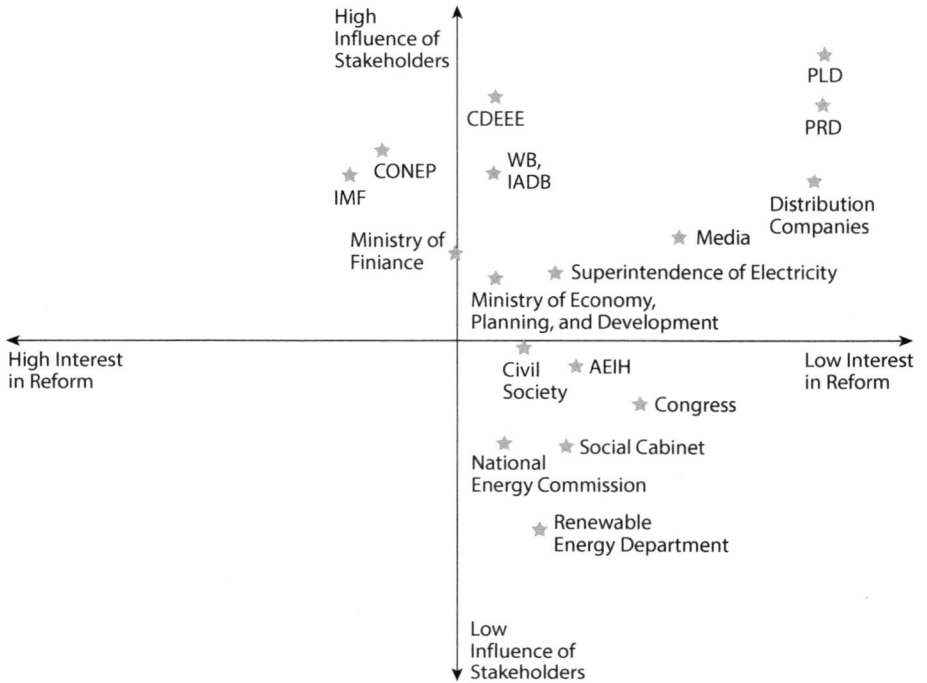

Source: Rufín and Zucchini 2010.
Note: AEIH = Asociación de Empresas Industriales de Herrera; CDEEE = Dominican Corporation of State Electricity Companies; CONEP = Dominican Republic's national business council; IADB = Inter-American Development Bank; IMF = International Monetary Fund; PLD = Dominican Liberation Party; PRD = Dominican Revolutionary Party; and WB = World Bank.

include the families and businesses that opt back in; the CDEEE; the Ministry of Finance; the MEPD; and the CNE; in addition to a more supportive stance by CONEP, and the media would at least not oppose the change.

Professionalization of EDE Management

In contrast to a rate increase, the professionalization of EDE management would bring together a strong pro-reform coalition (the CDEEE; the Ministry of Finance; the MEPD; civil society; and the private sector) as shown in figure 4.6.

Because distribution companies seem to be highly politicized, a certain degree of opposition should be expected by political parties and by the EDEs' management. However, an opening for this reform may occur immediately following congressional elections. In the Dominican Republic, as in many other countries, politicians have the greatest political capital directly after elections, and they are not yet wrapped up in the next campaign cycle. Although politicians may experience the strongest pressure to deliver benefits to their electoral supporters upon gaining power, they also enjoy greater credibility at that point than later in their mandates when prospective supporters can consider the politicians' behavior since the election. Furthermore, after elections, there are more incentives to form

Figure 4.6 Policy Alternative 2: Improve Management in EDEs First

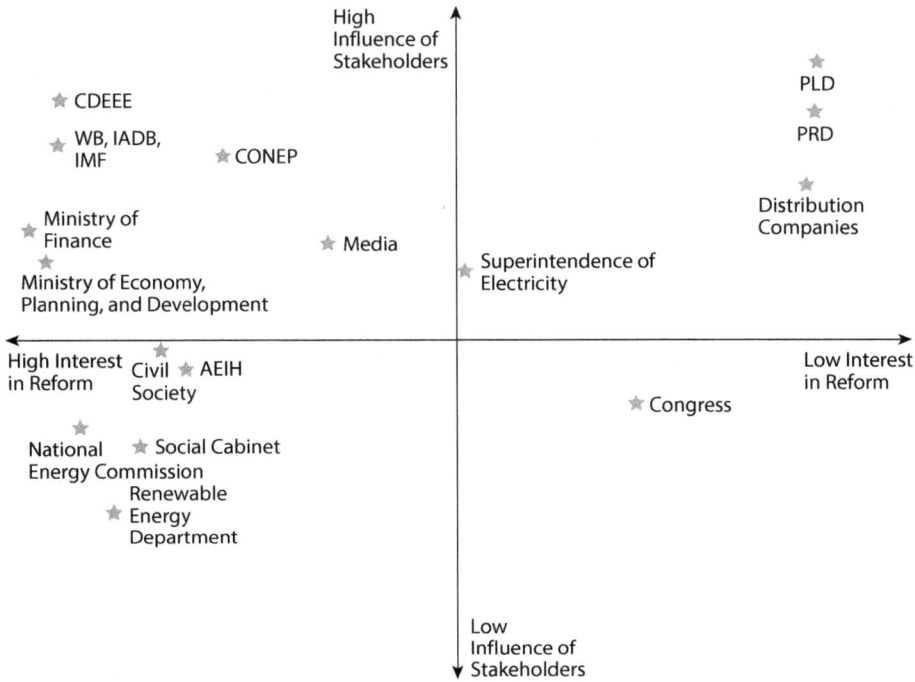

Source: Rufín and Zucchini 2010.

Note: AEIH = Asociación de Empresas Industriales de Herrera; CDEEE = Dominican Corporation of State Electricity Companies; CONEP = Dominican Republic's national business council; EDE = electricity distribution entity; IADB = Inter-American Development Bank; IMF = International Monetary Fund; PLD = Dominican Liberation Party; PRD = Dominican Revolutionary Party; and WB = World Bank.

a coalition, and the political cost of doing nothing may well exceed the cost of professionalization. Even for patronage and of constituency-building purposes, the indiscriminate electricity subsidies associated with doing nothing could well be redeployed more effectively after reform. Political parties could try to hamper the reform process, but to do so in a direct and visible way would diminish their electoral appeal, because corruption, nepotism, and influence peddling cases revealed by the media have created growing hostility among the public to political manipulation of the EDEs. A high degree of transparency during the reform process could help involve civil society and minimize the risk of subsequent disruption.

The recommendations following from the stakeholder analysis differed significantly from the general wisdom received from technical experts over the years. Instead of starting with an increase in tariff rates to allow distribution companies to collect enough revenue to provide adequate services and pay private generators, the political economy assessment suggested that professionalizing the distribution companies' senior management was a more feasible entry point for reform and should be prioritized. Professionalization could be carried out easily through the executive branch's powers of appointment and would not run into immediate popular political opposition, as might occur with tariff increases. In addition, improving transparency and accountability might have a secondary effect on weak collective action in the electric sector. Several scandals reported in the media had worked as a self-fulfilling prophecy. Because distribution companies had little credibility—and this lack of trust was reinforced by several scandals reported in the media—people opted out of the system and tolerated more fraud and theft. Greater transparency and accountability could help reverse this cycle, thereby encouraging electricity-consumers to rely more on the electricity network and, in turn, to work more closely with other customers and stakeholders to demand better service.

Implications for Country Dialogue and Implementation of World Bank Projects

Both Sánchez and Senderowitsch (2012) and Rufín and Zucchini (2010) shed light on broader factors that may inhibit collective action and the improvement of public services (the first study) as well as the specific coalitions that may form around particular technical reform options (the latter).

The discussion in Sánchez and Senderowitsch (2012) has served as a background paper for the Latin America and the Caribbean (LAC) flagship publication on mobility and the middle class (Ferreira et al. 2013). Rufín and Zucchini's (2010) concrete example of opting out behavior in the Dominican Republic has been discussed in several meetings and presentations by the chief economist for the LAC region. The paper has been discussed at the annual meetings in September 2011 with the Dominican delegation. It has also informed a recent publication in the Institutional and Governance Review Series (World Bank forthcoming), which analyzes the roots of poor public service provision by looking at the political economy of reform in the Dominican Republic.

Some of the policy recommendations derived from political economy analysis and presented in the second section of this chapter have helped justify certain courses of action and decisions in the field. Again, these recommendations included (a) enhancing capacity in civil society organizations to allow for more efficient and coordinated collective action, (b) introducing more redistributive policies and trying to reduce informality levels to bring the interests of the middle class and the poor closer again, and (c) increasing transparency mechanisms and moving into e-government formulas.

An interesting example is the Participative Anti-Corruption Initiative (IPAC) that originally was convened by private sector and civil society actors, 12 international donors, and government representatives. The goal of IPAC was to implement 30 recommendations aimed at fighting corruption, to improve transparency mechanisms, and to improve performance in 10 thematic areas such as health, education, public procurement, energy, water and sanitation, oversight institutions, and so forth. More broadly, however, the IPAC hopes to build a constituency to fight corruption, addressing recommendation (a), as the analysis of the middle class and its opting out behavior had highlighted the need to empower an otherwise disengaged civil society. The IPAC process started in August 2010, although a civil society observatory was not effectively constituted until March 2011, with a view to coordinating the different civil society actors and effectively monitoring the implementation of agreed recommendations. In the different IPAC-monitoring workshops, the civil society observatory assumed a leading role in signaling implementation deficiencies and putting pressure on government officials in charge of implementing the different recommendations. This observatory is a clear example of a mechanism aimed at empowering the civil society to channel demand for enhanced public sector accountability.

Another activity resulting from the recommendations that has been recently implemented is the launch of the budget transparency web-based portal "Consulta Amigable," which can help the government address citizen demands, identify system inefficiencies, and optimize the allocation of resources. This addresses recommendation (c) by making use of technology to increase citizen access to the government's spending priorities and programs.

Rufin and Zucchini (2010) provided operational recommendations in three key areas. First, their study contributed to a more detailed and rigorous understanding of which coalitions would arise from different policy scenarios. This understanding clearly changed the focus from the tariff issue, at least in the short term, to increasing professionalization of senior management, to improving transparency, and to setting a clear result-oriented framework that would address reduction in losses, number of employees per customer, and so forth. In this sense, it was a counterintuitive answer to the prolonged sector deficit: previous attempts to reduce the sector deficit by increasing revenues using tariff adjustments in a context of poor quality of service, little accountability, and lack of trust in distribution companies either failed or were reversed. Even though the sector needed to recover a sounder financial situation, the second-best alternative was a combination of professional management, better service (through programs like the 24-hour electricity program[13]), and a renewed client relation strategy that addressed the demand side of the problem.

To be sure, the World Bank and other actors favorable to reform had no more power to install a professional management team than they had to increase tariffs or to cut electricity losses. As a first step toward more comprehensive reform, the study did redirect the available leverage of the pro-reform coalition toward the appointment of professional management by the government rather than toward tariff increases or loss-reduction measures. This redirection is, in fact, what happened. As the government faced mounting financial costs from subsidization of electricity generation for the 2008 campaign in the midst of a major hike in international oil prices, the government agreed, as requested by multilateral financial institutions, to give up some political control over the sector in exchange for financial support.

Second, the analysis highlighted the need to combine investment in infrastructure to increase the reliability of the service with specific action to commit clients to paying their electricity bills. As noted by Rufín and Zucchini (2010), intertemporal considerations are fundamental in the electricity sector due to the long time span of economic transactions in the sector. Long asset lives combined with significant scale economies, particularly in generation and transmission, require lumpy investments whose benefits extend over decades. Institutions in the electricity sector have initiated a series of media campaigns and initiatives aimed at increasing the culture of payment. For instance, since 2011, an open website called "Portal de Circuitos" publishes information on programmed electricity blackouts; a number of neighborhoods with a higher propensity to payment have been granted 24-hour electricity supply. At the same time, this website also helps improve the quality and transparency of service provision. Again, the link between the political economy analysis and these outcomes lies in the reorientation of policy advice and financial support programs toward measures that combine carrots and sticks simultaneously, rather than in earlier attempts that focused on revenue-raising measures alone and promised service improvements only at a later stage. The political economy analysis increased the political sustainability of reforms by suggesting a reform package that would elicit a more favorable reaction from consumers and stakeholders.

Finally, in the early stage of the preparation of the political economy analysis of electricity reform, the authors of this chapter provided feedback to the team that was working in IPAC to understand the key constraints of the sector and helped produce valuable ideas for the debate on topics such as a transparency portal and a new procurement operational manual (implemented in 2011). The political economy and governance focus of the analysis has thus helped to contribute to increased social accountability. Clearly, the link between the anticorruption efforts and electricity reform is the weakest, because corruption is a complex phenomenon involving behaviors and incentives that are unlikely to change quickly. Nevertheless, the political economy analysis team understood very well that the longer-term viability of electricity sector reforms would be enhanced by initiatives that do not reward decisions similar to those that led to the dire situation of the sector in 2009.

In summary, the evidence derived from the political economy analysis focused on the constraints to public service delivery in the Dominican Republic and points to serious governance problems, clientelism, and the existence of blocking coalitions preventing certain reforms. Country-specific political economy analysis has contributed to identifying feasible actions to shift the Dominican Republic from an inefficient equilibrium by advancing the transparency and social accountability agenda in the nation. In the case of the electricity sector, the introduction of professional management (as opposed to political management), the provision of information to customers through a transparency portal, and the mounting of campaigns to raise public awareness and reduce nonpayment have already helped decrease sector losses.

Notes

1. The banking crisis resulted from poor supervision of domestic banks and led to a high level of nonperforming loans and several insolvencies among major banks. The crisis of confidence entailed a sharp drop in private consumption and investment, thereby leading just to a moderate decline in economic activity (–0.3 percent GDP growth in 2003), but also encompassing job losses that mainly affected the most vulnerable (World Bank 2006).

2. Data from the World Development Indicators (database) for the period 1991–2010, is incomplete, and averages may diverge compared to those calculated by the statistics services of the different countries considered. See World Development Indicators (database), World Bank, Washington, DC, http://data.worldbank.org/data-catalog /world-development-indicators. The education budget was increased to 4 percent of GDP in 2013.

3. Secondary completion rates are based on the Barro-Lee Educational Attainment Dataset, 2010, http://www.barrolee.com/data/full1.htm.

4. The six countries are Bolivia, Colombia, Guatemala, Panama, Peru, and República Bolivariana de Venezuela.

5. Even when citizen participation in associations and politics is high in the regional context, citizens tend not to participate in public protests, and effective demand for accountability seems limited, according to Latinobarómetro and AmericasBarometer opinion surveys. See Latinobarómetro, Latinobarómetro Corporación, Santiago, Chile, http://www.latinobarometro.org/latino/latinobarometro.jsp; AmericasBarometer, Latin America Public Opinion Project, Vanderbilt University, Nashville, TN, http://www.vanderbilt.edu/lapop/survey-data.php.

6. The middle class in the Dominican Republic would represent about 20 percent of the total population (Ferreira et al. 2013). The Dominican Republic would rank 11th of 14 Latin American and Caribbean countries in size of the middle class.

7. The so-called *inversores*, or electrical inverters, are used to supply energy stored in batteries (direct current) as alternating current. To ensure that the batteries are full in case of a blackout, one must charge them continually, resulting in roughly 30 percent higher costs than if they were not used. They are the cheapest and least sophisticated private solution to electricity shortages in the country.

8. See Instituto Nacional de Estadísticas y Geografía, ENIGH (Encuesta Nacional de Ingresos y Gastos de los Hogares, or National Income and Expenditure Household Survey), http://www.inegi.org.mx/est/contenidos/Proyectos/Encuestas/Hogares /regulares/Enigh/Enigh2010/tradicional/.

9. See ARS SENASA 2011, http://www.arssenasa.gov.do.

10. For more details, see SISDOM (database), of the Dominican Republic Ministry of Economy, Planning, and Development. http://dstats.net/download/http://www .economia.gob.do/UploadPDF/SISDOM/SISDOM_2.ZIP (accessed September 2011).

11. Estimate is by the National Energy Commission (CNE), as noted in Despradel (2009).

12. See reports by *El Nacional* (2011) and *Noticias Clave* (2010).

13. This program, managed by the three distribution companies and CDEEE, provides 24-hour continuous electricity in those sectors where payment rates are above 90 percent of the total bills for that specific geographic sector. See also http://circuitos .gov.do/About.aspx.

Bibliography

ARS SENASA. 2011. El Seguro Nacional de Salud (SeNaSa). http://www.arssenasa.gov.do.

Besley, Timothy, and Stephen Coate. 1991. "Public Provision of Private Goods and the Redistribution of Income." *American Economic Review* 81 (4): 979–84.

CONEP (Consejo Nacional de la Empresa Privada). 2008. "La economía dominicana: Algunos retos pendientes, macroeconómicos y sectoriales." CONEP, Santo Domingo. http://www.competitividad.org.do/wp-content/uploads/2009/01/la-economia -dominicana-algunos-retos-prendientes-macroeconomicos-y-sectoriales-conep-2008 .pdf.

Despradel, Julián. 2009. "Estudio de caso de la República Dominicana." Paper presented at the International Seminar "Acceso a la energía y reducción de la pobreza para alcanza los objetivos del milenio en América Latina y el Caribe." Santiago, October 20–22. http://www.eclac.cl/drni/noticias/noticias/6/37496/Despradel.pdf.

Diario Libre. 2009. "Solución a los problemas eléctricos en RD requirere de US$600 millones." *Diario Libre,* September 11. http://www.diariolibre.com/noticias/2009/09/11 /i215176_solucian-los-problemas-elactricos-requiere-us600-millones.html.

———. 2013. "Más de 500 mil clientes no pagan la luz a las empresas distribuidoras de energía." *Diario Libre,* February 1. http://www.diariolibre.com/economia/2013/02/01 /i369677_mas-500-mil-clientes-pagan-luz-las-empresas-distribuidoras-energaa.html.

Dominican Republic Central Bank. 2005. "Supply-Use Matrix." National Accounts, Santo Domingo.

El Caribe. 2013. "Lo robado sale caro … al país." *El Caribe,* April 3. http://www.elcaribe .com.do/2013/03/04/robado-sale-caro...-pais.

El Nacional. 2011. "Contratistas edes hacen fraudes." *El Nacional,* December 12. http:// www.elnacional.com.do/economia/2011/12/12/104582/aaaa.

Espinal, Rosario, Jonathan Hartlyn, and Jana M. Kelly. 2006. "Performance Still Matters. Explaining Trust in Government in the Dominican Republic." *Comparative Political Studies* 39 (2): 200–23.

Ferreira, Francisco, Julian Messina, Jamele Rigolini, Luis-Felipe López-Calva, Maria Ana Lugo, and Renos Vakis. 2013. *Economic Mobility and the Rise of the Latin American Middle Class.* Washington, DC: World Bank.

INEGI (Instituto Nacional de Estadísticas y Geografia). 2007. ENIGH. http://www.inegi .org.mx/est/contenidos/Proyectos/Encuestas/Hogares/regulares/Enigh/Enigh2010 /tradicional/.

Inter-American Development Bank. 2010. *La ruta hacia el crecimiento sostenible en la República Dominicana: Fiscalidad, competitividad, institucionalidad y electricidad.* Washington, DC: Inter-American Development Bank.

Inter-American Development Bank and World Bank. 2009a. "Plan de acción para mod-ernizar el sector eléctrico en la República Dominicana." Inter-American Development Bank and World Bank, Washington, DC.

———. 2009b. "Diálogo sobre el sector eléctrico." Inter-American Development Bank and World Bank, Santo Domingo.

Jones, Mark P. 2010. "Beyond the Electoral Connection: Political Parties' Effect on the Policymaking Process." In *How Democracy Works: Political Institutions, Actors, and Arenas in Latin American Policymaking,* edited by Carlos Scartascini, Ernesto Stein, and Mariano Tommasi. Cambridge, MA: Harvard University Press.

Luque, Javier, Cynthia Hobbs, and S. Carlston. 2010. "Education Sector Policy Note for the Dominican Republic." Policy Note, World Bank, Washington, DC.

Maurer, Luiz, Mario Pereira, and José Rosenblatt. 2005. *Implementing Power Rationing in a Sensible Way: Lessons Learned and International Best Practices.* Washington, DC: World Bank.

Morgan, Jana, Rosario Espinal, and Mitchell Seligson. 2010. "Political Culture of Democracy in the Dominican Republic, 2010: Democratic Consolidation in the Americas in Hard Times." Study by Latin American Public Opinion Project, AmericasBarometer, and Vanderbilt University, Nashville, TN.

Moya Pons, Frank. 1998. *The Dominican Republic: A National History.* Princeton, NJ: Markus Wiener Publishers.

North, Douglass C., John Joseph Wallis, Steven B. Webb, and Barry R. Weingast. 2007. "Limited Access Orders in the Developing World: A New Approach to the Problems of Development." Policy Research Working Paper 4359, World Bank, Washington, DC.

Noticias Clave. 2010. "Hasta contratistas de edes roban contadores." *Noticias Clave,* October 12. http://www.noticiasclaverd.com/2010/10/hasta-contratistas-de-edes -roban.html.

ONE (Oficina Nacional de Estadística). 2007. ENIGH (Encuesta Nacional de Ingresos y Gastos de los Hogares [National Income and Expenditure Household Survey]). ONE, Santo Domingo. http://enigh.one.gob.do.

Rufín, Carlos, and Davide Zucchini. 2010. *Political Economy of Policy Reform Study: The Dominican Republic's Electricity Sector.* Consultant's report, World Bank, Washington, DC.

Sánchez, Miguel E., and Roby Senderowitsch. 2012. "The Political Economy of the Middle Class in the Dominican Republic: Individualization of Public Goods, Lack of Institutional Trust, and Weak Collective Action." Policy Research Working Paper 6049, World Bank, Washington, DC.

Sánchez, Miguel E., and Edgar Victoria. 2012. "Budget Rigidities and Fiscal Space in the Dominican Republic." In "Improving the Quality of Public Expenditure in the Dominican Republic." Working Paper 71472, World Bank, Washington, DC.

Stokes, Susan C. 2009. "Pork, by Any Other Name ... Building a Conceptual Scheme of Distributive Politics." Paper for the Annual Meeting and Exhibition of the American Political Science Association, Toronto, September 3–6.

World Bank. 2003. *World Development Report 2004: Making Services Work for Poor People.* Washington, DC: World Bank.

———. 2006. *Dominican Republic Poverty Assessment: Achieving More Pro-Poor Growth.* Report 32422-DO. Washington, DC: World Bank.

———. 2009. *Implementation Completion and Results Report on a Loan in the Amount of US$150 Million to the Dominican Republic for a Programmatic Power Sector Reform Loan.* Report ICR00001260, World Bank, Washington, DC.

———. 2012. World Bank–IFC Enterprise Surveys (database). http://www .enterprisesurveys.org/Data.

———. Forthcoming. *Patronage or Reform? Political Economy of Policy Performance in the Dominican Republic.* Institutional and Governance Review Series. Washington, DC: World Bank.

CHAPTER 5

Using Political Economy Assessment to Reorient Sectoral Strategy: Infrastructure Reform in Zambia

Brian Levy and Patricia Palale

Introduction

Over the past half-dozen years, political economy assessments have played a far-reaching role in shaping the strategic direction of the World Bank's engagement in Zambia. Key activities included the following:

- A comprehensive country-level assessment was undertaken in early 2007 by two eminent political scientists, both of whom had long specialized in research on Zambian politics (Taylor and Simutanyi 2007).
- A series of sector-level assessments on electricity, telecommunications, urban water utilities, decentralization, agricultural land rights, mining, and tourism were performed. Each of these assessments used the country-level study as an analytical platform for drilling down into sectoral dynamics.
- An ongoing effort ensued over the subsequent four years by the World Bank's country program to ensure that the insights that emerged from the political economy work were incorporated into the design and implementation of operational work in the country.

The authors would like to thank Kapil Kapoor for his sustained support; Scott Taylor and Neo Simutanyi for generously sharing their insights on Zambia's political economy; Samuel O'Brien-Kumi and Ernest Matongo for guidance on the electricity sector; and Isabel Neto, Bjorn Wellenius, Marie Sheppard, and Aaditya Mattoo for their insights on telecommunications.

The findings, interpretations, and conclusions contained in this synthesis report are entirely those of the authors. They do not necessarily represent the view of the World Bank, its executive directors, or the countries they represent. The World Bank is not responsible for the contents of this research.

This chapter uses the examples of electricity and telecommunications to illustrate in-depth both how the effort unfolded and what was its value added. The first section describes the development challenge, confronted by the two sectors at the outset of the effort. The second section summarizes the national-level political economy assessment and details how the results at the national level were used to diagnose constraints to reform in the sectors. The third section lays out the recommendations of the sectoral assessment as to the possible entry points to reform that were better aligned with the country's political economy realities. The final section reports on the experiences with reform in the sectors in the years subsequent to the analytical work, and it suggests some broader lessons from the Zambia effort as to both the potential and the limits of approaching development programming in a donor agency such as the World Bank through a political economy lens.

The Development Challenges

The challenges confronting Zambia's electricity and telecommunications sectors were just two examples of a far-reaching conundrum that pervaded Zambia's development efforts. In the 1990s, Zambia had been something of a donor favorite as it took center stage as an African pioneer in a global trend away from centrally controlled politics and economics and toward democratization and market-based economic policies. The country moved from a one-party state to a multiparty democracy. Kenneth Kaunda, the president for the previous quarter century, was decisively defeated by Frederick Chiluba in an election held in 1991. Chiluba and his political party (the Movement for Multi-party Democracy, or MMD) embarked on a far-reaching program of structural adjustment, with the support of the World Bank and other donors. Over the subsequent years, there was seemingly a strong partnership between government and donors to sustain the reform effort.

However, a decade later, though there had been lots of action, very little seemed to have changed on the ground. A 2003 review of World Bank experience in the country described that challenge as follows:

> By and large, agreeing on policies and programs was the easy part of the Bank's relations with the government. The really difficult part was and continues to be implementation. (World Bank 2003)

This combination of great expectations and subsequent disappointment was vivid in the electricity and telecommunications sectors.

Electricity
A Legacy of Abundance
For many decades, electricity had been among the least of Zambia's problems. Electricity is provided by the integrated, monopoly parastatal company, the Zambia Electricity Supply Corporation (ZESCO). Between 1966 and 1976 (following the unilateral declaration of independence by then

Southern Rhodesia), the Zambian government developed 1,600 megawatts (MWs) of hydropower through multilateral funding. This translated into an exceptionally favorable supply situation for both ZESCO and its users. Zambia's electricity investments had been sized on the assumption of a continually growing economy. Instead, the economy stopped expanding in the early 1980s, with negative average growth rates over the subsequent two decades. In practice, there was thus no capacity constraint.

Under (almost) all circumstances, the combination of hydropower and excess capacity would translate into low electricity tariffs for users. Two additional decisions by ZESCO's state leadership created further scope for low pricing. First, ZESCO did not provide for the cost of replacement of its hydropower investments (hydropower investments are, of course, long lived). Second, ZESCO underinvested severely in ongoing operations and maintenance expenditures—as became evident subsequently in the unexpectedly high costs of ongoing rehabilitation of the power generation infrastructure. The combined result of the favorable endowment and the short-term-oriented managerial decision making was that, for many decades, Zambian users of electricity enjoyed among the lowest electricity tariffs in the world, with prices to residences, businesses, and mines (which accounted for about half of total power consumption) all below US$0.03 per kilowatt-hour.

With no expenditures being made to develop or maintain power generation (and with similar underinvestment in operations and maintenance of electricity distribution facilities), where was this US$0.03 per kilowatt-hour going? The short answer was to staff costs. In Zambia, commercialized utilities such as ZESCO have the discretion to set their own pay scales (subject, of course, to the oversight of their boards of directors). According to ZESCO's 2005 annual report, in that year staff costs amounted to over 50 percent of total annual turnover of approximately US$200 million.[1] As of 2006, ZESCO had over 5,000 employees, up from 4,000 in 2002.[2]

Two major drivers radically transformed the market for electricity in Zambia. First, in the 2000s, fueled by a close to fivefold increase in the price of its near-mono-export—copper—and a corresponding doubling of export volumes, the Zambian economy began growing at an accelerating rate, after a long period of stagnation. Much of this growth was driven by energy-intensive investments in mining. It did not take long for this energy-intensive growth to reverse the electricity supply-demand balance. Second, the broader Southern African market for electricity mirrored this pattern, with the supply-demand balance in South Africa—the behemoth consumer (and producer) in the market—also turning negative. Given an increasingly integrated Southern African grid, this situation created a potentially very large regional source of demand.

The Electricity Sector Reform Menu—and Its (In)digestibility

There is a standard technocratic menu of reforms for responding to electricity sector challenges of the kind confronted by Zambia. The menu includes unbundling power generation, transmission, and distribution (privatizing some, or all, parts of the system); rebalancing tariffs so that each part of the vertical network covers its own costs; creating competition in generation by opening access to the electricity grid; creating an impartial regulator as independent referee; and using public-private partnerships to attract equity and limited recourse debt financing for new investment (especially in generation), on the basis of precisely specified power purchase agreements from customers downstream.

Beginning in the mid-1990s, with strong support from the World Bank Group, Zambia began a process of putting this model in place. Though progress was uneven and slow, until 2003 this remained the model used for the World Bank Group dialogue in the sector. However, the following transpired:

- In April 2003, the Zambian government signaled to the World Bank and the International Monetary Fund (IMF) its unwillingness to proceed with the unbundling and privatization of ZESCO, despite earlier signals that it would do so. The Bank and the IMF subsequently accepted ZESCO commercialization as an alternative.
- In October 2003, the Zambian government instructed its Office for Promoting Private Power Investment (OPPPI) to terminate immediately its ongoing efforts to attract, through international competitive bidding, private concessionaires to the largest of the Greenfield hydropower investments on the table (Kafue Gorge Lower, 450–750 MW capacity). Instead, in late 2003, the Zambian authorities authorized ZESCO to begin actively engaging with Chinese power sector players and financiers on major hydropower investments.
- Despite the creation of an energy regulator in 1997, over the subsequent decade there were no significant moves to rebalance tariffs. As of 2007 (the time the political economy assessment of the sector was undertaken), tariffs to residential and business consumers remained below US$0.03 per kilowatt-hour. Long-term agreements struck in 2002/03 provided generated power to the mines at an exceptionally favorable price—ZESCO sold power to the private, Zambian-owned transmission intermediary, the Copperbelt Energy Corporation (CEC), for US$0.02 per kilowatt-hour, and CEC resold the power to the mines at US$0.03 per kilowatt-hour.

Telecommunications
Drivers of Change
Far more than for electricity, the drivers of change in the telecommunications sector have been global and technological. Until the early 1990s, telecommunications providers generally occupied a position in the economies of developing countries similar to that of electricity utilities. They generally were state-owned, monopoly providers, with substantial investments and major flows of revenues. Indeed, through the 1980s, telecommunications appeared to be the more dynamic public utility—an important, commanding presence and a prestigious employer, a parastatal crown jewel. The 1980s did see an impulse globally for institutional reform—notably privatization with regulation, plus the licensing of

a second fixed-line operator. But the opportunities for more radical vertical unbundling seemed fewer than in electricity.

Zambia's monopoly telecommunications provider, Zamtel, seemed well positioned. It had a staff of close to 3,000 employees and a strong revenue stream, including substantial payments in hard currency from international telecommunications providers to connect international calls terminating in Zambia. But two profound technological changes utterly transformed the telecommunications sector. First, the emergence of cellular telephony offered a relatively inexpensive route to creating multiple new networks for voice communications. In Africa, by 2001, the number of mobile phone subscribers had overtaken the number of fixed lines; in 2003, nearly 75 percent of telephone subscribers in sub-Saharan Africa used a mobile phone (GSM Association 2006a, 2006b). Second, the rise of the Internet has resulted in an explosion of digital communications, the emergence of a wide variety of new network services, and an accelerating demand for broadband communications infrastructure. Communications infrastructure has become ever more central to the global economy. Meanwhile, the market structures have become ever more complex— with high potential for competition, but only with effective regulation that ensures that it all works in a way to avoid monopoly control (and associated monopoly pricing to consumers).

False Dawn for Zambia's Telecommunications Reforms
In the face of this global transformation, Zambia seemed initially to be moving quite rapidly. Legislation to create a regulator, the Communications Authority of Zambia (CAZ), was promulgated in 1994. By 1998, Zambia had licensed two new cellular operators, in addition to Zamtel; as of 2007, these operators accounted for about two million subscribers (as compared with fewer than 100,000 for Zamtel's fixed-line service).[3] By 2001, five Internet service providers were operating. But thereafter, the momentum of reform ground to a halt[4]:

- The regulator was unable to establish a level playing field. Cost-effective arrangements for interconnection were not put in place, so (with a single, dominant mobile network accounting for over 80 percent of all local traffic) the costs of local calls remained high.
- Zamtel failed to expand services. Outside of Lusaka and the Copperbelt (which together currently account for only 30 percent of the population), access remained poor (see map 5.1). And the domestic telecommunications backbone had not been expanded rapidly enough to meet growing demand for broadband data services.[5]
- Zamtel held tight to its one remaining source of monopoly power, control over the international gateway. Despite a 2001 statute that formally permitted the licensing of a second gateway (for a fee of US$12 million), Zamtel maintained its monopoly position and set high charges for international connections; the costs of international calls remained upward of US$1 per minute.[6]

Map 5.1 Zambia

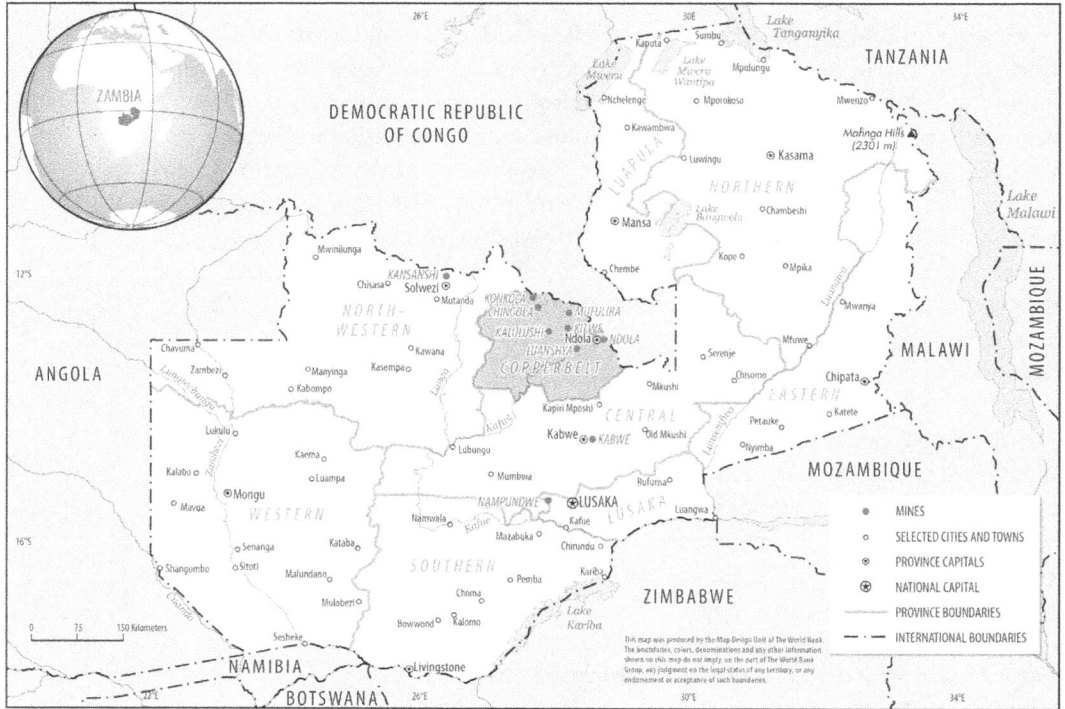

Source: Map number: IBRD 40248, September 2013.

- Technological innovation created bypass opportunities via a combination of V-SAT (very small aperture terminal) connections (which had been liberalized) and Skype (Internet telephony). For a period of time, in a desperate rearguard action, the Zambian authorities declared Skype illegal.

The World Bank Group and others embarked on a strong push to communicate the benefits of additional reform and to help identify specific decisions that could move the process forward. The efforts included sponsoring field visits of key Zambian telecommunications players to countries that had traveled the telecommunications reform path, continuing technical work, engaging multiple stakeholders and the media on the issue, and giving briefings at the highest level of government. But as of 2007, even though the costs of Zamtel's reluctance to adapt to a changing environment were well understood in Zambia by the leading local players, these efforts had yielded no new reforms.

Assessing the Political Economy Constraints

Why did the reforms in electricity and telecommunications prove so difficult to implement? To address this question, the technical features of each sector needed to be considered in a broader political and institutional context.

Political economy assessments were conducted at two levels. The most general level comprised an exploration of Zambia's country-level political economy drivers of decision making. That general analysis was then used to explore, from a political economy perspective, options and constraints at the sectoral level. The country and sectoral political economy analyses were, in turn, used to suggest politically feasible entry points for reform in each of the two sectors. This section summarizes the country- and sectoral-level political economy analyses. The following section details how these analyses were used to identify politically feasible entry points for reform.

The National Level: The Evolving Interaction between Political Management and Development Policy Making[7]

The Zambian state generally has been successful in its most important function. The country has not faced widespread violence—neither in the colonial period nor in the four decades following political independence in 1964. Although there are some 72 different tribes, or ethnic groups, in Zambia, there are multiple forms of cross-cutting identities that can militate against conflict. Zambians can identify themselves (and be identified by others) broadly by language group or narrowly by ethnicity, depending on the context. Further, none of Zambia's ethnic groups can exert power over the entire polity; consequently, intergroup contact at the elite level has always been high, and de facto coalitions and compromises have been essential components of political strategies.

En route to independence, there had been a successful first democratic election, which resulted in a legitimate elected parliament and president; there was a strong independent judiciary; and property rights were protected. As a country with a per capita income in 1964 of US$2,700 (in calendar year 2,000 dollars), among the highest on the African continent, and a thriving copper mining sector, Zambia's development prospects seemed good. Even so, during the early years of independence, Zambia was a postcolonial state whose integrity, cohesiveness, and sovereignty were quite fragile. In part, the fragility was a result of its location: freedom from colonial rule did not come as peacefully to its neighbors because both Zambia's location and its political commitments put it in the front-line of resistance movements in neighboring countries.

But there also were some fundamental disconnects that underlaid the institutional facade. Though political power had transferred to the African majority, in the years immediately following independence the patterns of ownership, control, and access to income opportunities continued to reflect those of the now-ended colonial order. Along with these economic inequities was an underlying tendency toward fragmentation in a recently independent country that had no natural national identity of its own. The result of these disconnects was that Zambia moved away from multiparty democracy.

The Rise and Fall of Dominant Party Patrimonialism

In 1972, a new constitution made Zambia a one-party state under the United National Independence Party (UNIP), led by President Kenneth Kaunda. Because of the fragility of state coherence, distributing patronage to key constituencies in the form of bureaucratic, managerial, and ministerial posts became an essential tool for consolidating both political power and the state itself. The economic dimensions of development policy making became increasingly subordinated to the imperatives of creating and allocating the rents necessary for political management. The beneficiaries of these rents were ethnic constituencies, represented by key elites, who were awarded positions in the Cabinet that were carefully balanced ethnically. Jobs in the parastatal sector and bureaucracy were key sources of patronage. Urban consumption was also subsidized as a means to placate potentially restive urban populations and centers of dissent.

But even as public spending grew, revenue collapsed. Throughout the period of UNIP rule, copper mining was the principal source of rents. In the immediate postindependence period, copper contributed up to 95 percent in total foreign exchange receipts and 45 percent in government revenue. Beginning in 1974, world copper prices fell sharply, and consequently, profits of Zambia's copper industry collapsed. Nonetheless, throughout the 1980s and early 1990s, copper revenue remained the most important rent that sustained various government operations. The government used its ownership and control of the copper mining giant, Zambia Consolidated Copper Mines, to finance recurrent expenditures and directed it to channel its funds to provision of welfare projects, such as passenger and commuter train transportation, clinics and schools, and operation of lodges.

Over the course of the 1980s, it became evident that neither Zambia's economy nor its polity had the resilience and flexibility to adapt to the changed economic circumstances. The patronage model of economic and political management continued and was accompanied by ever-more desperate measures to find the requisite rents. The now majority-government-owned mining industry was progressively deprived of revenues that ought to have been set aside for operations, maintenance, and replacement investment. And the country resorted to large-scale foreign borrowing, thus resulting in external debt increasing from 61 percent of gross domestic product (GDP) in 1980 to 317 percent of GDP by 1986. The country lurched from one half-hearted-and-then-abandoned reform effort to another.

Multiparty Democracy and Its Discontents

Following the collapse of the Berlin Wall in 1989, constituencies outside the one-party state became increasingly emboldened in their calls for multiparty democracy. Multiparty elections were held in October 1991, with the opposition MMD, under the leadership of Frederick Chiluba, winning the presidency and 125 of 150 seats of the National Assembly.

The MMD's victory ushered in a period of far-reaching economic reform and political change. The new government aggressively implemented the Washington Consensus package of macroeconomic reforms that included exchange rate and market liberalization and privatization. Though this recipe had been perceived by UNIP as politically infeasible, the MMD gave it credibility, both because the policies represented a sought-after radical departure from UNIP's half-hearted commitment to policy implementation and because people believed that these reforms would bring about economic growth and development.

But the early euphoria did not last. Less than two years after it came into power, the MMD split, with some of the most committed reformers leaving office. Further, the disintegration of UNIP, and its entire party and state planning apparatus, had left significant gaps in domestic policy-making capabilities, which neither the MMD nor donors initially perceived a need to fill. Policy making lacked coherence. Indeed, throughout the 1990s, Zambian policy making largely was a reactive combination of deference and resistance to initiatives sponsored by donors. The economy declined within four years of the first five-year term of the MMD government.

Top-down presidentialism and political management via the allocation of rents reasserted itself in the now-liberalized environment, but with important changes in the specific patterns of rent-seeking and corruption. A first change was in the sources of rent. With the troubled copper industry no longer a reliable moneymaker, the focus shifted to other sources of cash flow potentially under political control; to opportunities for discretionary provision of access to land and other resources; and to a subset of privatization, procurement, and other uneven transactions.

A second change was in the political role of rent allocation. Instead of using rents to buy group loyalty in the mold of the UNIP government, beneficiaries were less representative of their groups than individual entrepreneurs. Thus, a group of entrepreneurial political elites emerged, with less a sense of the national, public good and more an interest in individual gain and opportunities for patronage, which were almost always conditioned by their proximity to the president and ruling party.

The more overtly corrupt character of post-1991 rent management was due to multiple factors. The demise of the one-party state, and with it the Leadership Code, which had barred (albeit not altogether successfully) private business ownership and the appearance of impropriety by government ministers; the putative need to no longer placate ethnic constituencies (ethnic factionalism was successfully subdued under UNIP, and the MMD's genuinely pan-ethnic appeal diminished the urgency of such explicit patronage efforts); and a generous honeymoon period that enabled the MMD to shift substantial blame for rising hardships onto the donors and international financial institutions combined to create a free-for-all environment. Governance worsened further during the second five-year term of the MMD government, and the dysfunctional status quo could have persisted into a third term sought by the then-incumbent president, until determined social opposition persuaded him to step down.

Subsequent to President Chiluba's two terms, the MMD enjoyed two further terms in office led by Levy Mwanawasa and then (following President Mwanawasa's death in office) Rupiah Banda (who, in turn, was defeated in the 2011 presidential election by Michael Sata, leader of the Patriotic Front party). In the post-Chiluba period, the MMD government's approach to governance overall was in some respects closer to that of the UNIP government than to its first and second five-year terms. Top-down presidential decision making continued to be the norm, but with the role of patronage more subordinated to an overall policy vision. Efforts to combat corruption enjoyed a high public profile, but delayed prosecution and low conviction rates, coupled with continuing accusations of corruption against incumbent MMD officers, caused many members of the public to sour on the anticorruption effort.

How Zambia's Competitive Clientelism Worked

In sum, Zambia had long been characterized by a disconnect between its formal institutional structure and the informal rules of the game. The country had a full array of formal institutions characteristic of a liberal democracy, and all of them functioned to some degree, but the actors within them did not necessarily operate within a norm of being bound by rules. The following four propositions summarize the way the system worked in the first two decades of democratic rule and the implications for development decision making of this tension between formal rules and informal norms:

- *First, authority was centralized in the presidency, which enjoyed wide discretion.* When formal institutions are weak, patronage generally becomes the dominant mode of governance. As described previously, under the UNIP government, there was an explicit effort to engage particular ethno-linguistic groups as a means of ensuring their loyalty both to the new state and to the party. Under the first 10 years of the MMD government, these patterns of patronage became more oriented toward individuals. Over the subsequent decade, the pattern of patronage appears to have been somewhere between these two earlier patterns.

- *Second, checks-and-balances institutions created enough space for citizens' voices to ensure that impunity was not without limits.* In both the UNIP and MMD periods, the country's formal institutions were rather easily circumvented by the political class, but impunity has not been unlimited. Episodic adherence to the formal rules, as evidenced by the peaceful transition to multiparty politics in 1991 and by the dropping of a bid for a third presidential term in 2001, illustrates a degree of being bound by rules. The Office of the Attorney General, the Task Force Against Corruption, the Anti-Corruption Commission, and the Courts of Law, though subject to various degrees of political influence, nonetheless often attempted to enforce laws and rules in an environment that was not always hospitable to them.

- *Third, a consequence of Zambia's limited impunity was an extreme tilt toward the status quo.* A political culture that was neither fully rule based nor characterized by unbridled rent-seeking and corruption favored indecision and conservatism, rather than radical departures that could alienate fragile constituencies and provoke a wider reaction by civil society. Because reform potentially provokes more vocal public reaction or dilutes the power of the centralized state, the path of least resistance was to leave the system unchanged.

• *Fourth, elite economic nationalism emerged as a renascent part of Zambia's development discourse.* This proposition does not follow directly from the tension between formal rules and informal norms, but it has been a dominant feature across Southern Africa (via South Africa's Black Economic Empowerment initiatives and Zimbabwe's turbulent approach to land reform). It was also evident in Zambia, and turns out to be sufficiently pervasive in its implications for development decision making in some infrastructure sectors that it is worth noting explicitly.

Political Economy at the Sectoral Level

Analysis of electricity and telecommunications revealed how the politics of centralized discretion, the tilt toward the status quo, and the rebirth of elite economic nationalism contributed to the limited success of infrastructural reform efforts as of 2007.

Discretionary Control in Electricity and Telecommunications

Almost by definition, governance by centralized discretion requires access to discretionary resources for its efficacy. The electricity and, to a lesser extent, telecommunications utilities offered such resources to the political center in abundance.

Access to cash is the crucial discretionary resource. Both the electricity and telecommunications utilities enjoyed steady cash flows from service receipts—cash that was managed through their corporate treasuries, rather than through the control apparatus of the national budget. The volumes were large; ZESCO's 2005 annual turnover was equivalent to about 7 percent of the national budget—placing its revenue somewhere between the 2005/06 budget votes of defense (6.4 percent of the budget) and health (10.7 percent). Ready access to cash can be important to lubricate the political process—to help finance political parties, to respond rapidly to requests from influential constituents, and to signal to petitioning citizens and communities a readiness to respond to specific problems. (Note that none of these necessarily involve corruption in the sense of the top political leadership using public resources for private gain.)

In addition to cash, control over ZESCO and Zamtel also afforded access to procurement contracts and to jobs. Investments in capital equipment, or works directly under the control of a utility, can involve large sums of money, as well as fierce formal and informal competition among suppliers for potentially lucrative contracts. As for jobs, from an economy-wide perspective, the numbers were modest—5,000 for ZESCO and about 3,000 for Zamtel. But jobs in ZESCO in particular were high in both pay and stature.[8]

The means through which political leadership exercised control over these resources is simple: the power of appointment. Which appointments are key? Ministers and boards of utilities and of regulators (some reform-minded, some less so) come and go. But this can be second-order. Where the utility is an important source of discretionary resources, the crucial oversight relationships are not between its management and its formal government and regulatory overseers, but rather between the chief executive of the utility and the office of the president. Consider the following examples:

- In electricity, the same individual was chief executive of ZESCO throughout the 10-year Chiluba era; apparently his stature and influence rivaled that of senior cabinet ministers. President Mwanawasa followed a similar pattern by appointing a trusted confidante as successor.
- In telecommunications, President Mwanawasa also appointed a new and trusted chief executive of Zamtel upon acceding to power. Interestingly, though, in this case the chair of the board of the regulatory agency (CAZ)—himself an influential figure (former chairperson of the Zambian Association of Chambers of Commerce and Industry)—became tired of the chief executive's resistance to change and unilaterally fired him, making the announcement in a public arena. Within days, the board of the regulatory agency was dissolved.
- On a separate occasion, the responsible minister did not appoint a new board to CAZ for almost one year subsequent to the expiration of the term of office of the previous board, notwithstanding the fact that board approval is required for any regulatory decisions to be binding.
- In 2006/07, the electricity sector saw a complete change in oversight personnel—with a new minister replacing wholesale the boards of both ZESCO and the energy regulator—but with no apparent impact on the mandate and authority of the ZESCO chief executive.

The implications of centralized discretion for the conventional infrastructural reform agenda are stark. Reformers champion an independent regulator—a cornerstone of infrastructural reform—empowered to transparently set the rules of the game and to referee among competing interests. Interestingly, subsequent to their inception, both the electricity and telecommunications regulatory authorities became increasingly technically competent as regulators. But technical competence is relevant only insofar as the political rules of the game give that competence space to act professionally. In the Zambia case, as of 2007, such independence was limited; transparent, formal regulatory authority ran directly contrary to the rules of presidential discretion.

Reformers also champion sectoral restructuring to embrace competition. De-monopolization of the international telecommunications gateway was, as noted earlier, an especially high priority among donors and Zambia's private sector. But de-monopolization eliminates rents, and hence the moneymaker that produces discretionary resources. In the power sector, the priority restructuring is the unbundling of generation, transmission, and distribution to ensure that each part of a vertical network manages its costs effectively. But unbundling would make transparent the cross-subsidies in the system, that is, flows from rent-producing parts of a vertically integrated utility to either rent-absorbing (featherbedded) parts of the organization or rent recipients outside the organization.

The Politics of the Urban Status Quo

In all countries, utilities and their regulators face a tension between the preferences of consumers for lower tariffs and the economic imperatives of the utility. But for Zambian electricity, the combination of the economics of the sector and the dynamics of Zambian politics made this tension seem especially intractable.

An efficient electricity transmission and distribution system might perhaps be able to supply power to residential consumers at a price equal to about twice the cost of generated power, so if the generation cost is US$0.04 per kilowatt-hour, then the retail price to households would be US$0.08 per kilowatt-hour. Estimates suggested that the costs of new Zambian hydropower generation to meet expanded demand amounted to US$0.06–0.07 per kilowatt-hour as of 2007. Taken together, these numbers suggested that the cost-efficient marginal cost of supplying power to electricity consumers would be about US$0.011– 0.013 per kilowatt-hour.[9] But Zambians with residences linked to the electricity grid had become accustomed to very cheap power—US$0.03 per kilowatt-hour as of 2007. Clearly, moving from a price to residential consumers of US$0.03 per kilowatt-hour to a price capable of supporting sustainable system expansion was a large challenge.

The politics of Zambia suggests that realigning residential tariffs would be especially difficult. Among Zambia's elites, ZESCO was perceived as a high-cost organization. Efforts to raise electricity tariffs thus ran into the natural response that "ZESCO should improve its efficiency first." More fundamental was the challenge posed by Zambia's tilt toward the status quo. In the face of this tilt, any exercise in the wielding of discretionary power was thus something of an experiment: Who would react? How might these reactions affect the leadership's ability to orchestrate political control? With weak institutions, Zambia's political leaders seemed likely to rapidly retreat from any actions that provoked strong countervailing reaction.

The reactions that mattered most were those of urban residents. Zambia has long been among the most urbanized countries in Africa, with political power concentrated in the capital city, Lusaka, and the towns of the Copperbelt. Political leaders were thus especially wary of actions that would affect the interests and pocketbooks of white-collar urban residents. The technocratic logic of raising the price of electricity to urban residents from US$0.030 to US$0.075 per kilowatt-hour seemed impeccable. But the politics pointed in a different direction: few actions affect the interests and pocketbooks of urban elites as immediately—and can be as directly tied to government—as a decision to more than double utility prices.[10]

These urban constituencies decidedly were not Zambia's poor. Only about 40 percent of Zambia's urban population—and a meager 2 percent of the rural population—had access to electricity, implying an overall electrification rate of less than 20 percent of the country's roughly 2 million households. For most poor people, electricity pricing is irrelevant to their day-to-day lives.

In contrast to electricity, the obstacles to telecommunications reform did not involve resistance from consumers, even though reform was also likely to entail increases in the price of some fixed-line services. One reason these pricing issues were less contentious was that, with only 90,000 fixed-line subscribers, the numbers were smaller. In addition, there was a ready substitute: the overwhelming number of Zambians with fixed-line connections also used mobile phones, so were less dependent on the fixed-line service. Indeed, with two million mobile phone subscribers, but unusually high mobile phone charges from a comparative international perspective, the net welfare benefits of a competitive, liberalized, and efficiently regulated telecommunications sector could be very large. This is further discussed below.

Private Interests: The Rebirth of Elite Economic Nationalism

Consider the profile of the participants in the electricity and telecommunications proposals for sectoral reform that came suddenly, and unexpectedly, unglued:

- In electricity, in October 2003, after the OPPPI had succeeded in eliciting interest by competing North American and Nordic consortia in a major new hydropower investment at Kafue Gorge Lower, the Zambian government instructed the OPPPI to end its process and hand over responsibility for developing the investment to ZESCO.
- In telecommunications, a multiyear effort to provide compelling evidence as to the economic benefits to Zambia of a liberalized international gateway culminated, at a business-government retreat, in a scathing indictment by Zambia's then-president Levy Mwanawasa of the arrogance of the interests pushing for gateway liberalization.

In each case, international (Western) business interests—British, South African, and North American investment bankers seeking to structure electricity concessions and international mobile phone operators pushing for a liberalized telecommunications gateway—suddenly and unexpectedly found themselves on the wrong side of what seemed (from their perspective) highly attractive win-win development and business opportunities.

Yet consider these conflicts against the broader backdrop of Zambian history. In both cases, what was best for Zambia happened to coincide with leadership by international actors, with Zambian interests not directly part of the solution. The resonance with Zambia's earlier history of colonial rule is inescapable. Finally, consider the (short-term) denouement of each conflict: in electricity, authorization of the Zambian parastatal, ZESCO, to seek an alternative way forward; and in telecommunications, a rejection of donors' proposals for further gateway liberalization and a parallel authorization of Zamtel. Viewed together, these cases showed a common pattern that pointed toward—following the lead of Zambia's neighbors South Africa and (in an especially virulent form)

Table 5.1 The Relative Strength of Political Constraints to Infrastructural Reform

	Electricity	Telecommunications
Politics of discretion		
Resources	***	**
Featherbedding	***	**
Bias to status quo		
Residential tariffs	***	*
The private sector		
Capture	*	*
Economic nationalism	*	**

Significance level: * = modest political salience, ** = some political salience, *** = most politically salient.

Zimbabwe—the relevance of elite economic nationalism as a renascent part of Zambia's development discourse.

A Summary of the Sector-Level Political Constraints

Table 5.1 summarizes the previous discussion as to the relative strength of five sets of political constraints to institutional reform. Scanning down the columns of the table highlights the priority challenges for each sector. For electricity, the obstacles to reform seemed to derive from the politics of discretion and of the bias toward the status quo—for both of which key interests of the central political leadership were at stake. Given the centrality of ZESCO in the political calculus, it followed that unless ZESCO participated as a full partner in electricity reform, progress would not be feasible. For telecommunications, by contrast, the political constraints seemed less pressing, so long as a way forward could be found that was not inconsistent with the country's renascent economic nationalism.

Politically Feasible Entry Points for Electricity and Telecommunications Reform

A common underlying theme is evident in the failed reform efforts that predated the political economy work. For both electricity and telecommunications, the reform agenda had been to close the gap between the reality on the ground and a technocratic vision of optimal institutional arrangements. In such an approach, there is no room to incorporate the political economy realities. Yet, in each sector these political realities have confounded (to a greater or lesser extent) efforts to implement infrastructural reform.

The 2007 sectoral political economy assessment incorporated a series of proposals as to how the World Bank's approach to reform in electricity and telecommunications might be changed. This section describes these proposals. The following section details what actually happened subsequently.

The intent of the proposals derived from the political economy assessments was to suggest politically feasible approaches to reform, thereby loosening the grip of optimal models as a guide for reform design. The point is not to set them aside entirely: their normative logic is a useful point of reference—a north star to help navigate change. But a practical reform agenda cannot simply insist (repeatedly) that a normatively derived technocratic agenda of reform must (somehow) be implemented; to contend with political economy realities, the agenda needs to take the interests of stakeholders into account. How?

The key for jump-starting reform in Zambia's electricity and telecommunications sectors, the political economy assessment suggested, was to shift away from sweeping optimal solutions and to focus instead on much more narrowly targeted reforms and then to explore what might be the incentives of key actors vis-à-vis each specific proposal, that is, which, if any, of the narrower reforms might be politically implementable. Two key sets of stakeholders and their incentives are as follows:

- *Stakeholders with the incentive and influence to press for improved performance.* Who are they? How can they be crowded into the reform process? What institutional designs will empower them to sustainably hold key decision makers and implementers accountable for performance?
- *Top-level political decision makers.* What are the options for shaping the benefits and costs of the political calculus so that decision makers will opt on the margin for pro-development options?

The following three examples illustrate how careful attention to these questions can help uncover ways forward, even when political constraints seem severe.

Expansion of Electricity Generation: The Incentives of Mining Companies

As of 2007, Zambia's electricity sector confronted an urgent challenge of finding a revenue base to finance the expansion in generating capacity that, as long as the economy kept growing, was certain to be needed within a very few years. But the country's urban residential, commercial, and manufacturing constituencies seemed likely to be unresponsive to suggestions that they pay more for power. Further, given Zambia's political economy, their views seemed likely to be decisive in the minds of politicians.

The incentives of the mining sector were different. Copper mining accounted for close to 50 percent of Zambia's electricity consumption. This consumption was concentrated among a small number of large (in the Zambian context) companies that dominate the industry. Copper mining and processing are energy-intensive activities; uninterrupted flows of high-voltage power are necessary for profitability. The sector was highly profitable and it was growing at a very rapid rate, with the expansion projected to continue for the foreseeable future. Taken together, these facts imply that the link is inescapable for copper companies between, on the one hand, their decisions as buyers of electricity and, on the other, whether or not supply will expand to meet growth in demand. Specifically, recognizing the looming supply difficulties—and the political difficulties of getting other actors to cover the costs of expansion—the mining companies had every incentive to agree collectively to cover the full marginal costs of the additional generating capacity necessary to meet their surging demand. The policy implication was clear: move rapidly to lock in new generating capacity on the basis of full-cost pricing for the increment by mining companies. Do not hold such investment hostage to a broader reform of the pricing regime.

Pricing, Investment, and Productivity: Multistakeholder Bargains with Urban Electricity Consumers

Though the electricity sector urgently required new investment—both in generation and in urban electricity distribution grids—urban service users viewed (not without reason) utility staff members to be inefficient and overpaid, and so seemed unwilling to consider sympathetically the case for tariff increases. Finding a way out of the resulting low-level equilibrium is a classic chicken-and-egg problem.

Consider the three interdependencies highlighted in figure 5.1:

- *The interdependence of productivity and investment.* Investment can unlock binding performance constraints. In the absence of resources, a utility is unable to make even inexpensive productivity-enhancing investments.
- *The interdependence of productivity and pricing.* Increased electricity prices generate revenues—easing both financial stringency and pressure for performance. These prices typically are managed, so price setters need to strike a delicate balance—to both win consumer acceptance of price increases and make adequate resources available, without weakening pressure for performance. This is an especially salient tension in settings, such as Zambia, whose publicly owned enterprises have had a long history of endemic resource leakage through inefficiency and corruption.
- *The interdependence of investment and pricing.* Even with an implicit government guarantee, to attract private financing for new investment in electricity, a utility needs to be capable of a credible stream of future revenue that could cover debt repayment—thus requiring that prices be set sufficiently high.

Figure 5.1 A Utility's Pricing, Investment, and Productivity Interdependencies

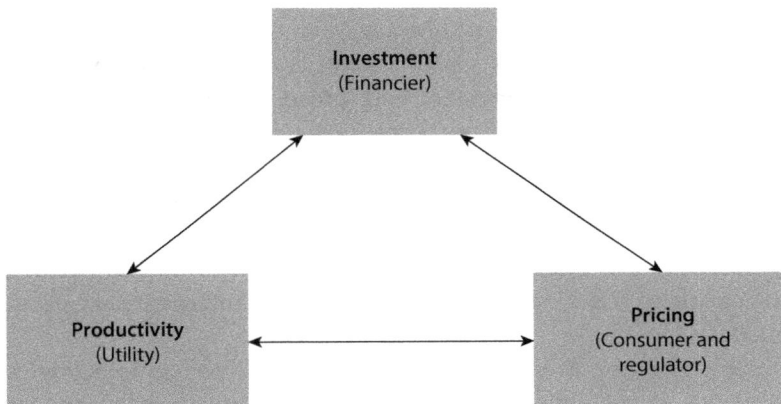

Figure 5.1 points to the possibility of a low-level equilibrium—one where the potential for investment and productivity gains is undercut by skepticism as to the efficiency with which a utility might use incremental resources and by associated resistance by urban residents to price increases. This appeared to be the prevailing Zambian pattern in electricity distribution.

But the figure also suggests a way out of the low-level equilibrium: a series of interlocking commitments—utilities committing to efficiency improvements, service users and regulators committing to sustainable prices, and donors and other financiers committing to make incremental resources available for investment. The incentives of urban consumers are key. Credible commitment that any injection of resources would indeed be used to improve the performance of the sector—rather than be siphoned off in inefficiency and rents—could overcome consumers' long-standing skepticism and associated resistance to price increases.

Given Zambia's institutional realities, how might such credible commitment be locked in? One key proposal was to make ZESCO an active partner in any effort to break out of this dysfunctional pattern. A second proposal was to find ways of engaging skeptical electricity users in dialogue on price increases.

Telecommunications: Enhancing Responsiveness to Citizens' Concerns

The dominant reform discourse in the sector centered around topics such as liberalization of the international gateway, regulatory regimes for interconnection, and provision of high-speed backbone for data transmission. Certainly, such reforms are priorities for innovation and development dynamism. But, as with all forward-looking reforms, the development benefits were likely to be evident only to a farsighted few. The cost of the highest profile of these reforms (gateway liberalization) would fall directly on one of the long-standing moneymakers of the political class. (Indeed, these costs would take the form of a seeming transfer from this Zambian entity to wholly foreign-owned companies—a potentially combustible dynamic in Zambia's climate of economic nationalism.) It was hardly surprising, then, that the political decision makers repeatedly ignored the recommendations of technocratic reformers.

Instead of prioritizing gateway liberalization, the political economy assessment pointed to an alternative reform priority for the telecommunications sector—one that both was consistent with broader reform goals and appealed more directly to politically salient constituencies. As noted earlier, a single, dominant provider had led the way in Zambia's cell phone expansion and had 80–90 percent of all subscribers. At close to US$0.50 per minute, Zambia also had among Africa's highest prices for local calls, signaling a lack of competition. Telecommunications reforms aimed at fostering entry, and competition thus seemed capable of reducing prices of both local and international calls to local consumers.

Were the regulator stronger technically and vis-à-vis legitimacy with consumers, such a dialogue could proceed straightforwardly on familiar technocratic lines. But as of 2007, neither was the case. Thus, the political economy assessment suggested that the key to successful reform was to make social benefits and costs transparent—and engage directly with influential local private sector and civil society players as to the merits of alternative policy options. Winning broad support from Zambia's cell phone users (who, though usage is broad based, certainly included the richer—therefore more politically influential—segment of the population) for an agenda of better service, with more choice and at lower prices, seemed to be an achievable objective.

Acting on the Assessment

This final section explores what impact the political economy assessment had on the World Bank's engagement in Zambia. It also offers some broader reflections—both on the impact on the ground of such changed engagement (although any direct imputation of causality is not feasible) and on the possible lessons to be learned from the Zambian experience as to the value added and the limitations of political economy assessments.

Whether a political economy assessment translates into a change in how World Bank teams engage with their government counterparts can depend critically on the extent of high-level support from the Bank management responsible for the country program. In the case of Zambia, the support was unusually strong. The reports were commissioned precisely because high-level management had come to the conclusion that business as usual was not working and was searching for an alternative way forward. There also was strong continuity over time; the commitment to anchor operational engagement in careful political economy analysis was sustained through the transition from one high-level Bank country program manager to another.[11]

For an illustration of the role the political economy assessment played in reframing the World Bank's engagement in Zambia, it is worth quoting at some length from the Bank's 2008 Country Assistance Strategy (CAS):

> As part of the new CAS and harmonization processes, the Bank has reassessed its strategic position in Zambia to determine where it should be active, passive, or disengaged, based on its strategy, resources, and comparative advantage....

> The new CAS gives priority to very specific interventions in which the beneficiaries are clear, with goals that unequivocally are supported by the political authorities...

> The Bank has undertaken a separate analysis that illuminates issues related to the political economy of reform, and this work has informed the preparation of the CAS. The analysis concludes that the World Bank's engagement in Zambia has been characterized by repeated attempts to promote far-reaching reforms, derived from first-best principles. It recommends that this CAS focus its engagement more narrowly and allow sufficient time for local coalitions for change to develop before

launching new initiatives. Accordingly, proposed analytical work will explore a variety of reform options that are feasible given Zambia's political economy and governance realities. (IDA 2008, 20–21)

So much for intentions. What happened in practice in the sectors under consideration in this chapter?

What Happened in Electricity and Telecommunications?[12]

In both sectors, subsequent to the political economy assessment, the World Bank teams realigned the ways they engaged—both on substance and in process. As per the recommendations, the telecommunications team reduced its heavy emphasis on liberalizing the international gateway and sought to reopen dialogue on the sector—with a broader focus on the high cost of telecommunications to Zambian users. The electricity team made a two-part adjustment: it intensified its commitment to working with ZESCO as a partner; and, with government (and ZESCO) approval, it began to explore options for a new, self-financing investment in electricity generation, anchored in take-or-pay purchase agreements with the mining companies.

On the process side, the Bank teams, working in partnership with a variety of local groups, initiated an intensive informational and public education campaign in both sectors. For telecommunications, the focus was on making explicit the substantially higher cost of telecommunications services (especially mobile calls) as compared with Zambia's neighbors. For electricity, the focus was on the very limited coverage achieved by Zambia's electricity system—rural areas and small towns were largely excluded—thereby highlighting the fact that Zambia's unusually low electricity prices, by starving the system of resources, were inhibiting expansion to lower-income groups, even as the benefits accrued overwhelmingly to elites.

In both sectors, the period subsequent to 2008 witnessed far-reaching changes on the ground, although it is, of course, impossible to attribute causality. Insofar as there was causality, at least some of the changes illustrate the workings of the law of unintended consequences.

In electricity, the Bank's focus on the broad, long-term objective of improving access to electricity services for a large part of the population, especially the rural population (as well as improving performance of ZESCO), transformed the dialogue. It provided a platform for engaging the government in a sustained discussion on politically sensitive issues relating to increases in electricity tariffs and institutional reforms. The Bank also supported a public education campaign that helped change how nongovernmental constituencies perceived the issues. This refocusing on the broader longer-term goals enabled the government to obtain the political support needed for increasing tariffs significantly.

A series of major tariff increases were implemented in 2009 and 2010—increases of 27.0 percent in January 2009, 35.0 percent in August 2009, and 25.6 percent in August 2010. These tariff increases have allowed ZESCO to improve its financial performance, putting the company on the path to financial sustainability, while at the same time increasing the number of people connected to the electricity grid.[13]

In turn, reforms of electricity pricing and institutional arrangements provided the necessary platform for attracting private investment into electricity to meet the surge in demand that had come from the country's copper-mining-led economic boom. Between 2009 and 2012, the energy sector attracted upward of US$2 billion in foreign direct investment—much of this targeted directly to the mining sector. Electricity generated in the country is projected to double between 2013 and 2017.

For telecommunications, the story is more complicated. After years of limited results, the political economy diagnostic led to a refocusing of policy dialogue, from the improvement of efficiency to the adverse impact of high telecommunications costs on Zambia's competitiveness, both by contributing to the high cost of doing business and by contributing more broadly to high telecommunications costs for the many citizens who now enjoyed access to mobile telephone services. This subtle change in message resulted in a general consensus that the telecommunications sector needed to be reformed.

But, contrary to the principal thrust of the political economy diagnostic—the importance of regulatory reforms to foster competition among providers of mobile services as a way of bringing down their rates—and for underlying motivations that cannot be readily discerned by outsiders, the reform agenda gave priority to the privatization of the state-owned (fixed line and mobile) operator, Zamtel. The privatization process moved forward very rapidly, with a Libyan company, LAP Green (also active in Rwanda and Uganda) becoming the new owner. Initially, the privatization effort was hailed by some as a new Zambia success story. But when the Patriotic Front government under Michael Sata (who had been an opponent of the privatization) took power in September 2011, it appointed a Commission of Inquiry to take a second look. In response to the commission's disturbing findings, the privatization was reversed, without compensation.[14]

Some Broader Lessons

Viewed from the perspective of proponents within the World Bank of political economy assessment, the Zambia experience is as good as it gets. The commitment of high-level leadership of the country program was strong, sustained, and well resourced.[15] The experience thus offers some clear lessons as to both the potential and the limits of approaching development programming in a donor agency such as the World Bank through a political economy lens. Four lessons are highlighted here—the first two lessons focus on content, and the next two focus on process.

First, the example of Zambian infrastructure underscores that to be operationally useful, political economy assessments need to bridge the national and the sectoral levels. A country-level study on its own is too general to offer operationally helpful guidance. But only with a clear understanding of the country-level political economy dynamics do the incentives and constraints confronting sector-level decision makers become clear.

The second lesson is that much of the value added of sector-level political economy is in the details. To be operationally useful, sectoral assessments need to incorporate both detailed knowledge of the relevant sector and strong familiarity with the sector's technical menu of reform options. Different reform options have different implications for the various sector-level stakeholders. If the team conducting the political economy assessment is to offer constructive, practical guidance—potentially including help in coming up with innovative ways forward that are both politically feasible and technically sound—then it needs to be comfortable with not only the political dimensions but also the specialist technical dimensions of the challenge. Without this sectoral knowledge, it is all too easy for sector-level assessments to offer little more than yes or no judgments of the feasibility of the best practice technocratic option.

The third lesson is that cross-disciplinary collaboration is vital. It is the sectoral specialist teams, not the political economy experts, who take the lead in operational engagement with country counterparts on sectoral reform. To have operational impact, political economy assessments thus need to be undertaken in close collaboration among political economy experts and the specialist teams responsible for the sectoral reforms. This in turn requires the sectoral teams to be open to the political assessments. As was evident in the electricity and telecommunications examples, sectoral political economy studies can help technically oriented task teams better understand and articulate some of the political drivers and incentives that they experience day to day and that often, from a narrowly technocratic perspective, seem to be irrational but can be important inputs into finding creative alternatives.

The fourth and final lesson is that high-level commitment from leadership of the country program is crucial for realizing the potential synergies between political economy and technical expertise. A political-economy-oriented way of approaching development problems is unfamiliar to many sectoral experts and sometimes raises complexities and challenges that make the task ahead more problematic than it might appear from a narrow, technical perspective. Sometimes, the professional commitment of sectoral teams is sufficient to ensure that the insights are taken on board. But, often, it may be necessary for higher-level leadership to insist that the political dimension be fully internalized in the proposed approach to design and implementation.

Leadership of the World Bank's Zambia country program was strongly supportive (in both the electricity and the telecommunications sectors and more broadly) of anchoring operational initiatives in a sophisticated understanding of the relevant political economy dimensions—and in bringing into the reform process constituencies with whom sector specialists might not otherwise have engaged. Even so, it took considerable effort to bring the sectoral teams (and other senior management staff within the Bank) on board. The results of these efforts speak for themselves.

Notes

1. Total turnover in 2005 was reported in the annual report at 783 billion kwacha (K) and staff costs at K 396 billion. The published audited annual accounts were found to be inaccurate. An independent consultancy (IPA Energy Consulting 2007) came to the conclusion that, for example, 2006 reported profits of about K 130 billion actually amounted—on recalculation to exclude exceptional items—to a loss of more than K 50 billion.

2. This amount includes about 3,800 permanent full-time staff members plus 1,200 temporary full-time staff members; all of the increase was in temporary full-time staff members (IPA Energy Consulting 2007).

3. The largest mobile operator, Celltel, accounted for about 80 percent of the market. As of 2007, its annual revenues exceeded US$200 million; 42 percent of these revenues were paid in taxes (corporate, value-added tax, and others) to the government.

4. For details, see Arnold, Guermazi, and Mattoo (2007).

5. The power utility ZESCO recently began investing in a fiber-optic telecommunications backbone.

6. Mobile operators are charged 80 percent of Zamtel's retail price as an interconnection fee for the delivery of an international call. As of 2006—after a unilateral 40 percent reduction—Zamtel's price was US$1.15.

7. This section draws extensively on Taylor and Simutanyi (2007).

8. Note that patronage employment need not necessarily translate into mediocrity. ZESCO's permanent employees apparently enjoy a strong sense of esprit des corps and professional pride—more as engineers than as cost-efficient corporate managers.

9. Note that the break-even price level depends on the assumptions made as to how to incorporate into the pricing structure the preexisting, fully depreciated hydropower generation facilities. A comprehensive study, completed in 2007, uses US$0.075 as its cost-reflective base case for residential consumers (see IPA Energy Consulting 2007).

10. This is especially true given that the incomes of most members of the white-collar elite in a low-income country such as Zambia are not high.

11. For those familiar with the internal workings of the World Bank, it is perhaps worth noting that, at the time, Zambia was part of a joint country management unit with Malawi and Mozambique. But, in this instance, the Country Director was based in Mozambique and delegated substantial control over the design and implementation of the Bank's engagement to the Bank's country manager.

12. This section draws on a series of presentations on reform progress made in 2011 and 2012 by Kapil Kapoor, World Bank country manager for Zambia from 2008 to 2012.

13. For fiscal years 2006–08, ZESCO reported an operating loss of K 84 billion (US$21 million). Losses after interest charges over the same period amounted to K 160 billion (US$41 million), and negative net cash flows (after borrowings) reached K 39 billion (US$10 million). Following the tariff increases, ZESCO reported a net profit of K 354 billion (US$70.1 million) on revenues of K 1,713 billion (US$342.6 million).

14. Among the findings of the Commission of Inquiry were the following: the then-Minister of Communication appointed, on a sole source basis (and against the advice of other public officials), a Cayman Islands company, RP Capital, as the transactions adviser. RP Capital de facto directly managed the transactions process. LAP Green's winning bid for the asset was US$275 million, of which all but US$43 million was to

cover prior obligations, but the Zambian government, although itself the owner (and with a residual 25 percent equity), put in an additional US$335 million, so that LAP Green could inherit the assets debt free, and with more than US$40 million cash on hand (see *Times of Zambia* 2012).

15. As with other examples in this volume, and as per the discussion in the introductory synthesis in chapter 1, a major share of these resources came from the Governance Partnership Facility funded by the Department for International Development of the United Kingdom.

Bibliography

Arnold, Jens, Boutheina Guermazi, and Aaditya Mattoo. 2007. "Telecommunications: The Persistence of Monopoly." In *Services Trade and Development: The Experience of Zambia*, edited by Aaditya Mattoo and Lucy Payton, 101–54. New York: Palgrave Macmillan; Washington, DC: World Bank.

GSM Association. 2006a. *Universal Access: How Mobile Can Bring Communications to All*. Universal access report, London.

———. 2006b. *Regulation and the Digital Divide*. London.

IDA (International Development Association). 2008. *Country Assistance Strategy for the Republic of Zambia*. Report 43352-ZM, World Bank, Washington, DC.

IPA Energy Consulting. 2007. *Revised ZESCO's Cost of Service*. Report to the Energy Regulation Board, Edinburgh.

Taylor, Scott, and Neo Simutanyi. 2007. *Governance and Political Economy Constraints to Development Priorities in Zambia: A Diagnostic*. Unpublished report prepared for the World Bank, Washington, DC.

Times of Zambia. 2012. "Zambia: Zamtel Saga—Corrupt Deal Backfires." January 25.

World Bank. 2003. *Zambia: Completion Report for 1999–2003 Country Assistance Strategy*. Washington, DC.

ZESCO (Zambia Electricity Supply Corporation). 2005. *2005 Annual Report*. Lusaka.

PART 3

Political Economy Challenges of National-Local Interactions in Sectors

CHAPTER 6

Developing Commercial Agriculture in Ghana

David W. Throup, Chris Jackson, Katherine Bain, and Rachel Ort

Strengthening an Enabling Environment for Investment in Commercialized Agriculture

Ghana has reached lower-middle-income status with an estimated per capita income of US$1,342 in 2010 (World Bank 2012, 1). Poverty decreased from 52 percent in 1992 to 20 percent in 2008, and Ghana has made significant progress against Millennium Development Goals on poverty, hunger, primary completion, gender parity at schools, and access to water (World Bank 2012, 1). Development gains, however, have not been distributed evenly across the country, with the north of Ghana increasingly characterized as a lagging region (World Bank 2012, 1). According to a recent Poverty Assessment undertaken by the World Bank and the government of Ghana, "regional imbalances persist with higher and more extreme poverty rates in the northern sector" (World Bank 2012, 2–3). Promoting more inclusive development, especially along regional lines, will be important if Ghana hopes to continue on its current growth trajectory.

One avenue for achieving this goal is through the expansion of the agricultural sector. New investment in commercialized agriculture, in particular, could add substantial development value, providing new opportunities for economic diversification in an area of (underexploited) potential comparative advantage for Ghana. Furthermore, it provides an opportunity for more equitable, inclusive growth—especially if it can incorporate smallholder farmers. Yet, despite its attractiveness, commercialized agriculture has grown slowly, especially in the North and Central regions and outside of the cash crop cocoa. As the chapter will detail, recent experiences with commercial agriculture have been characterized by insecure access to land as well as difficult relationships with local communities. Some communities have been excluded from job opportunities and have lost access to critical resources under their control.

In addition to the challenges within Ghana, the wider context of commercial agriculture in Africa presents risks. Increased interest in Ghana's agricultural potential occurs during a rush by foreign companies, governments, and local investors to acquire large tracts of land in African countries. As a recent World Bank report explains, such initiatives can benefit developing countries, for example, by bringing increased government revenue, access to technology, or jobs for rural citizens (Deininger et al. 2011). The report notes, however, that given the context of low state capacity, undefined property rights, and weak regulatory institutions, large-scale investments in land frequently come at the expense of local people. Cotula et al. (2009) points out that rural citizens can lose access to land and seasonal resources critical to their livelihoods. Moreover, in some cases, instead of using revenue from land transactions for developmental purposes, government officials may divert new revenue, either for clientelist ends or into their own bank accounts. The balance of benefits and costs—and their distribution across stakeholders—depends on the specific country context as well as the particulars of each investment. Thus, it is important to understand the balance between the benefits of activating the commercial agriculture sector in Ghana and the risks that these gains will be captured by foreign companies or by the domestic political elite rather than reaching the local population.

Given this context, when considering how best to support Ghana's agriculture agenda, the World Bank's country team in Accra felt that it needed a deeper understanding of the political economy drivers of decision making at both the national and the sector levels. Were the factors that led to the collapse of previous investments in agriculture still at play? Given the climate of large-scale land acquisition, was it reasonable to expect outcomes that would benefit the local people and increase the inclusiveness of Ghana's growth? What steps could be taken to make it easier for investment but more difficult for malfeasance? How might transparency and accountability be fostered in the sector without challenging existing structures? The sector team, in particular, hoped to document in a formal way some of the informal knowledge that they acquired by working with stakeholders in the agriculture sector, and therefore facilitate a more concrete and structured conversation within the country management unit (CMU) about how to move forward.

As a result, the agriculture team decided to build on some country-level political economy work done earlier that year. This country-level analysis, undertaken by the CMU with support from the Governance Partnership Facility, provides a historical and structural overview of Ghana's political economy. Its aims are twofold: first, to help illuminate the longer-run patterns of continuity and change that are the backdrop of contemporary Ghanaian politics; and second, to provide an analytical platform for follow-on, sector-level, problem-driven political economy work. The analysis of commercial agriculture was one of these sector-level pieces and was undertaken to inform the design of projects in Ghana. It was also part of a broader focus on mainstreaming governance and political economy considerations across the portfolio, under the Global Partnership Facility Trust Fund. This sector-level study explores the political and institutional challenges facing commercial agriculture—both conceptually and empirically—from the perspective of the Accra Plains and the Northern Region (map 6.1).

Based on the analysis in these studies, this chapter argues that for Ghana to move forward successfully with its commercial agriculture agenda, it needs to address two sets of risks. The first is the lack of credible commitment needed to attract investment. The second is the possibility of predatory capture (benefiting outsiders or rent-seekers in government). Careful analysis of Ghana's national-level political economy provides reason for cautious optimism on both fronts. However, as the chapter discusses, the risks associated with credible commitments for investments at the local level are substantial. These risks largely arise out of the complicated and opaque patterns of land ownership in Ghana.

Thus, the policy recommendations of this chapter address how best to strengthen an enabling environment for inclusive investment in commercial agriculture at the local level. In the short term, a model in which new investments by commercial operators are complemented by outgrowing arrangements offers an attractive way forward, not in the least because it builds on existing land use patterns. Multistakeholder engagement should be supported, with a focus on building consensus and ensuring that stakeholders with potential veto power are not left out. In the longer run, it will be helpful to complement these adhoc local initiatives with more systematic efforts to build formal institutions to support agriculture, such as clarified property rights or farmers associations capable of creating a more level playing field vis-à-vis corporate agribusiness.

The second section of this chapter provides a historical overview of the country-level political economy dynamics in Ghana, focusing on those especially relevant to commercialized agriculture. The third section reviews the immediate sector-level constraints to fostering inclusive commercialized agriculture. The fourth section discusses the implications of this analysis and proposes several policy recommendations for moving forward with investments in agriculture. The final section highlights the impact of the political economy work on the World Bank's operational engagements in Ghana.

Ghana's National Political Economy

This section provides an overview of Ghana's national-level political economy. It explores the origins of Ghana's contemporary political system and the interaction between rents and politics in Ghana. It concludes with a discussion of the possibilities for national-level support to commercialized agriculture generally and outgrower arrangements specifically. Broadly, this section finds that Ghana's national-level political economy provides two reasons for cautious optimism.

First, over the past 30 years, consensus has emerged among Ghana's political elite over the rents that can be extracted from the agriculture sector without discouraging the initiative or production of smallholder farmers. This middle way

Map 6.1 Accra Plains and Northern Region, Ghana

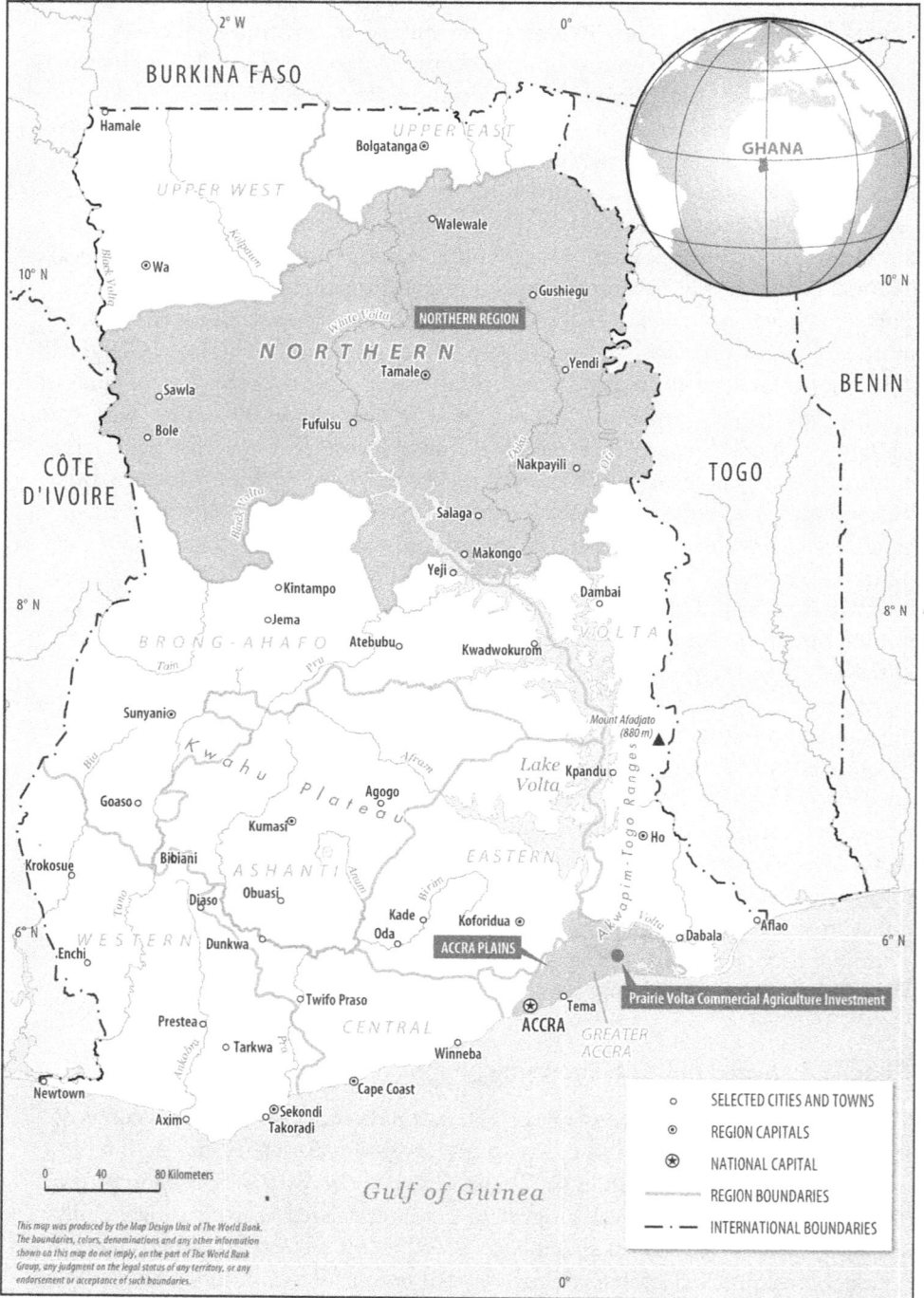

Source: Map number: IBRD 40241, August 2013.

means that parties are unlikely to create strong distortions in commercial agriculture through rent-seeking. Second, there is intense political competition between Ghana's two main political parties, the New Patriotic Party (NPP) and the National Democratic Congress (NDC). Support for these two parties in the rural areas has varied by up to 10 percent over the past few elections, which indicates that both may have an incentive to be responsive to rural constituencies. The NPP and NDC have moved closer to programmatic competition than parties in other parts of Africa. The NDC is the dominant force on the center-left, while the NPP represents the more right-leaning, market-oriented side of the political spectrum. The NPP, originally founded in opposition to Kwame Nkrumah and his Socialist policies, is now considered the party of "successful businessmen, or 'big men'" (Keefer 2007, 180). The NDC, which inherited the interventionist ideology of Nkrumah, draws its support mainly from the Volta Region and northern Ghana although it also has a strong basis of support in most of the Akan-populated south.

Ghana's Political and Economic History

It is heuristically helpful to think of Ghana's history in terms of two concentric circles of political, economic, and social concentration. Using this structural divide as a lens, Ghana's political history can be divided into three distinct periods (1874–1951, 1951–81, and 1981–present) during which different sociopolitical coalitions held power and pursued different policies.

During the first period, the fundamental structural divide in Ghana's polity was between a core, long-standing elite of Akan chiefs and cocoa farmers, especially in Ashanti, and everyone else. The inner circle in historical terms, although not necessarily in terms of relative contemporary political power, comprised the Akan polity.[1] The outer circle of Ghanaian politics comprised multiple other actors—geographically on the periphery of the Akan cocoa heartlands, but potentially politically decisive. These include the North, as well as the Ewe and other communities in the Volta Region, Ghana's less-developed labor reserves, which supplied migrant workers to cocoa farms and the southern cities.

By the 1940s, Akan society had become differentiated as a result of complex social, economic, and ethnic stratification.[2] Cocoa production intensified internal social divisions, creating a new class of prosperous peasants with links to the global economy, while bolstering the power of the royal families and Native Authorities. Profits from cocoa created a Western-educated elite who in the 1940s emerged as leaders of the United Gold Coast Convention (UGCC). They saw themselves as leaders of the nationalist movement and the soon-to-be independent state. Profits also attracted migrant labor from the northern savannah to the cocoa areas, further differentiating the rainforest Akan communities. The early advent of commercial agriculture at the end of the 19th century in part explains why class identities in rural Ghana are stronger than in most of Africa, but more significant is the survival of the power of the chiefs and Native Authorities over land.

The second period of Ghanaian political and economic history (1951–81) saw the collapse of elite dominance, the growing polarization in Akan societies, the emergence and triumph of the populist Convention People's Party (CPP), and a series of governments alternating between military and civilian rule. By the late 1940s, the Akan societies had become deeply polarized over land, cocoa profits, the rights of migrant laborers, and the frustrations of emerging elementary school departers. These cleavages, representing aristocrat-commoner, indigenous-migrant, and elite-mass divisions within the societies, tended to be reinforcing. As a result, the Akan elites lost control of political affairs.

From the beginning, Nkrumah sought to increase pressure on the colonial state and create a radical mass party, appealing to Accra's underemployed, peasant farmers and the so-called verandah boys with limited education. In 1949, he launched the CPP, taking with him the UGCC youth-wing and trade unionists.[3] Nkrumah's CPP was able to mobilize poorer and less-privileged Akan—and some non-Akan groups—into an effective political coalition to win the 1951, 1954, 1956, and 1960 national elections, which in the rainforest south transcended ethnic and regional factors. The CPP's victory transformed Ghanaian politics and handed power to a new kind of politician from modest social backgrounds and without ties to the Akan royal families or traditional elite. Relatively few had university education; some were active in the trade union movement; and others had been village schoolteachers. They were much closer in background to commoner and migrant smallholders in the cocoa belt, to the unemployed war veterans, and to the urban masses than were the elite gentlemen of the UGCC.

Demands for the rents generated by cocoa-growing smallholders and the pace of modernization were intensified under the new African-controlled state. The CPP government had an ambitious development agenda and was even more willing to intrude into peasant agriculture than was the colonial state. One of the new government's first acts in May 1951 placed statutory bodies, including the Cocoa Marketing Board, more fully under state control. The three producer representatives on the board were no longer to be selected by producers' organizations, but instead were selected by the governor. In 1954, the government announced that it planned to freeze cocoa payments at 134 pounds (£) per ton for the next four years even though the international price was now over £500, further alienating the Ashanti with its seizure of so-called cocoa rents.

The CPP remained dominant until 1966. Opposition parties made fitful, largely ineffective efforts to regroup, but remained part of the formal political landscape, at least until 1964, when Kwame Nkrumah was declared "President for Life." But the populist policies that he adopted—largely funded by cocoa rents—resulted in growing economic chaos. Nkrumah was overthrown by a military coup in 1966. This ushered in a period of alternation between military and civilian rule as a series of governments were overwhelmed by the economic problems facing the nation. These governments maintained the control-oriented economy created in the late colonial era and strengthened by the Nkrumah government. The rival factions were locked in battle, not to control the government's policies, but to control jobs, contracts, and corruption. Their rent-seeking as well as the structural impediments of the economy became increasingly apparent.

Cocoa prices in the mid-1970s had reached new highs, but the regime still used the Cocoa Marketing Board as a form of taxation and refused to increase prices to producers. By 1978, there were huge balances of payment and budgetary deficits and acute shortages of foreign exchange. Consumer goods and industrial and agricultural inputs were in short supply. The inflation rate was pushing 100 percent, and the purchasing power of workers' wages had fallen to one-quarter of what it had been in 1972 (see Boahen 1989, 8–16; Jeffries 1989, 76–81). Only a privileged few profited from the system of control rents, but for the fortunate few with the right contacts, cedi fortunes could be made by acquiring import licenses or foreign exchange to buy commodities at the official rate and sell them on the black market.[4]

At the beginning of the third period of Ghanaian political and economic history (1981–present), the Ghanaian economy reached rockbottom. In 1981, Flight Lieutenant Jerry Rawlings came to power in a military coup. His response to this economic crisis marks the beginning of a stable rule of the game with regard to cocoa rents specifically and economic management more broadly. His April 1983 budget announced a series of fundamental reforms, including a 65 percent increase in cocoa producer prices, a doubling of retail gasoline costs, and a major cut in the government's budget deficit. A process of gradual devaluation commenced through a system of export bonuses and import surcharges, which amounted to a devaluation of 990 percent. In October 1983, a further devaluation was announced, thus making a total devaluation of 1,500 percent. Market liberalization and exchange rate devaluation shifted terms of trade in favor of agriculture, and cocoa growers in particular (see Jeffries 1991, 164; see also Herbst 1993, 38–94).

The Economic Recovery Program (ERP), which required accepting the conditionalities of the international financial institutions and their structural adjustment program (SAP), was politically difficult and socially painful, threatening the cohesion of Ghanaian society.[5] Rawlings' Ewe ethnic bailiwick was too small and economically and socially peripheral to hold the state together without the benefit of control rents.[6] The middle classes, both business people and members of the professions, who had been alienated by the regime's actions in 1981–83, remained hostile. The ERP and SAP hit particularly hard at the urban population, alienating both urban workers and their trade unions as well as the urban poor who depended on the informal sector to survive. The farmers, who were the main beneficiaries of the depreciation of the cedi and the dismantling of the marketing boards, by contrast, lived far from Accra, were both geographically and institutionally dispersed, and could provide little practical backing to the regime during the years of crisis. Few people, however, dared to criticize the regime with its reputation for autocracy. Rawlings's party was "suspended in mid-air," lacking any institutional roots (Jeffries 1991, 165; see also Ninsin 1991, 54–63). To legitimize his rule, Rawlings was persuaded that there was no alternative but to hold elections in 1992.

Problem-Driven Political Economy Analysis • http://dx.doi.org/10.1596/978-1-4648-0121-1

Since 1992, elections have been hotly contested, and there are large groups of potentially nonaligned voters spread throughout the country. Patronage politics and rent distribution still remain a part of the political and economic order, now with the direct aim of purchasing electoral support. As will be described in more detail, in the run up to recent elections (in 2000 and 2008), successive Ghanaian governments have found it difficult to refrain from opening the spigot of public spending in the 18–24 months before an election. Short-term gains in consumer confidence and employment are necessary to secure reelection, and the ruling party's allies in the business community demand a last tranche of government contracts before their party risks losing power. Peaceful changes in the governing party have taken place in 2000 (NDC to NPP) and 2009 (NPP to NDC). After elections, state employment has seen high turnover. Prior to the 2000 election, for example, key figures in the civil service, the military, and the business world had enjoyed nearly two decades of privilege access to the government's coffers and to rents. In the wake of John Kufour's victory, these were stripped away and handed over to a new set of individuals aligned with the NPP.

In sum, the structure of Ghanaian politics provides a relatively strong basis for programmatic politics. Political contestation has coalesced around two broad coalitions with distinctive interests and distinctive ideologies (center-left NDC and center-right NPP). Consensus among the two major parties exists on some core policy areas. It is possible that good economic policies can provide an alternative basis for politicians to win political support rather than relying on a system of discretionary rents. A developmental approach, diversifying the economy and creating new sources of wealth, provides new possible resources for consolidating political power. Further, more so than in many other African countries, these interests and ideologies cut across potentially polarizing lines, such as ethnicity and regionalism (Booth et al. 2005).

The Role of Economic Rents in Ghana

As highlighted above, contestation over access to economic rents has shaped Ghanaian politics in three distinct ways. All continue to be salient, though their relative importance has fluctuated over time.

Discretionary Government Controls

First, discretionary government controls have been a long-standing important source of rents. This rent source was especially central from the latter 1950s to the mid-1980s—with a combination of overvalued exchange rates and price controls creating enormous opportunities for arbitrage in both currency and goods markets through "black marketeering." The public rationale for these control rents was to protect urban consumers, but the rents also undermined the incentives for rural producers.

Liberalizing reforms in the 1980s, described above, largely ended these sources of rents. Nevertheless, even in the contemporary period, echoes of these earlier discretionary control rents are evident in two other areas: decision making surrounding privatization and private foreign investment (most recently in the contentious 70 percent sale of Ghana Telecom's landlines to Vodafone), and narcotics rents (illegal cocaine and heroin transshipments since 2000 have grown to an estimated 3–5 percent of gross national product). President John Atta Mills (a member of NDC who held office from 2009 to 2012) has drawn attention to the corrosive effects of drug money on key state institutions, and recent prosecutions suggest that it is becoming a new source of political funding and rents (Price 1984).

Discretionary Public Expenditure

Second, public expenditures continue to be a key source of discretionary rent allocation. Both main political parties have used public spending in a variety of ways to build support, including by providing patronage in the form of public employment and by financing discretionary public procurement. Both parties have organized around these rents, both vertically by providing jobs and horizontally through the issuing of contracts and via high-level appointments. Both parties, consequently, have some incentive to maintain this rent-based mechanism for orchestrating political support.

The importance of access to rents for winning the presidency, even today, cannot be exaggerated. The 1992 Constitution of the Fourth Republic was carefully structured to preserve the interests of then-Chairman Rawlings of the Provisional National Defense Council. The powers of the presidency penetrate to all levels of the administration down to the villages, while the system of legislative scrutiny remains extremely weak. The president directly appoints some 4,050 individuals, including the executive officers of the 110 District Assemblies and 30 percent of the members of nonpartisan local government institutions. Most of the revenue for these local governments, amounting to 7 percent of central government spending, flows from central coffers. Presidential patronage is used to fill these positions with party loyalists and to award contracts and official positions at all levels of the civil service, from senior presidential advisers down to local assistant postmasters, as well as in the state enterprises.

The oil sector in Ghana is an emerging new source of rents and will likely be decisive in the future (see Cook 2010). Expectations of oil revenue are already spurring a growth in public spending (see Breisinger et al. 2009; Cook 2010). Parliament has just approved a large public sector wage increase. Members of the National Assembly had already awarded themselves a 17 percent salary increase in October 2010, retroactive to 2008. Parliament has debated government plans to go ahead with a US$1.12 billion loan from a little-known consortium, and a US$10 billion deal with the government of the Republic of Korea and the STX Group to construct housing. The government has also agreed to a US$15 billion package of loans from Chinese enterprises. Foreign debt borrowing has risen, just as the International Monetary Fund (IMF) has lowered its forecast of future oil earnings. All of this is eerily reminiscent of Kwame Nkrumah and the CPP. It suggests that little has changed in the political system; oil rather than cocoa is now seen as the motor of transformational development.

Changes in the governing party, for example, those that took place in January 2000 with the inauguration of President Kufour and in January 2009 with the inauguration of President Atta Mills, witness a major shift in jobs at all levels. State contracts are awarded to rival consortia of party-aligned businesses, and both parties when in office have permitted a preelection spending boom to bribe voters and to provide last-minute contracts to loyal associates in the business community. The NPP government in 2001 and the NDC government since 2009 faced serious economic problems, requiring assistance from the IMF and stringent fiscal cuts to rectify the economic damage. Party activists also expect that the incoming government will investigate deals negotiated by their rivals and will bring court cases to embarrass and perhaps convict senior officials of the former government, creating a cycle of legal cases that undermine the impartiality of the judiciary. Most Ghanaians, however, continue to have faith in the judicial process, a faith that is bolstered by the fact that both the NDC and the NPP in opposition have complained that the judiciary is biased in favor of the government.

Cocoa Rents

Finally, there has been a long-standing zero-sum conflict over cocoa rents between the elites of the cocoa regions and others, though the relative importance of this conflict has diminished since 1983—and will perhaps continue to diminish as oil rents come online. This conflict has played out in three interrelated domains: (a) over the distribution of cocoa rents (to farmers; to the central state as taxes to finance public spending and development); (b) within the marketing board (for stabilization funds to finance research, the introduction of new cocoa varieties, and the provision of services to farmers); and (c) over the setting of exchange rates, and whether rates should be pro-export—thereby providing an incentive to cocoa farmers to produce more—or overvalued in order to subsidize imports and maintain urban living standards and political stability.

As described above, during the 1980s, the Rawlings regime put in place a balanced mix of policies—devaluation, market liberalization, modified state controls over cocoa marketing, and a transparent revenue-sharing formula (in 2011, 70 percent of the net free on board export price went to farmers) for sharing rents between cocoa famers and the government. Since then, contestation over cocoa rents has been less polarizing than in the previous 35 years. Stable rules of the game vis-à-vis the cocoa sector have been a key underpinning of the political peace of the past quarter century. Though strident voices and policy prescriptions continue to be heard at both the urban populist and the pro-cocoa-farmer ends of the spectrum, the mainstream political discourse has been between less-polarizing center-left (NDC) and center-right (NPP) options. Two underlying reasons for the depoliticization of cocoa sector policy can be identified. First, Chairman Rawlings' reputation as a pro-poor reformer convinced elements of the urban poor to back the reforms even during the difficult mid-1980s, when their adverse effects hit the urban population and the benefits of increased rural production and prosperity had yet to become apparent (Jeffries 1989). Second, the importance of the cocoa sector to Ghana's economy has declined with the growth of manufacturing, services, and mining, especially gold (as production increased after 2004) and now potentially oil (with the discovery of significant reserves in 2007).

In sum, from the 1950s into the 1980s, conflicts over rents had disastrous economic and political consequences. Subsequently, though, these conflicts have become more muted; there has been some convergence over a few core areas, most notably the need not "to kill the goose that lays the golden egg"—that is, the cocoa sector and now presumably oil—and not to push ethnic rivalries to extremes. The central reason is that both the conservative market-orientated elite and the populist socialist elite have mixed motives vis-à-vis rent maintenance. On the one hand, access to patronage resources is part of the allure of power. On the other hand, Ghana's history reveals that pushing too hard can be destabilizing, and both coalitions share an interest in maintaining stability by not straying too far from the center. Or, to put it differently, there exists a continuing tension for each group between the attraction of pushing its sectional interests and the risk of creating instability, which might result in the coalition losing power as a result of overreaching. The power of urban Ghana, moreover, means that both groups have been extremely cautious about introducing reforms that would engender urban opposition.

As a result, both the NDC and the NPP have reached consensus on some key policies: the peasantry must be encouraged, nontraditional crops must be promoted, development must be brought to the North, and investment on infrastructure should be prioritized. But neither party is capable of abandoning clientelism, which remains the way that both groups of party leaders interact with their followers and the wider electorate. Kwame Nkrumah recognized this in 1949, when he told his supporters, "Seek ye first the political kingdom, and all will be added unto it."

Propitious Environment for Inclusive Commercial Agriculture?

With regard to the prospects for inclusive commercial agriculture in Ghana, one important question exists: what will be the balance of Ghana's contemporary and future political economy between the clientelistic allocation of rents and the programmatic efforts to pursue win-win development initiatives? Almost every economic policy decision can usefully be interpreted through the lens of a choice between a discretionary rent distribution route and a development-enhancing, quasi-rent creation route.[7] The outcome is uncertain, but there are some grounds for optimism that the latter can play a quite dominant role with regard to agriculture. Two key questions arise. First, what are the political untouchables that are beyond reform—that is, what are the key elements of Ghana's political economy that need to be preserved, with no more than incremental efforts at reform? Second, what are the clear potential development win-wins or opportunities?

Regarding the first question, consensus over the relationship between the cocoa industry and the state and especially over the prices that smallholders should receive, which can be termed the cocoa *equilibrium*, is best viewed as an untouchable that needs to be preserved, with no more than incremental efforts at reform. The cocoa equilibrium remains vital to agrarian politics and thus to Ghana's political economy more broadly. Remarkably, Ghana's earlier antiagricultural bias of national politics and policy has turned around decisively. The key policy shifts—eliminating the overvaluation of the currency and increasing the share of the export price going to cocoa farmers from less than one-third to more than two-thirds—have endured. A policy consensus in both of Ghana's two contemporary political parties has gradually emerged during the past 20 years with regard to agrarian development. Both parties have learned from past failures, with the NDC repudiating the state-led, mechanized farming schemes of Nkrumah's CPP and the heavily subsidized strategies of the regime of Ignatius Kutu Acheampong, while the NPP seems convinced that commercial enclave farming will not succeed.

The development of outgrowing agribusiness and of nontraditional crops seems to be a clear win-win. Both parties agree that it is important that Ghana should be more self-sustaining in food production in order to promote the country's food security; both are agreed that irrigation will open up potentially productive areas in the relatively sparsely populated Accra Plains and in the Northern Region to cultivation; both recognize that large-scale investment is required; both want to diversify Ghana's exports by developing horticulture and high-value vegetable and fruit exports to Europe; both are concerned about the problems of acquiring land and ensuring sustained labor supplies to develop and operate the schemes, given the difficulties in securing both aspects in the past; and both are responsive to the demands of the rural electorate for development in "our area" and to the demands of urban voters for more abundant, cheaper food.

This eagerness of both political parties to deliver has two further positive consequences going forward for the implementation of an agricultural development strategy. First, it reduces the risks of land-related corruption by national political elites undermining the effort. Given the importance of the rural swing vote in Ghana's highly contested electoral system, the costs would be high to either political party of being associated with corrupt practices involving commercialized agriculture.[8] Second, it should be possible to avoid holding agriculture hostage to the timing of the political cycle. To be sure, given heightened political competition, each of the two parties has a strong incentive to be perceived as the party that delivered on the promises of commercialized agriculture—and to prevent their rival from being so perceived. This raises a risk that the party out of power will continually seek pretexts for delaying action. But, again, the risks of being so perceived are high, especially in light of the seeming consensus of both parties to move forward. Meanwhile, the party out of power is well positioned to ensure that hasty, badly designed initiatives that short-circuit local rights and responsibilities do not move forward prematurely. Local actors could usefully leverage this consensus to lock in agreement to move forward, and thereby ensure that it is not held hostage to the vagaries of the political cycle.

In sum, at the national level the environment is propitious for moving forward with a growth- and productivity-oriented—and equitable—set of commercialized agriculture initiatives in Ghana. But nothing should be taken for granted. As the next section details, there is much difficult work to be done at regional and local levels. The gap is large between a positive national vision and effective follow-through on the ground. As always, the "devil is in the details."

Political Economy of Agriculture in the Accra Plains and the Northern Region

This section lays out the political and institutional challenges to commercialized agriculture—both conceptually and empirically—from the perspective of the Accra Plains and the Northern Region. The section begins by describing the experience of recent commercial investors, and then moves on to explore attitudes toward outgrower arrangements in the Accra Plains and the Northern Region. In broad terms, although the national drivers of politics are potentially aligned with the expansion of commercial agriculture, the risks at the local level are much more substantial. The section concludes by examining these sector- and local-level risks, as well as the need for credible commitment mechanisms between nucleus farms and smallholders.

Experiences with Commercial Agriculture in Ghana

Despite the enormous potential of commercial agriculture in Ghana, with the exception of cocoa, the sector has grown slowly. Looking back to the colonial era, when investment in infrastructure and agriculture focused on cocoa-growing regions, neither the Accra Plains nor the Northern Region received significant resources. The pattern changed somewhat after independence, when efforts were made in both regions to establish large-scale commercial agriculture, but with limited success. In the first decade following independence, the principal focus was on state farms, but these efforts subsequently collapsed. There was then a major push in the Northern Region to promote large-scale private agriculture, but again with only modest success. By mid-1965, the state had acquired 1,114,315 acres for state farms, of which only 114,136 acres were actually planted. Though subsequent governments made available cheap loans for putative private commercial farmers, uptake was relatively modest. Access was skewed away from smallholders, with the loans going disproportionately to urban-based residents.

Recent large-scale investments in commercial agriculture have also proved problematic. Investors lack credible assurances that they will have access to land they acquire, and communities have lost out both on job opportunities arising from new ventures and on access to land that they previously used for cultivation. The following example from the Accra Plains is particularly illustrative of these challenges.[9]

Prairie Volta is a joint venture between two U.S. entrepreneurs who own 40 percent of the equity, and the government of Ghana and the Ghana

Commercial Bank, which each has a 30 percent share. Initiated in 2008, the venture had 750 acres of rice in production by 2011 (Anderson 2011). Prairie Volta uses land that was acquired earlier by the government under a process of compulsory acquisition in the early 1970s with the intention of developing large-scale mechanized cotton cultivation. Although the land was never developed and the enterprise was abandoned, it remained under government control. Local people were permitted freely to cultivate it until commercial farming activities commenced on some of it in the late 1990s. At that time, the government leased the land to the Quality Grains rice-growing scheme, which subsequently failed. Much of the money provided to Quality Grains by the Ghanaian authorities was imprudently spent; the company collapsed in 2000, and three senior NDC government officials were sent to prison for imprudent management of state money after the NPP came to power in 2001. Equipment was abandoned for seven years.

The government leased the land (formerly leased to Quality Grains) and physical capital to Prairie Volta. When Prairie Volta took over the moribund business in 2008, local youth prevented their vehicles and machines from getting to the rice fields. Although Prairie Volta signed a land lease with the government, based on the 1970 compulsory purchase order, the lease has not prevented repeated problems with the company's access and land rights, some of which continued three years after the transfer was completed. Three clan heads argued that they had never been compensated when the government initially acquired the land in the 1970s or when land rights were transferred to Quality Grains in 1998. The matter is now before the courts. Subsequent attempts to make restitution have been equally compromised.

Development is continuing, but Prairie Volta finds it difficult to expand production or to raise additional capital. The company's initial output projections were far too optimistic, and it is facing serious cash flow problems. Banks are unwilling to make further loans until the additional land acquisition is ratified. Prairie Volta has certified that it has reached an understanding with the chiefs, clan heads, and government on the expansion, but this has not satisfied creditors. Discussions have continued with clan heads to resolve the dispute and to permit the company to clear some portions of the land for cultivation. Title deeds still have not been agreed to because urban residents who belong to the clans are refusing to approve the agreement. The police have been called in to ensure Prairie Volta's access to the land. Prairie Volta has now decided not to employ people from the local community because attempts to discipline them have serious repercussions on the company's already-precarious standing with local residents.

The example of Prairie Volta illustrates that many of the challenges faced by commercial investors revolve around their relationship to the communities in which they are located and around access to land. Ghana has not clarified and formalized property rights in land, and as a result, each attractive piece of land has multiple interested parties who can potentially veto a new commercialized agriculture initiative (either ex ante, through noncooperation, or worse, once the investment is underway). In effect, this situation means that investors lack reasonable assurances that they will be able to access and farm the land that they acquire. However, any attempt to formalize or clarify land ownership would set members of local communities against one another, leading to sociopolitical tensions (or even violence) that would be disruptive to commercial agriculture in their own right. Because it makes use of existing patterns of land ownership, an outgrower model may thus offer an inviting way forward. Though they bypass some of the risks around access to land, these arrangements also bring their own set of challenges at the local level. They need institutions that can support contract reliability and ensure a balance of bargaining power between the agribusiness hub and smallholder farmers.

Consultation with Stakeholders in the Accra Plains and the Northern Region
The Accra Plains[10]

Ghana Irrigation Development Authority officials, representatives of the District Authority, local councilors, chiefs, and church leaders in the Accra Plains were in nearly universal agreement that the area needed to attract investment and to generate jobs. They were eager to see a larger area irrigated and the current irrigation system modernized and improved to open up a larger area to year-round cultivation. They recognized that this would mean large-scale production by Ghanaian or international agribusiness ventures and considered that land could be made available. Some of the current agribusiness companies operating in the area also endorsed the plans, but they were concerned that increased commercial production would overwhelm the area's transport system and its capacity to provide labor.

Studies and interviews in the Accra Plains suggest that local community leaders are convinced that a nucleus outgrower or contract farming model would prove most attractive to the area. Land is available—after careful and transparent negotiation with all stakeholders—for commercial farming, but the density of population and smallholders is sufficiently high enough to foster the development of an outgrower model of contract farming. The local people who own the land are accustomed to producing (to some extent) for the market and are sufficiently driven by commercial factors to respond positively to the introduction of new techniques and skills by a neighboring agribusiness. They would be attracted to participate by the prospect of securing higher, more stable incomes, and especially by the training possibilities and access to processing and marketing down-market chains.

Officials of the local District Authority, District Councilors, church leaders, and chiefs all agreed that such a scheme would facilitate local agreement to the acquisition of land for a nucleus commercial farm on a lease-hold basis and would encourage members of the local community to become wage laborers on the commercial farm, while guaranteeing supplies to the agribusiness from smallholder producers. In addition, bringing new agricultural investors into the district could increase the local revenue base and secure assistance in improving local facilities, such as schools, clinics, community centers, roads, and bridges, either by grants to the District Authority or through direct work by the commercial venture. Local leaders hoped that major agribusiness investors would help lobby the government to improve drinking water supplies, to update the road network, and to bring electrification.

The Northern Region

The Northern Region's Savannah Accelerated Development Authority (SADA) was inaugurated by President Atta Mills in December 2010. The "Synopsis of Development Strategy (2010–2030)," released by SADA on October 22, 2010, seeks to achieve "a Forested North" by 2030:

> A model for the modernization of agriculture that starts from generating a market impetus as the main catalyst for stimulating farmers to produce, using a market-based out-grower system with improved technology and timely inputs. By this strategy, farmers do not wait to find markets after they have produced; rather the market defines their production targets and quality. This strategy is also mindful of food security requirements, especially in the most vulnerable areas. (SADA 2010)

The development strategy also proposed construction of a circular road network to link Upper West, Upper East, and Northern regions, to open up the area in between, which is watered by tributaries of the White Volta River, for "brisk farming and economic activities." It proposed that "the road network and network of drainage canals will be accompanied by an appropriate irrigation infrastructure, especially drip-irrigation which can be owned by smallholder farmers to facilitate cultivation of cereals, fruits and vegetables all year-round (concept of a green North)" (SADA 2010). This "pro-poor growth model" sees a sequential development of agriculture that factors into policy the fragility of the soils, the short rainy season, and the vagaries of the weather associated with climate change through a growth strategy that enables local residents "to provide for themselves" (SADA 2010).

The agenda pursued by SADA was endorsed by both main political parties before the December 2008 general election, and although President John Mahama, who comes from the North, has adopted it with great enthusiasm, there seems little doubt that an NPP government would follow the same strategy as the current NDC administration. The Institute for Policy Alternatives in Tamale, which had been working on a development strategy for the Northern Region for a number of years, lobbied assiduously before the 2008 elections to ensure that both main parties accepted this general plan. The SADA strategy has been endorsed by a number of civil society nongovernmental organizations (NGOs), including SEND-Ghana, the Integrated Social Development Center (ISODEC), and the Foundation for Grass Roots Initiatives in Africa, which have urged the government to "show more commitment to the implementation process" (*Ghana Business News* 2010). The *Ghana Business News* (2010) referred to the various attempts in the past to promote development in the northern regions, lamenting that "all these failed to make the desired impact because of mismanagement" and hoped that "SADA would not go the way of its predecessors."

Access to Land in the Northern Region and the Accra Plains

For both large- and small-scale commercial farming, an immediate task is to provide potential investors with access to land. In a mature market economy, the institutional challenge is straightforward: clear assignment of, and respect for, property rights provides the framework within which potential investors can purchase land from its recognized owners. However in Ghana, as in many other developing countries, the route for getting "from here to there" is not a direct one. National institutions alone are not strong enough to carry the weight of the necessary credible commitments. Although Ghana has among the better judicial systems in Africa (indeed among low-income countries worldwide), as explored immediately below, continuing ambiguity in the allocation of property rights in Ghana's rural areas implies that judicial enforcement is unlikely to be of much help in resolving the commitment problems associated with commercialized agriculture. The success (or otherwise) of a commercialized agriculture project in the Accra Plains and the Northern Region thus depends crucially on the performance of subnational institutions.

Partly as a result of indirect rule, during which little effort was made to restructure ambiguous property rights, and partly as a result of the regions' remoteness from the centers of power and economic dynamism, the question of securing access to land in the Accra Plains and the Northern Region is a complicated one. There are some parallels—but also some very large differences—in the socioeconomic structures that the Accra Plains and the Northern Region inherited from the precolonial period. In both regions, at the most local of local levels, there are multiple stakeholders with some claim to control over land. However, in the Northern Region—but not in the Accra Plains—there is also the overlay of a quite tightly defined traditional social hierarchy.

The Northern Region

The Northern Region's social structure has evolved over more than 600 years through complex patterns of migration and conquest, and still engenders significant tensions:

- The long-standing cultivators of the land comprise acephalous (segmentary lineage) populations; authority, such as it was, resided principally among *tengdanas* (earthpriests) who were the guardians of the land. There seem to have been no secular chiefs.
- Around about the 1500s, invading horsemen from the north (likely present-day Burkina Faso) conquered the area. They created four new centralized kingdoms, of which their descendants formed the aristocracy; each kingdom was ruled by a Paramount Chief, appointed from the aristocracy.
- The kingdoms extracted revenue from long-distance trade, but for the most part made little effort to transform the local economy. Day-to-day control and allocation of land for cultivation remained with the tengdanas.[11]

Problem-Driven Political Economy Analysis • http://dx.doi.org/10.1596/978-1-4648-0121-1

- In subsequent centuries, Christianized immigrant communities moved into the region, bringing with them their own set of chiefly leaders.

The Northern Region's complex social structure erupted into conflict in the 1990s in response to changes in land law and a perception that the value of land (and hence of controlling it) was increasing. These changes reawakened tensions between the chiefs and the local tengdanas over precisely who had the authority to allocate land: the aristocratic officials of the four kingdoms in the Northern Region or the traditional earth priests of the local communities who were the key mediators with the ancestors and local spirits. This tension remains and will complicate the process of negotiating access to land for commercial farming activities throughout the Northern Region (Gariba 1989, 232–33). The most serious of these conflicts, known as the Guinea Fowl War (January 1994–September 1995), resulted in 4,000 people killed and 150,000 displaced.

Overall, historical evidence suggests that land is part of the safety net extended to families. Cultivators in the Northern Region seem to have successfully resisted the process of peasantization[12] and incorporation into market production. The social organization of production remains fluid, drawing on immediate and extended family members (and neighbors as needed) to secure the harvest, differing from year to year because of the rains and because of the life-cycle of the smallholder and his or her household. Farm and nonfarm labor coexist uneasily, with smallholders benefiting from external cash but weighing nonfarm work against lost time cultivating. Seasonal migration continues, although less pronounced than in the colonial era and more localized, with many seeking work in nearby towns or in other parts of the Northern Region rather than migrating to the gold mines or the cocoa farms of the south. Smallholders are well attuned to their local soils and climate conditions, determining their farming strategies through the prisms of experience and local histories. They employ both extensive and intensive forms of production and have frequently been resistant to the demands of agrotechnology.

The Accra Plains

In the Accra Plains, there is also some tension between the formal chief-oriented structure and the local family and clan arrangements as to who controls land. A chief is appointed by the head of the traditional state. A clan head is the hereditary leader of a lineage and has nothing to do with traditional authority in colonial terms or the remnants of the precolonial state. In interviews conducted in the Accra Plains as part of a recent study,[13] state officials suggested that commercial investors would find it impossible to deal directly with all interested parties, including the different clan heads, and might better deal with the government and, through them, the chiefs. Such opinions reflect the desire of the state to control the process, an approach that might have difficult consequences for investors and communities. By contrast, local councilors, NGO representatives, and academics suggest that although the village chief may be the entrypoint for negotiating access to land, it is imperative also to negotiate and agree on appropriate compensation directly with clan and family heads. As highlighted by the example of Prairie Volta, outlined earlier, these ambiguities of control continue to complicate land transactions even into the present day.

The complexity of the land question in the Accra Plains can be seen from an analysis provided by officials of the North Tongu District Authority. In this district, land was under the control of individual clans or families, was not owned by the chiefs, and was not under the chiefs' control. Although a chief claimed in an interview that he controlled the land in the proposed irrigation project and could allocate it to government or to commercial interests, the district officials and councilor insisted that it was, in fact, owned by a number of individuals, most of whom belonged to a local clan. There was a clan head, sometimes called "a chief," who held political authority over the area, but each extended family head controlled the family's land. Only the clan head could lease land and had to be consulted about all land transactions, although he would take potential investors to the clan chief. The chief held political authority but had no economic control over land.

In the face of the ambiguity of property rights to land in the relevant regions, the reality is that the ambiguity cannot straightforwardly be resolved by fiat; for large-scale commercial farming investment to proceed, two interrelated institutional challenges will need to be addressed. First, given that there are multiple potential claimants on land, institutions are needed to assure investors that, once a deal is complete, no new claimants will emerge with the potential to veto the arrangement. Second, the distribution of benefits from the sale of land—both the price paid by the buyer and the division of revenues among potential claimants—will need to be viewed as fair and legitimate by all of those involved.

With regard to outgrower initiatives, one of their key advantages is that they are based largely on the existing allocation of land.[14] Consequently, such a scheme can circumvent some of the challenges associated with unclear or informal land use and ownership rights. However, outgrower schemes potentially confront their own set of hold-up problems that can be addressed only through appropriate local institutions.

Challenges with Outgrower Schemes

For any farming done to produce for a market, smallholders need access to inputs at the start of the growing season, but will earn revenue to pay for them only once the crops are sold. In principle, there are two seemingly straightforward methods to address this challenge, but neither is workable in contemporary Ghana. In the first method, well-developed input markets (including credit and crop insurance markets) could enable the input transactions to proceed independently of crop sales. However, as is now thoroughly understood, these markets are endemically weak in low-income countries, with smallholder farmers in particular lacking access to them. In the second method, public sector agricultural extension, financing, and input marketing arrangements could potentially fill the gap. However, with rare exceptions, public provision of agricultural input and marketing services to smallholder farmers has failed the world over, and outside of cocoa,

Ghana does not have a track record of successful provision of such services. Thus, these public sector solutions have been discarded as unsuccessful.

A nucleus-outgrower arrangement seemingly offers a third institutional method: the nucleus farmer supplies inputs and extension support, in return for which small farmers grow the crop and then resell to the nucleus farmer. This method is especially attractive because it can connect a well-capitalized nucleus with extensive marketing skills and knowledge of European supermarket requirements with the production capacity of smallholders (see Kleeman 2011; see also Nankani 2009). But this option, too, brings with it the following inter-related institutional challenges:

- Given that outgrowing transactions are separated in time, institutional arrangements will be needed to mitigate the risk of side-selling, that is, smallholders take inputs from the nucleus, but then (in return for better terms) renege on their agreement and sell for better terms to an alternative outgrower (or independent trader). (Note that in many low-income settings, likely including Ghana, there is no credible likelihood of assuming this problem away by simply asserting the sanctity of contract as enforced by the judiciary.)

- Agreement will be needed at the outset of each season's outgrowing transaction as to what price will be paid by the nucleus farmer to smallholder farmers. The agreement also will need to be sustained across the lifetime of each season's outgrowing transaction, even though market conditions may have changed between the time of the initial agreement and the moment of sale. This is a pure zero-sum conflict (if one presumes, of course, that the investments have been made in the first place).

In principle, a nucleus-outgrower arrangement has the advantage of continuous physical proximity between the nucleus commercial farm and the smallholder outgrowers. This is in contrast to other models in which a trader provides funding for seeds and then returns at the time of harvest to pick up the produce. The nucleus-outgrower arrangement might increase the ability of each party to monitor the other. However, there is still ample scope for tension and disputes over prices and the distribution of risks.

Overall Implications: Options for Institutional Evolution Needed to Develop Commercial Agriculture

This section suggests some implications of the analysis presented in previous sections. It concludes that some first-best policy options are not immediately available in the Ghanaian context, and so this section charts a path forward based on several feasible second-best options.

As discussed previously, at the national level, it is possible to be optimistic about the prospects of outgrower initiatives in the Northern Region and the Accra Plains. There is agreement by both national political parties about the importance of agriculture. In general, the rules of the game, by which no party pursues rent distribution to such a degree as to drive important sectors into crisis, bodes well for agriculture. Also, given the increasingly competitive nature of Ghanaian politics, politicians may be responsive (whether on a programmatic or a clientelist basis) to demands for development in these areas. When one turns to the local level, for all of the seeming enthusiasm among the population and leadership in both the Accra Plains and the Northern Region for agricultural investment in general, and nucleus-outgrower schemes in particular, the evidence discussed in the previous section suggests that formidable institutional challenges lie ahead if these optimistic visions are to be transformed into thriving, sustainable, commercialized agriculture.

Exploring these challenges further, one notes the parallels and interdependencies among the institutional risks associated with both access to land and outgrower arrangements: for each of them, institutions will be needed that can deliver both *enforceability* and *legitimacy*. Enforceability is key to giving the first movers to the relevant transaction (that is, investors—in land or in the provision of inputs to small farmers) assurance that the rights and commitments associated with the initial transaction will be honored. Legitimacy is key to ensuring that the second mover stakeholders (that is, stakeholders who surrender rights to land or who receive inputs on credit in return for delivering crops) fully acknowledge and accept the fairness of the relevant transaction—and their associated obligations to act (that is, by providing crops)—or refrain from acting (that is, from using the land provided to the investor or seeking a new round of compensation ex post). Said differently, successful investment in commercialized agriculture—large-scale or outgrower—creates quasi-rents, or development-enhancing investments that yield social and private benefits in excess of the up-front cost. The dilemma is how to share them. Unless there are clear and credible arrangements in place to achieve this, either the investment will not happen or it will end badly.

To move forward, institutions will be needed that can address the twin challenges of legitimacy and enforceability. Given the marginalization of the two regions from Ghana's heartland, even less than in other parts of the country, central- and national-level institutions have decisively superseded preexisting arrangements. Yet, local-level institutions in both the Northern Region and the Accra Plains are characterized by a combination of complexity and ambiguity. The task, then, is one of institutional innovation: to draw on the institutional assets that are available to construct arrangements capable of meeting the challenges of legitimacy and enforceability. The available assets will be a combination of national- and local-level resources, with the latter being different in the Accra Plains and the Northern Region. Broadly speaking, the options can be unbundled into two categories: (a) hierarchical or participatory and (b) formal or informal.

Access to Land

Consider first the potential role of formal state institutions. Here, there are two constraints. The first constraint is that, even if rule-of-law institutions were unequivocally strong, the ambiguities as to how property rights are vested imply that recourse to formal law is likely to complicate rather than simplify the process. As the example of Prairie Volta demonstrates, the existence of multiple claimants on a single tract of land can slow down the legal process considerably, and in the meantime, lenders can be unwilling to extend credit while investors' right to the land is in question.

The second constraint concerns the legacy of prior state action in Ghanaian agriculture. Again, the Prairie Volta case is salient. Some clan heads and urban residents claim they were not properly compensated when the state acquired the land in the 1970s. This circumstance has made it difficult for Prairie Volta to settle its court case and build a positive relationship with the community. Given difficult prior experiences (in the Accra Plains and the Northern Region, as well as elsewhere in Ghana) with nationalization of the land by exercising the state's right of eminent domain, direct action by government to acquire land is likely to alienate the local communities and create major problems in the future, thus leading to conflict over land access and reluctance to provide labor. Such action would not be helpful as the way forward.

Now consider the role of informal social hierarchies. There is, indeed, a strong hierarchical overlay in the Northern Region (though not in the Accra Plains). Even so, although gaining access to land for commercial farming in the relatively lightly populated Northern Region is far from impossible, the process is not straightforward. As described earlier, land allocation is not simply the responsibility of the traditional chiefs, although they have an important role to play, but is part of a complex matrix of responsibilities.

Thus, while clarifying and formalizing property rights in land and making it possible to rely on formal state institutions alone would be a first-best option, it is not feasible in the short run in the Ghanaian context. Instead, the key operational recommendation of this analysis is, in the nearterm, that the principal focus of efforts to build institutions capable of supporting commercialized agriculture should be on semiformal, participatory and inclusive approaches, involving multiple stakeholders. These semiformal approaches generally will be investment specific. They will place significant demands on government, the putative investor, and the local stakeholders involved in the relevant transaction.

Arrangements between Communities and Investors

For any land transactions, including the acquisition of property for nucleus farm hubs, a focus on participatory and inclusive options is key vis-à-vis both the process and the content of agreements:

- *Process:* Due diligence and fully transparent negotiations by the commercial investor with all of the local stakeholders involved will be key to ensuring that the land is acquired with the full agreement of the local communities, and hence that the land transaction is credible. Investors should maintain close relations with the local communities and practice good corporate citizenship, but not become too identified with particular chiefs, clan heads, or, indeed, political parties and factions. Relations with all levels of authority should be transparent, and the local communities should be fully consulted and their approval secured at each step of the process.

- *Content:* A structured, transparent set of payments and compensation to the local community and smallholder cultivators who were working the land would be essential. Investors will need to be proactive in ensuring that the process is transparent and that all stakeholders—including those who actually cultivated the land as well as the clan and family heads who were the putative landowners—have been fully compensated and so, hopefully, have a vested interest in the success of the enterprise. Members of the local community should also be given the first option to employment on commercial farms.

For outgrower schemes, aggregator arrangements provide a potentially attractive institutional arrangement for the near term.[15] They have the potential to do the following:

- Build high-trust relationships with farmers;
- Add value directly, by doing bagging, transporting, marketing, and so on;
- Enhance the transparency in transactions, by providing clear information systematically to all farmers on, for example, pricing (information that farmers themselves can corroborate via cell phone access to international market prices); and
- Use peer-group pressure as a means of holding farmers who do not abide by agreements to account.

Finally, on both land acquisition and outgrower arrangements, the national and subnational governments can potentially play a key monitoring and facilitation role, supporting and strengthening the two semiformal, multistakeholder approaches described above. The government can assist in reaching and sustaining agreements between commercial investors and local farmers, reassuring smallholders as to the desirability of the schemes and explaining how their interests are protected. It can help ensure that agribusiness ventures play fair and meet their contractual obligations, delivering the inputs and downstream services at fair prices to the local cultivators. Specific tasks the government could undertake in support of semiformal approaches include the following:

- Monitoring and regulating negotiations between investors and local actors;
- Providing information to the local communities on commercialized agricultural transactions, their benefits, and risks;
- More broadly, helping establish an informational clearinghouse through which participants can learn about the reliability (or otherwise) of both nucleus and smallholder participants in outgrower arrangements;
- Devising model contracts; and

- Providing brokerage underwriting of the community's business involvement, thereby leveling the negotiating playing field between agribusiness investors and local smallholders, and ensuring that the lease agreements reflect its strategic land use perspectives.

Smallholders (especially in the Northern Region) will need careful guidance as they attempt to craft the production contracts, which they will be expected to fulfill. Most have little understanding of what the contracts will require and have virtually no access to legal or commercial information. This role could potentially be filled by government, but also by civil society organizations or advocacy agencies.

Regional Differences

How best to implement these recommendations will vary somewhat for the Northern Region and the Accra Plains. In the Northern Region, despite the seeming straightforwardness of the prevailing hierarchies, careful consideration will need to be given to the rights of all stakeholders in the land, including the chiefs, the traditional tengdanas (or earthpriests), the clan heads of the lineage networks that currently cultivate the land, and the actual cultivators themselves. In addition, Fulani cattle herders follow a pattern of seasonal migration across large parts of the Northern Region and must be explicitly included in any system of compensation, or they will be overlooked as outsiders; they have the capacity to cause significant financial damage if they permit their herds to wander through cultivated crops. More broadly, the local population in the Northern Region has been less integrated into the market—in terms of producing for the market and working as wage laborers—than have smallholders on the Accra Plains. This situation has some key implications:

- Commercial agribusiness will face greater constraints in educating local producers to satisfy the quality standards demanded by many retailers and in inculcating new farming methods.
- Obstacles also exist in transporting produce from the farming sites to the main shipment centers to market. Many of the potential irrigation sites are isolated, and road communications are poor, especially in the rainy season.
- Participants in commercialized agricultural initiatives are likely to be the bigger local landholders, less concerned than their poorer neighbors about growing sufficient food to meet their own household requirements. Poorer farmers may lose out, becoming wage laborers on the plots of their more prosperous neighbors. Given the complex ethnic divisions in the Northern Region and the all-too-many examples over the past 30 years of links between commercialization of land and ethnic violence, this may have serious repercussions.

Land rights also are dispersed in the Accra Plains, so, at the surface, land and contracting problems appear as intense there as in the North. But the Accra Plains is much closer to Ghana's economic heartland than the north; so, although complicated, the process of land acquisition for commercial farming activities is well established. The local administration, the chiefs, and the local people are fairly accustomed to the idea. Local people have developed a sophisticated conception of the kind of compensation they want. Outright, single payments to the chiefs, as were customary in the past, are no longer deemed appropriate. Although local chiefs insist that only they have the authority to lease land, they acknowledged that the structure of payments agreed to in the past had created dissension and would not be accepted by other stakeholders today, that is, the smallholder cultivators actually working the land to be leased. Chiefs were determined to protect their authority over land, but were willing to accede to popular pressures for a diffusion of payments.

The recommendations presented in this section chart a feasible path forward for commercial agriculture in the near term. However, investment-specific, ad hoc arrangements can carry the process of agricultural commercialization only so far. Such a process is cumbersome and is vulnerable to breakdowns—both idiosyncratic, investment-specific breakdowns that would nonetheless risk damaging the reputation of the endeavor as a whole and breakdowns that result from the inevitable incompleteness of informal arrangements that depend heavily on a combination of trust and hope. A longer-term strategy should consider how best to expand the reform space and increase the possibility of achieving first-best policies, focusing on building sustainable institutions for the sector. These institutions might include farmers associations to provide a platform for equalization of bargaining power between an agribusiness nucleus and smallholder outgrowers, sustainable monitoring and facilitation capabilities by the government, and clarified formal rules around property rights.

Implications and Impact on the World Bank's Operational Engagements

The political economy analysis described in the preceding sections shaped World Bank engagement with the government of Ghana and had a direct impact on Bank operations surrounding commercial agriculture. The country- and sector-level political economy analysis was part of a three-pronged approach aimed at improving the effectiveness of the Bank in Ghana through better consideration of governance and political economy considerations. The three-year program was funded almost entirely by the Global Partnership Facility Trust Fund.

The country-level analysis provided context for recent political and economic developments. This was especially critical for CMU management, which was relatively new to Ghana at the time. The sector analysis identified at what level and with which groups risks to engagement were highest, which was also important to CMU management. As discussed in the introduction, there were concerns about moving ahead on commercial agriculture given the regional context of investors and political elite capturing key benefits. If operations went poorly, engagement in agriculture might involve a major reputational risk for the Bank.

Problem-Driven Political Economy Analysis • http://dx.doi.org/10.1596/978-1-4648-0121-1

Because of its optimism toward national-level drivers of decision making in Ghana and its recommendations for building support at the local level, the political economy analysis helped address some of the concerns within the CMU about whether the Bank should become involved in a potentially controversial sector.

For the sector team, the analysis was influential during the design and preparation phase of a US$100 million loan to Ghana for a commercial agriculture. Because it was a comprehensive and complicated operation, the team engaged a number of experts, including those from the social development, water and irrigation, environmental protection, and political economy practices. The orientation of the team toward accepting advice from outside of its technical specialization facilitated the integration of political economy recommendations into the project. For the sector staff, the political economy study was seen as an opportunity for more rigorous analysis of its assumptions about whether commercial agriculture could be made feasible at the local level. Though staff members informally tracked the political dynamics of the sector quite regularly, they felt it was important to formalize this process and subject their assumptions to critique. The analysis largely corroborated the team's knowledge of the agricultural sector and validated the basic concept for the project, which was to build on existing patterns of land ownership by supporting outgrower arrangements where possible. Key findings were also presented to government and local NGOs during a two-day workshop. This was especially helpful for building consensus among stakeholders about a project for which there was much enthusiasm and many ideas about how to move forward.

Through the loan proposed by the sector team and approved by the World Bank's Board of Directors, the CMU seeks to support and enable progress in developing commercial agriculture in a socially inclusive and sustainable way. As the Project Assessment Document (PAD) describes, the sector analysis provided "guidance [to the CMU] as to the conditions under which [investments in commercial agriculture, especially outgrower arrangements,] would be consistent with wider Ghanaian social norms and in particular, would be acceptable to communities" (World Bank 2012, 13). Though the PAD and the recommendations of the analysis are structured in slightly different ways, key recommendations from the political economy analysis were incorporated into the loan. For example, on land transactions, communities will receive support to determine whether and how they wish to engage in commercial agriculture, facilitated by local civil society organizations. They will receive guidance on

> the preparation of a community platform with which investors could engage, adoption of community participation in decision-making, and requiring investors to adopt a community-level publish what you pay approach. Where necessary—for example in the case of emerging investors—support will be provided to investors on engagement with communities including corporate social and environmental responsibility. (World Bank 2012, 25)

Regarding the content of agreements around the acquisition of land and the development of outgrower arrangements, the PAD proposes

> carefully screening potential investment locations, deploying relevant safeguards instruments and providing support for land use right inventory, participatory planning, enhanced consultation, strengthened negotiation capacity and contract design. (World Bank 2012, 19)

Finally, the political economy analysis identified a number of first-best policy options for supporting the larger institutional environment for commercial agriculture. Although it suggested that these could not be relied on or achieved in the short run, they would be important for sustaining successes. Building on the recommendations of the study, the loan incorporates these institutional changes as *long-run* goals. They include, "clarifying who holds allocative authority over land targeted for investment," "identifying the full range of rights and uses affecting land," "transparency in land governance processes," "clarifying the status of land previously acquired by the state," and "ensuring meaningful negotiations between communities and investors leading to clear and enforceable contracts" (World Bank 2012, 112).

As of May 2013, the project is in the early phases of implementation. Though it is still too early to assess the impact of the political economy recommendations on project outcomes, it is clear that the analysis shaped CMU management thinking around the desirability of intervening in commercial agriculture, the Bank's engagement with key partners, and the sector team's strategic design of the recent US$100 million loan.

Notes

1. The Akan formed (and continue to form) roughly 49 percent of Ghana's population.
2. For the best account of precolonial Ashanti, see Wilks (1975). See also Boahen (1966, 212–22).
3. See Rooney (1988, 29–59), which remains the best modern biography. A good, brief biography is Birmingham (1990, 8–36), which covers the same period.
4. The best account of Ghana's economic failure remains Rimmer (1992) and of Ghana's recovery, Herbst (1993).
5. See Jeffries (1991, 164–70). For a critical view by future NPP Minister, Mike Oquaye, see Oquaye (2004). This 600-page account is uniformly hostile to Rawlings and his government's policies. See also Opoku (2010).
6. Control rents are created through discretionary government controls that can be used to allocate benefits to individuals or groups; these can be used for political or private gain.
7. In economic terms, a rent is a return that an asset receives that is in excess of its opportunity cost or, more intuitively, its cost of production (for example, natural resource rents; rents that accrue to entertainers or sports players). If rents were reduced, but returns were still above the opportunity cost or cost of production, then the asset

would still be supplied in the same quantity. A quasi-rent has those characteristics—but only over the shorter term. For example, if one has made a large fixed investment, returns on the investment could be partially expropriated with no effect on supply in the short term (but with damage to the prospect of reinvestment).

8. Although the Accra Plains and the Northern Region are not swing areas, they do contain important swing voters. The Northern Region especially is becoming increasingly politically competitive, and the NPP's strategy in 2008 and 2012 was to build on their success in those regions.

9. Similar experiences have characterized investments in the Northern Region: Bio Fuel Norway's attempt to cultivate 38,000 hectares for production of jatropha around the village of Alipe in Kuswagu, Central Gonja District, about 20 miles from Tamale, provoked widespread opposition as the forest was cut down, destroying people's income from forest products such as shea nuts, and endangering local rainfall (Nyari 2008).

10. This section is largely based on interviews conducted by David Throup in March 2011.

11. The earthpriests still exist and act as intermediaries between the living, the dead, and those still to be born. They are the key religious leaders of the indigenous population, a sizable portion of whom have not been converted to Islam or Christianity.

12. The transition from subsistence farming to partial production for the market to commercial farming.

13. Based on interviews conducted by David Throup in March 2011.

14. In the case of nucleus-outgrower arrangements, the investors would only need to acquire and maintain access to a small tract of land. In the case of contract farming, the investor would acquire no land at all.

15. The Institute for Policy Alternatives in Tamale, in the Northern Region, offers one example of what such an organizational arrangement might look like.

Bibliography

Anderson, Everett. 2011. "Rice Farming in Ghana: What's Wrong, Can It Be Fixed?" Public Private Partnership Presentation, World Bank, Washington, DC, March 1–2.

Birmingham, David. 1990. *Kwame Nkrumah*. London, U.K.: Sphere Books.

Boahen, A. Adu. 1966. "A New Look at the History of Ghana." *African Affairs* 65 (260): 212–22.

———. 1989. *The Ghanaian Sphinx: Reflections on the Contemporary History of Ghana, 1972–1987*. Accra: Sankofa Educational Publishers.

Booth, David, Richard Crook, E. Gyimah-Boadi, Tony Killick, and Robin Luckham, with Nana Boateng. 2005. "What Are the Drivers of Change in Ghana?" CDD/ODI Policy Brief 1, Ghana Center for Democratic Development, Accra, and Overseas Development Institute, London.

Breisinger, Clemens, Xinshen Diao, Rainer Schweickert, and Manfred Wiebelt. 2009. "Managing Future Oil Revenues in Ghana—An Assessment of Alternative Allocation Options." Kiel Working Paper 1518, Kiel Institute for the World Economy, Kiel, Germany.

Cook, Nicolas. 2010. *Ghana, an Emergent Oil Producer: Background and U.S. Relations*. Congressional Research Service, Washington, DC.

Cotula, Lorenzo, Sonja Vermeulen, Rebeca Leonard, and James Keeley. 2009. *Land Grab or Development Opportunity? Agricultural Investment and International Land Deals in Africa.* Rome: Food and Agriculture Organization of the United Nations; London: International Institute for Environment and Development; Rome: International Fund for Agricultural Development.

Deininger, Klaus, and Derek Byerlee, with Jonathan Lindsay, Andrew Norton, Harris Selod, and Mercedes Stickler. 2011. *Rising Global Interest in Farmland: Can It Yield Sustainable and Equitable Benefits?* Washington, DC: World Bank.

Gariba, Sulley. 1989. "The Peasantry and the State in Ghana: The Political Economy of Agrarian Stagnation and Rural Development in Northern Ghana." PhD thesis, Carleton University, Ottawa.

Ghana Business News. 2010. "SADA—Urgent Need for Sustainable Funding." September 29. http://www.ghanabusinessnews.com/2010/09/28/sada-urgent.

Herbst, Jeffrey. 1993. *The Politics of Reform in Ghana, 1982–1991.* Berkeley, CA: University of California Press.

Jeffries, Richard. 1989. "Ghana: The Political Economy of Personal Rule." In *Contemporary West African States*, edited by Donal B. Cruise O'Brien, John Dunn, and Richard Rathbone, 75–98. Cambridge, U.K.: Cambridge University Press.

———. 1991. "Leadership Commitment and Political Opposition to Structural Adjustment in Ghana." In *Ghana: The Political Economy of Recovery*, edited by Donald Rothchild, 157–72. Boulder, CO: Lynne Rienner Publishers.

Keefer, Phil. 2007. "Political Economy." In *Ghana: Meeting the Challenge of Accelerated and Shared Growth: A Country Economic Memorandum*, edited by Zeljko Bogetic. Vol. 3, 171–214. Washington, DC: World Bank.

Kleeman, Linda. 2011. "Organic Pineapple Farming: A Good Choice for Smallholders?" Kiel Working Paper 1671, Kiel Institute for the World Economy, Kiel, Germany.

Nankani, Gobind. 2009. *The Challenge of Agriculture in Ghana.* Accra: Institute for Democratic Governance.

Ninsin, Kwame A. 1991. "The PNDC and the Problem of Legitimacy." In *Ghana: The Political Economy of Recovery*, edited by Donald Rothchild, 49–67. Boulder, CO: Lynne Rienner Publishers.

Nyari, Bakari. 2008. "Biofuel Land Grabbing in Northern Ghana." February. http://biofuelwatch.org.uk/docs/biofuels_ghana.pdf.

Opoku, Darko Kwabena. 2010. "From Quasi-Revolutionaries to Capitalist Entrepreneurs: How the PNDC Changed the Face of Ghanaian Entrepreneurship." *Commonwealth and Comparative Politics* 48 (2): 227–56.

Oquaye, Mike. 2004. *Politics in Ghana, 1982–1992: Rawlings, Revolution and Populist Democracy.* Accra: Tornado Publications.

Price, Robert. 1984. "Neo-Colonialism and Ghana's Economic Decline: A Critical Assessment." *Canadian Journal of African Studies* 18: 163–93.

Rimmer, Douglas. 1992. *Staying Poor: Ghana's Political Economy, 1950–1990.* Oxford, U.K.: Pergamon Press.

Rooney, David. 1988. *Kwame Nkrumah: The Political Kingdom in the Third World.* London, U.K.: I.B. Tauris.

SADA (Savannah Accelerated Development Authority). 2010. "Synopsis of Development Strategy (2010–2030)." Policy Unit, Office of the Vice-President, Government of Ghana, Accra.

Wilks, Ivor. 1975. *Asante in the Nineteenth Century: The Structure and Evolution of a Political Order.* Cambridge, U.K.: Cambridge University Press.

World Bank. 2012. *Project Appraisal Document on a Proposed Credit in the Amount of SDR 64.5 Million (US$100 Million Equivalent) to the Republic of Ghana for a Commercial Agriculture Project.* Report 66499-GH, Washington, DC.

CHAPTER 7

Continuity and Change in Postconflict Sierra Leone: Why Politics Matters for Infrastructure Sector Reform

Marco Larizza, Vivek Srivastava, and Kavita Sethi

Introduction

Since the end of conflict in 2002, Sierra Leone has been rebuilding itself with the assistance of the international community. It has held three rounds of competitive multiparty elections at both the national and the subnational levels, which were judged as free and fair by international observers and national players (EU EOM 2012). Despite significant progress in the consolidation of peace and postconflict state building, the country still faces serious development challenges. Slow progress on several dimensions of governance has limited the government of Sierra Leone and its development partners from effectively reducing poverty and improving development outcomes. This observation coincides with an increasing recognition by international development scholars and practitioners that the obstacles to effective reform are often political and that technical solutions are not enough (Williams, Duncan, and Landell-Mills 2007; Fritz, Kaiser, and Levy 2009; Carothers and de Gramont 2013).

Though in principle the development community now largely accepts that politics matters, in practice the design and the implementation of many projects continue to follow traditional approaches that overlook the context in which economic policies and reform initiatives take place. The analysis presented in this chapter is based on the assumption that understanding the complex world of politics is a necessary—albeit insufficient—condition to improve the developmental impacts of aid and other donor-funded operations.

Summarizing key findings from a set of multisectoral political economy studies that were carried out between 2008 and 2011 by the World Bank for Sierra
Leone, this chapter shows how political economy analysis can support donors'
efforts to understand why reform strategies have not produced their desired
results, as well as what can be done differently to improve aid effectiveness and
to unlock development potential. Such analysis is particularly important in postconflict and fragile countries in which policy coordination and implementation
capacity is relatively weak and where the security, political, and development
spheres are closely intertwined.

Specifically, the analysis presented here sought to understand (a) how the
country-level drivers of electoral politics evolved since the end of the conflict in
2002, (b) how they affect the potential for improving the delivery of public
goods and services, and (c) what they imply for recent efforts to improve outcomes in critical infrastructure sectors. The central argument is that ethnically
driven patterns of competitive clientelism persist in the postconflict period and
define a suboptimal equilibrium whereby politicians continue to have strong
incentives for diverting resources to themselves for political purposes or for narrowly targeting goods that benefit a few citizens at the expense of the larger
public. Looking at the roads and power sectors, the chapter draws implications
for what these country-level dynamics imply about the prospects for reform, and
it suggests how the Bank and development partners can change their strategies
to better align with the existing incentives and to improve the likelihood of successful reforms.

Whereas the political equilibrium in Sierra Leone is unlikely to shift in the
short term, the analysis suggests that the process of institutional change generated by decentralization reform might be leading to the emergence of alternative
social forces and new interest groups. It is possible that this approach, in turn,
might renew the politics of electoral competition and might help overcome
inherited constraints.

It should be noted that since the original analysis presented in this chapter was
conducted, the situation on the ground in Sierra Leone continues to evolve. In
national politics, a new round of elections took place in November 2012 and saw
the reelection of President Ernest Bai Koroma and the victory for the All People's
Congress (APC) in parliament. For roads, new legislation regarding governance
of the sector is being implemented. If new research were conducted today, it
might shed further light on the evolution of Sierra Leone's political economy.
The purpose of this chapter, however, is not to provide the most current inter-
pretation of those dynamics but rather to present the analysis and recommendations as shared with the World Bank country team and sector experts in early
2012, as well as to explore how these may impact policy dialogue and change.

The rest of this chapter is organized as follows. The second section provides a
brief overview of Sierra Leone's postconflict development outcomes and suggests that the country underperforms relative to its potential. The third section
argues that the country's lack of development outcomes has its roots in Sierra
Leone's political conditions as well as the incentives these conditions generate

for politicians and key decision makers. Specifically, it shows how the political incentives of the national elite shape the possibilities for service delivery and concludes with operation recommendations to the World Bank and other development partners for how to best navigate the current environment and align with existing incentives. The fourth section presents evidence of how the political strategies of the elite shape progress and opportunities in infrastructure reforms through examples from the road and power sectors. The final section concludes by looking at the overall impact of the analysis and by making suggestions for future research.

Defining the Problem

The development challenges facing Sierra Leone today have a long legacy. The country's postcolonial history has been marked by exceptionally poor governance and development results. Even in the 1960s and 1970s, growth of per capita incomes was barely positive, and it turned negative during the 1980s. The political economy of development was characterized by a strong urban bias and the marginalization of wide sectors of the population, especially youth. With the abolition of elected local councils (LCs) in 1972, power was further centralized in the hands of elites in Freetown, perpetuating the ethno-regional divide and generating an increasing reliance on patronage and state violence as a means of political control. The ruling elites engaged in systematic repression of political opponents, adopted predatory practices, and privatized state resources such as diamond wealth (Kpundeh 1995; Reno 1995; Davies 2007). The erosion of state institutions and the subsequent collapse of public services led to widespread deprivation and popular distrust of the government, especially among unemployed youth, who had little voice and limited opportunities in a society controlled by urban elites allied with traditional chiefs. The endemic conditions of marginalization made youth easy recruits for the Revolutionary United Front (RUF), driving the country to a terrible civil war that lasted from 1991 to 2002 and resulting in an estimated 70,000 people killed and about 2.6 million displaced (Richards 1996; Truth and Reconciliation Commission 2004; Humphreys and Weinstein 2008).

Since the end of the civil war in 2002, much has changed in Sierra Leone's political landscape: democracy—at least in its electoral form—is now in place. With a large international presence—including successive United Nations peacekeeping and peace-building missions as well as substantial bilateral engagement, in particular from the United Kingdom—peace has been consolidated, and the country held multiple rounds of competitive multiparty elections at both the national (2002, 2007, 2012) and the subnational (2004, 2008, 2012) levels. In September 2007, political power was peacefully transferred for the first time in the country's history. Former combatants have been disarmed and re-integrated into society. These are notable achievements for a postconflict country. The country has also benefited from significant aid flows, receiving the same or more official development assistance than other recent postconflict countries (Liberia being the exception; see figure 7.1).[1]

Figure 7.1 ODA-to-GDP Ratio, 2000–10 Average

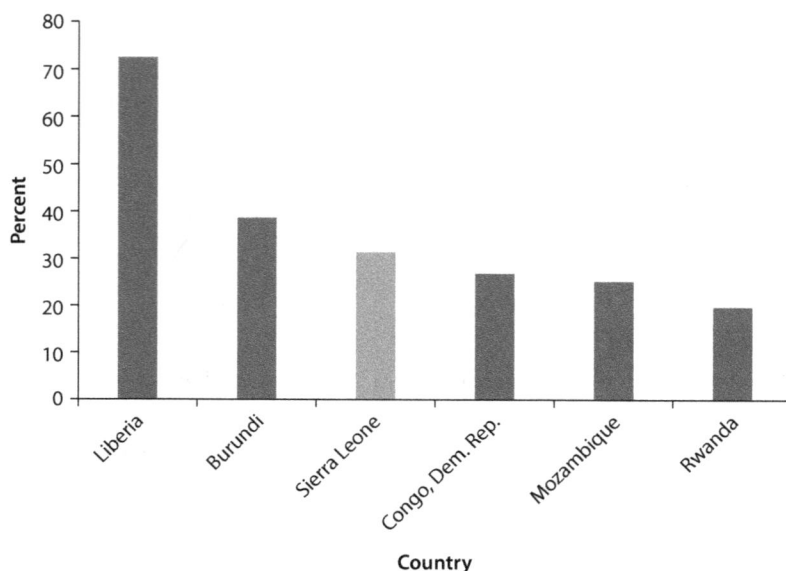

Source: OECD 2012.
Note: GDP = gross domestic product; ODA = official development assistance.

Table 7.1 Social Development Indicators: Sierra Leone in Comparative Perspective

Country	Adult literacy rate, % (2010)	Ratio of young literate females to males, % ages 15–24 (2010)	Infant mortality rate, per 1,000 live births (2011)	Under-five mortality rate per 1,000 live births (2011)	Improved sanitation facilities, % of population with access (2010)	GNI per capita (PPP), constant 2005 US$ (2010)
Sierra Leone	42	73	119	185	13	946
Burundi	67	100	86	139	46	526
Congo, Dem. Rep.	67	90	111	168	24	294
Mozambique	56	83	72	103	18	815
Rwanda	71	101	38	54	55	1,068
Liberia	61	116	58	78	18	396
Guinea	41	82	79	126	18	—

Source: World Bank, World Development Indicators (database) 2012.
Note: — = not available; GNI = gross national income; PPP = purchasing power parity.

And yet, the provision of public goods and services continued to fall short of regional standards. As table 7.1 illustrates, only 13 percent of the population has access to improved sanitation facilities and almost two-thirds of the population is illiterate. Sierra Leone ranks 158th of 169 countries in the 2010 edition of the UN's Human Development Index, with life expectancy standing at 41 years, well below the average (57 years) of low-income countries. The under-five mortality rate is 185 deaths for every 1,000 live births, nearly double the average for low-income countries (95 for every 1,000). Poor performance in service delivery is complemented by uneven progress along several dimensions of governance (see figure 7.2): despite significant improvements on political stability and citizens' political rights associated with elections (voice and accountability), Sierra Leone remains at the bottom 10th percentile on other critical governance indicators such as government effectiveness, rule of law, and control of corruption. This position is well below the average for African countries.

As discussed in the fourth section, infrastructure development is also lagging, with only 7 percent of the population (mainly located in Freetown and the Western peninsula) having access to power and a road density of only 0.22 paved kilometer (km) per 1,000 people (the Sub-Saharan African average is 0.79 km per 1,000 people). The performance of the road sector is particularly disappointing compared to the increasing volume of resources made available to the sector. According to the estimates reported in the 2010 *Sierra Leone Public Expenditure Review* (World Bank 2010a), the share of budgetary allocations directed to the road sector was the second-largest expenditure item for the period 2004–09.

Figure 7.2 Sierra Leone Governance Indicators, 2011

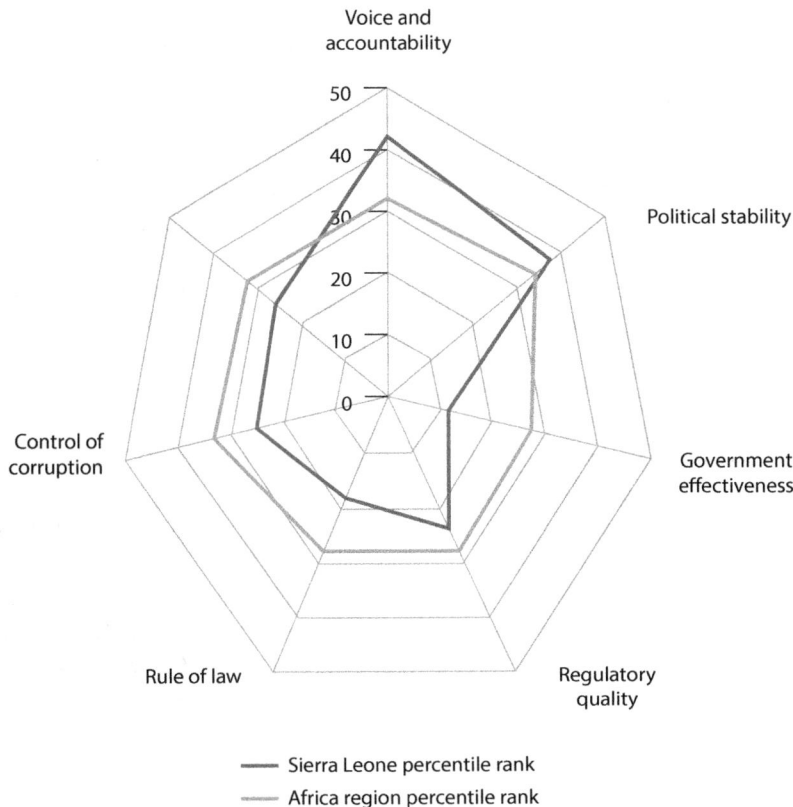

Source: World Bank, Worldwide Governance Indicators (database), 2010b.
Note: 0–50 represents percentile ranking.

This evidence suggests that the observed poor performance cannot be explained by lack of financial resources. Explanations must be found elsewhere.

Political Economy Analysis and Findings

Approach, Data, and Methodology

The analysis presented here aims to provide a more systematic understanding of how existing power relationships influence decision making in Sierra Leone and how these relationships in turn impact public policies and development outcomes. It does so by exploring the structure of politicians' incentives and interests that lead to the adoption of particular political strategies, explaining (a) where and how these interests can be in conflict with development and poverty reduction objectives and (b) whether and to what extent they may be influenced by external partners. Given the importance of historical legacies in a postconflict environment, the analysis also addresses the degree of continuity (or change) in the strategies developed by the national elites, showing to what extent key features of the prewar period endure in the postwar environment.

The work presented in this chapter benefits from previous efforts to understand the political economy of development in Sierra Leone and complements the previous work with field research carried out by the team in the country between 2010 and 2011.[2] Whenever possible, efforts have been made to move beyond subjective statements and support the arguments with the best available evidence, including (a) reviews of existing literature, including relevant sector-specific studies; (b) official statistics, and household surveys; (c) stakeholder interviews; and (d) more than 20 focus group discussions with politicians and civil servants, as well as representatives of nongovernmental organizations and local communities.[3] In addition, two workshops were convened in Freetown with the World Bank country team and representatives from leading development agencies (the U.K. Department for International Development, the European Union (EU), and the African Development Bank) to discuss and validate the findings from the analysis.

Politics and Development in Sierra Leone: Major Patterns

Prewar Environment (1962–91)

Subsequent to gaining independence from the United Kingdom in 1961, Sierra Leone's politics came to be shaped by an ethno-regional divide and the use of patronage and state violence as a means of political control. This political divide was particularly evident under Siaka Stevens' regime (1967–85).[4] Stevens openly rewarded areas where support for his ruling party—the APC—was strong, while discriminating against the regional heartland of the opposition party, the Sierra Leone People's Party (SLPP). Under his rule, power was concentrated in the executive branch of government, the formal institutions of democracy were suspended, and a one-party authoritarian system was established. In 1972, elected LCs were abolished, and political power was centralized in the hands of urban elites in Freetown. Moreover, Stevens manipulated traditional political institutions such as the Paramount Chiefs (PCs), thereby granting autonomy and control over local resources in exchange for political support. During this period, the ruling party engaged in systematic repression of political opponents, a number of whom were imprisoned, killed, or forced to flee the country.[5] The regime adopted predatory practices and privately appropriated state resources, including revenue derived from alluvial diamonds (Kpundeh 1995; Reno 1995).

When Stevens retired in 1985, this strategy for governing Sierra Leone continued under President Joseph Momoh (also from the APC). The deterioration of state institutions further accelerated, corruption became pervasive, and a high degree of kleptocracy was tolerated. Basic services at the local level were undersupplied, and the rule of PCs was perceived as being increasingly arbitrary and predatory.[6] Frequent victims of this system were young men, targeted by chiefs seeking free labor and the revenue from large fines.

Political Economy of the Civil War (1991–2002)

The tendency to confer paramount chieftaincies to party loyalists regardless of their ruling house credentials often generated prolonged local protest and campaigns of civil disobedience (Fanthorpe 2006; Reno 1995). Combined with the overcentralization of power in the hands of a single party (APC) in Freetown, the authoritarian tendencies of the chiefs magnified popular discontent. The governing style marginalized wide sectors of the population and provided a ready opening for youth conscription into the fighting rebel factions when the RUF crossed the border from Liberia, eventually bringing the country to civil war (Hanlon 2004; Humphreys and Weinstein 2008; Richards 1996).

Postwar Environment (2002–11)

One notable aspect of the postwar setting is that the same two parties present during the prewar period continued to dominate the political landscape. The postwar elections in 2002 were won by the SLPP, and President Ahmad Tejan Kabbah was reelected to a five-year term in a landslide victory. The RUF political wing, the RUFP, failed to win a single seat in parliament. Kabbah obtained 70 percent of the vote, compared with 22 percent for the APC's presidential candidate, Ernest Bai Koroma. The SLPP also dominated parliamentary elections, winning 83 of the 112 available seats in parliament. Voting patterns in many ways mirrored the prewar period and confirmed the strong influence of regionally based ethnic identities; the APC won in the northern regions (dominated by Temne and Limba), while the SLPP attracted most of its support from the south and east of the country (dominated by Mende).

The political economy of civil war generated large pressures in the aftermath of the conflict for a rapid peace dividend in the form of a reestablished state presence and improved access to basic services outside the Western peninsula. These popular demands were common across a broad spectrum of societal groups and accounted for the early articulation of decentralization reform as a national objective of the SLPP-led government. In this regard, a notable achievement was the passage of a local government act in 2004. This passage appears to

have been based on a twofold motivation: (a) to create an institutional set-up
that would reduce the potential for a return to the prewar political economy of
overcentralization and reduce the influence of the traditional leadership (geron-
tocratic) and chieftaincies, which the youth had resisted during war, and (b) to
meet popular expectations and win political support (Robinson 2010; Larizza
and Glynn forthcoming). However, the government was not able to reform the
chieftaincy institution. Accordingly, the 2004 Local Government Act reestablished both LCs and—at the same time—restored the institution of PCs.[7]

Whereas the Kabbah government achieved significant progress in some
areas, overall its performance was disappointing. Kabbah's presidency successfully demobilized over 70,000 combatants and rehabilitated security services,
improved public financial management, and restored elected local governments (abolished in 1972). But the SLPP government generated few tangible
benefits for the population and made little headway to reduce endemic
poverty in rural areas.[8] Moreover, the government largely failed to control corruption and even intervened to prevent the Anti-Corruption Commission
from acting vigorously to enforce the government's anti-corruption strategy
launched in 2005.[9] As president, Kabbah was not eligible to run again in the
2007 elections, and an internal leadership contest emerged within the SLPP
that eventually triggered a split of the party. The internally defeated candidate,
Charles Margai, decided to leave and create his own party, the People's
Movement for Democratic Change. A further blow to the SLPP's reelection
chances came when some of Sierra Leone's major donors decided to end
direct budget support out of frustration over the limited degree of effort
being made to curb corruption, which was seen as widespread within government and public services[10] (Kandeh 2008). The 2007 elections were consequently won by the APC, the prewar ruling party, with its candidate Ernest
Bai Koroma winning 54.6 percent of the popular vote in a second-round
runoff race and winning 40.7 percent of votes for parliament (receiving 59 of
112 eligible seats).[11]

The government of Koroma won in part on a platform of governance and
service delivery improvements. It sought to create a number of programs
designed to ensure support from key constituencies. In Freetown, provision of
electricity has improved, and "on the whole, the capital is far cleaner and
more robust than it was previously" (Gberie 2010, 1). As will be discussed in
the fourth section, after multiple delays, the government was able to complete several donor-funded road projects that had been initiated since 2002,
and in 2010, it embarked on several new ones. It launched a popular initiative
to provide free medical care for children under five and lactating mothers,
and it sought to demonstrate its commitment to improving governance by
passing a set of amendments to the Anti-Corruption Act in 2008.[12] At the
same time, many reform initiatives were initially limited to the drafting of
new acts (for example, the Freedom of Information Act), proposals for
institutional reform (for example, of the National Power Authority [NPA]),
and the formal enhancement of existing agencies' powers (for example,

the Anti-Corruption Commission). In November 2012, Koroma won a second mandate, thereby granting to APC an overwhelming majority in the new
parliament.

Understanding the Political Equilibrium

As discussed above, political competition in postconflict Sierra Leone continues
to be marked by striking continuities that affect the extent to which those in
government have been motivated and able to improve the delivery of public
goods and services. This section provides a closer look at the underlying drivers
of the political equilibrium, analyzing what factors are thought to shape the
preferences of national elites and influence their decision to adopt neopatrimonial strategies to maintain power and ensure political survival. Three main factors
are discussed below: (a) the role of ethnic identities in shaping the party system
and driving national electoral politics, (b) the use of informal patronage networks
to gain political support, and (c) the use of violence as a means to ensure societal
control and political survival.

Though Sierra Leonean society has been characterized by continuity, it is not
static. Decentralization has given rise to a new generation of politicians, which is
emerging at the local level. Often, these are independent candidates with strong
links to local communities who are not necessarily aligned with either the APC
or the SLPP. This new class of local politicians could lead to the emergence of a
new elite representing alternative social forces and new interest groups, with the
potential to play a central role in shaping the country's development outcomes
and renewing the political system in a way that may help overcome weaknesses
inherited from the past.

How Ethnic Identities Shape Electoral Politics, Politician's Incentives, and Policy Outcomes

In principle, the dynamics of political competition under a democratic regime
increase the opportunities for citizens to keep the government accountable and
so constrain the behavior of politicians. But this constraint is weakened if people
vote on the basis of ethnic or regional appeal instead of a party's performance
(Horowitz 1985). Indeed, when people vote on the basis of fixed characteristics
(such as ethnicity), it significantly reduces the extent of electoral competition—
support is guaranteed, regardless of performance—and increases the ability of
politicians to gain support in exchange for rewarding specific ethnic groups with
jobs and other private goods. In turn, this ability tends to undermine government
incentives to deliver broad investment in public goods (Keefer 2010). As long as
a large share of voters vote on the basis of affiliation rather than performance, the
likelihood that citizens will collectively be able to hold governments to account
for their performance is reduced. Sierra Leone's electoral politics provides broad
evidence to bolster this argument: similar to several other countries in Sub-
Saharan Africa, ethnic affiliations continue to shape political alignments in Sierra
Leone (Kandeh 2003, 2008). A particular aspect of Sierra Leone's political landscape is that these affiliations are aligned in relatively large regionally based

ethnic groups and, to date, have resulted in a competition dominated by two parties (rather than a larger number of smaller parties).

In Easterly and Levine's (1997) list of the most ethno-linguistically fractional- ized countries in the world, Sierra Leone ranks fifteenth, suggesting a high level of ethnic fragmentation at first sight. However, the three largest ethnic groups (Mende, Temne, and Limba) command roughly 70 percent of the population, whereas none of the other 10 ethnic groups exceed a 10 percent share of the population. Moreover, the distribution of the major ethnic groups is highly con- centrated by region. As shown in map 7.1, panel a and panel b, respectively, Temne (and Limba) are located almost exclusively in the northern and western regions, and Mende are largely located in the southern and eastern regions. This regional distribution provides a strong incentive for political parties to mobilize their constituencies along ethnic lines. The regional distribution of electoral results for the national parliamentary elections in 2002, 2007, and 2012[13] pro- vides strong empirical support to this argument, revealing that the APC remains strongly associated with the Temne (and Limba) in the north and the west, whereas the SLPP is strongly associated with the Mende in the south and east. For example, in 2007 the APC captured 36 of the 39 seats (92 percent) in the north, while getting no seat at all in the Mende-dominated Southern Province. Conversely, the SLPP gained only three seats in the Northern Province and no seat at all in the Western Area (including Freetown).[14] In map 7.1, panel c and panel d visually illustrate this point, based on self-reported electoral results.

How the Supply and Demand of Patronage Shapes the Way Political Power Is Used and Maintained

A further aspect of the political incentive structure in Sierra Leone—itself closely intertwined with the ethnic dimension of politics—is the apparent enduring strength of neopatrimonial structures (see box 7.1) and the use of patronage networks as attractive strategies to gain power and maintain political support. The research confirmed that many citizens demanded and expected rewards from the ruling party based on their ethnic identity. However, given that ethnic divisions are structured in Sierra Leone with no group having a majority, politicians of the two main parties have to combine a simple ethnically based appeal to their core constituencies with strategies to attract and retain support from smaller ethnic groups as well as from the urban electorate in Freetown. The reestablishment of the PCs in 2004 is also part of this pattern. The PCs maintain strong links with the ruling national elites and have traditionally been granted authority in exchange for their political support and their ability to deliver votes. When the institution of PCs was reconfirmed in 2004, it was done in such a way as to give national politicians considerable influence over who would be chief in a given jurisdiction. In turn, chiefs are seen as being able to influence voter participation and preferences. By some estimates, it appears that PCs are able to influence 10–20 percent of the voters in their jurisdictions (Robinson 2010). Working with and through chiefs can allow national politicians to maintain targeted patronage networks in districts so that they can maximize electoral benefits.

Map 7.1   Ethnicity as a Key Driver of Political Identities

IBRD 40247

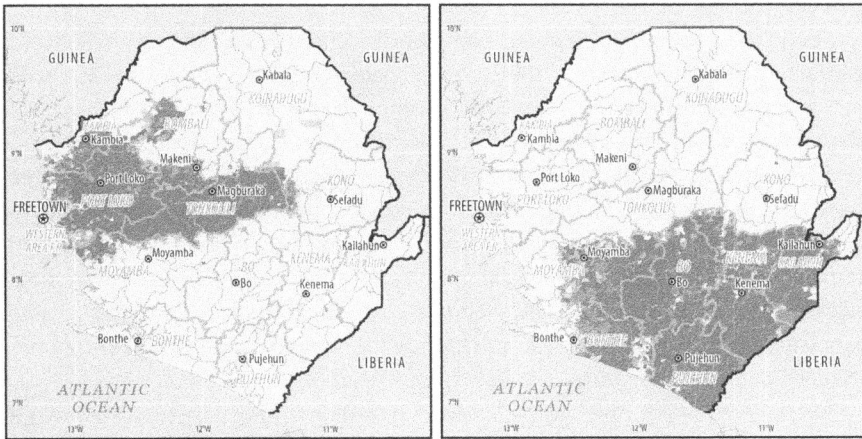

a. Percentage of respondents who identified as Temne

b. Percentage of respondents who identified as Mende

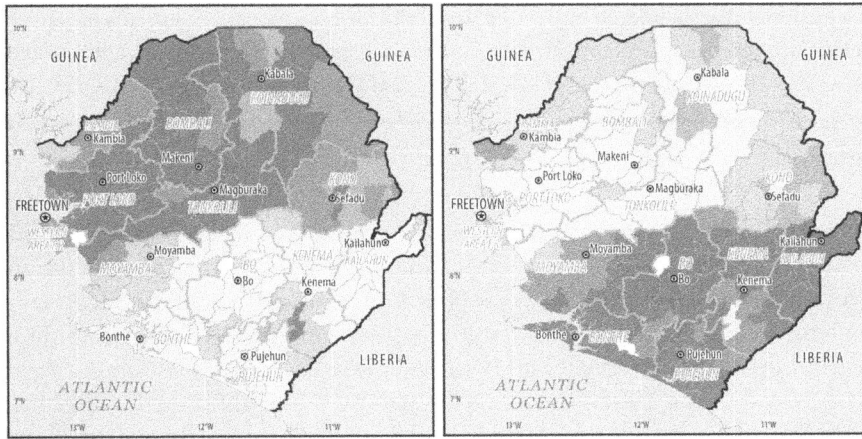

c. Average percentage of respondents by chiefdom who voted for APC

d. Average percentage of respondents by chiefdom who voted for the opposition

80%	CITIES AND TOWNS
60%	DISTRICT CAPITALS
40%	NATIONAL CAPITAL
20%	CHIEFDOM BOUNDARIES
	DISTRICT BOUNDARIES
	INTERNATIONAL BOUNDARIES

This map was produced by the Map Design Unit of The World Bank. The boundaries, colors, denominations and any other information shown on this map do not imply, on the part of The World Bank Group, any judgment on the legal status of any territory, or any endorsement or acceptance of such boundaries.

Sources: Map number IBRD: 40247, September 2013; Sacks and Larizza 2012; data from the 2008 National Public Services (NPS) Survey, IRCBP 2010.

Note: Panels a and b reflect the percentage of heads of households by chiefdoms who identified themselves as Temne or Mende, respectively, according to Sierra Leone's 2004 National Population and Housing Census. Panels c and d show the average percentage of respondents by chiefdom who voted for the All People's Congress (APC) and the opposition—either the Sierra Leone People's Party (SLPP) or the People's Movement for Democratic Change (PMDC)—in the 2007 national elections, respectively, according to the NPS 2008 survey.

Box 7.1 The Implications of (Neo) Patrimonialism

Neopatrimonialism is the coexistence of patrimonial relationships with a modern administrative structure. For the purposes of this study, neopatrimonialism is understood as a style of governance in which politicians maintain power through a system of personal relationships in which they, as patrons, provide favors to clients in exchange for political support.

In this framework, private goods are politically desirable, because they can be targeted to supporters and withheld from opponents. Public goods, on the contrary, are not politically attractive ways of generating support and thus are generally undersupplied (Bates 1981). Patrimonial regimes create distortions in market prices to create rents, which can then be politically allocated. When supply falls short of demand, that which is demanded becomes a great political resource for those who can allocate it. This market creates massive economic distortions, but it can be good politics (Cammack 2007, 600).

Under patrimonialism, the law is applied in discretionary ways, thereby following and reproducing hierarchical and asymmetrical relationships between patrons and clients. The very notion of "equality before the law" is denied by the "un-rule of law" (O'Donnell 1996). Finally, patrimonialism undermines the coherence of the bureaucracy. This occurs because the bureaucracy represents a potential source of political opposition to patrons, with the consequence that bureaucrats are continually shuffled so that they cannot conspire against rulers.

Available evidence suggests that as part of the need to secure political support, direct vote-buying has also been used in Sierra Leone, as is the case in a number of countries (see chapter 8 on Papua New Guinea in this volume). According to Kandeh (2008), the initial postwar government engaged in vote-buying during the early days of government and then again as a last-resort solution during the runoff round of the 2007 elections. This activity is also confirmed by Robinson (2008, 25) who relates the following: "When asked what was the most important determinant of election outcomes I was told by a senior local APC politician in Freetown 'money.' I asked, but surely someone who provided a new school or built drains ... and roads would win votes, he said: 'maybe, but this was less good than money.'"

In turn, identity politics has shaped how politicians have governed once in power. After its victory in 2007, the APC pursued a policy of "northernization" of key positions, in a winner-takes-all approach to the national government (Gberie 2010). According to Robinson (2010), after the change in government, there was "a pattern of southerners and easterners being dismissed from parastatal agencies and, where possible, from civil service." Dismissals included the governor of the Central Bank, the commissioner of the National Revenue Authority, the commissioner and deputy commissioner of the National Commission for Social Action, the ombudsman, and the chair of the telecommunications commission, among others. Such practices of handing positions to supporters and dismissing existing office holders is quite common in patronage-driven environments. Given the dearth of qualified civil servants that characterizes Sierra Leone's postconflict environment (see Srivastava and Larizza 2013), such practices are particularly concerning; they could have adverse implications for the country's ability to rebuild the public administration and enter a higher trajectory of governance and performance.[15]

Ethnic patterns are still significant drivers of voting behavior in Sierra Leone, but politicians also need to reach beyond their core group of constituencies to win office or stay in power. They need to do so by using a variety of means, including patronage links with PCs and efforts to buy votes. With some exceptions, performance on service delivery does not appear to play a primary role in voting behavior, although—as noted above—poor performance did provide a target for the opposition campaign and its bid to win. In the language of political economy, there seems to be ex post, but not ex ante accountability: in Sierra Leone, swing voters might be able to remove incumbents whose past performance is seen as bad (as in the case of the 2007 elections) even when they cannot count on the newly elected to do better.

How the Threat of Violence Provides a Means for Political Control and Survival

The presence of low-level violence in Sierra Leone continues to mobilize ethnic constituencies and promote patronage networks, although there has been no larger-scale eruptions of violence since the end of the war in 2002. As Kandeh (2010) points out, violence as a tool of intimidation and marginalization is not inconsistent with the other strategies and may well be employed in areas that are traditionally hostile to the ruling party in power (such as Kailahun and Kenema districts in the east and Pujehun, Bo, and Bonthe districts in the south), and hence these areas are less likely to receive resources in the forms of patronage. Recent episodes seem to support this hypothesis: for example, the SLPP headquarters in Freetown and other major urban areas had been attacked by APC mobs several times following the 2007 elections (Kandeh 2008). These episodes parallel the intimidation of SLPP voters reported in the 2008 local elections (NEC 2008a). More recently, episodes of political violence have been registered in the SLPP strongholds (for example, following President Koroma's 2011 visit to Kenema and Kailahun districts).[16] According to a recent report by the United Nation Commissions for Africa, such incidents of violence have mostly been perpetrated by civilians (mainly youth), and although the security forces have not been directly implicated, they have been accused of bias in handling incidences (Lavali, Hughes, and Suma 2011). However, widespread fears that greater violence would erupt ahead of or during the 2012 elections[17] did not materialize. The relative stability suggests that large-scale political violence might have become too costly for the elites as a strategy either to intimidate voters (preelectoral violence) or to reject results and target the winners (postelectoral violence).

Problem-Driven Political Economy Analysis • http://dx.doi.org/10.1596/978-1-4648-0121-1

Evolving Intergovernmental Relations: Some Promise Despite Mixed Incentives

In addition to analyzing political incentives at the central government level, the analysis also considered the drivers shaping decentralization and the relationships across levels of government. As discussed above, the civil war generated large demands and pressures for a rapid peace dividend in the form of a reestablished state presence across the country and improved access to basic services outside the Western peninsula. These popular demands were common across a broad spectrum of societal groups and account for the early articulation of decentralization reform as a national priority program. In 2004, the Local Government Act reestablished LCs and formally revised the country's territorial organization (box 7.2). Since then, decentralization has come to be relatively far advanced.

The political economy analysis of decentralization found two trends that include the positive as well as the more problematic aspects of how decentralization has evolved[18]:

- In 2004, central government decision makers adopted decentralization (with a considerable degree of central control) more as a political strategy than as an instrument for improving service delivery. Robinson (2010) argues that the incentive to decentralize some portion of resources to LCs was driven by the fact that the SLPP elites maintained strong links with the ruling families in the chiefdoms. The institutional form adopted seemed reasonable, but in fact it suffered from several shortcomings. LCs were and continue to be underresourced and remain in constant tension with the chieftaincy.
- Decentralization has been positively perceived by citizens (as intended by national politicians), and it has opened up space for engagement of groups (such as women and youth) that tend to be less represented at the national level.

The original decision to decentralize was made by the SLPP in 2004. It appeared to have been motivated by a mix of memories about institutional legacies during its initial postindependence government[19] and by the notion that

---

Box 7.2 The Territorial Organization of Sierra Leone

Sierra Leone is composed of three provinces—the Northern Province, the Southern Province, and the Eastern Province—and one other region called the Western Area. The provinces are further divided into 12 districts (map B7.2.1), and the districts are further divided into chiefdoms, except for the Western Area (which includes a rural council and a city council for Freetown, the nation's capital). Whereas district and town councils are responsible for service delivery, chiefdom authorities maintain their own infrastructure of police and courts, which are also funded by local taxes.

box continues next page

Box 7.2 The Territorial Organization of Sierra Leone *(continued)*

Map B7.2.1 Districts of Sierra Leone

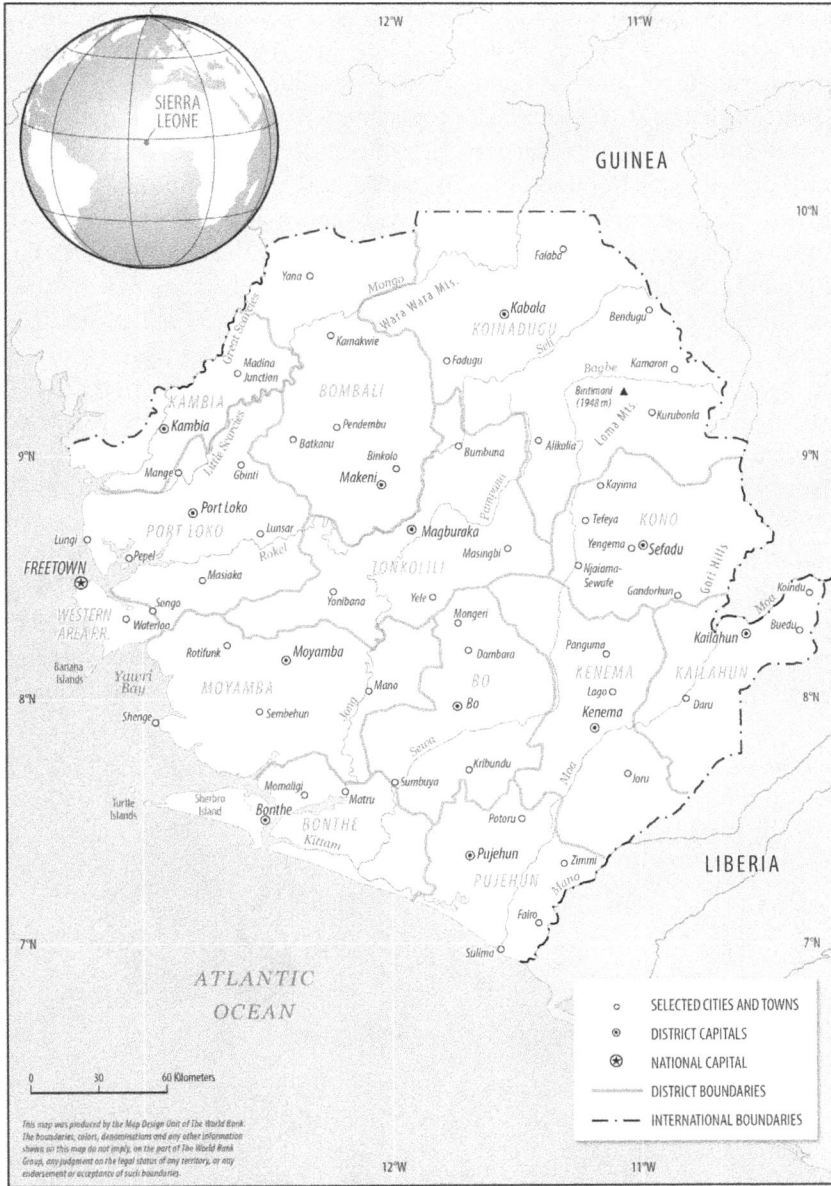

Source: Map number: IBRD 40246, August 2013; Zhou, 2009.

decentralization would be popular in a country in which rural areas have traditionally been neglected by central government. However, the specific design was made to facilitate (a) playing the traditional authorities (PCs) against the local authorities through a divide-and-rule style of governance and (b) providing only limited autonomy of LCs over the control of financial and human resources. In particular, the distribution of powers and responsibilities between PCs and LCs was not clarified, and PCs retained responsibility for collecting local revenues to be shared with local governments (which in addition received transfers from the central government). Robinson (2010) concludes that the continuing presence of chieftaincy creates the potential for a divide-and-rule equilibrium that would strengthen the bargaining power of the ruling party with both PCs and LCs.

Despite these limitations, public perception surveys indicate that by the end of the first decade of the 2000s, citizens held positive views of decentralization and also perceived improvements in service delivery, such as the reduced distance to primary schools, drivable roads, and available market areas (IRCBP 2010). Furthermore, local elections have offered space for political participation among traditionally marginalized groups such as women and youth. In 2004, women occupied 12.7 percent of council seats in council elections, but in 2008, this number increased to 18 percent, a higher rate of representation relative to the 12 percent share of women's seats in the national parliament (NEC 2008b). This positive trend is confirmed if we consider the rate of participation of women candidates in local versus national elections: in the 2007 national elections, 12 percent of total candidates running for parliamentary seats were women, and elected women were 11 percent of total MPs (figure 7.3). In the 2008 local

Figure 7.3 Women's Representation in National and Local Elections

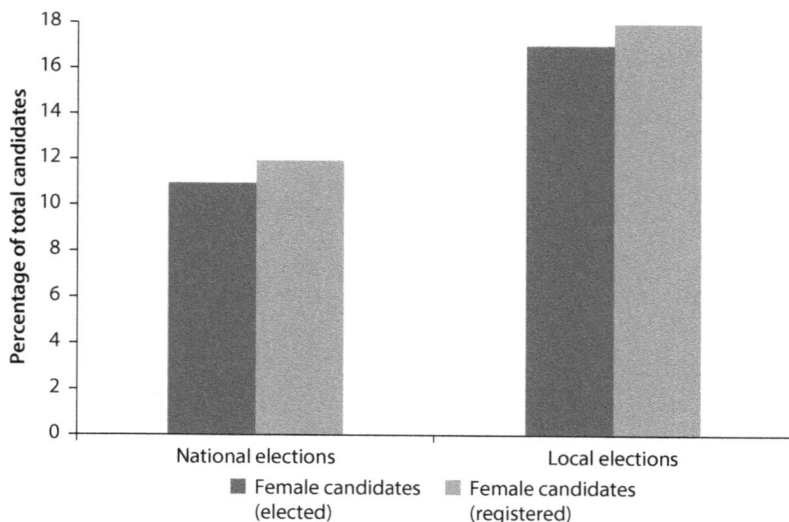

Source: NEC 2008b.
Note: National elections refers to 2007 parliamentary elections; local elections refers to 2008 local elections for councilors and mayors.

elections, 18 percent of total candidates running for council seats were women, and women councilors accounted for 17 of total elected councilors.

Two rounds of subnational elections—in 2004 and 2008—reported an increasing level of political competition[20] and managed to create a new class of local politicians whose interests might be better aligned with the development of their own constituencies. Moreover, figures from the 2008 Decentralization Stakeholders Survey suggest that only about half of the councilors who had reported their intentions to run for reelection were actually reelected to a second term (IRCBP 2008; Zhou 2009). The turnover of incumbent councilors attests to the anchoring of local representational politics and the growing role that local elections play as a channel of vertical accountability. One reason for that might be that—relative to the national level—playing the ethnic card is likely to be less relevant at the local level because most voters share a common identity. Also, evidence from qualitative research suggests that ordinary citizens are better able to organize at the local level and participate in the decision-making process to protect their collective interests (Larizza and Glynn forthcoming). A recent study confirmed that ordinary citizens can be quite vigilant in monitoring government performance at the local level, rewarding better-performing governments with a higher level of trust (Sacks and Larizza 2012). This vigilance in turn might generate incentives for political parties to recruit high-quality candidates who—once in power—deliver on their electoral promises. Overall, this evidence suggests that local elections are more likely to be about policy issues such as service provision or development. These findings are consistent with the conclusion of recent research on local political strategies and voting behavior in Sierra Leone that shows that decentralization can "break a country out of the low accountability equilibrium in which citizens cast their votes blindly across partisan lines" (Casey 2010, 1) and can contribute to change the political equilibrium.

Implications of Country-Level Political Economy Analysis

Overall, Sierra Leone's postconflict political economy presents a mixed picture. On the one hand, the ability to preserve the peace, to achieve peaceful turnover in government in 2007, and to avoid a return of violence during the 2012 elections are remarkable achievements. On the other hand, the political strategy adopted by the elite has shown considerable continuity with the past and relatively less evidence of a shift to a better equilibrium in which the delivery of public goods and government performance dominate. Comparatively, governance in Sierra Leone has not been as difficult as in other postconflict countries (such as, for example, the Democratic Republic of Congo) where violence and political survival have constantly preoccupied the attention of the political leadership. But there are also few signs of coherent efforts at building a more effective state as has happened in Rwanda. However, the specific geographic distribution and clustering of ethnic groups in Sierra Leone has provided strong incentives for politicians to mobilize voters across ethnic lines and to rely on patronage to appeal to voters rather than to improve government performance in providing public services and developing the country's minimal infrastructure. Given the limited incentives for government performance, achieving development objectives has had limited relevance for elected officials. Such dynamics, in turn, allow elected officials to allocate scarce resources elsewhere for personal or political ends.[21]

The broad conclusion drawn from the analysis is that these basic drivers of the political economy dynamic in Sierra Leone need to be taken as a given, at least in the short term. Basing operational design on assumptions about rapid gains in government effectiveness would be unrealistic and would result in failure. Yet there are still a number of ways in which development partners can engage to pursue progress on development results as well as to gradually shift political incentives toward a stronger focus on service delivery.

First, the study recommended adopting approaches such as (a) results targets and (b) performance-based lending or similar financing modalities and support (for example, conditional cash transfers, results-based aid, and so on). These approaches provide incentives for political leaders to make things work in order to access aid funds that are needed for political survival. In contrast, providing general budget support or using more traditional (input-oriented) lending instruments may have presupposed an unrealistic alignment of incentives.

Second, the analysis suggested to invest further in strengthening institutions for horizontal accountability such as the Anti-Corruption Commission, the parliament, and the judiciary, whose organizational capacity and political legitimacy could be enhanced to prevent abuses and mismanagement in the use of public resources. This analysis implies the need to overcome the executive bias that traditionally characterizes donor interventions and think about innovative ways to develop the policy dialogue, including renewed efforts to target interventions to change the balance of power between the executive and other key institutions of the state.

Third, development partners need to complement supply-side interventions with the promotion of demand-side initiatives that—by improving the information base available to the poor—facilitate collective action and support citizen's efforts to mobilize, to form organizations to protect their interests, and to assess the performance of the incumbent government. This action would ultimately strengthen the role of elections as a mechanism of political accountability.[22] Over time, political accountability will likely increase the costs of underperformance and, in time, shift incentives toward public goods provision. In the Sierra Leonean context, this strategy could, for instance, indicate support for the newly established independent Sierra Leone Broadcasting Corporation, as well as promote the loosening of restrictions on the media and the rapid implementation of the Freedom of Information Act. At the same time, increased support could be provided to civil society organizations such as the Sierra Leone Association of Journalists in their advocacy efforts to improve the pluralism of the media and reduce the risk of abuses of the 1965 Public Order Act.

Fourth, and probably most important, the study suggested that development partners focus on strengthening the process of decentralization by providing LCs the financial and technical aid required to perform their mandates. The main rationale for this approach is existing evidence that the barriers to collective action appear more easily overcome at the local level (Larizza and

Glynn forthcoming), and that because a majority of voters at local levels have a common identity, those seeking political office cannot simply rely on making ethnic appeals.[23] As Casey (2010) shows in her study of local elections, greater information on the performance of political candidates does lead voters to cross the party lines and to cast their votes for better-performing candidates. In turn, the growing electoral weight of the swing voters might gradually shift political incentives toward demonstrating performance in providing public goods. Finally, by supporting decentralization reform, the development community can create the conditions to give opposition politicians access to more resources to distribute a greater stake in the system, thereby reducing the risk of violence and promoting political stability.

Drivers of National Decision Making and Infrastructure: Examples from Roads and Power

As set out in the first section, widespread destruction caused by the civil war left Sierra Leone with the challenging task of reconstructing and rehabilitating its infrastructure. In the road and power sectors, a decade of war led to a general lack of repair, the vandalism of equipment and, ultimately, the collapse of both the road network and the electricity generation and distribution capacity. The Sierra Leone government responded to this challenge with ambitious development plans, identifying the reconstruction of destroyed infrastructure as top priorities for development.[24] Both power and roads have seen increased levels of funding from domestic as well as external sources and some effort to improve sector governance. This increase in funding has not been commensurate with achievements.

As discussed in the second section, political incentives in Sierra Leone have been mixed. There is a focus in the public debate and in election campaigns on the poor state of infrastructure. Yet at the same time, incumbent claims about progress made, ethnic- and patronage-based voter allegiances, and vote-buying practices (Utas 2007; Robinson 2010) have overall weakened citizen demands for accountability and effective delivery of public goods. This section explores how successive governments have gone about rebuilding public infrastructure—in particular roads and power—in Sierra Leone and how some of the governance challenges and apparent underlying drivers affect these efforts.

Attempts to introduce first-best reforms to create checks and balances and greater accountability have met with limited results, in part because the reforms would reduce politicians' ability to manage appointments and rents. As argued above, it is unlikely that the incentives supporting the status quo will change in the short run. This knowledge guides the recommendations for a combination of results-based lending and support for decentralization to LCs where possible.

The State of Infrastructure in Sierra Leone

Although the Sierra Leone government has signaled the importance of directing attention and investment into infrastructure, progress has been weak and below potential. The analysis suggests that the reasons for this weak progress are the same reasons that drive the national political incentives and equilibrium. Accordingly, strategies for doing better in this environment would include results-based and calibrated donor support along with decentralized provision where technically feasible.

Roads

According to the estimates of the World Bank (2010a), the quality of Sierra Leone's road network is well below regional standards. Sierra Leone's road density is 2.0 km per 1,000 people compared to the regional average (measured across 19 countries) of 3.6 km per 1,000 people. Likewise, Sierra Leone's paved road length of 0.22 km per 1,000 people is about one-fourth the Sub-Saharan African average (World Bank 2010a, 155–56; table 7.2).

National survey data indicate citizen dissatisfaction with the notable lack of improvement in road quality: almost one-third of the households surveyed rated the quality of the roads as "poor," and a further 38 percent considered them "very poor." Moreover, the national average masks subnational differences, indicating that the perceived quality of roads is especially a concern of small towns and villages (see table 7.3). These findings are further confirmed by the focus group interviews carried out across districts: especially outside the Freetown area, the poor conditions of roads and the lack of a comprehensive road network were raised by all participants as issues of primary concern. This finding is not surprising. Roads are typically something that citizens care a lot about and are clearly attributable to government action. So the issue of road quality could be a good

Table 7.2 Road Network: Sierra Leone in Comparative Perspective

	Sierra Leone	Sub-Saharan Africa
Road density		
Km/1,000 people	2.0	3.6
Km/km²	158–61	204
Road quality (% paved)	11–12	25
Road density (paved)		
Km/1,000 people	0.22	0.79

Source: World Bank 2010a.
Note: km = kilometer; km² = square kilometer.

Table 7.3 Road Quality in Sierra Leone: The Citizen's View

	Percentage of households				
	Freetown	Large town	Small town	Village	Total
Very good (reasonably smooth tarmac)	**40**	14	13	3	12
Good (rough tarmac)	29	**43**	16	10	17
Poor (reasonably smooth unpaved)	22	35	**43**	35	33
Very poor (rough unpaved)	9	9	27	**53**	38

Source: IRCBP 2010.
Note: Bold values represent the majority response.

entry point for encouraging performance-based electoral accountability (see chapter 9 on the Philippines in this volume).

Despite recognition that road sector investments are urgently needed, progress has been halting. The government sought to allocate substantial resources to the sector, on average about 17 percent of its total annual budget between 2004 and 2012 (table 7.4). However, in most years, planned progress has fallen short, and there have been significant delays in the execution of projects, including those funded by development partners.

By 2009, the Sierra Leone Roads Authority (SLRA), the agency responsible for planning, development, and maintenance, was able to rehabilitate less than 300 km of urban roads, falling short of the national development target of 600 km. Similar shortfalls characterized the rehabilitation of feeder roads.

The execution of externally funded projects—mainly for the rehabilitation of key road connections—has also seen significant delays. The SLRA was diagnosed as one of the weakest performers in using donor funds compared to other Sierra Leone agencies (World Bank 2010a, 159–68). In several instances, previously committed funding had to be suspended or cancelled. For example, concerns over contractors' supervision and management led the German government–owned development bank KfW to cancel funding for some 24 projects scheduled for 2010 (Srivastava and Larizza 2011b). In another example, the EU began a project to rehabilitate the Freetown-Conakry Highway in 2003. Because of

Table 7.4 Budgetary Allocations to the Road Sector

	2004	2005	2006	2007	2008	2009	2010	2011	2012
Total roads (leones billions)[a]	120.0	128.1	108.3	181.6	158.6	246.8	312.9	378.3	460.4
Ministry of Works, Housing, and Infrastructural Development (leones billions)[b]	109.6	106.3	76.9	144.4	104.7	190.6	255.6	313.0	384.0
External financing (leones billions)	106.6	97.9	68.9	134.9	85.0	175.2	182.2	230.8	291.6
Domestic financing (leones billions)	3.0	8.4	8.0	9.5	19.7	15.5	73.3	82.1	92.4
Road fund (leones billions)[c]	10.4	21.7	31.4	37.3	53.8	56.2	57.3	65.3	76.4
Total (US$ millions)	44.4	44.3	36.6	60.8	53.2	74.4	85.7	100.6	118.9
External financing (US$ millions)	39.5	33.9	23.3	45.2	28.5	52.8	49.9	61.4	75.3
Domestic financing (US$ millions)	4.9	10.4	13.3	15.6	24.7	21.6	35.8	39.2	43.6
Memo items									
Roads (% of total budget)[d]	15.6	15.5	12.0	16.4	14.1	18.3	19.2	19.9	21.4
Education (% of total budget)[d, e]	17.2	18.8	19.6	18.4	18.9	18.3	17.3	17.0	17.0

Sources: World Bank 2010a; Sierra Leone Ministry of Finance and Economic Development; and World Bank staff calculations.
a. Excludes the National Commission for Social Action and the Ministry of Agriculture, Forestry, and Food Security because of lack of detailed information.
b. Development budget only. Excludes nonroad expenditures.
c. Recurrent transfers only. The road fund is included in the allocations for the Min. works in 2004 and 2005.
d. Total allocations excluding debt service and net lending.
e. Includes allocations to local councils.

serious delays, the project was temporarily terminated in July 2007 (Delegation of the EU to Sierra Leone 2013). The rehabilitation restarted in March 2009 with an expected completion date of March 2011. After further delays, the road eventually opened in late 2012.[25]

Power

Recovery has also been a challenge in the power sector. In principle, Sierra Leone could take advantage of an extensive network of rivers with an estimated hydroelectric potential of 1,200 megawatts (MW). Despite this relative abundance of hydro-energy potential, Sierra Leone's postconflict history has been characterized by an underdeveloped power sector. For example, the consumption of public power in 2005 was 8 kilowatt-hours (kWh) per capita, compared to a regional average of 541 kWh. Even after a hydropower project, the Bumbuna Hydro-Electric Power Plant, was completed (which had first been conceived in the 1980s), the country still had an installed generating capacity of only 80 MW in 2010. Less than 6 percent of the population has access to grid electricity.

Moreover, particularly for the power sector, but also for roads, infrastructure provision has been strongly concentrated in and around the capital city, Freetown. Grid power is available only in the capital and two other cities, Bo and Kenema, and only 21 percent of the rural population lives within 2 km of an all-season road (Pushak and Foster 2011).

Apart from inadequate generation capacity, challenges in the sector also include poor transmission and distribution systems and resulting high system losses. Technical and commercial losses in the distribution network are estimated at 42 percent (Srivastava and Larizza 2011b). The NPA, the country's sole power utility, has weak technical, operational, and financial management capacity. Despite having one of the highest retail tariffs in the world, the NPA is unable to cover its operating costs and relies on government subsidies.

As in the road sector, the power sector has similarly been marked by a combination of some progress being achieved, but also considerable inefficiencies. As a report by Pushak and Foster (2011) notes, Sierra Leoneans paid three times as much for power as did residents of African countries that relied on hydropower, even after the completion of the Bumbuna plant reduced costs somewhat. It is also striking to observe that shortly after the 2012 elections, power production from Bumbuna had to be significantly scaled back because of problems with the plants' two turbines.

Institutional Arrangements and Underlying Drivers Affecting Infrastructure Development

Roads

In the road sector, the first round of institutional reforms was undertaken in the early 1990s, during the onset of the conflict period. In 1993, the government established the SLRA, an independent statutory body responsible for planning, development, and maintenance of all roads in Sierra Leone that took over most of these responsibilities from the Department of Works.[26] The intention of the reform was to create an autonomous, commercially oriented agency with substantially reduced staff and professional management. Road construction and maintenance were to be contracted to private companies, with the SLRA performing quality control and oversight functions. In practice, the SLRA established monopoly control over the sector. For example, the allocation of resources among various categories of the road network (rural roads, urban roads, and so on) came under the control of the SLRA, outside the government's general budgetary framework and control.

The SLRA also had total control over resources from the road fund. This fund had been established by a cabinet decision in 1989 to finance regular, periodic, and emergency maintenance of the main road network through the collection of road user charges, such as fuel levies, vehicle licensing, and registration fees. Though limited in absolute terms, the resources available to the SLRA are still significant given the context of a poor economy. According to available information, between 2004 and 2008, an average of US$1 million per year was unaccounted for when being transmitted from the road fund to the main SLRA account (World Bank 2010a, 170). These losses would have taken place before any additional potential rent extraction through procurement or contracting practices.

According to the 2004 Local Government Act, the responsibility for maintenance of primary feeder roads and chiefdom roads was supposed to be transferred to local authorities. To date, however, the involvement of LCs in the sector remains limited because of strong resistance within the SLRA to transfer the control of feeder roads to LCs.[27] This lack of local authority makes it more difficult for road users—especially those living in rural areas—to ensure that service providers adequately respond to their needs. The chairman of the Bo LC called on the central government to enforce the devolution of feeder roads and noted that the delay by SLRA in transferring responsibility for rural roads is the "bane to rural development" (*Sierra Express Media* 2013). The justification provided by the SLRA is the lack of technical capacity in the LCs and of contractors at the local level. But responsibility of decision making does not necessarily mean that the LCs have to take responsibility for execution.

Following a pattern similar to other countries (Wales and Wild 2012), informal links have marked the relationship between the SLRA and political leadership in Sierra Leone. Participants in the focus group discussions widely shared the view that appointments of contractors are typically made on the basis of partisan and business connections rather than technical competency. For example, local councilors reported that a government-affiliated firm had received a number of contracts for road rehabilitation since 2007 and that contracts were regularly given to politically connected firms, often based in Freetown. This practice is seen as part of the elite's efforts to maintain the patronage network and grant benefits in exchange for political support (Robinson 2010).[28]

There is also evidence that key appointments are made on the basis of patronage. For example, the selection of a director general of the SLRA, appointed in

2008, was allegedly made outside of the formal process on the basis of personal connections and in contravention of formal procedures and over other more qualified candidates (Kandeh 2010).[29]

Robinson (2010) records the close personal connections between the head of the National Commission for Privatization that was charged in 2002 to co-oversee the SLRA jointly with the Ministry of Works, Housing, and Infrastructural Development, the director general of the SLRA, and key politicians. At the same time, the head of the SLRA has been a relatively prominent representative of the opposition SLPP. The constellation of dual oversight over the SLRA is also seen as having made effective management more challenging.[30] Such patronage practices appear to be quite frequent in the road sector across several countries (Wales and Wild 2012; see also chapter 9 on the Philippines in this volume). Their primary cost can be distortions and greater inefficiencies in a sector. In Sierra Leone, observed inefficiencies include the significant delays in several road projects noted in the third section, as well as various reported cases of corruption and ghost contracting.[31]

Power

Under both SLPP and the APC governments, control over appointments in the power sector has been used to advance political strategies. This control has had an effect at all levels, from senior-level appointments to regular staff recruitment, and on transfers and promotions in the power sector. President Kabbah's appointees to the Ministry of Energy and Water Resources (MoEWR) and NPA were implicated in corrupt procurement contracts for the Bumbuna Hydro-Electric Power Plant project. When the APC government took over in September 2007, significant changes were made in the leadership of the MoEWR and the NPA. At the NPA, Zubairu Kaloko was appointed as the general manager.[32] Kaloko was a member of the Sierra Leonean diaspora in the United States. While in the United States, he had worked as an economist for a regulatory authority in Pennsylvania, and his services had been terminated.

Recent Reform Initiatives
Roads

On April 9, 2010, parliament passed the Road Maintenance Fund Administration (RMFA) Act. This act establishes a formal separation between the SLRA and the road fund and could strengthen spending oversight. One important question is whether the implementation of the act will significantly change governance of the road sector. Early evidence remains mixed. After the act was signed into law in 2010, parliament approved the members of the board of the RMFA in June 2011, and the managerial staff of RMFA was in place by December 2012. The 2010 RMFA Act provides for an eight-member board; all but one are appointed by the president, subject to parliamentary approval. The board chairman is also appointed by the president rather than chosen by board members. Furthermore, the RMFA Act assigns the appointment of the chief executive to the president rather than requiring an open, competitive process. This system leaves substantial room for presidential control over the road fund.

Both the SLPP and the APC governments have kept tight control over the power sector. With the passage of the NPA Act of 2002, Sierra Leone adopted the model of a vertically integrated electricity utility. Under the act, the NPA was established as the sole utility in the sector with wide-ranging powers and authority, responsible for the generation, transmission, and distribution of electricity and for the setting of prices.

Power

In 2004, the government of Sierra Leone embarked on reforms aimed at introducing competitive market mechanisms in the investment, management, and operation of the sector. The objectives of power sector reforms (MEP 2004, 2006, 2007) included the following:

- Ensure the role of the MoEWR as the main policy-making authority in the sector to draw up a new electricity policy.
- Establish an independent sector regulator to oversee entry into the electricity sector and the technical and safety performance of sector operations and tariff adjustments.
- Restructure the NPA by transforming it into a corporate, self-financing entity devoted mainly to the transmission and distribution of electricity and called the National Power Company (NPC); in the transition to the new structure, the management of the NPA would be awarded—through a performance-based management contract—for resurrection of its operational status through institutional reforms, introduction of appropriate commercial practices, and downsizing of staff.
- Facilitate private sector involvement through the establishment of independent power producers that will sell power to the revamped NPA.

Reforms have proceeded tentatively and have not managed to effectively strengthen oversight. The sector, like roads, has faced significant irregularities in contracting. In 2007, a US$7 million donor-financed project supported the provision of 15 MW of power equipment to be procured through an international competitive bidding process. Evidence suggests that the new leadership in the MoEWR and the NPA, appointed by the then recently elected APC government, actively interfered in the procurement process. Thus, while Global Trading Group NV was awarded the contract through the formal bidding process in November 2007, another company—Income Electrix Ltd.—was, in parallel, awarded another contract on a sole-source basis. This contract imposed a take-or-pay obligation on the NPA. The government was unable to withdraw from the contract and continued to make payments to the company even though it used little or no energy from its plant. The Anti-Corruption Commission investigated the government's contract with Income Electrix and cast doubts on the legitimacy of the award, noting it seemed that "there was a premeditated plan to award the contract to Income Electrix Limited even before the bidding process had commenced."[33] It also recommended that institutional clarification be made regarding the role of the MoEWR, which is supposed to oversee the NPA and the NPC.[34]

Operational Implications at the Sector Level

Overall, the two infrastructure sectors provide interesting, although largely anecdotal and incomplete, illustrations of how political elites in Sierra Leone across successive governments have sought to maneuver between public policy promises of improvements and increases in spending within constrained resource envelopes. The illustrations also reveal political elites' efforts at maintaining close political control through the use of appointment powers and some apparent efforts to facilitate interelite sharing of rents and benefits available in the two sectors.[35]

If sector governance is a key roadblock to achieving better performance in infrastructure, then the first-best policy option would be to seek reforms of the formal institutional arrangements and to strengthen the resulting institutions. According to the analysis, national elites have a big stake in protecting the status quo, because they benefit from the systematic dysfunctions and governance failures characterizing these sectors. Therefore, although recent reforms have the potential to significantly improve the prospects of sector governance, implementing those reforms remains difficult. It follows that the scope of change that can be expected in the behavior of key players (such as the SLRA and the NPA) is limited, at least in the short term.

Given that politics at the national level has shown considerable continuity through the pre- and postwar environment, how the sectors are managed de facto is unlikely to change even when changes to formal institutional arrangements are put in place. Given these challenges, the recommendations emerging from the sector analysis are (a) to use results- and performance-based instruments where possible, (b) to calibrate World Bank engagement relative to observed governance scenarios in the two sectors, and (c) to support decentralization of roads and power services to LCs where technically feasible. In addition, the analysis emphasized the need for seeking a more intensive dialogue with reform supporters and constituents.

The study identified three illustrative governance scenarios for each sector and suggested calibrating the extent of engagement depending on which level of actual reform traction would actually be observed. Furthermore, the study suggested using forms of results-based lending, whereby donors agree to provide funding against observable delivery of progress. For example, government and donors could agree on a program of road maintenance or rehabilitation with disbursements being made upon verification of completion of work or of stages of work.

On the devolution of responsibility, the study recommended that development partners should focus on empowering subnational authorities as a way to reduce the concentration of power in the sectors. The study also suggested that partners should promote a greater orientation toward providing infrastructure services to rural areas of the country that would also reduce the current urban bias in provision and access.

In the road sector, this focus would take the form of support for the devolution of feeder road maintenance to LCs. For power, mini- and microgeneration and distribution networks potentially could be developed at the level of LCs. This redistribution of responsibility is consistent with the conclusions from the national analysis. For roads especially, this recommendation represents a desirable policy option from the technical perspective. The study acknowledges that powerful actors whose vested interests are directly challenged by the devolution of the road sector's functions (such as the SLRA or NPA) would likely resist the change and that the devolution would only represent a relatively small solution that would not necessarily alter the architecture of the road sector. Continuing efforts to strengthen the compact would thus also be desirable.

Overall Impact of the Analysis

When the study was completed, it could not be shared beyond a relatively small core group of World Bank staff members because of not only the perceived sensitivity of the findings but also the approaching 2012 elections. Despite this limitation, some opportunities for translating the operational recommendations into strategic actions at the policy level and into inputs for the design of new operations materialized.

Ongoing engagement in the road and power sectors has benefited from the insights provided by the analysis, including through both a new project supporting reforms and expansion of access in the power sector and the development of a transport sector strategy. The study has also led to eventual follow-up work on another key area of rent generation and distribution—the management of natural resources in the country—that was not covered in the original analysis. The study also led to an overall scaling-up of the World Bank's engagement in governance, including closer coordination with other main development partners.

The study's emphasis on the critical need for donors to remain engaged in decentralization and continue supporting subnational government has informed the design of the Decentralized Service Delivery Project (Phase II, US$50 million). Doing so helped the team advocate for joint-financing mechanisms that were eventually granted with an EU contribution to the project.[36] The support to the subnational level increased during the country programming period (2010–13) through the Rural Community and Health Project, which also works through local governments.

At the policy level, the emphasis on the emerging threats to the sustainability of the local government system has led the country management unit to intensify the policy dialogue with the government of Sierra Leone, giving mandate to Poverty Reduction and Economic Management and Human Development task teams to organize a multisector study to review progress and challenges of decentralization reform. Drawing on the findings from the present analysis, the Bank team has successfully ensured the government's support for the Economic and Sector Work (ESW). The ESW is expected to provide a platform for intergovernment dialogue to mediate diverging interests among key domestic stakeholders (local councilors, PCs, Ministry of Local Governance, and civil society groups) with the expectation of gradually realigning their incentives to keep the momentum of decentralization reforms and to manage present and future challenges in the implementation process.

Finally, the analysis' emphasis on the risks associated with the nature of national politics and its suggestion to manage these risks by promoting results-based lending proved to be critical during the design of the new Public Sector Reform project (approved in May 2012). This project uses a results-based modality to support civil service reforms, an area in which donors have had limited success so far. The project is in early stages of implementation, but the progress is promising.

In conclusion, although the initial impact of political economy analysis was limited, it is now beginning to influence the thinking about development efforts and aid effectiveness in the Bank. Moreover, with the passage of some time, concerns about the sensitivity of the findings of the report have decreased and selective findings have been published (for example, Srivastava and Larizza 2011a, 2013; Acemoglu, Reed, and Robinson 2013; Roseth and Srivastava 2013; Larizza and Glynn forthcoming), creating a public record and generating further debate.

Conclusion

The main goal of this chapter has been to present the findings of a political economy study that explored the incentives of key players, the impact the incentives had on national decision making, and, ultimately, their impact on sector-level policy outcomes in Sierra Leone. The analysis suggests that the status quo is difficult to change in the short term. Indeed, a key finding of this study is how little impact even dramatic events—such as the civil war—appear to have had on changing the structural features of national politics in Sierra Leone. In particular, ethnic alignments continue to play a significant role in how political competition is taking shape. In addition, informal patronage practices remain a resilient strategy for exercising political power and managing relationships between the state and society. Finally, violence, although limited in Sierra Leone, remains a threat made against political opponents.

As a result of these drivers, rent allocation, targeted provision of private goods (such as jobs, contracts, and political appointments), and a bias against investments in broader public services continue to be salient in Sierra Leone's political economy (Acemoglu and Robinson 2008). It would have been unrealistic to expect that such strategies would be rapidly reduced with the return to peace and a democratic government. The specter of recurrent violence generates strong incentives for government leaders to use patronage relationships rather than to seek impersonal relationships. In addition, government leaders are willing to tolerate rent-seeking among elite groups in return for their support or, at a minimum, agreement to refrain from renewed violence (North et al. 2013). However, to the extent that these patterns hold back greater progress on development and an ability to meet popular expectations, over time they become a growing threat to political stability and government legitimacy.

Therefore, the challenge for the development community is to be aware of how this political environment evolves, to calibrate its support so efforts to improve service delivery are effective despite a constrained environment, and, where possible, to engage in improving the accountability dynamics. The analysis suggests two main strategies for donors to follow: (a) navigate the current environment and (b) try to change the status quo. Regarding (a), donors should accept that the nature of national politics in Sierra Leone—as in most politically competitive, low-income countries with weak institutions—is likely to remain largely patrimonial. At the same time, patrimonialism per se might not be bad for growth and development, but rather the specific form that neopatrimonialism often takes and the specific ways in which rent-seeking is organized. With this perspective, it might be possible to reach agreement with a patrimonially oriented political leadership on results targets, performance-based lending, or similar financing modalities. These approaches might create conditions for a form of "developmental patrimonialism" (Kelsall and Booth 2010) in which the political leadership is successful in centralizing control over rents, while it also takes a long-term approach to maximizing rents (Khan 2000, 2010; Levy 2010). While doing so, donors should also try to promote policies that—by redistributing power within the Sierra Leonean society—empower drivers of change and increase their level of influence over the decision-making process. This empowerment and increase of influence, in turn, is expected to change the strategies of both politicians and citizens and to alter the current equilibrium.

Note that Sierra Leonean society is not static. Despite the persistence of certain strategies for managing political support, a new generation of politicians may be emerging at the local level. As highlighted previously in the chapter, these individuals are often independent candidates with close ties to local communities, unaffiliated with the APC or SLPP. It is possible that these individuals may signal the emergence of a new elite representing alternative social forces and new interest groups. These dynamics are relevant for donor engagement in the country, as they might open up opportunities for a "circulation of elites" (Mosca 1939) and create an environment fostering institutional change (Acemoglu and Robinson 2008). Whether decentralization will eventually succeed in enabling the development of a new national leadership is not known. However, the analysis presented in this chapter suggests that there is greater scope for accountability and collective action at the local level. Accordingly, another implication would be to direct resources away from the central government to the local authorities through increased support of decentralization.

The study as described in this chapter should be treated as a first contribution to efforts to integrate political economy analysis into the design and implementation of policy reforms in Sierra Leone. Further research is needed to validate the findings and confirm that the conclusions presented in this chapter are indeed representative of a larger trend. This additional research is important because the current political landscape may evolve in ways that cannot yet be foreseen, and future events have the potential to generate new dynamics that alter the strategies and motivations of the key political actors described here.

Notes

1. Especially in the initial postwar years, governments have had to work within very limited resources. In 2002, total central government revenue amounted to only US$123 million (for a population of 4.5 million at the time), rising to US$414 million by 2012. Annual official development assistance contributed on average just over US$400 million per annum. This reflects Sierra Leone's significant dependence on aid.

2. The team included Bank staff members and a group of three academics who prepared a set of four background papers based on the available data, the focus group discussions, and stakeholder and informant interviews.

3. The focus groups were divided into six categories: general public, civil society, councilors, paramount chiefs, parliamentarians, and, in Freetown, tribal heads. A total of 160 individuals participated in these discussions. Each focus group discussion was guided by a list of questions designed to stimulate ideas and enable the task team to enhance its understanding of power relationships and inner dynamics of decision-making processes in both formal government institutions and informal public and private networks.

4. Stevens became prime minister in 1967 and then president in 1971; he remained in power until 1985.

5. As one example, Alfred Akibo-Betts, the former chairman of the Freetown City Council, played a key role in exposing some of the worst excesses during the Stevens administration. Akibo-Betts was dismissed, was physically assaulted, and ultimately had to flee the country (Kpundeh 1995, 98).

6. Much of the exploitation of the people by the chiefs had related to their prerogative to identify those who were indigenous to the chiefdom (indigenes) and to guarantee their rights to local residence, land use, and political and legal representation (Fanthorpe 2006).

7. PCs were given more than just symbolic significance and retained some rights to collect revenues.

8. According to the 2002–03 "Sierra Leone Integrated Household Survey" (GoSL 2007), nearly 80 percent of the rural population fell below the poverty line, in contrast to 28 percent of Freetown and 63 percent of other urban areas.

9. When the Anti-Corruption Commission chairman, Val Collier, attempted to investigate cases of political corruption, he was quickly replaced by Henry Joko-Smart, the brother-in-law of President Kabbah. As reported by the International Crisis Group (ICGR 2007, 9), "While Collier brought charges against ministers, an appeals court judge, and several senior civil servants, Joko-Smart has focused almost exclusively on junior and mid-level officials."

10. During the 2007 presidential election campaigns, the opposition-controlled media widely reported alleged cases of bureaucratic embezzlement of development funds, corruption in the awarding of government contracts, and widespread impunity granted to offenders—alongside corruption among police and in the courts (ICGR 2007; Wyrod 2008).

11. An additional 12 seats in the 124-seat legislature are decided by PCs.

12. The amendment established obligations for all public officials to declare their assets, introduced new crimes for indictment and stiffer penalties, and gave the Anti-Corruption Commission greater independence to investigate cases and more prosecutorial powers.

13. In the November 2012 presidential elections, the geo-ethnic voting pattern was again repeated, with the incumbent APC president winning between 70 and 90 percent in Northern and Western districts, while carrying only 10–20 percent of the electorate in the South. In terms of aggregate votes, the presidential race was decisively won, however, with over 1.3 million votes for Koroma versus 830,000 votes for the SLPP challenger Julius Maada Bio.

14. Similarly, in the presidential run-off, Koroma took 80 percent of the vote in the traditional APC areas, while Berewa (the SLPP candidate) won heavily in the south and east.

15. According to *Africa Confidential*, "more than 200 qualified, competent southeasterners have been fired from public services and replaced by his kinsmen, cronies, and party stalwarts with little regard for their competence, experience, or qualification" (2009, 5; ICGR 2008).

16. When Koroma visited Kenema, the area where he stayed experienced an unexpected blackout. In the following days, small, armed groups of APC supporters attacked civilians, including the watchmen at the power station. The failure of the president to condemn the event and call for the prosecution of those responsible confirms suspicion of connections between the presidential security guards and criminal elements involved in the assaults.

17. In a recent report, data from 135 expert interviews and countrywide focus group discussions showed that 81 percent of respondents agree that violence is a major feature of political campaigns and fear that the 2012 elections will be rocked by electoral violence (Lavali, Hughes, and Suma 2011).

18. This section summarizes findings from a subset of studies undertaken by the World Bank team on the subject, including Robinson (2010), Srivastava and Larizza (2011a), and Larizza and Glynn (forthcoming).

19. LCs existed in the postindependence period until they were abolished in 1972 under then president Siaka Stevens. President Kabbah had been a district commissioner in the late 1950s and early 1960s.

20. Of the 1,112 total candidates registered with the National Electoral Commission in the 2004 elections, 84 of 394 (21 percent) constituency councilors were elected unopposed. In the 2008 local elections, the number of uncontested seats dropped to 38 of 394 (9.6 percent).

21. Keefer and Vlaicu (2008) provide a rigorous empirical test of this argument and demonstrate that sharply different policy choices across democracies can be explained as a consequence of differences in the ability of political competitors to make "credible pre-electoral commitments" to voters. According to the authors, in democracies where political competitors can make credible promises to only small segments of the electorate (such as, for instance, their own ethnic group), governments prefer to pursue clientelistic policies, high targeted spending, high rent-seeking, and low public goods provision.

22. The concentration of swing voters in Freetown and the Western Area seems to support this line of argument, suggesting that where citizens can regularly access

information through the media (newspapers and radio), policy issues tend to play a greater role in citizens' voting behavior. This reasoning suggests that some of the voters may be willing to withdraw their political support to punish poor performance (Kandeh 2008). Outside the Freetown area, however, the availability of information remains poor, and citizens are simply unable to assess the impact of government action (or inaction) on their daily lives. Imperfect information makes it difficult to assign credit or blame by voting a government in or out. It follows that politicians tend to have larger incentives to seek rents and provide targeted (private) goods rather than to deliver broad public goods and services. At the level of local elections, however, citizens seem willing and able to use greater information available during election campaigns to punish underperforming candidates (Casey 2010).

23. "In Port Loko nearly everyone is Loko and candidates cannot succeed in council elections by running on a Loko platform. Thus it is far more likely that local elections will be about nonidentity issues such as service provision or development. This argument suggests that decentralization will lead to less patronage and more public goods being provided in Sierra Leone" (Robinson 2010, 20).

24. *An Agenda for Change* (GoSL 2008) identified the development of a national road and transportation network and the development of the power sector as two of four strategic priorities for reducing poverty and stimulating economic development for the sector.

25. Several additional EU road projects also experienced significant delays. According to the Delegation of the European Union to Sierra Leone (2013), the Masiaka–Bo Highway was scheduled for completion in 2009 but opened in mid-2010. The Songo–Moyamba Junction Road was scheduled for completion in January 2009, but has yet to be completed.

26. Until 1993, the Department of Works was responsible for road sector coordination, policy formulation, sector planning, development, maintenance, monitoring, and oversight.

27. This level of involvement might change soon, because the new Feeder Roads Policy approved by the Cabinet in December 2010 states that maintenance of feeder roads will be devolved to LCs immediately upon its approval.

28. Moreover, evidence from focus groups also suggests that the contracting system is not transparent and that procurement information is very limited outside the Freetown area, thereby making it difficult for local contractors to compete and for local authorities to understand the technicalities of the process. Focus group discussions were held in August 2009.

29. Team interview, Freetown, August 4, 2009. In the words of one of the technical advisers in the SLRA: "The SLRA Board was involved in drawing up the Director General's job description. Top people applied for the position, but the current one was selected despite the established criteria."

30. The relevant issue here is not to publicize the specific individuals concerned, but rather to illustrate the type of networks and appointment practices that can facilitate political use of funds.

31. The problem of ghost contractors was highlighted in most of the focus group discussions to underscore the endemic corruption in the sector. As summed up by one of the participants: "The contracting system is broken because it lacks transparency" (focus group discussion, Makeni, August 4, 2009). A case cited throughout most of the interviews was the collapse of a bridge in Kailahun because of the shoddy work of contractors.

32. Kaloko's father was an associate of former president Siaka Stevens, who died in a car crash while campaigning for President Koroma, and to whose family, apparently, the president owes a huge debt of gratitude.

33. See research team interviews in Freetown in 2011.

34. The Anti-Corruption Commission investigations into the Income Electrix scandal seems to be evidence of its growing oversight capacity. But overall, it has only just begun programs that would help ministries and public sector agencies establish effective internal monitoring systems against corruption. According to its deputy director: "The investigation of such a high risk area showed that we could influence the course of the anti-corruption debates. We engaged all stakeholders in the energy sector; our report contributed to the renegotiation of the power contract" (team interview, Freetown, August 5, 2009).

35. Note that the most significant rents in the Sierra Leonean economy are to be found in the natural resource sector that was not analyzed during the initial round of political economy analytic work, but for which a political economy analysis was carried out more recently.

36. The EU participated in the consultation workshop where findings from the original political economy analysis studies were shared, thereby providing participants a chance to react to initial findings. The final report and recommendations were also shared.

Bibliography

Acemoglu, Daron, Tristan Reed, and James A. Robinson. 2013. "Chiefs: Elite Control of Civil Society and Economic Development in Sierra Leone." NBER Working Paper 18691, National Bureau of Economic Research, Cambridge, MA.

Acemoglu, Daron, and James A. Robinson. 2008. "Persistence of Power, Elites, and Institutions." *American Economic Review* 98: 267–93.

Africa Confidential. 2009. "More Power to Freetown." *Africa Confidential* 50 (20): 4–5.

Bates, Robert H. 1981. *Markets and States in Tropical Africa.* Berkeley, CA: University of California Press.

Cammack, Diana. 2007. "The Logic of African Neopatrimonialism: What Role for Donors?" *Development Policy Review* 24 (5): 599–614.

Carothers, Thomas, and Diane de Gramont. 2013. *Development Aid Confronts Politics: The Almost Revolution.* Washington, DC: Carnegie Endowment for International Peace.

Casey, Katherine. 2010. "Crossing Party Lines: The Effects of Information on Redistributive Politics." Unpublished working paper, Department of Economics, Brown University.

Davies, Victor A. B. 2007. "Sierra Leone's Economic Growth Performance, 1861–2000." In *The Political Economy of Growth in Africa, 1960–2000*, Vol. 2, edited by Benno J. Ndulu, Stephen A. O'Connell, and Robert H. Bates. New York: Cambridge University Press.

Delegation of the European Union to Sierra Leone. 2013. "Roads and Transportation." Freetown. (accessed June 22, 2013), http://eeas.europa.eu/delegations/sierra_leone/eu_sierra_leone/tech_financial_cooperation/infrastructure/roads_and_transporation/index_en.htm.

Easterly, William, and Ross Levine. 1997. "Africa's Growth Tragedy: Policies and Ethnic Divisions." *Quarterly Journal of Economics* 112: 1203–50.

EU EOM (European Union Election Observation Mission). 2012. "Peaceful and Well-Conducted Elections Represent an Important Step towards Consolidation of Democracy, Despite Unequal Playing Field." Press release, EU EOM, Freetown, November 19. http://www.eueom.eu/files/pressreleases/english/eueom-sierra-leone-press-release-19112012_en.pdf.

Fanthorpe, Richard. 2006. "On the Limits of Liberal Peace: Chiefs and Democratic Decentralization in Post-War Sierra Leone." *African Affairs* 105 (418): 27–49.

Fritz, Verena, Kai Kaiser, and Brian Levy. 2009. *Problem-Driven Governance and Political Economy Analysis: Good Practice Framework*. Washington, DC: World Bank.

Gberie, Lansana. 2010. *Situation Report—Sierra Leone: Business More than Usual*. Pretoria, South Africa: Institute for Security Studies.

GoSL (Government of Sierra Leone). 2007. *Sierra Leone Integrated Household Survey (SLIHS) 2003/2004*. Final Report, Freetown.

———. 2008. *Sierra Leone: An Agenda for Change—Second Poverty Reduction Strategy (PRSP-II) 2008–2012*. Freetown.

Hanlon, Joseph. 2004. "Is the International Community Helping to Re-Create the Preconditions for War in Sierra Leone?" *The Round Table* 94: 459–72.

Horowitz, Donald. 1985. *Ethnic Groups in Conflict*. Berkeley, CA: University of California Press.

Humphreys, Macartan, and Jeremy M. Weinstein. 2008. "Who Fights? The Determinants of Participation in Civil War." *American Journal of Political Science* 52: 436–55. doi: 10.1111/j.1540-5907.2008.00322.x.

ICGR (International Crisis Group Report). 2007. *Sierra Leone: The Election Opportunity*. Africa Report 129, Brussels.

———. 2008. *Sierra Leone: A New Era of Reform*. Africa Report 143, Brussels.

IRCBP (Institutional Reform and Capacity Building Project Evaluation Unit). 2008. *Report on the Decentralization Stakeholder Survey*. Freetown.

———. 2010. *Report on the IRCBP 2008 National Public Services Survey: Public Services, Governance, and Social Dynamics*. Unpublished manuscript, Freetown.

Kandeh, Jimmy. 2003. "Sierra Leone's Post-Conflict Elections of 2002." *Journal of Modern African Studies* 41 (2): 189–216.

———. 2008. "Rogue Incumbents, Donor Assistance and Sierra Leone's Second Post-Conflict Elections of 2007." *Journal of Modern African Studies* 46: 603–35.

———. 2010. "Governance Constraints and Challenges to State Building in Post-Conflict Sierra Leone." Unpublished paper, World Bank, Washington, DC.

Keefer, Philip. 2010. "The Ethnicity Distraction? Political Credibility and Partisan Preferences in Africa." Policy Research Working Paper 5236, World Bank, Washington, DC.

Keefer, Philip, and Razvan Vlaicu. 2008. "Clientelism, Credibility, and Democracy." *Journal of Law, Economics, and Organization* 24 (2): 371–406.

Kelsall, Tim, and David Booth. 2010. "Developmental Patrimonialism? Questioning the Orthodoxy on Political Governance and Economic Progress in Africa." APPP Working Paper 9, Africa Power and Politics Programme, Overseas Development Institute, London, U.K.

Khan, Mushtaq H. 2000. "Rents, Efficiency and Growth." In *Rents, Rent-seeking and Economic Development: Theory and Evidence in Asia*, edited by Mushtaq H. Khan and Jomo K. Sundaram, 21–69. Cambridge, MA: Cambridge University Press.

———. 2010. "Political Settlements and the Governance of Growth-Enhancing Institutions." Paper prepared for the U.K. Department for International Development, London, U.K.

Kpundeh, Sahr. 1995. *Politics and Corruption in Africa: A Case Study of Sierra Leone.* Lanham, MD: University Press of America.

Larizza, Marco and Brendan Glynn. Forthcoming. "Sierra Leone Case Study: Local Councils." In *Institutions Taking Root: Building State Capacity in Challenging Contexts*, edited by Elisabeth Huybens, Lorena Viñuela, and Naazneen Barma. Washington, DC: World Bank.

Lavali, Andrew, Charlie J. Hughes, and Mohamed Suma. 2011. "Sierra Leone: Elections and Diversity Management." United Nations Economic Commission for Africa, Addis Ababa.

Levy, Brian. 2010. "Development Trajectories: An Evolutionary Approach to Integrating Governance and Growth." Economic Premise 15, Poverty Reduction and Economic Management Network, World Bank, Washington, DC.

MEP (Ministry of Energy and Power). 2004. *The Energy Policy for Sierra Leone.* Draft report, Freetown.

———. 2006. "Sierra Leone NPA Recovery Strategy." Report submitted to the Minister of Energy at a wrap-up meeting of the International Development Association Mission, Freetown, October 5.

———. 2007. "Energy Sector Strategy Note." Paper presented at the Development Partnership Committee meeting, Freetown, March.

Mosca, Gaetano. 1939. *Elementi di Scienza Politica* [The Ruling Class]. Translated by Hannah D. Kahn. New York: McGraw Hill.

NEC (National Electoral Commission). 2008a. *Summary of Results of 2008 Local Elections.* Freetown: NEC. http://www.nec-sierraleone.org.

———. 2008b. "Final Local Councils Nomination Statistics." NEC, Freetown. http://www.nec-sierraleone.org.

North, Douglass C., John Joseph Wallis, Steven B. Webb, and Barry R. Weingast, eds. 2013. *In the Shadow of Violence: Politics, Economics, and the Problems of Development.* New York: Cambridge University Press.

O'Donnell, Guillermo. 1996. "Illusions about Consolidation." *Journal of Democracy* 7 (2): 34–51.

OECD (Organisation for Economic Co-operation and Development). 2012. *Fragile States 2013: Resource Flows and Trends in a Shifting World.* Paris: OECD. http://www.oecd-ilibrary.org.

Pushak, Nataliya, and Vivien Foster. 2011. "Sierra Leone's Infrastructure: A Continental Perspective." Policy Research Working Paper 5713, World Bank, Washington, DC.

Reno, William. 1995. *Corruption and State Politics in Sierra Leone.* New York: Cambridge University Press.

Richards, Paul. 1996. *Fighting for the Rainforest: War, Youth and Resources in Sierra Leone.* Oxford, U.K.: Oxford University Press.

Robinson, James A. 2008. *Governance and Political Economy Constraints to World Bank CAS Priorities in Sierra Leone*. Washington, DC: World Bank.

———. 2010. "The Political Equilibrium in Sierra Leone." Unpublished manuscript, World Bank, Washington, DC.

Roseth, Benjamin and Vivek Srivastava. 2013. "Engaging for Results in Civil Service Reforms: Early Lessons from a Problem-Driven Engagement in Sierra Leone." Policy Research Working Paper 6458, World Bank, Washington, DC.

Sacks, Audrey, and Marco Larizza. 2012. "Why Quality Matters: Rebuilding Trustworthy Local Government in Post-Conflict Sierra Leone." Policy Research Working Paper 6021, World Bank, Washington, DC.

Sierra Express Media. 2013. "Chairman Condemns SLRA Devolution." January 11. http://www.sierraexpressmedia.com/archives/51801.

Srivastava, Vivek, and Marco Larizza. 2011a. "Decentralization in Postconflict Sierra Leone: The Genie Is Out of the Bottle." In *Yes Africa Can: Success Stories from a Dynamic Continent*, edited by Punam Chuhan-Pole and Manka Angwafo, 141–54. Washington, DC: World Bank.

———. 2011b. "Governance and Political Economy Constraints in Emerging Postconflict Sierra Leone: A Multilevel Analysis." Unpublished paper, World Bank, Washington, DC.

———. 2013. "Working with the Grain for Reforming the Public Service: A Live Example from Sierra Leone." *International Review of Administrative Sciences* 76 (3): 458–85.

Truth and Reconciliation Commission. 2004. *Final Report of the Truth and Reconciliation Commission of Sierra Leone*. Freetown: Truth and Reconciliation Commission.

Utas, Mats. 2007. "Watermelon Politics in Sierra Leone: Hope Amidst Vote Buying and Remobilized Militias." *African Renaissance* 4 (3/4): 62–66.

Wales, Joseph, and Leni Wild. 2012. *The Political Economy of Roads: An Overview and Analysis of Existing Literature*. Overseas Development Institute, London, U.K.

Williams, Gareth, Alex Duncan, and Pierre Landell-Mills. 2007. "Making the New Political Economy Perspective More Operationally Relevant for Development Agencies." Policy Practice Brief 2, The Policy Practice, Brighton, U.K.

World Bank. 2010a. *Sierra Leone Public Expenditure Review*. Report 52817-SL, Washington, DC.

———. 2010b. Worldwide Governance Indicators (database). http://info.worldbank.org/governance/wgi/index.asp.

———. 2012. World Development Indicators (database). http://data.worldbank.org/data-catalog/world-development-indicators.

Wyrod, Christopher. 2008. "Sierra Leone: A Vote for Better Governance." *Journal of Democracy* 19: 70–83.

Zhou, Yongmei, ed. 2009. *Decentralization, Democracy, and Development: Recent Experience from Sierra Leone*. World Bank: Washington, DC.

CHAPTER 8

Formal Rules, Clientelism, and the Allocation of Project Funds across Villages in Papua New Guinea

Zahid Hasnain, Philip Keefer, and Nicholas Menzies

Introduction

Confronted with intractable political and capacity constraints that undermine the implementation of top-down development initiatives, reformers in some countries have turned to programs that funnel resources directly to local governments. The World Bank alone loaned more than US$85 billion over the past decade to local participatory development (Mansuri and Rao 2013). Typically, these programs allocate funds for local infrastructure development to communities, leaving it to the communities to identify spending priorities and to oversee use of the funds. The programs vary widely in how they are governed and in the eligibility requirements that communities must meet. At one extreme, social protection funds might be run by an independent agency of the government and make few requirements of communities, other than that they submit detailed plans to implement some project. At the other extreme, community-driven development programs typically require participatory, usually elected bodies to request funds and to supervise their expenditure. In all cases, however, program design tends to assume that formal, de jure institutional arrangements will have a substantial effect on the incentives and discretion of decision makers at all levels of government regarding fund disbursement and project implementation.

Using evidence from the decentralization of infrastructure resource allocation in Papua New Guinea, we find that in clientelist political settings, apparently substantial formal institutional arrangements have little effect on

The authors wish to thank Paul Barker, Marjorie Andrew, Laura Bailey, Nicole Haley, Mathew Allen, Yasuhiko Matsuda, Stuti Khemani, and colleagues from the World Bank's Justice for the Poor program for contributing to the research and this report. We are especially grateful for significant assistance from Quynh Nguyen in the construction of the database.

The findings, interpretations, and conclusions contained in this synthesis report are entirely those of the authors. They do not necessarily represent the view of the World Bank, its executive directors, or the countries they represent. The World Bank is not responsible for the contents of this research.

infrastructure allocations. In particular, central government authorities (members of parliament) who were influential before the decentralization of infrastructure spending remain influential afterward. The community characteristics that matter most for infrastructure allocation are those that define their relationship with their member of parliament (MP) rather than those that relate to their participation in the institutional arrangements that formally frame local infrastructure allocation.

The basis of the analysis is a survey covering almost 1,100 households across 49 wards in 9 districts in Papua New Guinea. It was undertaken with the explicit aim of examining community access to infrastructure and the community's relationship with higher-level government. This is the first detailed empirical analysis to investigate communities' access to outside public works financing as a function of the electoral behavior of candidates in the locality, households' own knowledge of the formal institutional arrangements through which projects are distributed, and the extent of group activity in the communities.

Previous studies have shown that the central funding of subnational governments can be politicized. Schady (2000) concludes that the Peruvian social fund (Cooperation Fund for Social Development, or FONCODES) exhibited signs of politically motivated allocation (for example, allocations were highest before elections and heaviest in the most competitive electoral districts), but that equity and political criteria seemed to overlap, because poorer districts were nevertheless privileged. His research looks at the outcomes of the program, not at the effect of program design on those outcomes.

Khemani (2007), in contrast, considers program design explicitly. She compares central government transfers to state governments in India when they were undertaken directly by the central government to transfers mediated by an independent fiscal agency. Her evidence indicates that the participation of the independent agency muted partisan influences on allocations. Litschig (2012) also examines the effect of nonpartisan rules on transfers, but with a different conclusion. He observes that in Brazil, fiscal transfers to municipalities are based on rigid, population-based criteria, apparently leaving no room for political influence. He finds, however, that in the presence of rigid, population-based criteria for making transfers to local governments, officials engaged in significant manipulation of population numbers.

As with Litschig (2012), our evidence indicates that new formal institutional arrangements that should have increased the influence of communities and curbed the influence of central government politicians in the allocation of resources appear, in practice, to have been insufficient. Our data allow us to go beyond previous work and to trace the presence of new projects in communities to precise features of the electoral and institutional landscape. In particular, the data allow us to show that MP interaction with communities is a significant determinant of whether communities have new projects. In contrast, whether or not community members are informed about the new institutional arrangements has no relationship at all with whether communities are able to obtain new projects.

The chapter analysis highlights the important role that political economy analysis can play in understanding when development interventions will succeed. One aspect of success is whether reforms are implemented. Another is whether they achieve their intended effects. The reforms in Papua New Guinea arguably succeeded under the first definition, but not under the second. The incentives of higher-level politicians play a powerful role, shaping both the design and the implementation of the program. In particular, in increasing the role of communities (actually, wards, which constitute one or a small group of villages) in local infrastructure provision, MPs adopted institutional arrangements that formally obligated them to pay greater attention to community demands, but informally permitted them to continue to exercise significant control over the allocation of funding. We present substantial evidence that, as a consequence of continued MP influence, the formal procedures for ward access to local infrastructure funding are substantially less important than are the clientelist links between communities and the MPs—the same links that have previously characterized ward access to the resources of the central government.

The analysis has implications for how reformers should think about the design of policies that allocate resources to communities. First, small statutory details can play a significant role. Originally, the national parliament and, to a lesser extent, provincial governments determined the infrastructure allocations across communities. Parties matter little for political competition in Papua New Guinea. Instead, the political success of individual MPs depends on their ability to build up clientelist networks and on the strength of the clans that they represent. Their decisions over the allocation of infrastructure financing across communities were guided by these considerations.

A key institutional reform, however, shifted responsibility for the allocation of some infrastructure funds to the district level and to new, district-level committees. In principle, these committees gave communities greater influence over infrastructure allocations, because they had direct representation on the committees. However, the specific rules governing these committees endowed the MP with significant authority. The MP for the district is the chair of the committee, can pick several of its members, and has strong agenda-setting authority. Moreover, because travel to district committee meetings in Papua New Guinea is exceptionally difficult, the MP's agenda control has an exaggerated effect, so that the MP in fact exerts significant continuing authority over spending allocations.

However, our analysis provides strong support for reformers who seek to deepen participation at the local level. As Keefer, Hasnain, and Menzies (2013) document, communities in which members are more active in church and non-church groups are more likely to report new infrastructure projects. That is, the capacity of communities to act collectively has a significant effect on the ability of communities to influence the decisions of higher-level political actors, even in clientelist settings where formal institutional arrangements impose only weak constraints on political discretion.

The next section briefly describes the formal local-level government institutional arrangements. The section following describes the survey instrument and presents some descriptive statistics on the basic characteristics of the households that participated, their knowledge of local-level institutions, their participation in groups, and their voting behavior. Thereafter, the analytical core of the paper presents the results from the regression analysis on the determinants of infrastructure projects in Papua New Guinea wards.

The Planning and Budgeting Process for Local Projects

Prior to 1995, infrastructure spending in Papua New Guinea was entirely determined by the provincial and national governments and, in particular, the national parliament. The parliament is composed of MPs elected in so-called open seats, each representing one of the 89 districts in the country. An additional 20 seats in parliament are held by members elected from province-wide constituencies (Regional MPs). There are 20 provinces,[1] and these Regional MPs also serve as the governors of the province in which they are elected.

Formal responsibility for infrastructure allocation changed significantly with the 1995 passage of the Organic Law on Provincial Governments and Local-level Governments (hereinafter Local Government Law), which provides the overarching framework for the planning and budgeting of local project delivery. The law mandates that, within this broad framework, a detailed set of cascading plans and budgets be produced, starting at the bottom with the wards. Each ward elects a ward councilor, who sits on the Local-level Government (LLG). Every district contains one or more LLGs (commonly, three or four) and each LLG contains, on average, approximately 20 wards (see figure 8.1). Each ward is also

Figure 8.1 Governmental Units in Papua New Guinea

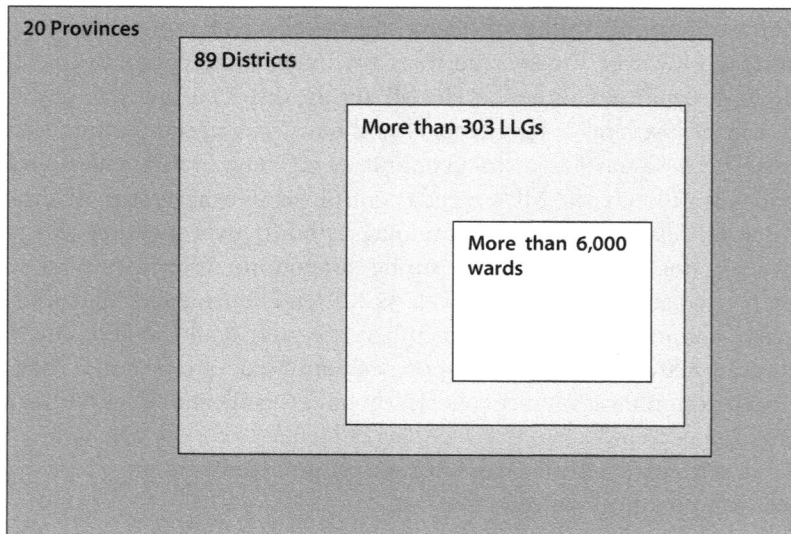

Note: LLG = local-level government.

meant to have a Ward Development Committee (WDC) and to prepare a ward development plan outlining the development priorities for the ward. Each LLG is tasked with preparing five-year LLG plans that take into account the ward development plans in their area. District-level plans are then prepared incorporating the plans of the constituent LLGs.

The Joint District Planning and Budget Priorities Committee (JDPBPC), was then created by a 1996 amendment to the Local Government Law. The JDPBPC was intended to bring government closer to the people when compared with the efforts of national and provincial service providers. It would do this by concentrating resources and decision-making power at the district level.

At the apex of this system, then, sits the JDPBPC, which is responsible for overseeing all aspects of planning and budgeting for each district. The JDPBPC distributes significant resources because of its authority over two infrastructure grant programs, the District Support Grant and the District Services Improvement Program. The latter involved appropriations to each district of 4 million kinas (K) in 2007, K 6 million in 2008, and K 4 million in 2009 (between US$1.3 million and US$2.1 million),[2] with reports of significant additional financing for selected districts. In contrast to this, funding for LLGs appears to have fallen away, with LLG officials regularly reporting a lack of funds beyond the bare minimum to pay the salaries of a handful of core staff members and sitting fees for council meetings. LLG and ward officials interviewed during this research often questioned the utility of preparing development plans when so little money was in the hands of LLGs and wards to actually implement projects.

The lack of resources is associated with many gaps in the planning apparatus envisioned in the legislation. For example, one report has noted that in the province of New Ireland, only one of the many required ward, LLG, and district plans existed (Kalinoe 2009). From our own research, almost half of the ward officials and more than a quarter of LLG officials interviewed reported an absence of ward and LLG plans, respectively. This is probably underestimated, because they are responsible for preparing these plans and have an incentive to overreport their existence. These results have emerged despite significant efforts by the government of Papua New Guinea and development partners to assist local officials in making this structure work.

At the same time, although the significant institutional changes were meant to increase local influence over infrastructure spending allocations, the MP continues to wield significant authority. Not only is the MP the chair of his or her JDPBPC, but he or she[3] also appoints three of the members who sit on the committee, in addition to the heads of each LLG who serve on it. In effect, then, the result of decentralization under the Local Government Law has been the concentration of decision-making power and resources with national MPs, who chair the JDPBPCs, at the expense of provincial and local-level governments. This appears to confirm some assessments that the real objective of the 1995 reforms was a drive by open-seat MPs to substantially increase the resources at their disposal (and hence their ability to gain reelection) at the expense of provincial governors and local-level officials (Allen and Hasnain 2010,).

Nevertheless, formally, the de jure institutional changes endowed wards with significantly more influence over infrastructure allocations than they had previously. First, directly or through their LLG representative, they had a seat on the committee. Second, they had more information and greater certainty about the funds available (because funds allocated by the JDPBPC cannot be shifted across districts, unlike funds allocated at the national government level). Third, in contrast to previous parliamentary procedures, the JDPBPC was legally enjoined to take ward preferences and plans into account in making its allocation decisions.

The central development question is therefore whether the new system for allocating local infrastructure funds, under the JDPBPC, had an effect on how funds were actually allocated. We get at this question indirectly, by asking whether the determinants of access to JDPBPC-funded infrastructure projects appear to be those related to politics as usual (vote-buying, clientelism, and the capacity of ward residents to act collectively—their participation in church and nonchurch groups) or whether the new institutions mattered (in the sense that wards with greater awareness of and adherence to the formal distribution rules were also more likely to receive infrastructure funding). In fact, we find that politics as usual matters most, while knowledge and adoption of the formal procedures have little effect on whether wards report recent infrastructure projects. This finding leads us to conclude that the wards that gain access to JDPBPC projects are roughly the same as the wards that would have received local infrastructure allocations prior to the decentralization of infrastructure finance.

Methodological Options in Political Economy Analysis

Every analysis of the political economy of policy implementation and effectiveness requires, as in the foregoing section, a careful discussion of the key decision makers and the formal institutional arrangements within which they operate. Analysts then have several choices to make about how to proceed from this starting point. Those choices are informed by judgments about which policy issues are most pressing and which determinants of political incentives are likely to matter most, and by constraints on the types of information that can be collected to undertake the analysis.

The first choice concerns the outcomes that analysts should care about. In the case of the local government reforms in Papua New Guinea, at least three issues are relevant for policy makers. Did the reforms change the identity of key decision makers and their incentives regarding infrastructure allocation? Did the reforms improve the capacity of community members to act in their collective interests? And did the reforms lead to a closer match between local community preferences and infrastructure allocations? Given the resources and data available, we could investigate variants of the first two questions, but not the third.

The second choice concerns the determinants of these outcomes that analysts should examine. Political decisions are the product of myriad influences, and only in rare cases can an analyst hope to capture all of them. However, the failure to take into account significant factors that actually matter can lead the analysis astray. If we observe that only projects supported by a recommendation from a WDC are approved, then we might conclude that the local government reforms in Papua New Guinea succeeded. However, if we undertook a more thorough analysis, then we might note that only wards with strong family ties with the MP bothered to set up WDCs. In this case, our conclusion would be the opposite: as in the pre-reform period, clientelist and clan ties are key to project allocation. The analysis here uses theory and the knowledge of experts on politics in Papua New Guinea to draw well-informed conclusions about the major factors that are most likely to influence political decision making in the country.

The third choice is how to prove which of the factors that we think *might* matter for political decision making actually *do* matter. This is largely a question of the types of information that analysts have the opportunity and resources to collect. At one end of the spectrum, analysts can pursue a purely qualitative strategy, relying on structured interviews of key informants who are chosen according to whether they are in a position to observe actual decision making by politicians. Qualitative research has many advantages, not the least of which is the ability to extract detailed information on the mechanisms through which particular factors of interest (clan membership, ward group activity, and so on) affect political incentives. One significant disadvantage, however, is the possibility that the key informants have only incomplete information. For example, they may all know about the behavior of a few notorious MPs or be very familiar with particular parts of Papua New Guinea, but this knowledge may not generalize more broadly. It can also be difficult to trace the incentives of political decision makers, as depicted by key informants, through to the specific, concrete decisions related to the policy in question (here, local infrastructure allocations).

Quantitative, empirical analysis is the other strategy, broadly speaking, that analysts can employ. The advantages and disadvantages are nearly the mirror image of qualitative work. Analysts can use surveys to extract the opinions of many individuals, and not only key informants, thus allowing them to have information from a broader array of sources and giving them greater capacity to draw general conclusions. However, while surveys draw opinions from a large group of respondents, their advantage is ambiguous when the respondents are less knowledgeable than the key informants. Surveys and other approaches can also be used to collect a broad array of objective information (for example, "Exactly what projects were provided where and across how many jurisdictions?"). In general, surveys are costly and are uninformative about mechanisms (for example, "Why are clans so important to MPs?"), but they can offer greater capacity to draw general conclusions and to control for biases and noise in the information provided by respondents.

Qualitative analysis is more common in operational political economy analysis. The decisions in question are typically large and singular (for example, "Under what conditions will the government approve tax reform?"), and opportunities for quantitative analysis are scarce (there are no data sets nor is there the possibility of conducting surveys to collect systematic data on which politicians supported or opposed tax reform and on the characteristics of politicians that could explain their support or opposition). Significant resource constraints also tend to confront most political economy analyses. Budget allocations are typically sufficient to allow a consultant to review the secondary literature and to undertake two or three weeks of interviews, leading to a bias toward qualitative analysis.

Both the nature of the question in the analysis here and the budget permitted more quantitative analysis, however. The question was not (for example), "What is the level of central government support in Papua New Guinea for the effective implementation of local government reform?" Instead, it was, "What determines which wards receive infrastructure allocations under the new, decentralized system governing infrastructure spending?" The latter question relates to hundreds of decisions that lend themselves to quantitative analysis; the former question relates to only one. At the same time, we had the budget necessary to undertake a large survey to examine the determinants of those allocation decisions.

Unfortunately, the budget was insufficient to permit the adequate implementation of associated qualitative research that would have more deeply informed the mechanisms underlying the results that we report below. Wards in Papua New Guinea are often remote and difficult to reach. We were able to field a survey team that had the experience and ability to navigate in this tricky terrain, both geographically and culturally. The team was efficient and accurate in deploying a structured survey instrument. However it did not have a comparative advantage in pursuing more open-ended, qualitative research. Resources were insufficient, to field a separate team of scholars to undertake this qualitative work.

Both qualitative and quantitative political economy (or any other) analyses must grapple with whether the information upon which they rely can yield robust conclusions. In the case of the analysis that follows, we conclude that the introduction of the JDPBPC (district committee in charge of infrastructure allocation) did not change the way in which infrastructure is allocated.

A qualitative analysis might reach this conclusion based on reports from key informants who describe, in detail, the power of MPs on the JDPBPC, the relative weakness of community representatives, and the way this influence is approximately the same as the authority they had over local infrastructure in the prior system. This analysis would be successful to the extent that the analysts could defend the assumption that the key informants were knowledgeable about infrastructure allocations before and after local government reform and across different parts of Papua New Guinea.

A quantitative analysis might reach this conclusion by comparing infrastructure allocations before and after local government reform, holding constant the identity of the MPs and district-specific characteristics other than the introduction of the JDPBPC that might have changed and that could also account for shifting allocations. However, we had no information and no ability to collect information on pre-reform allocations. Instead, the analysis takes a more indirect approach, comparing wards with more and fewer projects and asking whether they differ in ways that would be consistent with the efficacy of the JDPBPC system.

For example, if the JDPBPC system were salient, then wards with more projects would be more knowledgeable about it. We find that they are not. If ward representation (direct or indirect) on the JDPBPC is critical, then we would expect that the presence of WDCs should be associated with wards that exhibit more projects. They are not. If the JDPBPC system were meant to attenuate the authority of national-level officials in the allocation of infrastructure, then interactions with district MPs should matter little in the allocation of projects. In fact, these interactions are highly significant.

Descriptive Statistics and Summary Indications that Politics as Usual Prevails

Data for the analysis come from a household survey conducted during April 2010 in nine districts (Namatanai, Kairuku-Hiri, North Fly, Kokopo, Chuave, Usino Bundi, Goroka, Koroba–Lake Kopiago, and Maprik) and covering approximately 1,100 households (map 8.1). The districts were chosen to represent a range of experiences across a number of criteria, including access to services;

Map 8.1 Survey Districts, Papua New Guinea

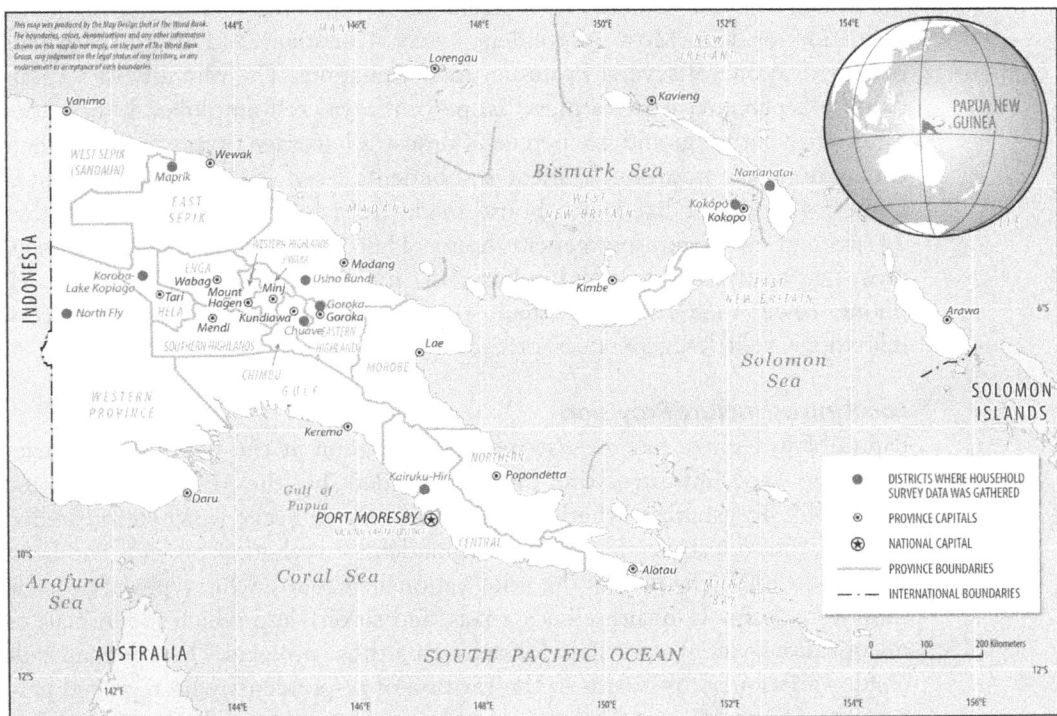

Source: Map number: IBRD 40243, September 2013.

Problem-Driven Political Economy Analysis • http://dx.doi.org/10.1596/978-1-4648-0121-1

reputed performance of resource allocation processes; access to benefits from mining; regional representation (Highlands, Islands, Papua, and Momase); and overall disadvantage. While a survey sampling of 1,100 households is almost sufficient to have been nationally representative, we did not choose our households randomly from among all households nationally. We cannot say, therefore, that they are representative of Papua New Guinea as a whole. We can, however, be confident that they represent a diverse cross-section of the country. Indeed, consistent with common views of Papua New Guinea, a diversity of experience districts is readily apparent in the results.

Table 8.1 presents a fuller picture of the district characteristics and criteria for selection. The survey asked for basic respondent information, including household assets; respondents' level of engagement with social and community groups; household perceptions of service delivery; respondents' knowledge and households' media access; and respondent and household voting behavior. Additional instruments used in the research include a key officials' questionnaire and a ward profile.[4]

Most of the households interviewed were rural, with limited means and education. The respondent households appear to be representative of the types of households that reforms intend to benefit. Most (67 percent) of respondents were men, which is not surprising given that 75 percent of the respondents were heads of the household. The median age of the respondents was 40, and the median household size was six. Reflecting the troubled education sector in Papua New Guinea, 64 percent of respondents had an eighth grade education or less. Most respondents were Christian, and most Christians belonged to one of several Protestant denominations. The plurality of respondents (45 percent) were farmers; 20 percent were self-employed in activities other than farming; and 15 percent (almost all women) reported that their occupation was housework. Most respondents lived in cheaply constructed homes: 42 percent lived in a house made from bush material and another 34 percent in a semi-permanent house. Half of the households had pigs, most had mattresses, half had radios, and, interestingly, 64 percent had a cell phone. Fewer than 20 percent had other durable assets such as refrigerators, televisions, vehicles, generators, or cookers.

Local Infrastructure Provision

Papua New Guinea has no systematic information at the national or district levels on new infrastructure projects funded by the district committee (JDPBPC). To establish whether wards had new projects, we therefore relied on numerous questions that probed respondents on whether projects had been built since 2007 (the date of the prior national election), what types of projects they were (schools, health clinics, roads, and so on), and which individuals or organizations were responsible for delivering those projects. There was considerable variation across wards in the fraction of respondents who reported new projects. This fraction is the main variable we use to judge whether a ward has new projects: the larger the fraction of respondents who report a new project,

Table 8.1 Research Districts

District	Province and region	Rationale for selection
Usino Bundi	Province: Madang Region: Momase	New mine (in construction); mine site, pipeline, and refinery; 30-year mine life, yet little research to date Memorandum of Agreement between landowners, mine developer, and the state negotiated with Minerals Resource Authority assistance, including women's association Four landowner associations Second-most-disadvantaged district in Papua New Guinea[a]; considered "extremely disadvantaged"[b] Access to services—2[c]
Koroba–Lake Kopiago	Province: Southern Highlands Region: Highlands	Established water-use payment regime Fifteen-year engagement with Porgera gold mine Had two by-elections using the newly introduced LPV system prior to research Good longitudinal election data In the bottom 13 districts in Papua New Guinea; considered "extremely disadvantaged" Access to services: 2 (1)
Kairuku-Hiri	Province: Central Region: Southern	Special Purpose Authority Kokoda Development Program Considered "seriously disadvantaged" Access to services: 4
Maprik	Province: East Sepik Region: Momase	Government systems reported to be working well, including the JDPBPC Full complement of district staff and service improvements Considered "slightly disadvantaged" Access to services: 4
Namatanai	Province: New Ireland Region: New Guinea Islands	Significant resources from mining Considered "slightly disadvantaged" Access to services: 3
Chuave	Province: Chimbu Region: Highlands	Had one LPV by-election prior to the research Good longitudinal election data Considered "slightly disadvantaged" Access to services: 4 (2)
Goroka	Province: Eastern Highlands Region: Highlands	Good election data Partly urban/partly rural Among the top five districts in Papua New Guinea; considered "not disadvantaged" Access to services: 5
Kokopo	Province: East New Britain Region: New Guinea Islands	Good election data Among the top five districts in Papua New Guinea; considered "not disadvantaged" Access to services: 5
North Fly	Province: Western Region: Southern	Significant resources from mining Considered "extremely disadvantaged" Access to services: 3

Source: Based on survey data.

Note: Much of the data used for the ranking come from the mid-1990s and as such do not reflect current service levels in some districts. An updated estimate (by the research team) of current conditions is indicated in parentheses for some districts.

a. Hanson et al. (2001).

b. Hanson et al. (2001) rank district "disadvantage" on five factors (land potential, agricultural pressure, access to services, income from agriculture, and child malnutrition) into five categories: "extremely disadvantaged," "seriously disadvantaged," "moderately disadvantaged," "slightly disadvantaged," and "not disadvantaged."

c. Hanson et al. (2001) rank districts according to access to services (one factor within the ranking of disadvantage—noted in note b). A value of 1 represents very poor access to services; a value of 2 represents poor access to services; a value of 3 represents moderate access to services; a value of 4 represents good access to services; and a value of 5 represents very good access to services. JDPBPC = Joint District Planning and Budget Priorities Committee; LPV = Limited Preferential Voting.

Problem-Driven Political Economy Analysis • http://dx.doi.org/10.1596/978-1-4648-0121-1

the more likely it is that a new project was actually built. Variation is substantial. In 15 of the 49 wards we surveyed, more than 80 percent of respondents indicated that the ward had received a new project; in 17 of the 49 wards, fewer than 20 percent of respondents believed that the ward had received a new project.

Consistent with the main conclusion of the analysis, respondents perceive MPs to be the main actors responsible for funding projects. Fifty-four percent of respondents stated that the most important project in the community was funded by the MP, as compared with 7 percent who stated that it was funded by the LLG, 13 percent by a company, 13 percent by a donor, and 9 percent by the community.

Media Access and Knowledge of Institutions

In addition, and also consistent with the continued importance of the MP, respondents know their MP, but have very little knowledge of the formal procedures under which local infrastructure funds are supposed to be allocated. This reflects the continued de facto importance of the MP in the allocation of benefits from the national government. Almost all respondents (93 percent overall: 97 percent for men; 83 percent for women) knew the name of their MP, the pivotal government figure for localities. Knowledge of the MP's political party was much lower (although with considerable interdistrict variation), reflecting the well-known weakness of political parties in Papua New Guinea. Knowledge of other aspects of local government arrangements was markedly lower (see table 8.2). Fifty-two percent of respondents had knowledge of when and where LLG meetings take place. Under the Local Government Law, however, and also in practice, the entity with the most resources to allocate for local infrastructure is the JDPBPC. However, many fewer respondents, only

Table 8.2 Knowledge of Local Government Institutions
Percentage saying "yes"

District	Know of local-level government meetings?	Heard of the JDPBPC?
Namatanai	35	33
Kairuku-Hiri	33	45
North Fly	83	18
Kokopo	79	52
Chuave	92	72
Usino Bundi	30	44
Goroka	41	24
Koroba–Lake Kopiago	19	12
Maprik	77	57
Overall	52	39

Source: Based on survey data.
Note: JDPBPC = Joint District Planning and Budget Priorities Committee.

39 percent, report even having heard of it, with a significant difference between men (47 percent) and women (20 percent).

Fewer than half of respondents (41 percent) stated that a WDC was functioning in their ward, and only 17 percent of all respondents had ever attended a WDC meeting. This is significant because the WDC is charged with preparing and submitting proposals for local public works to their LLG and then on to the JDPBPC. The interdistrict variation on this point is considerable—Chuave, Goroko, and Koroba–Lake Kopiago, the three surveyed districts in the Highlands, appear to have largely nonfunctional WDCs. In general, about half of the respondents who report that a WDC is operating also report that they attended a meeting. The fraction of respondents who report having attended a meeting ranged from 0 to 35 percent.

The lack of respondent knowledge regarding local government institutions is not a consequence of lack of media access (surprisingly, given the remoteness of many of the wards). Over 50 percent of households stated that they listened to the radio, and one-third stated that they read the newspaper (daily or several times a week). This pattern of reporting was fairly uniform across the districts. There was some variation between male and female respondents on both radio listening (58 percent of men compared with 44 percent of women) and newspaper usage (37–28 percent).

Group Participation

More organized communities—those better able to mobilize citizens for collective action—should be better able to condition their political support for incumbents on incumbent performance with respect to the delivery of local infrastructure financing. Keefer, Hasnain, and Menzies (2013) find that wards reporting more respondent activity in community and social groups are indeed significantly more likely to report new infrastructure. This reflects substantial variation across wards and districts in the extent of social capital.

The survey made a distinction between statutory local associations, such as landowner associations, and other local bodies. Sixty-four percent of respondents stated that they were active in the latter type of local group (school boards, producer cooperatives, or churches), and about half stated that these groups met on a weekly basis. Unsurprisingly in highly religious Papua New Guinea, church participation was by far the most common group in which respondents said they were active (45 percent of respondents), followed by youth groups (22 percent of respondents), women's groups (43 percent of female respondents), and sports clubs (17 percent of respondents). Chuave, in the Highlands, was the only district that had limited group activity, with only 12 percent of respondents stating that they belonged to a group. Table 8.3 displays the range of group participation across districts.

The survey yields several indications that group activity is a meaningful sign of collective action. First, social fragmentation can be a significant deterrent to collective action. Within wards, a key source of fragmentation is along kinship or clan lines. If group activity facilitates collective action in a ward, then it should

Table 8.3 Group Membership
Percent

District	Active in a group[a]	Frequency of group meeting		
		Weekly	Monthly	Other
Namatanai	92	62	15	23
Kairuku-Hiri	85	30	40	30
North Fly	57	64	13	23
Kokopo	60	20	47	33
Chuave	12	31	15	54
Usino Bundi	46	44	18	38
Goroka	59	41	44	15
Koroba–Lake Kopiago	57	68	14	18
Maprik	90	37	8	55
Overall	64	47	23	30

Source: Based on survey data.
a. Producer cooperative, school board, hospital board, microfinance organization, church, youth group, women's group, or sporting club.

be the case that groups include members from multiple clans. If one acknowl-edges the inherent difficulties in defining these categories and the different conceptions of "clan" that likely exist between respondents, it is still notable that 59 percent of respondents stated that two or more clans belonged to the group (respondents were asked this about one particular group they mentioned), and 25 percent stated that more than 10 clans participated.

A second indication that groups are meaningful indicators of collective action is that the majority of respondents (90 percent) stated that "big" financial deci-sions of the group were made by multiple people. Similarly, 84 percent stated that that all members of the group are involved in voting for the leaders of these groups, and 90 percent stated that the group leaders tell members how much money they spent and in what areas. Therefore, not only is participation in com-munity groups high, but also these groups appear to be run in a reasonably democratic and transparent manner.

Voting Behavior

The survey documented that politics as usual in Papua New Guinea is clientelist and that the currency of electoral competition is the delivery of narrowly tar-geted private benefits in exchange for electoral support. In the survey, 95 percent of males and 92 percent of females of voting age reported voting in the 2007 elections. Consistent with clientelist electoral transactions, they reported that ballot secrecy was low and variable. Thirty percent of respondents answered that their ballot was not secret and that other individuals could see or hear how they cast their vote. Districts varied widely in the answer: from a low of 11 percent of respondents in Chuave who claimed that others could observe their vote, to a high of more than 60 percent in Namatanai and Goroka.

Table 8.4 Views of Candidate to Whom First Preference was Given in 2007 Elections

| District | First preference candidates | | | | |
	Had personal interaction	Were related to respondent	Brought projects to area	Gave gifts	Received cash for votes?
Namatanai	73	20	26	21	3
Kairuku-Hiri	69	40	30	23	5
North Fly	88	46	43	37	9
Kokopo	90	42	24	9	0
Chuave	85	46	38	27	47
Usino Bundi	64	42	14	50	0
Goroka	62	40	17	29	21
Koroba–Lake Kopiago	62	32	11	52	38
Maprik	97	76	45	29	6
Overall	75	40	27	32	47

Source: Based on survey data.

The survey provides other, even more direct evidence of the importance of clientelist strategies of electoral mobilization. As shown in table 8.4, 75 percent of respondents stated that they personally knew their most preferred candidate (the candidate they allocated their first preference vote to in Papua New Guinea's Limited Preferential Voting system) and 40 percent said that they were related to this candidate. A large number of respondents, 32 percent, reported that their preferred candidate had provided them with gifts.

Sizable interdistrict variation was also observed on a related question, where respondents were asked whether they themselves received cash payments from candidates. Although overall, 47 percent of respondents stated they received cash for votes (21 percent of men and 9 percent of women), the numbers varied from none in Kokopo and Usino Bundi to 38 percent and 47 percent in Koroba–Lake Kopiago and Chuave, respectively (both in the Highlands).[5]

The Determinants of Infrastructure Allocation

The remainder of the analysis investigates more rigorously whether the formal institutions introduced by local government reform, and in particular the institutional arrangements for allocating local infrastructure, have a large effect on allocations. Our concern, here, is not whether particular ward characteristics *cause* wards to receive more infrastructure.[6] Instead, we examine the relative correlation of two kinds of ward attributes with ward infrastructure. One set of ward attributes defines the political influence of the ward, including the ward's relationship to the MP. The other set defines the ward's relationship with the formal institutional arrangements for infrastructure allocation (for example, the JDPBPC). The first set of attributes should have a small association with ward infrastructure to the extent that the second set of attributes, the formal institutional arrangements for infrastructure allocation, are binding.

Table 8.5 Correlates of Functional New Projects

Dependent variable: Presence of new project	Personal contact with MP (1)	Cash for vote (2)
MP has visited the ward	0.169* (0.0752)	0.135 (0.0857)
Respondent received cash to vote for a candidate in last election	n.a.	−0.821* (0.365)
A ward development committee is active in the ward	0.247 (0.242)	0.311 (0.221)
Knows who chair of JDPBPC is	−0.0860 (0.718)	0.0146 (0.647)
Knows what the JDPBPC is	−0.230 (0.724)	−0.230 (0.687)
Count (number) of common household assets	0.526 (1.745)	0.414 (1.505)
Does household have cash income?	0.916 (0.765)	1.048 (0.833)
Does household raise cash crops?	−0.0837 (0.203)	0.00491 (0.276)
Does household have cash income from nonagricultural activities?	−0.115 (0.293)	−0.0485 (0.324)
Housing quality (bush, semi-permanent, or permanent)	−0.380*** (0.112)	−0.456*** (0.125)
Does respondent earn a salary?	0.261 (0.833)	0.325 (0.832)
Is respondent a farmer?	0.795 (0.817)	0.961 (0.805)
Is respondent self-employed?	0.678 (1.098)	0.933 (0.973)
Number of observations	44	42
R^2	0.42	0.47
Number of districts	9	9

Source: Based on survey data.
Note: Robust standard errors, clustered by district, are in parentheses; estimates are based on ordinary least squares with district fixed effects. JDPBPC = Joint District Planning and Budget Priorities Committee; MP = member of parliament; n.a. = not applicable.
***$p < 0.01$, *$p < 0.1$

Table 8.5 reports estimates of regressions that allow us to disentangle the relative associations of the two different sets of ward characteristics from the presence of a new project in the ward. A number of ward characteristics define its political influence independent of the formal institutions of local government. Has the MP visited the ward? And, were ward residents likely to be targeted with vote-buying? These variables capture the usual elements of political competition in Papua New Guinea and should matter less to the extent that the formal local government institutions have a binding effect on infrastructure allocation. If they do not have a binding effect, then infrastructure allocation is determined by MPs. Decision making by MPs is then influenced by their relationship to a ward (for example, whether they have visited it) and their perception whether infrastructure provision is the best way to mobilize support in the ward (for example, whether it is more efficient to mobilize residents instead through vote-buying).

In contrast, if the formal institutional arrangements matter most, then ward knowledge of those arrangements, and ward compliance with them, should be highly correlated with whether wards report new projects. To capture whether the formal institutional features of the process are relevant for infrastructure finance, the regressions in table 8.5 therefore control for average respondent knowledge of the JDPBPC and the chair of the JDPBPC and for the presence of a WDC.

The regressions also control for various measures of household wealth and income. Wards with richer households are likely to have more influence over MPs. However, they are also likely to be able to better navigate the formal system of infrastructure allocation through the JDPBPC. In part because nearly all households and wards are poor, these variables have no robust association with infrastructure allocation. One immediate conclusion from table 8.5, regardless of the particular regression that one considers, is that formal arrangements for the allocation of infrastructure projects are, by and large, irrelevant. Respondents' knowledge of the institutions for allocating project funds (of the JDPBPC and the identity of its chair) is entirely uncorrelated with whether wards have new projects. Although wards must, formally, establish a WDC to be eligible for project grants, the presence of a WDC is also insignificantly related to new projects, with the exception of column (2). In other words, there is no sign that the formal institutional arrangements for infrastructure allocation play any role at all in determining which villages receive new projects.

In contrast, variables that capture politics as usual are highly significant. The regression in column (1) shows that MP visits are, by themselves, somewhat significantly associated with new projects. Column (2) introduces a direct measure of clientelism, whether respondents reported receiving money for their votes. It is *negatively* associated with the presence of a new project. As Keefer, Hasnain, and Menzies (2013) explain, MPs optimize the resources at their disposal: in wards where they cannot easily buy votes, they supply infrastructure. Keefer, Hasnain, and Menzies (2013) also show that wards with greater group activity—greater capacity to act collectively—are likely to exert greater leverage on the political process and extract greater resources from it. That analysis shows that both church and nonchurch activity are highly significant predictors of whether wards report new projects.

The results in table 8.5 indicate, therefore, that politics as usual continues to matter much more for infrastructure allocation compared with the formal institutions of local infrastructure allocation. One might have expected the reforms, which formally increased local participation in allocation decisions, (a) to improve the actual capacity of communities to act collectively and to defend their own interests or (b) to increase the weight given to developmental criteria and to local preferences in allocation decisions. To the extent that the new institutional arrangements matter little, it is unlikely that these deeper objectives have been achieved.

For example, communities least exposed to the most clientelist form of electoral mobilization—vote-buying—are also the most likely to benefit from new infrastructure projects. Ideally, then, new formal institutional arrangements would have made it more difficult for politicians to reduce infrastructure allocations to constituencies where they preferred to buy votes. The evidence suggests that this has not happened.

Conclusion and Policy Implications

Ideally, by simply adopting different formal institutional and organizational arrangements, countries would be able to shift the incentives of decision makers toward a more pro-development stance. The decentralization of responsibility for infrastructure spending has the potential to be a catalyst for just such a shift. However, new de jure institutions are nested in a preexisting political setting. On the one hand, incumbent political actors shape the institutions to their advantage; on the other hand, de jure innovations may not disrupt the relationship between incumbent politicians and voters. The evidence from Papua New Guinea (and elsewhere) indicates that both of these issues are key and are revealed only when the political constraints on de jure reforms are explicitly analyzed.

One objective of policies to transfer resources to local communities is to ensure that the most deserving communities are prioritized or, at least, to ensure that allocations are made according to the preferences of local communities rather than the electoral strategies of national politicians. The Papua New Guinea experience has demonstrated two lessons in this regard. First, development strategies must pay more attention to the details of de jure innovations. Subtle rules governing LLGs and the JDPBPCs serve to reinforce the dominance of the MP and traditional modes of interaction between MPs and their constituencies. Different rules, such as increasing the presence of community representatives and limiting the agenda-setting power of the MP on the JDPBPC, although not sufficient to ensure greater local determination of infrastructure allocations, appear to be necessary. We cannot exclude, however, that tighter de jure restrictions on the MP's influence over infrastructure allocation could precipitate more informal efforts to circumvent the restrictions, such as Litschig (2012) reports in Brazil, a much less clientelist setting.

Second, however, as suggested by the results from Keefer, Hasnain, and Menzies (2013), a highly robust determinant of whether communities report new infrastructure projects is whether the communities exhibit greater capacity for collective action. This condition implies that measures to increase the capacity of communities to act collectively should play an important role in any effort to increase community influence over the allocation of infrastructure resources.

There could be merit in developing additional accountability and feedback measures to link MPs and the district development committees that they chair more closely with citizens. These procedures could include relatively straightforward measures to increase transparency, such as policies to publicize JDPBPC allocations, budgets, and meeting minutes in the newspaper, on the radio, and on church notice boards and at other community points. More involved measures such as performance monitoring and citizen and community scorecards, participatory budgeting, and expenditure tracking have been implemented in many countries, but they remain largely absent from the service delivery landscape in Papua New Guinea.

However, measures such as these are more likely to succeed in communities that already exhibit greater capacity for collective action—a characteristic that seems, according to Keefer, Hasnain, and Menzies (2013), to vary significantly across wards in Papua New Guinea. Nevertheless, it is difficult for donors to promote collective action at the local level. Until such capacity emerges, future programs might target grants directly to wards, such as block grants to WDCs.

On the one hand, such grants might be based on objective development criteria that do not require collective action by wards. On the other hand, ward councilors seem likely to be responsive to ward residents. They are already well known by both men and women. Residents concerned about poor (or nonexistent) service delivery are significantly more likely to register these concerns with ward councilors than with other authorities. Such grants could be tied to matching grants to LLGs and districts to encourage collaboration across wards and better integration between levels of government. A process of direct grants would have to consider means of mitigating potential costs, such as a weakening of links (and associated oversight and implementation support) between provincial and district officials and the wards.

These implications do not touch on the question of how program design can best encourage wards to make good use of infrastructure funds. The analysis in Keefer, Hasnain, and Menzies (2013) indicates that better-organized wards are more likely to attract funds, but the data do not allow us to discern whether they are also better able to use them efficiently. Still, it seems most likely that reforms aimed at supporting those wards with limited group activity should both improve their capacity to attract infrastructure resources and use it efficiently to produce actual infrastructure.[7]

The analysis reported here, and its recommendations, were well received by the donor community in Papua New Guinea. However, though the recommendations flow directly from our analysis of the difficulties of strengthening local government in Papua New Guinea, and although such strengthening is a priority, the recommendations have not been easy to implement. In a country like Papua New Guinea, donor participation in the implementation of such recommendations is essential, both to facilitate technical support and to drive the process forward in an environment where political incentives to strengthen local governments are weak. Yet during and since the study, Papua New Guinea has seen ever-increasing natural resource rents and a corresponding reduction in government reliance on donor advice and funding. These factors have slowed implementation of the policy advice that flows from the political economy analysis we conducted.

Notes

1. In addition, there is one Autonomous region (Bougainville) and the National Capital District.

2. K 1 = US$0.40 (approximately). See Allen and Hasnain (2010).

3. Generally "he," although there are now three women in parliament.

4. This research was a collaboration between the Papua New Guinea Institute of National Affairs, academics from the Australian National University, and the World Bank. The survey was implemented by a team of Papua New Guinean researchers. Research of this type invariably presents challenges, many of which were amplified in this case (including translating interview questions and concepts across multiple languages and contexts, the remoteness of many research localities, security issues, and the challenges of implementing a mixed-methods research methodology within a limited time frame).

5. The amount of cash reported was also significant, averaging (though with huge interdistrict variation) K 1,300 per respondent, or about five months of per capita income in 2007. These are very high amounts, but in mining districts, elected positions have a very high value. Some evidence from the Philippines suggests that there, as well, vote-buying is especially lucrative in mining areas.

6. Keefer, Hasnain, and Menzies (2013) conclude, however, that a ward's ability to act collectively makes it more likely that politicians will allocate infrastructure to the ward.

7. Our data describe whether wards have new projects, but note nothing about how much these projects cost and how large the infrastructure allocations were to the wards. These are critical issues, as well. We cannot exclude the possibility, for example, that the results in table 8.5 tell us the determinants of wards that were most likely to turn infrastructure resources into actual projects. However, the field work revealed no perverse relationship between these two variables; that is, the field work suggests that wards that are most likely to have infrastructure projects are also most likely to receive infrastructure funding.

Bibliography

Allen, Mathew, and Zahid Hasnain. 2010. "Power, Pork and Patronage: Decentralisation and the Politicisation of the Development Budget in Papua New Guinea." *Commonwealth Journal of Local Governance* 6 (July): 18.

Hanson, Luke, Bryant Allen, Michael Burke, and Timothy McCarthy. 2001. *Papua New Guinea: Rural Development Handbook*. Canberra: Australian National University.

Kalinoe, Lawrence. 2009. "A Review of the OLPLLG [Organic Law on Provincial Governments and Local-level Governments]: The New Ireland Provincial Government Experience 2002–2007." Unpublished paper, Port Moresby.

Keefer, Philip, Zahid Hasnain, and Nicholas Menzies. 2013. "How Does Community Collective Action Affect the Mobilization Strategies of National Politicians? Vote-buying versus Infrastructure Provision in a Clientelist Country." Development Research Group, World Bank, Washington, DC.

Khemani, Stuti. 2007. "Does Delegation of Fiscal Policy to an Independent Agency Make a Difference? Evidence from Intergovernmental Transfers in India." *Journal of Development Economics* 82 (2): 464–84.

Litschig, Stephan. 2012. "Are Rules-Based Government Programs Shielded from Special-Interest Politics? Evidence from Revenue-Sharing Transfers in Brazil." *Journal of Public Economics* 96: 1047–60.

Mansuri, Ghazala, and Vijayendra Rao. 2013. *Localizing Development: Does Participation Work?* Washington, DC: World Bank.

May, Ron. 2004. *State and Society in Papua New Guinea: The First Twenty-Five Years.* Canberra: ANU E Press.

Schady, Norbert R. 2000. "The Political Economy of Expenditures by the Peruvian Social Fund (FONCODES), 1991–95." *The American Political Science Review* 94 (2): 289–304.

CHAPTER 9

Strengthening Local Service Delivery in the Philippines: The Use of Political Economy to Craft Bank Operational Strategies

Yasuhiko Matsuda

Introduction: Decentralization and Development Challenges in the Philippines

Composed of more than 7,000 islands and with as many as 175 local dialects, the Philippines is one of the most geographically diverse nations in the world. Although the central government has established firm control of most of the national territory, geographic disparity and diversity as defining features of the Philippine state make some form of decentralization a fact of life. From a development perspective, the effectiveness of local government units (LGUs) as providers of key public services becomes a high priority.

The current form of decentralization in the Philippines follows the passage of the 1991 Local Government Code (LGC). The LGC devolved a number of sectoral functions such as health, agriculture, and social welfare to LGUs—while curiously retaining basic education at the central level—and assigned for each level of LGU (province, city or municipality, and barangay [village]) revenue sources by a combination of intergovernmental transfers (a revenue sharing arrangement called Internal Revenue Allotment [IRA]) and each level's own source tax and nontax revenues.

The passage of the LGC was a major political landmark in the Philippines, coming in the wake of the collapse of the Marcos dictatorship by "People Power" in the mid-1980s. The code represented another form of democratizing trend and reflected the optimism that engulfed the country. Democratically elected

---

local chief executives (LCEs) were expected to be more responsive than rulers of the past to citizens' needs and demands through functional electoral processes. These hopes notwithstanding, the process of devolution has since remained incomplete.

A number of studies that have examined the LGC (for example, Llanto 2009; Manasan 2004) have pointed out a variety of structural problems emanating from both its design and its implementation. A majority of LGUs remain heavily dependent on fiscal transfers from the national government, which in turn dampens their incentive to invest in raising their own revenues, often a prerequisite for effective democratic accountability and service delivery. Horizontal and vertical imbalances persist in revenue assignments because of both inefficient allocation of taxing authorities (for example, limited taxation by province despite its larger expenditure needs) and the distribution formula of the IRA, which is unresponsive to the spending needs of LGUs.[1]

The LGU structure is highly fragmented into large numbers of relatively small jurisdictions at each of the three levels—80 provinces immediately below the national government, 143 cities and about 1,500 municipalities below the provinces, and more than 40,000 barangays below the cities or municipalities, each with its own elected executive and legislature (box 9.1).[2] Furthermore, parochial politics that often encourage feuding local political clans to settle their disputes not by election but by agreeing to carve out respective bailiwicks have led to further proliferation of LGUs, thereby exacerbating the geographic fragmentation and reduced economies of scale in provision of public services.

The Philippines has yet to develop a reliable system for measuring and tracking service delivery performance of LGUs, but available evidence suggests the quality of local services is uneven across LGUs. Although some cities and provinces have established solid reputations as islands of good governance with

---

Box 9.1 Levels of Subnational Governance

The Philippines has the following levels of subnational governance:

- *Province*—Immediately below the national government. The entire national territory, except Metro Manila, is organized into 80 provinces.
- *City or municipality*—Provinces are divided into cities and municipalities. There is a total of 143 cities and about 1,500 municipalities in the national territory.
- *Barangays*—All cities and municipalities are further divided into barangays. There are a total of 40,000 barangays in the national territory.

In addition, the Philippines archipelago is subdivided geographically into three broad divisions: Luzon in the north, Visayas in the middle, and Mindanao in the south (map B9.1). These divisions denote geographic areas, but are not themselves administrative levels.

---

box continues next page

Box 9.1 Levels of Subnational Governance *(continued)*

Map B9.1 Subnational Governance Levels, the Philippines

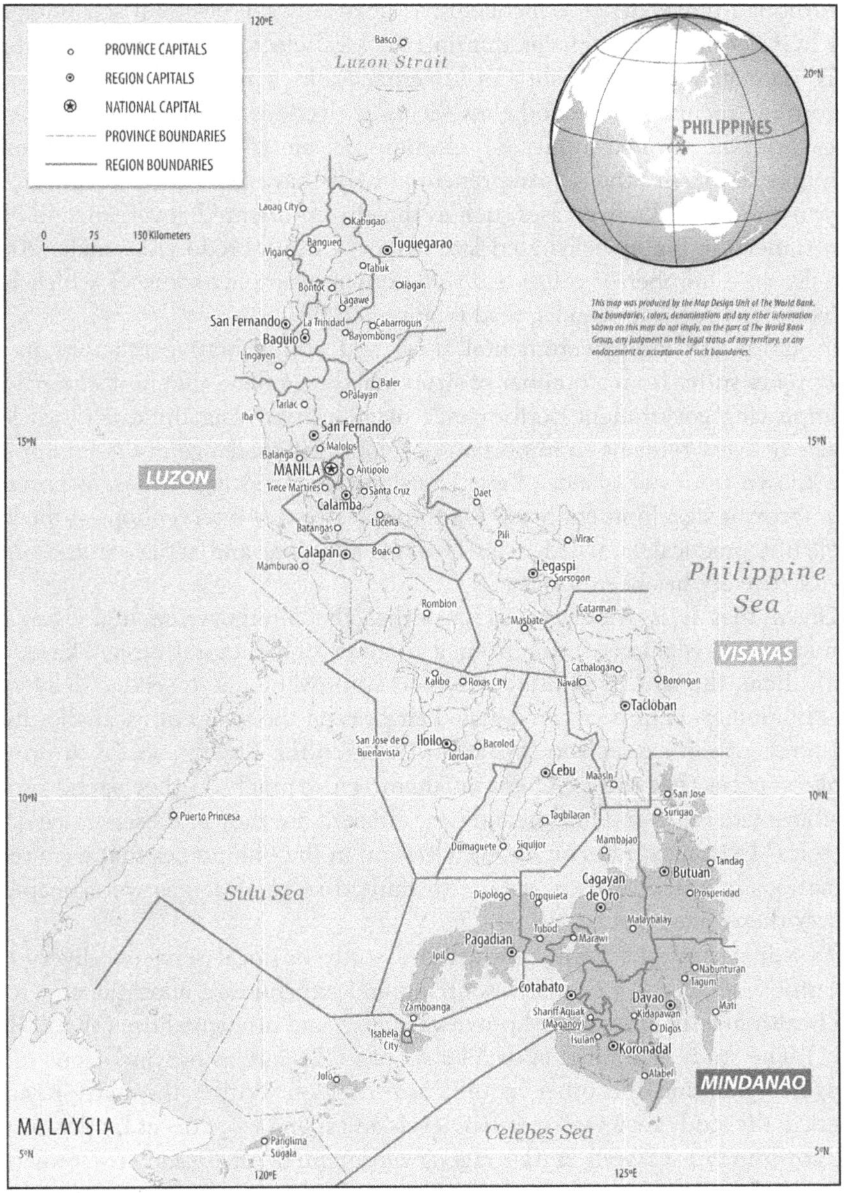

Source: Map number: IBRD 40244, August 2013.

progressive and reform-minded chief executives at their helms, many localities are still dominated by traditional political dynasties with limited accountability to their local constituents.

Although the evidence is inconclusive, links between electoral accountability and LGU performance appear thin in that local electoral outcomes are apparently unrelated to the quality of governance. In a number of LGUs, poor-performing incumbents nonetheless secure reelections relatively easily, thereby suggesting the limited utility of elections as an accountability mechanism (Capuno 2008). In others, entrepreneurial LCEs have led local innovations, not only in a few well-known cases such as the citizen-oriented governance in Naga City under the highly celebrated late mayor Jesse Robredo (Kawanaka 2002), but also in a number of other less well-known examples, some of which have actively been replicated and spread (Capuno 2008).

In short, the intergovernmental fiscal and administrative relations in the Philippines suffer from a number of structural design flaws that limit the efficacy of improving government performance overall. Improving the quality of local service delivery remains an important development challenge in the Philippines. The known stories of islands of good local governance suggest there is potential for improving development prospects through effective interventions at the local level. But practical knowledge on how to stimulate and replicate good local service delivery has been scarce.

Given that it is widely recognized that the intergovernmental fiscal and administrative relations suffer from a number of structural design flaws, the World Bank thought its efforts to support improvements to service delivery in the Philippines required more detailed analysis on the issues of fiscal allocations and levels of service delivery. What do LGUs in the Philippines do to provide public services that the LGC assigns them? How much do they spend on key functions like roads and health, and how efficient are they in these service delivery roles? Existing studies on decentralization in the Philippines that have relied on nationally available fiscal data with limited sectoral details were unable to answer these questions.

As a first step, the Bank conducted a study on local service delivery that undertook detailed reviews of resourcing and expenditure allocations in roads and health in a small sample of provinces, cities, and municipalities (World Bank 2011). The study examined in detail a set of LGUs in two provinces, one in the Visayas region and the other in the Luzon region. Within the two provinces selected, the study reviewed resource levels and spending patterns by the provincial government, as well as the city government of the respective provincial capital (which is independent of the provincial administration) and one or two municipalities. The findings of this study and its key technically focused policy recommendations are summarized in the second section of this chapter.

As a second step, given that not all technically desirable reforms are always politically feasible, the World Bank followed up on this study with a political economy analysis (PEA). This analysis examined the incentives LGUs face for providing adequate road and health services. The results of this PEA are presented in the third section of this chapter, and the operational recommendations resulting from the analysis are discussed in the fourth section. This chapter concludes with a discussion of the Bank's ongoing efforts in the Philippines to use PEA to inform operations.

Background: Unpacking the Challenges Facing Local Service Delivery

This section provides a summary of the findings and the key resulting policy recommendations that are focused on how resource allocations could be improved from a technical perspective. This summary offers a more granular picture of the problems faced by local service delivery.

Local Roads

On local roads, insufficient funding for the costs of devolved services (for example, costs to maintain local roads) has often been raised as a key constraint to better service delivery. The resourcing and expenditure study confirmed this view, revealing highly uneven levels of service provision across levels of LGUs and among the same types of LGUs. The middle column in table 9.1 shows the formula-based shares of the general purpose transfer IRA across the four types of LGUs while the second column indicates the shares of local roads.[3] The data clearly indicate that the levels of IRA funding are not directly related to the share of roads the LGUs are required to maintain. For example, cities and municipalities are assigned large shares of the total IRA resources but have relatively few local roads under their responsibility. By far, the greatest gap between resources and need is at the level of barangays to which the greatest share of the local road networks is assigned.

Furthermore, data on the selected LGUs analyzed in detail (table 9.2), which take into account both IRA allocations and own resources, suggest that even among the same type of LGUs, the available resources relative to the length of the road network vary greatly. For example, the total length of the provincial road network in the province in the Visayas region is more than twice the total length of the provincial road network the Luzon region but the latter has a significantly larger IRA allocation as well as higher own revenues. This imbalance translates

Table 9.1 Local Government Code: Vertical Distribution of IRA versus Distribution of Local Roads

Percent

LGU level	IRA formula share	Local roads as a share of total road networks in Philippines (2000)
Provinces	23	16
Cities	23	4
Municipalities	34	9
Barangays	20	71

Source: JICA–DPWH 2003.

Note: IRA = Internal Revenue Allotment; LGU = local government unit.

Problem-Driven Political Economy Analysis • http://dx.doi.org/10.1596/978-1-4648-0121-1

Table 9.2 Case Study LGUs: 2003–07 Income per Kilometer

Case study LGU	Land area, 2000 (km²)	Population, 2007 (thousands)	LGU local roads (km)	IRA (real 1985 pesos, thousands)		Total income (real 1985 pesos, thousands)	
				Total	Per km	Total	Per km
Province A	4,117	1,230	971.4	452,743	466	499,955	515
Province B	8,926	1,647	428.1	633,076	1,479	839,918	1,962
City A	33	92	66.6	106,369	1,597	203,840	3,061
City B	83	236	20.0	173,954	8,698	297,209	14,860
Municipality A1	76	44	6.7	24,284	3,624	43,140	6,439
Municipality A2	34	18	6.2	14,553	2,347	18,462	2,978
Municipality B	245	128	11.9	58,853	4,946	75,215	6,321

Source: Official web sites of the respective local government units, Engineering Offices of the respective local government units, the Local Budget Preparation Forms of the respective local governments units.
Note: "A" LGUs are located in the Visayas region. "B" LGUs are located in the Luzon region. IRA = Internal Revenue Allotment; LGU = local government unit; km = kilometer; km² = square kilometer.

into the Luzon region having nearly four times as large an income per kilometer (km) of road as does the Visayas region. Similar discrepancies are observable between the two cities and, to a lesser extent, among the three municipalities in the sample.

In addition to supporting the contention that divergent service levels follow unequal distribution of revenues, the study also revealed that LGUs adopt strategies for enhancing the level of resources available to the roads sector beyond what they choose to allocate from IRA. LGUs can lobby national government agencies (NGAs) to allocate discretionary funds to finance roads. This effort generally means turning to the Department of Public Works and Highways (DPWH), which implements road projects with funding from the Priority Development Assistance Fund (PDAF; so-called congressional pork-barrel funds[4]). As a consequence of the uneven allocation of NGA funds, the province in Luzon, for example, was able to spend only a very small fraction (2 percent) of its total budget on roads over the four-year period that the study examined, yet it still outspent the province in Visayas per km of road nearly eightfold because it received significantly greater NGA funding for its provincial road network. At the city level, the provincial capital in the Visayas region received greater NGA funds, but had far fewer LGU resources relative to the extent of its road network. Again, this imbalance resulted in much higher spending per km of road in the provincial capital located in the Luzon region (see table 9.3).

The study notes that in relative terms, NGA funding is most important for barangays, whose road networks are considered a no man's land. Because barangays lack financial capacities to maintain their own roads, other government levels step in at times and locations of their choosing. National government spending on barangay roads is remarkably consistent across our sample cities and municipalities (except for one municipality in Visayas). This observed pattern is consistent with anecdotal evidence that funds for barangay roads are often spread among a large number of barangays in similar amounts (for example, allocations of 1 million pesos [₱] or ₱500,000 regardless of the needs).

Table 9.3 Case Study LGUs: Expenditures versus Income, 2004–07

Road class	LGU income per km (real 1985 pesos, thousands)	Road and bridge expenditures as percentage of LGU expenditures	Road and bridge expenditures per km (real 1985 pesos, thousands)					
			LGU expenditures		NGA expenditures		Total expenditures	
			LGU roads	BGY roads	LGU roads	BGY roads	LGU roads	BGY roads
Provincial roads								
Province A	418	14	55	—	12	—	67	—
Province B	1,588	2	29	—	495	—	524	—
City and municipality roads								
City A	2,471	7	171	0	25	34	196	34
City B	12,163	10	745	171	14	33	760	204
Municipality A1	5,270	2	73	1	0	30	73	31
Municipality A2	2,436	4	23	3	0	5	23	9
Municipality B	5,118	2	63	1	11	36	74	38

Source: Provincial and City Engineering Office Accomplishment Reports for Luzon city; Local Budget Preparation Form No. 152 and the Statements of Allotments, Obligations, and Balances of the respective local government units for the remaining areas.
Note: "A" LGUs are located in the Visayas region. "B" LGUs are located in the Luzon region; — = not available; BGY = barangay; LGU = local government unit; km = kilometer; NGA = national government agency.

Key technical policy recommendations that emerged from this study centered on rearranging both administrative and fiscal aspects of intergovernmental relations for the road sector. First, the study recommended that the government clarifies administrative responsibilities over barangay road networks by assigning them either to cities and municipalities that are relatively well-funded for their own spending needs or to the national government that currently implements the majority of barangay road projects through DPWH. Second, the study called for reforms to the intergovernmental fiscal arrangements by (a) mitigating the vertical and horizontal imbalances in fiscal capacities among LGUs; (b) strengthening incentives and technical capacities for local road planning, budgeting, data collection, and management; and (c) strengthening accountability for local road service provision. Both of these sets of reforms would involve amendments to the LGC. As a possible supplementary measure, the study suggested using conditional block grants for local road construction and maintenance, although it stopped short of proposing specific details. Nor did the study probe the question of how such grants would be compatible with the prevailing political incentives that include a mutual dependence of national and local politicians.

Health

A particular issue in health is the relative underprovision of local health services, especially by cities and municipalities that are in charge of primary care. Centrally available data (shown in the columns "National average" in table 9.4) show that subnational levels of government allocate relatively small shares of their total spending on health. The exceptions to this pattern are the provinces because of the large costs that maintenance of provincial hospitals entails. Generally in

Table 9.4 Case Study LGUs: Expenditures by Functional Categories, 2003–07

	Provinces			Cities				Municipalities			
	National average	Visayas Region	Luzon Region	National average	National average (non-NCR)	Visayas Region	Luzon Region	National average	Visayas A1	Visayas A2	Luzon B
Average annual expenditure (real 1985 pesos, thousands)	76,439	95,594	176,258	91,215	56,143	40,046	68,966	6,356	8,553	3,055	13,629
Share of annual expenditure (%)	100.0	100.0	100.0	100.0	100.0	100.0	100.0	100.0	100.0	100.0	100.0
General public services	35.0	37.5	28.6	41.4	43.0	54.1	43.4	51.7	43.8	53.3	40.1
Debt service	2.6	0.9	1.4	4.5	4.9	9.5	5.2	1.7	7.6	0.0	1.7
Economic affairs	16.9	29.9	13.0	16.4	18.0	22.0	21.8	13.3	20.0	12.4	24.7
Transport and other infrastructure	—	16.7	7.5	—	—	14.4	17.7	—	7.2	5.4	17.5
Health	18.6	20.1	39.4	7.6	7.0	7.8	6.3	8.1	17.1	9.2	11.8
Housing and community amenities	1.3	0.9	0.7	3.4	2.2	5.6	0.4	1.2	8.9	16.4	6.8
Social protection	1.6	4.0	2.9	2.3	3.0	3.0	5.4	3.1	3.3	3.2	9.4
Education	5.0	3.1	10.6	10.9	6.7	5.8	15.0	3.4	2.4	1.2	4.6
Other purposes	21.6	4.5	4.9	18.0	20.1	1.7	7.6	20.0	4.6	4.2	2.8
Annual expenditure per capita (real 1985 pesos, thousands)	87	78	107	346	301	434	292	165	192	170	106
General public services	30	29	31	144	130	235	127	86	84	90	43
Economic affairs*	15	23	14	57	54	96	64	22	38	21	26
Health	16	16	42	26	21	34	18	13	33	16	13
Housing and community amenities	1	1	1	12	7	24	1	2	17	28	7
Social protection	1	3	3	8	9	13	16	5	6	5	10
Education	4	2	11	38	20	25	44	6	4	2	5
Other purposes	19	4	5	62	60	7	22	32	9	7	3

Note: ₱1,000 (1985) ~US$54. — = not available; NCR = National Capital Region. "Other purposes" incorporated expenditures for environmental protection; peace and order; and recreation, culture, and religion.
*Includes roads and other infrastructure.

LGU budgets, the catchall categories of "General public services" and "Other purposes" dominate the allocations (see table 9.4).[5] Although the statistics do not allow us to identify the exact nature of spending covered under these categories, the spending sometimes includes large public investment projects such as construction of city or municipal halls.[6]

More disaggregated data collected from the case study LGUs (shown in the Visayas and Luzon columns in table 9.4) reveal further variation across the LGUs. The Luzon province that allocated relatively little on roads spent a lion's share of its budget on health, at a level far higher than the health spending by the Visayas province in both absolute terms (spending per capita) and as a share of its total spending. This expenditure on health was because the Luzon province runs a tertiary hospital, whereas the Visayas province does not. The cities and the municipalities in the sample, with the exception of the Visayas A municipality that runs its own municipal hospital, spent relatively little on health, preferring to prioritize general public services, economic affairs, and housing and community amenities.

The study also found weak functioning of institutional mechanisms intended to foster increased accountability of service providers to the local clientele. For example, the LGC mandates each LGU to establish a local health board (LHB) to advise the local chief executive and the local council. None of the LHBs in the case studies' LGUs met on a regular basis; at most, they met twice a year. In the Visayas city, instead of convening the entire LHB, the city health officer preferred to consult with the national Department of Health (DOH) representative and the chairman of the local council's health committee before presenting a proposal or problem to the mayor. In the Luzon city, the LHB met once or twice a year, but only city health office personnel, members of the local council, and a representative of the mayor normally attended the meetings. LCEs rarely attended meetings, and nongovernmental organizations (NGOs) were seldom present in meetings and typically acquiesced to the agenda of the rest of the LHB.[7] The LHB of the Luzon municipality did not even convene during 2003–07.

The technical policy recommendations stemming from the analysis (including on findings not reported here) focused on continued use of financial incentives and procedural requirements set by the national DOH to coordinate behavior of different tiers of LGUs and compensate for funding gaps in DOH discretionary spending among LGUs, especially between those with and without tertiary hospitals. The study was not able to go beyond qualitative assessments based on anecdotal evidence to gain understandings of the incentives of the front-line primary care provisions by cities and municipalities.

Understanding Underlying Drivers and the Feasibility of Reforms: Political Economy Constraints and Incentives

The findings on local road and health service provision pointed to the widely recognized problem of design flaws in revenue and expenditure assignments in the LGC. What the study did not reveal, however, were finer understandings of the LGUs' incentives to prioritize and provide adequate road or health services within the available resource constraints. This information pointed to two lines of political economy inquiry to supplement the findings of the detailed technical study. One political economy question is whether an overhaul of, or at least limited specific amendments to, the LGC could be politically feasible and hence a viable reform objective. The other political economy question is what prompts politicians to allocate resources for better road and health service provision at the local level. To address these questions and further deepen our understanding of operational frontiers in local service delivery improvements, the Bank conducted a set of political economy studies addressing each of these questions.[8]

This section is divided into three parts. The first examines the national-level drivers of decision making in the Philippines, the second addresses the feasibility of reforming the LGC, and finally, the third assesses the incentives for better road and health service provision.

National-Level Political Economy: The Macro Politics of Center-Local Relations[9]

The performance of local governments is embedded in the politics of center-local relations. Therefore, a proper appreciation of these relations is a prerequisite for being able to formulate a coherent and viable strategy to support improved local governance and service delivery. A first defining characteristic of the Philippine politics relevant to this chapter's topic is that it is a consolidated electoral democracy where every three years more than 40,000 jurisdictions hold elections for their executive and legislative positions.[10] Politicians constantly invest large amounts of time and resources to be elected.

Another characteristic is that the Philippines lacks institutionalized political parties with nationwide reach, coherent ideological programs and policy platforms, and internal organizational discipline. Although parties do exist, the membership tends to be fluid, with many members switching sides depending on the outcomes of particular elections (especially presidential elections). In the absence of clear and contrasting policy platforms, candidates compete on the basis of patronage, personality, and even outright vote-buying or coercion in some cases (Hutchcroft 1998; Hutchcroft and Rocamora 2003; Montinola 1999). Under these circumstances, elections often fail to serve as a credible mechanism either to punish poor performing incumbents or to reward candidates who offer credible policy platforms.[11]

A third feature that stands out in the Philippines is the role of family ties and other personal networks as the basic unit of politics (Landé 1965; McCoy 1994). Especially at the local level, politics is treated literally as a family business where elected positions in the area under the influence or control of a family or clan are shared among and passed from one family member (for example, the family patriarch) to another (for example, a son or a niece). According to the Philippine Center for Investigative Journalism, close to 200 such clans exist in the entire country, dominating local politics and, in many cases, holding positions of influence in national politics.[12] Clans use access to elected positions and the public power that comes with them as a means to expand their economic interests and, in turn, use the enlarged economic resources to further solidify their power through elections (Sidel 1999).

These stylized facts lead to the following implications for center-local relations in the Philippine politics. For politicians at the local level, winning elections and holding on to the power and largesse that elected positions offer them are often essential elements of securing their (and their clans') economic fortunes. Successful politicians create a circle of power and wealth, feeding each other to perpetuate their status in their area of influence and establish dynasties by sharing and passing on one or more elected positions among a close circle of family members (Querubin 2010). In a typical LGU that heavily depends on fiscal transfers from the national government, accessing these central resources forms a part of the core strategy for dynasty building, or mere political survival, as the case may be. In this stylized situation, stakes are high for local politicians to continue their access to public resources and power.

For politicians at the national level—many are those who have their own constituencies within their own local bailiwicks but not beyond—especially for presidential and senatorial candidates who need to gather votes nationwide, there is a critical need to establish efficient ways of capturing votes from all corners of the archipelago. Political parties scarcely play this role in the Philippines because of their organizational weaknesses. Well-entrenched local politicians serve the role of vote collectors for national politicians within their respective areas of influence. The combination of local politicians' dependence on national resources and national politicians' need to rely on local dynasties for securing votes creates strong symbiotic incentives for both national and local politicians to sustain interdependent relations.

Use of public resources by both national and local politicians is a principal tool in building and sustaining interdependent relations. At the local level, patronage and electoral considerations often dominate LGUs' decisions on how much local service to deliver to whom and to where. National politicians in turn direct fiscal resources at their disposal to electorally targeted areas and constituencies. They do so typically through local-level allies for the dual purposes of securing votes for themselves and of allowing their allies to claim electoral credits. The situation leads to an equilibrium where neither national nor local politicians, under normal circumstances, have strong incentives to suspend use of public spending, among other public resources at their disposal, for patronage-driven political purposes. Local service delivery unfolds within this political economy panorama.

Exploring the Political Feasibility of Reforming the Local Government Code[13]

There is a perception that major legislative reforms are difficult in the Philippines. Given this perception of low probability of success, the Bank has typically sought to avoid explicit support for a legislative change. According to a recent tally in a study by a political scientist, the Philippine Congress has managed to enact only about 3 percent of the bills submitted by its members in either house since 1987

Table 9.5 Bill Enactment Rates in the House of Representatives, 1987–2004

Congress/administration	National application (passed/introduced)	Enactment rate (%)	Local application (passed/introduced)	Enactment rate (%)
8th/Aquino (1987–92)	191/5,237	3.6	809/30,183	2.7
9th/Ramos (1993–95)	156/3,184	4.9	306/11,448	2.7
10th/Ramos (1996–98)	147/3,785	3.9	393/6,766	5.8
11th/Estrada (1998–2001)	67/4,197	1.6	348/8,738	3.9
12th/Arroyo (2001–04)	89/2,920	3.0	84/3,764	2.2
Total	650/19,323	3.4	1,940/60,899	3.2

Source: Kawanaka 2010.

(when the constitution created today's political structure) (Kawanaka 2010; see table 9.5). Given this context, part of the analytic effort focused on whether any amendments to the LGC as suggested by the technical analysis could be feasible.

First, Matsuda (2011) reviewed the political history of the decentralization reform in the Philippines and tried to understand (a) the context and the prevailing incentives that led to the decision to decentralize and (b) the specific content of the reform. He concluded that the specific historical conditions, such as the democratic euphoria of the immediate aftermath of the fall of the Marcos dictatorship, had played an important role in leading to the passage of the LGC, but that such conditions were no longer present.

Second, Matsuda (2011) sought lessons from other countries about conditions under which governments have tended to launch decentralization reforms such as a major political change (for example, the fall of dictators in Indonesia and Peru). He also sought lessons from countries that faced a major fiscal crisis associated with profligate subnational fiscal behavior (for example, Brazil and Colombia) and asked if similar conditions existed in the Philippines today. The answer, again, was no.

Third, Matsuda (2011) reviewed legislative activities that have occurred since the passage of the LGC in 1991 to ascertain the extent to which attempts had already been made to reform aspects of the code, as an indicator of latent demand for reforms. He then asked what changes had already been adopted and what other reform proposals with some prospect of success were still pending. Interestingly, the review of the bills showed that more than 700 bills, including some intended to address fundamental features of the LGC, had been filed since the early 1990s, of these, however, only four were passed into legislation (table 9.6). Most of those passed into law dealt with issues tangential to the design of the intergovernmental fiscal relations. For example, one law reduced the amusement tax rate LGUs could charge from 30 percent to 10 percent in an apparent bow to the local movie and other entertainment industries.

Fourth, just because the congress had not passed a major decentralization law since 1991 did not mean that it would never do so. Therefore, Matsuda (2011) attempted to conjecture the likelihood that a majority coalition might form to support one of the simpler legislative reform options: the increase in the LGU

Table 9.6 Bills Related to LGC by Category, House and Senate, 1987–2010

Congress (years)	Expenditure assignment	Tax assignment	Local capital finance	Local financial management	Omnibus amendment	Intergovernmental transfer	Total
8 (1987–91)	6/1	4/5	0/0	1/2	1/2	11/8	23/18
9 (1991–95)	17/12	14/6	1/0	4/2	0/0	9/9	45/29
10 (1995–98)	23/14	19/8	1/0	4/10	0/1	27/19	74/52
11 (1998–01)	22/5	27/8	7/1	3/1	4/0	33/10	96/25
12 (2001–04)	14/14	23/13	4/3	1/8	0/4	29/11	71/53
13 (2004–07)	14/16	34/12	2/5	0/6	0/3	28/14	78/56
14 (2007–10)	14/16	31/20	2/4	1/15	0/5	30/9	78/69
Total	110/78	152/72	17/13	14/44	5/15	167/80	465/302

Source: Matsuda 2011.

share of national revenue from the current 40 percent to a slightly higher rate.[14] It was not possible to know each and every legislator's preference, and so the study used a simple assumption: those legislators who had relatives running LGUs as LCEs and those who had been LCEs themselves and expected to return to those posts after their congressional terms ended would be more inclined to support measures to enhance LGUs' resource bases at the expense of the national government. As tables 9.7 and 9.8 show, the number of legislators who either had been LCEs themselves or had relatives running LGUs was relatively small—in the House with 286 members, the number fell short of a simple majority, although in the 24-member Senate, the number met the 50 percent +1 threshold. Even a smaller number of the members of the 14th Congress (2007–10) aspired to local elected posts in the 2010 elections. With these data, the study concluded that a voting bloc in Congress large enough to push for even a simple, pro-LGU amendment to the LGC was unlikely to emerge: the voting block that could be put together would be unable to overcome the expected strong resistance from the national government. Prospects for forging a consensus on more complex legislative options looked even weaker.

The conclusion and the implications from all these strands of investigation pointed in the same direction. As important as a fundamental reform of the LGC may be from a purely technical perspective, Kawanaka (2010) concludes that the likelihood that serious investments of our resources and efforts would result in a meaningful change was nil. A more promising entry point to strengthening local governance seems to be to support strengthening of the LGUs' incentives for service delivery within the existing fiscal framework.

Political Economy of Local Service Delivery

With regards to the second question about the LGUs' political incentives for service delivery, a pair of empirical studies on health and roads revealed an interesting contrast between the two sectors.[15] A key question is whether politicians' incentives to pursue consolidation of their positions through reelections are compatible with pro-poor service delivery. To gain insights into political

Table 9.7 Members of Congress Who Are Former LCEs or Have Relatives Who Are Former LCEs

Category	Representatives	Senators
Former LCEs	21	1
Former LCEs with relatives who are former LCEs	18	6
Members with relatives who are former LCEs	58	6
Total	97	13

Source: Matsuda 2011.
Note: LCE = local chief executive.

Table 9.8 Distribution of National Legislators by Positions Sought in 2010 Elections

Classification of national legislators	Position sought in 2010			
	LCE post (governor or mayor)	Local legislative post (vice governor or vice mayor)	Senate	President or vice president
House members (of 286)				
First term	9	1	1	—
Second term	2	1	2	—
Third term	30	6	3	—
Total	41	8	6	—
Senate members (of 24)				
Mid-term (elected 2007–13)	—	—	—	4
End term (elected 2004–10)	1	—	4	4
Total	1	—	4	8

Source: Carizo 2009.
Note: — = not applicable; LCE = local chief executive.

incentives for local service delivery, we designed and implemented original survey-based research in the province of Isabela in the northern tip of the Luzon region (map 9.1). The survey covered 1,200 households in 30 of the province's 35 municipalities. We chose Isabela because of the large observed variance in certain health outcomes after controlling for municipal incomes and poverty levels. We hypothesized that some of the unexplained variance in the health outcomes would be due to variations in political economy conditions across the municipalities.[16]

Our studies showed that politicians' incentives were not aligned directly with objective needs of communities. Those studies also showed that the observed politician behaviors in health and roads were systematically different, even though they ought to be operating on the basis of the same political incentives (that is, these are the same politicians who pursue their political gains through their actions in the health and roads sectors as well as in other areas of public and private actions). This contrasting finding, as elaborated on later in this chapter, suggests a need for differentiated approaches to pursue improvements in these sectors. In general, local politicians in the Philippines appear less interested in providing health services for political (that is, electoral) ends. As a result,

Map 9.1 Isabela Province, the Philippines

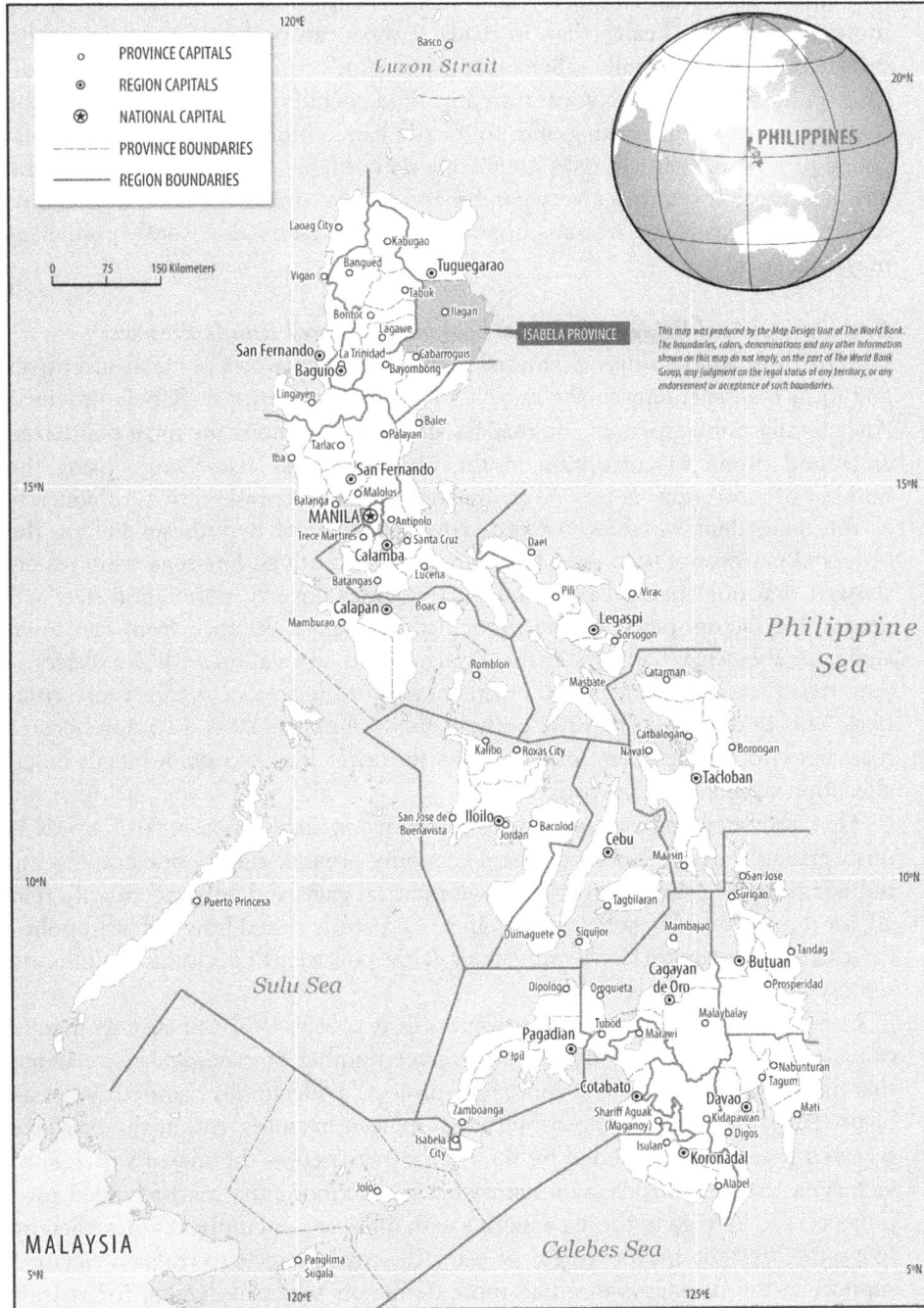

Source: Map number: IBRD 40245, August 2013.

municipalities generally underprovide health services. Ironically, however, this may mean that enhancing politicians' incentives to improve service delivery is more promising in health than in roads, if ways can be found to make health service delivery electorally salient in a given locality. In contrast, evidence indicates politicians are deeply interested in road spending but apparently for the wrong reasons—rent-seeking and political alliance building rather than public goods provision. Political risks are significantly higher in the roads sector, and any intervention requires a very careful and creative mix of additional accountability mechanisms to restrain opportunistic behaviors that some politicians may engage in.

Building Political Bridges? Political Economy of Local Roads Projects[17]

One of the paired studies examined relationships between political incentives and local road spending in the sample of 30 municipalities in Isabela province. Anecdotally, public spending on roads is known to be among the most politicized areas and prone to corruption in the Philippines (as elsewhere). Using the number of road projects funded by mayors and area representatives of congress as the dependent variables, we tested for a variety of hypotheses linking the observed patterns of road spending to political incentives. The regression results showed that objective measures of needs such as poverty, population size, and geographic factors (such as the particular barangay's distance from the town center, or *población*, had no statistically significant correlation with the observed patterns of road spending by either the mayors or the area's congress representatives. This finding is no surprise because the Philippines lacks a comprehensive road network master plan, especially at the local level, to guide needs-based allocation of spending on roads.

That the spending pattern does not follow available measures of needs is unsurprising if one follows a political economy premise that politicians allocate public resources primarily for their own political gains and only secondarily, if at all, for the supposed beneficiaries' welfare. Our study tested how different political calculations might have interacted with politicians' decisions to allocate resources for local roads.

By measuring electoral competitiveness in two ways—(a) the average margin of victory by the winner and (b) the average number of candidates—we found that mayors tended to allocate more road projects to electorally competitive areas. Figure 9.1 shows that the probability that a given barangay within the province received road projects funded by the mayor increased as the mayor's margin of victory in the previous election narrowed. Furthermore, the mayor-funded road projects tended to go to those barangays with more anti-incumbent votes, thereby suggesting that the mayors might be using the road projects to (re)gain electoral support in the barangays that had more detractors while neglecting (or at least giving lower priorities to) those where they had a more solid support base.[18]

The hypothesis that the mayors used road projects to buy votes was supported further by another result on the relationship between the propensity of the mayors to fund road projects and their terms in the office. If one of the reasons that

Figure 9.1 Road Projects and Electoral Competition

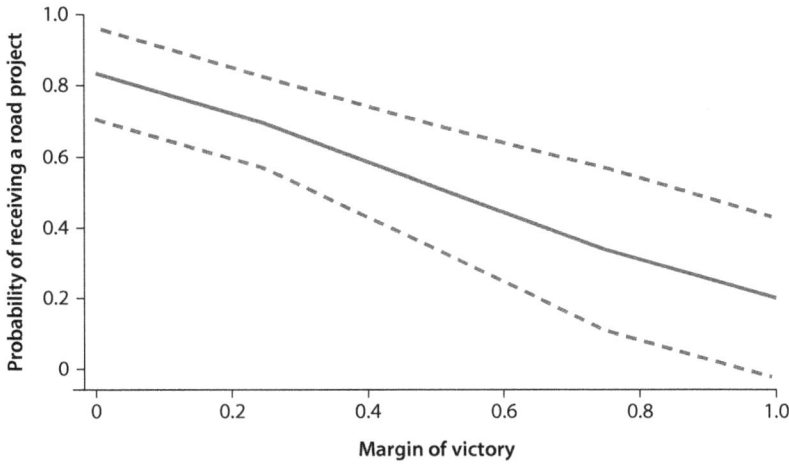

Source: Based on survey data.
Note: Margin of victory is measured as the difference in vote share between the winner and the next runner-up such that if the winner ran unopposed, the score would be 1 and if two candidates shared the exact same number of votes, the score would be 0, though highly unlikely in practice. The solid line represents the predicted probabilities of a barangay receiving road projects at different levels of margin of victory, holding all of the other variables at the mean. The dashed lines are confidence intervals that indicate the reliability of the estimates.

the mayors increased the number of road projects was to protect themselves against potential electoral vulnerability, we might find some systematic pattern, and we did. Third-term mayors were more likely to fund road projects, whereas second-term mayors were significantly less likely to do so. This finding may be because in the Philippines, third-term mayors are constitutionally banned from seeking reelection. Under normal circumstances, this situation might lead to reduced spending in politically valuable goods such as road projects because incumbents should have no electoral incentive of their own.[19] In the specific context of the Philippines' clan politics, however, elected posts are often handed down among family members or their close friends and allies. In such situations, the incumbents are likely to be endorsing their handpicked successors, who are often less politically established than the third-term mayors themselves.[20] In contrast, the same mayors who would serve a full three terms are practically on automatic pilot for reelection from their second to third term and, hence, face less incentive to buy votes with road projects. The first-term mayors who are seeking their first reelection are likely to include both those well-entrenched politicians who will go on to serve a full three terms as well as those with a more tenuous support base who will end up losing their reelection bid for the second term. Therefore, we would expect no clear relationship between the first-term mayors and their behavior in the aggregate.

Area congress members, through their PDAF, or pork barrel, are another major source of funding for works on local roads (especially barangay roads).[21] Unless the area member of congress is explicitly allied with a particular mayor, however, we would not necessarily expect the PDAF spending pattern by the representative to be statistically correlated with outcomes of the mayoral elections.[22] Our regression analysis in fact showed no such correlation.

Other results of the analysis pointed to interesting possibilities and suggested that congress members used PDAF spending (at least on roads) primarily as a means to forge political alliances in specific circumstances and also as a means of rent-seeking. First, the data showed that members of congress tended to increase road project spending in those municipalities characterized by presence of political clans. Similarly, more congress-funded road projects were found in municipalities where the mayors were allied with the congress member. Interestingly, PDAF spending on roads also increased in those municipalities where the mayors reported having alliances with other higher-tier politicians such as the governor, senators, and the president. It may be that mayors who are relative political heavy weights (that is, members of clans and well-connected to higher-tier politicians) are in better positions to attract PDAF resources.[23]

Finally, evidence showed that members of congress also directed funding for roads to municipalities where there was a hardware or construction business *owned by the mayor*. This targeted funding may occur because the presence of a mayor-owned construction company provided congress members with opportunities to receive kickbacks from infrastructure projects. Furthermore, splitting the sample according to whether the mayor and the congress member were allies revealed that a positive association between a mayor-owned construction company and congress member–funded projects was driven by cases in which the mayor and the congress member were allies. The relationship between the presence of any hardware or construction company (not necessarily owned by the mayor) and congress member–funded road projects disappeared once the mayor–congress member alliance was taken into account. The analysis leads one to conclude that congress members funded road projects only in areas where an *allied* mayor owned a construction or hardware business.

Buying Votes versus Supplying Public Goods in Health[24]

Health is one of the devolved services that LGUs are responsible for delivering. Although some aspects of local health spending such as provision of nutritional supplements, centrally mandated vaccinations, and construction of health facilities are often heavily or wholly subsidized by the national government, a broad range of primary health services are still exclusive responsibilities of the LGUs. Arguably, primary health care is the closest thing to a broad-based pro-poor public service for which LGUs in the Philippines are responsible.[25] Past research has shown that variation in several indicators of child health and development was strongly correlated with variation in the availability of health and early childhood development (ECD) services in the barangay. Research also has shown that unobserved village characteristics accounted for a large variation in ECD outcomes among barangays and reduced substantially the estimated effect of family background such as poverty and mother's education. Ghuman et al. (2005) posited that the "blackbox" of barangay fixed effects might be a reflection of local politics, especially of the presence of clientelism, reputed to be wide-spread across the Philippines but in varying degrees from one locality to another.

The analysis (Khemani 2013) tested a host of variables hypothesized to have effects on health service delivery and outcomes. These variables include house-hold size, number of children, duration of residence in the municipality, age of population, level of education, proxy measures of income and poverty (received remittances, experienced hunger, owned durable assets), access to mass media, possession of social capital and political connectivity (holding of political or public office; membership in groups; and participation in local collective action, or *bayanihan*), and so on. Similar to the findings on roads, the study also tested for associations between various measures of local politics such as the level of electoral competitiveness, the presence of entrenched clans, the economic domi-nance of the mayor, and the extent of the mayor's political affiliations. The regression results in different specifications consistently revealed that only one variable, vote-buying, had a systematic, significant, and robust correlation with a variety of measures of the quality and availability of public health services. These relationships were negative; that is, the more vote-buying, the less health services and the worse health outcomes. In barangays where more respondents reported instances of vote-buying, households had lower access to maternal health services (trained assistance at birthing) and, frequently, lower access to nutrition supple-ments. Quite strikingly, as a measure reflecting the quality of health services, village health records showed a higher percentage of young children with below-normal weight. Village data also showed fewer health workers and fewer health projects where reports of vote-buying were higher (figure 9.2). At the municipal

Figure 9.2 Health Outcomes and Vote-Buying

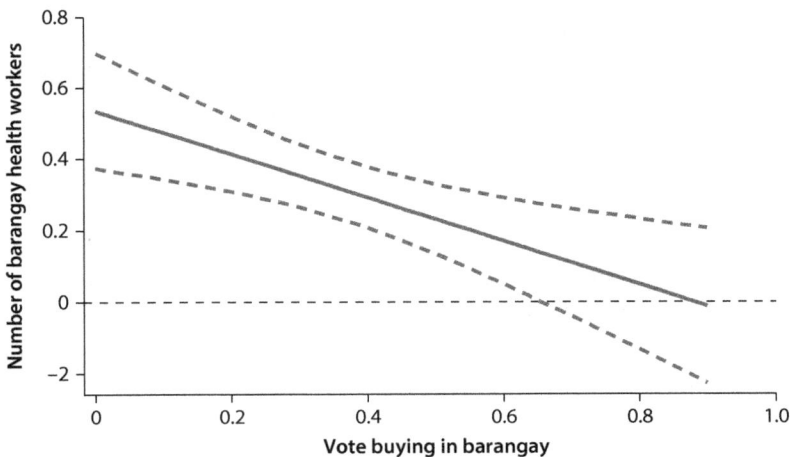

Source: Based on survey data.
Note: The solid line represents the predicted number of barangay health workers in a given barangay at different levels of reported incidence of vote-buying by the respondents in that same barangay, holding all of the other variables at the mean. The dashed lines are confidence intervals that indicate the reliability of the estimates.

level, greater reporting of vote-buying was associated with a lower proportion of municipal spending allocated to health, controlling for a host of socioeconomic and political variables.[26]

Curiously, other political variables had no systematic relationship with the measures of health service delivery. For example, following theories of democratic accountability, we might expect that, everything else being equal, the more competitive the elections, the more pressure these will put on the politicians to woo voters, including by improving service delivery (at least in certain circumstances). The results of the study showed no such relationship between health service delivery in the sample municipalities and different measures of electoral competitiveness—the number of mayoral candidates in a given municipality in a given election and the vote margin of the winning candidate. These results suggest local politicians in the Philippines (or at least in Isabela province) do not use health spending as a direct means to appeal to voters, unlike spending on roads.

Local clans are a prominent feature of the local political scenes in the Philippines. Entrenched clans, or political dynasties, are considered an anathema to democratic development and are even prohibited, in principle, in the country's constitution. However, anecdotes have suggested that the mere presence of entrenched clans is not a good predictor of the quality of governance in a given local jurisdiction. Some of the well-known reformers are themselves scions of or founders of dynastic clans. Reflecting these conflicting realities, the results of our analysis were also somewhat inconsistent. The presence of a dominant political clan in the municipality is associated with a higher access to birthing assistance but a lower access to supplements and with a higher share of municipal spending in the category containing construction projects.

Operational Implications

The empirical studies on political incentives for road spending and health service delivery have shown that politicians approach both sectors with clear political motivations as opposed to the objective of enhancing the welfare of the population. But the specific findings differ, suggesting different political uses of the two sectors by politicians.

Road infrastructure is a type of public spending that is relatively visible and easy to target to specific geographic areas and constituents. Hence, it is one of the types of government spending that political economy theorists predict to be oversupplied in clientelist settings (Keefer and Vlaicu 2008). Although the amount of public spending on local roads is insufficient compared to the massive absolute needs (partly because of the tendency to neglect routine maintenance), road infrastructure is one of the prioritized items in a typical municipal budget compared to other sectoral needs. Our results were consistent with a plausible set of expectations about politicians' behavior in the specific local context of the clientelist politics in the Philippines. That is, mayors use road projects as a means of securing votes (and probably rent-seeking, as amply supported by abundant anecdotes, although we have no data to test this hypothesis). In contrast, members of congress see road projects as a means of political alliance maintenance (because they rely more on indirect ways of securing votes by enlisting friendly mayors and barangay captains as vote aggregators) and rent-seeking.[27]

Health, in contrast, is an example of a pro-poor public service with a broad reach. It is among the high priorities of the public, especially among mothers, and yet available evidence indicates that local health services, some of which are not particularly costly, are underprovided at the local level. Our evidence shows that politicians deliberately trade off direct vote-buying with health service delivery but that they do not target health services geographically to garner votes. In other words, political incentives for providing health services, even for electoral reasons, are weak at the municipal level in the Philippines. This again is consistent with theories of clientelism that predict underprovision of broad public services, especially for the poor if they are unorganized. Politicians in a patronage-driven environment use political strategies that focus on winning political support by providing private benefits that are more easily targeted, such as relatively visible road projects. Such clientelist strategies go hand in hand with lowering the political effort toward providing broad public services such as primary health care.

So what are the operational implications of these findings? Two broad approaches take into account the central roles of clientelist politics. One is to take the prevailing political rules of the game as a given and try to maximize the welfare effect of public interventions within the existing constraints. The other is to introduce an intervention aimed at disrupting the clientelist equilibrium. The contrasting findings between roads and health, within the exact same sociopolitical and institutional context of the 30 municipalities in Isabela province, offer clues to how we might be able to devise different strategies to deal with the perverse political economy of deficient local service delivery.

Roads

The evidence suggests that politicians—mayors as well as members of congress—see road spending as a valuable political tool for the multiple purposes of securing votes from areas where the mayors receive less support, thereby cementing political alliances and capturing rents. All of these are common strategies for securing a politician's (and his or her clan's) long-term political survival. Based on our knowledge of the politics of the Philippines, it seems unlikely that incentives for vote-getting, alliance formation, and rent-seeking could be altered. Therefore, the recommended measures are to focus more on constraining some of the opportunistic behaviors through a combination of external restraints such as extensive use of mandatory information disclosure; participatory governance tools and third-party monitoring; or an intensified program of random audits by the national audit authority, Commission on Audit, as successfully demonstrated in Indonesia (Olken 2007).

One of the biggest challenges is the lack of precise information about the actual distribution of political risks across LGUs. It is logical to assume that not all

LGUs are equally politicized in their management of public resources. But it is also generally understood that road spending is among the areas most vulnerable to political use. The exact distribution of the risks across LGUs is practically impossible to measure ex ante without the kind of detailed data we gathered in this survey for each LGU in the entire country. One available means to begin to screen LGUs according to the quality of governance is to rely on proxy measures of good governance such as the Seal of Good Housekeeping of the Department of Interior and Local Governments.[28] Another option may be to encourage LGUs to conduct participatory budgeting for capital expenditures following a robust, yet simple participatory process for identifying relative needs. For example, it may be possible to extend the participatory method used in the national Community Driven Development Program to encompass all (or at least a large portion of) infrastructure spending by LGUs. Actual execution should also be closely scrutinized through third-party monitoring as well as mandatory disclosure of details of the bids and awards.

A key recommendation is to make adherence to transparency and participation measures strictly voluntary. A program of support could then use the LGUs' voluntary compliance with a stringent set of transparency and participatory requirements not as an additional risk mitigation measure but as a screening device to identify those LGUs that are less prone to political risks of the kinds identified in our study.

A complementary approach would be to take (at least some) decision-making authority away from LGUs by imposing decision criteria that are transparent and rule based. For example, it may be desirable for the national government to step in and develop technically sound plans for a portion of local road networks. For certain selected purposes, the national government could specify that at least the national government subsidies and congressional funding for local roads follow those network plans. Examples of this approach that the government has considered are local roads for promoting tourism in certain designated areas. Knowing in advance where roads are supposed to be built or repaired and with what design specifications (length, width, and so on) is essential for any third party that monitors road works. Whether the national government can actually impose and enforce such rules depends on the politics of center-local relations. But it may be feasible if applicability of such rules is limited to a subset of local roads—those that are of strategic interest to the national government's specific policy objectives such as tourism development—while still leaving a bulk of public spending on local roads to the prevailing clientelist criteria.

Health

In health, the overwhelming need is not to restrain politicians from misallocating public spending, although the efficacy of allocating available funding is, no doubt, an important consideration in any public spending. Instead, the primary challenge is to entice the mayors to spend more on high-return public health interventions such as child immunization and prenatal care services (for example, by deploying an adequate number of trained midwifes and nurses). The fact that politicians are generally less interested in health, however, may be a blessing in disguise. It means that with regard to general health, spending has not been seen as important a source of rent as have roads and other infrastructure spending. If health is less politically salient, there is in principle more room to improve technocratic targeting (for example, by using the existing National Household Targeting System that is already used to identify beneficiaries of the Conditional Cash Transfer Program) because allocating more health spending to areas where needs are the greatest is less likely to involve zero-sum trade-off with vote-getting or rent-seeking opportunities elsewhere. It may also be possible to enhance politicians' own interest in providing more (and better) health services if they realize that improving health service delivery can enhance their ability to attract support from some voters. That is, health, precisely because of its lower political salience, may be a promising ground for experimenting with an intervention to disrupt the clientelist equilibrium in local service delivery.

One possible way is to try a carefully designed information campaign to provide beneficiaries with reliable information on LGUs' performance in various aspects of health care delivery. An approach similar to one developed in Peru that ties performance assessment with a common service performance standard may be worth trying. Such an approach would be consistent with the implications drawn from theories of clientelist political competition. These theories see a key impediment to effective functioning of an electoral market in the inability of citizens to organize their demands on government around broad public goods. Whereas some of the underlying causes for such lack of coordination and organization may be deep seated, such as poverty, lack of education, or entrenched inequalities in institutions, recent experiments by civil society organizations in a diverse range of countries—from Benin to Brazil and from India to Nigeria—suggest that short-term information and advocacy campaigns can have a striking effect in shifting citizen demands (Ferraz and Finan 2008; Pande 2009, provides a review).

Information campaigns, however, do not work in every circumstance. Campaigns are unlikely to have the desired effects when, for example, citizens perceive that barriers to improving government performance are insurmountably high compared to their own ability to mobilize for change (Banerjee et al. 2006) or simply when they do not expect the government to effectively provide certain services based on their experience. The findings of the study reported here do not shed any particular light on the question of constraints to effective participation and mobilization of external pressure for LGUs to improve service delivery. But some additional information in the data collected in Isabela province provides a rationale for using expert-generated performance information as an indirect way of reducing the appeal of petty vote-buying and of mobilizing voters around relevant performance indicators that appeal to them.

The particular sample of respondents targeted by the survey—young mothers— is especially likely to care about health services; indeed, 80 percent of respondents put health in the top three services when asked to prioritize what municipalities should do, followed by 76 percent for education. In contrast, only 38 percent put cash or in-kind transfers or jobs provision in the top three. Yet, scattered bits of evidence suggest that even these respondents are constrained in evaluating municipal performance in delivering health services: their ranking of health services is not correlated with more objective indicators of access to services, for example. In several instances (about 19 percent of respondents), a household ranks municipal performance in delivering health services very high while responding on a separate question about perceptions of child health outcomes that more than half the children in the municipality are likely to be severely malnourished. Although 93 percent of respondents think the municipal administration could improve maternal and child health services, the greatest consensus on how to improve lies in the area of providing more medicines and supplements (85 percent think more medicines and supplements should be provided). Far fewer people (17 percent) think service quality or performance could be improved.

There also appears to be substantial heterogeneity in the respondents' views of what criteria to use when evaluating politicians and whether to vote for them. Although the criteria for voting cited most frequently in the top slot is performance of politicians (47.0 percent) followed by campaign promises and speeches (20.5 percent), the preferences of friends and family also matter (18 percent). It is not clear what the respondents consider as key criteria of politician performance. Furthermore, receiving gifts from candidates before the elections is one of the top three reasons for voting for them (19 percent of respondents). Interventions focusing on greater information about performance in delivering broad public goods could potentially shift more voters toward considering performance criteria in their evaluation of politicians and reduce the viability of clientelist strategies for politicians.

Our general assumption for most LGUs is that improving the quality of health service delivery is not excessively costly and hence affordable within most LGUs' current resources, although it would certainly require a degree of reallocation among spending items. If our assumption holds, then the information campaign alone might suffice to change LGU behavior, at least in some cases where the mayors are particularly sensitive to voter pressure. Here, the level of electoral competitiveness might make a difference. However, if improving health service provision requires a significantly greater injection of fiscal resources—perhaps because the particular LGU needs to construct health facilities or hire staff members—then the availability of additional resources from the national government tied to some measure of performance might be an effective supplement to the information campaign. The DOH has already been experimenting with schemes to tie its budget transfers to LGUs to predefined performance criteria. So far, these schemes are not combined with any systematic approach to coordinate voter demand for more and better services. There is a potential to design a combined scheme to strengthen LGU accountability for health service delivery in two directions: toward the citizens and toward the national government as a partial provider of critical funding.

Using Political Economy to Inform Operational Decisions: The Bank's Ongoing Efforts in the Philippines

Use of Political Economy in the Philippines Country Team

The studies described above on the political economy of decentralization and local service delivery were developed in parallel to efforts by the World Bank's Philippines Country Team (CT) to institutionalize use of PEA in its operational decison making as a part of its enhanced approach to governance and anticorruption at the country level. With the intent of mainstreaming governance concerns across the country program and portfolio, in 2009 the Philippines CT introduced an innovative internal review of proposals for Bank-financed operations with an explicit focus on governance-related risks. This procedure has its roots in the CT's recognition that weaknesses in the team's project portfolio had often resulted from political risks such as (a) weak commitment by political leaders to the proposed operation, (b) diluted effects of technocratic interventions for failure to take into account underlying political incentives, or, in a few cases, (c) corruption cases related to issues of political capture.

The procedure, called Pre-Identification Note (PIN) review, precedes the mandatory review of a Project Concept Note (PCN) and is a discussion of anticipated governance-related risks to the proposed new operation before this formally becomes part of the CT portfolio after the approval of the PCN. Both PIN and PCN review meetings are chaired by the country director, and the director's clearance is required for the team to proceed to the next phase of project preparation. The difference is that at the PIN stage, the team proposing a project has not worked out all the details of the proposed project concept. Nonetheless, the team has identified key parameters of the proposed project such as (a) the sector or the subsector, (b) the broad development objective, (c) the identity of the government agency that will execute the project, and (d) the risks related to the sector and the agency. The PIN reviews are expected to screen out project proposals that are deemed too risky from governance perspectives. Some of the PINs reviewed so far have had background political economy studies to inform their governance risk assessments.[29]

The teams are required to prepare a five-page note that describes the main thrust of the proposed operation and discusses its governance risks based on available information. Much of that information is tacit knowledge of the team members, who typically have years of engagement in the sector. In this case, some team leaders willingly sought support and advice from the Manila-based governance team to conduct background political economy studies to better inform their project identification, whereas other teams conducted discussions on governance risks without systematically studying political economy constraints in the sectors in which they operated.[30] The limited take-up of political economy studies reflects that findings from PEAs can remain challenging to integrate into the operational approaches developed by sector teams for a variety of reasons.

In those cases where background studies were conducted, the additional insights were seen to enrich the PIN review discussions and to lead to more strategic decisions by the country director. Those decisions included delaying processing of the project identification and delaying adjustments to operational design. But the cases show that the systematic incorporation of explicit political economy considerations still faces some internal incentive barriers.[31]

Operational Use of the Studies on Local Service Delivery

The two political economy studies on local service delivery described in this chapter were not prepared as background to a particular PIN review. Instead of informing a specific operational design, the studies, which made use of original survey data and took significantly longer to complete than the studies conducted for the PIN reviews, were expected to inform the World Bank's overall strategy and approach to local service delivery issues as a supplement to the more technical study also described early in this chapter. The technical study on local service delivery and the political economy studies were parts of a package of analytical studies that the CT conducted on decentralization and local service delivery from 2008 to 2010. Together, these studies provided an analytical basis for an internal local governance strategy in the Philippines.

The strategy, as prepared by a multisectoral team of Bank operational staff members working on the Philippines, offers a systematic framework to organize Bank engagements at the local level in the Philippines with strengthening of LGU accountability as a central theme. This strategy is expected to help inform the Country Partnership Strategy for the Philippines that is currently being prepared.

Notes

1. IRA is a revenue sharing arrangement that transfers 40 percent of the national taxes to the LGUs based on a clear and simple formula, but the formula ignores costs of providing devolved services and thus favors cities, and to some extent municipalities, at the expense of provinces.

2. In general, cities are larger, more urban agglomerations than municipalities, although the extent of urbanization is limited in some of the smaller cities.

3. IRA is a formula-based general purpose transfer. Each year, 40 percent of the national tax collection is distributed among the four tiers of LGUs following the formula indicated in table 9.1. Within each tier, the total amount is distributed among the LGUs based on population (50 percent), land area (25 percent), and equal sharing (25 percent). For most LGUs, IRA is the most important source of revenue, given the generally weak local revenue generation.

4. In the Philippines, each member of the lower house, elected in a U.S.-style small district, is appropriated a Priority Development Assistance Fund (PDAF) of 70 million pesos (₱) each (around US$1.6 million at the exchange rate of late 2012) for constituent services. Senators, that is, the delegates elected to the upper house, are elected on a nationwide ballot and receive ₱200 million each.

5. Data centrally available from the Bureau of Local Government Finance of the Department of Finance does not allow further disaggregation of functional categories than reported in this table. So for example, it is not possible to ascertain what share of Economic Affairs spending goes to the road sector.

6. In visits to several LGUs, the author frequently witnessed new city and municipal hall construction as the LGU's flagship public investment project.

7. Explicit provisions on the selection of an NGO representative were not included in the LGC or DOH's implementing regulations.

8. These studies have been published as World Bank Policy Research Working Papers: Matsuda (2011), Khemani (2013), and Cruz and Matsuda (2013).

9. For a more nuanced and comprehensive discussion on this topic, see de Dios (2007).

10. In the Philippines, the president and the national senators are elected by a single national constituency for a term of six years. The president cannot run for reelection, whereas senators can serve up to two consecutive terms. All the other posts (members of the national congress; provincial governors; city and municipal mayors; barangay captains; and provincial, city, municipal, and barangay council members) are elected for three-year terms and can serve up to three consecutive terms.

11. Although the Philippines is an ethnically and linguistically diverse country, voting based on ethno-cultural identities is considered not to be a defining feature of electoral behavior.

12. Querubin (2010) estimates that more than 50 percent of the national representatives to congress have relatives who have served in congress or as provincial governors in the previous 20 years.

13. Based on Matsuda (2011).

14. The LGC defines the source of the IRAs as 40 percent of the national taxes.

15. See Khemani (2013) and Cruz and Matsuda (2013) for details.

16. For lack of data, we were unable to use road sector performance as a criterion for selecting the province.

17. This section draws on Cruz and Matsuda (2013).

18. In political science parlance, this scenario could be characterized as mayors targeting swing voters. The study does not show how the mayors reward their core supporters, or how they keep the latter's allegiance. But one plausible scenario, also given our findings on the health sector, is that the mayors rely on more economical clientelism methods like vote-buying (costing around ₱500 (about US$12) per person in Naga City) to ensure votes from secure areas.

19. Of course, the incumbents could engage in electioneering to support their political allies such as party mates.

20. We often encountered numerous cases where the departing third-term mayors endorsed a politically inexperienced family member (wife, son, daughter, niece, and so on) to keep the family in the business of running the LGU.

21. PDAF is appropriated in the annual budget (General Appropriations Act). Each member of congress receives ₱70 million of discretionary funds, which can be used to fund development projects of the member's choice. Once the legislator determines the use, the fund will be transferred to the executing agency, which could be DPWH, a particular LGU, or any other government agency.

22. Our survey did not measure electoral competitiveness of congressional elections by barangay.

23. Area congress members are also more likely to fund road projects in those barangays with high rates of voting against the mayor, but only for those mayors who are allies of the congress members.

24. This section draws on Khemani (2013).

25. Another example of a broad-based pro-poor public service is basic education, but by law, this is a national government responsibility in the Philippines.

26. Anecdotes abound of reported instances of direct vote-buying in the Philippines. The most crude and apparently widespread method entails a simple exchange of cash for a voter's promise to vote for a particular candidate. Going rates reportedly vary from ₱200 (US$5) to ₱500 (US$12), depending on factors such as the type of office being sought. Given the reported prevalence of such practices, many (or most?) of the survey respondents are likely referring to this form of direct vote-buying. However, a variety of other means to nullify the effects of secret ballots have been reported in the Philippines, including frequent use of violence and intimidation. Indeed, the only municipality in our sample for which a significant number of household respondents reported witnessing violence during elections is also the municipality with the highest reported instances of vote-buying. Therefore, some of the respondents possibly were referring to other less direct methods of vote-buying.

27. From a public welfare perspective, politically directed projects still can have positive pro-poor effects, for example, if the mayors are receiving fewer votes from poorer barangays and are directing road projects preferentially to gain more votes from them (Schady 2000). But it is obvious that rent-seeking always results in net welfare loss.

28. The Seal of Good Housekeeping is a policy introduced by the national Department of Interior and Local Governments (DILG) to encourage LGUs to disclose a set of basic financial and planning documents to the public and to achieve certain levels of internal governance such as establishment of an internal audit office, institutionalized partnerships with NGOs, and so forth. However, the seal does not capture information that matters most for judging how the LGUs are likely to use fiscal resources—namely, reporting on expenditure execution and service delivery in a standardized format. As of late 2011, DILG had awarded the seals to 25 of the 80 provinces, 39 of the more than 150 cities, and 395 of the more than 1,600 municipalities.

29. As of January 2013, the CT had carried out 11 PIN reviews. Of the 11 proposed operations, 8 were allowed to move to the next phase of the project cycle, that is, the PCN review.

30. A background political economy study is not mandatory because a study imposed on a team that is not convinced of its need is unlikely to be a wise use of resources. In principle, the risk of not having a political economy study as background is borne by the team itself.

31. For a long time, however, many Bank staff members have taken political economy considerations into account based on their tacit knowledge. But because such knowledge is not collectively scrutinized openly and systematically and because the quality of individual insights varies, explicit use of such insights in informing the Bank's operational decisions has been infrequent.

Bibliography

Banerjee, Abhijit, Rukmini Banerji, Esther Duflo, Raschel Glennerster, and Stuti Khemani. 2006. "Can Information Campaigns Spark Local Participation and Improve Outcomes? A Study of Primary Education in Uttar Pradesh, India." Policy Research Working Paper 3967, World Bank, Washington, DC.

Capuno, Joseph J. 2008. "The Spread of Local Government Innovations under Decentralization: A Case Study of Four Philippine Provinces." Paper presented at the 11th International Convention of the East Asian Economic Association, Manila, November 15–16.

Carizo, Jay. 2009. "Policy Champions and Political Incentives: The Prospects of IRA Reform in the 14th Philippine Congress." Unpublished background paper.

Cruz, Cesi, and Yasuhiko Matsuda. 2013. "Building Political Bridges with Roads: Political Linkages, Electoral Strategies, and Local Roads Projects." Draft working paper, World Bank, Washington, DC.

de Dios, Emmanuel. 2007. "Local Politics and Local Economy." In *The Dynamics of Regional Development: The Philippines in East Asia*, edited by Arsenio M. Balisacan and Hal Hill, 157–203. Northampton, MA: Edward Elgar Publishing.

Ferraz, Claudio, and Frederico Finan. 2008. "Exposing Corrupt Politicians: The Effect of Brazil's Publicly Released Audits on Electoral Outcomes." *Quarterly Journal of Economics* 123 (2): 703–45.

Ghuman, Sharon, Jere R. Behrman, Judith B. Borja, Socorro Gultiano, and Elizabeth M. King. 2005. "Family Background, Service Providers, and Early Childhood Development in the Philippines: Proxies and Interactions." *Economic Development and Cultural Change* 54 (1): 129–64.

Hutchcroft, Paul D. 1998. *Booty Capitalism: The Politics of Banking in the Philippines*. Ithaca, NY: Cornell University Press.

Hutchcroft, Paul D., and Joel Rocamora. 2003. "Strong Demands and Weak Institutions: The Origins and Evolution of the Democratic Deficit in the Philippines." *Journal of East Asian Studies* 3: 259–92.

JICA-DPWH (Japan International Cooperation Agency–Department of Public Works and Highways). 2003. "Roads in the Philippines." JICA-DPWH, Tokyo.

Kawanaka, Takeshi. 2002. *Power in a Philippine City*. Tokyo: Institute of Developing Economies.

———. 2010. "Interaction of Powers in the Philippine Presidential System." IDE Discussion Paper 233, Institute of Developing Economies–Japan External Trade Organization, Chiba, Japan.

Keefer, Philip, and Razvan Vlaicu. 2008. "Democracy, Credibility, and Clientelism." *The Journal of Law, Economics, and Organization* 24 (2): 371–406.

Khemani, Stuti. 2013. "Buying Votes vs. Supplying Public Services: Political Incentives to Under-Invest in Pro-Poor Policies." Policy Research Working Paper WPS 6339, World Bank, Washington, DC.

Landé, Carl H. 1965. *Leaders, Factions, and Parties: The Structure of Philippine Politics*. Vol. 6 of Southeast Asia Studies, Yale University, Monograph Series. New Haven, CT: Yale University.

Llanto, Gilbert M. 2009. "Fiscal Decentralization and Local Finance Reforms in the Philippines." Discussion Paper, Series No. 2009–10, Philippine Institute for Development Studies, Manila.

Manasan, Rosario G. 2004. "Local Public Finance in the Philippines: In Search of Autonomy with Accountability." Discussion Paper, Series No. 2004–42, Philippine Institute for Development Studies, Manila.

Matsuda, Yasuhiko. 2011. "Ripe for a Big Bang? Assessing the Political Feasibility of Legislative Reforms in the Philippines' Local Government Code." Policy Research Working Paper 5792, World Bank, Washington, DC.

McCoy, Alfred W., ed. 1994. *An Anarchy of Families: State and Family in the Philippines.* Madison, WI: University of Wisconsin Press.

Montinola, Gabriella. 1999. "Politicians, Parties, and the Persistence of Weak States: Lessons from the Philippines." *Development and Change* 30 (4): 739–74.

Olken, Benjamin A. 2007. "Monitoring Corruption: Evidence from a Field Experiment in Indonesia." *Journal of Political Economy* 115 (2): 200–49.

Pande, Rohini. 2009. "Can Informed Voters Enforce Better Governance? Experiments in Low-Income Democracies." Working Paper, Kennedy School of Government, Harvard University, Cambridge, MA.

Querubin, Pablo. 2010. "Family and Politics: Dynastic Persistence in the Philippines." Massachusetts Institute of Technology, Cambridge, MA.

Schady, Norbert R. 2000. "The Political Economy of Expenditures by the Peruvian Social Fund." *American Political Science Review* 94 (2): 289–304.

Sidel, John. 1999. *Capital, Coercion, and Crime: Bossism in the Philippines.* Stanford, CA: Stanford University Press.

World Bank. 2011. "Philippines—Study on Local Service Delivery." Policy Note 68625, World Bank, Washington, DC. http://documents.worldbank.org/curated /en/2011/03/16275262/philippines-philippines-study-local-service-delivery.

About the Contributors

Editors

Verena Fritz is a Senior Governance Specialist with the Poverty Reduction and Economic Management unit in the World Bank's Africa region and previously was with the Public Sector Governance anchor. She coauthored *Problem-Driven Governance and Political Economy Analysis: Good Practice Framework* (World Bank 2009) and led the World Bank's political economy community of practice for several years. In various capacities, she has also worked on state building and on public financial management reforms. Her current focus is on governance and political economy diagnostics for World Bank programming and operations in various African countries and on new approaches to public sector and governance reforms in ways that seek to engage productively with political economy dynamics and to combine the delivery of results with strengthening institutions. She holds a doctorate from the European University Institute and has authored a range of reports, articles, and books on issues related to her areas of work.

Brian Levy is the Academic Director of the Graduate School of Development Policy and Practice at the University of Cape Town and a Senior Adjunct Professor at the School of Advanced International Studies, Johns Hopkins University. His 23-year career at the World Bank included five years as leader of the Africa Public Sector Reform and Capacity Building unit and four years as head of the secretariat responsible for the design and implementation of the World Bank Group's Governance and Anticorruption strategy. He was the founding champion of the World Bank's political economy community of practice. He has authored, coauthored, and coedited numerous books and articles on the interactions between public institutions, the private sector, and development. He has a doctorate in economics from Harvard University.

Rachel Ort is a consultant with the Public Sector Governance and the Social Development units at the World Bank. Her research interests include the political economy of decentralization and collective action in fragile states. Before joining the World Bank, she spent a year in Botswana on a U.S. Fulbright grant researching the relationship between civil society and democratization. She has worked with the AFL-CIO Solidarity Center in Johannesburg, South Africa; managed workforce training and grant development for a nonprofit in northern

Nevada; and worked as a community organizer on U.S. political campaigns, where she coordinated fundraising, voter registration, and get-out-the-vote efforts. She holds a master's degree in international development and international economics from the Johns Hopkins School of Advanced International Studies.

Authors

Katherine Bain is Senior Governance Specialist with the World Bank. She has led regional work on the demand for good governance in Africa as well as country-, sector-, and project-level political economy work on Ghana, Nigeria, and Tanzania. She holds a master's degree in social policy and planning in developing countries from the London School of Economics and Political Science.

Dorothée Chen is a Health and Social Protection Specialist at the World Bank. Her interests are in public financial management and political economy in the Social Protection and Health sectors, and she has worked in the Middle East and North Africa region and in Africa. She holds several master's degrees, including in political science from Sciences Po (Paris).

Zahid Hasnain is a Senior Public Sector Specialist at the World Bank, where he has been since 2002. His interests are in public financial management, public administration, and political economy, and he has worked on projects on Indonesia, Mongolia, Pakistan, Papua New Guinea, and the Philippines. He holds a doctorate in political science from the University of Chicago.

Chris Jackson is Lead Rural Development Specialist at the World Bank in the East Asia and Pacific region. His research interests include the political economy of development, and he has previously worked in Africa and South Asia. He holds a master's degree and a doctorate from the University of Nottingham.

Philip Keefer is a Lead Research Economist in the Development Research Group of the World Bank whose work has appeared in journals ranging from the *Quarterly Journal of Economics* to the *American Political Science Review*. His research focuses on collective action, political credibility, and economic development in democracies and autocracies.

Judith Krauss is currently a Doctoral Researcher at the Institute for Development Policy and Management, University of Manchester. Previously, she worked in North Africa and the Middle East for the German Agency for International Cooperation (GIZ), which encompassed a secondment to the World Bank's Rabat office beyond her principal engagement in a GIZ forest policy and climate change program.

Marco Larizza is a Public Sector Specialist in the Poverty Reduction and Economic Management Network in the Africa region of the World Bank and a Visiting Fellow at the Institute for Democracy and Conflict Resolution, University of Essex. His research interest focuses on the interaction between political institutions and provision of public goods and service in postconflict countries.

Andrea Liverani is currently with the World Bank working on sustainability issues. He has published on the political economy of climate policy, state building in North Africa, and aid effectiveness and evaluation systems. He has a master's degree and a doctorate from the London School of Economics and Political Science.

Yasuhiko Matsuda is a Senior Public Sector Specialist with the Poverty Reduction and Economic Management unit in the World Bank's East Asia and Pacific region. He holds a master's degree from the University of Kansas and a doctorate from the University of Pittsburgh both in political science. His research interests include the political economy of institutional reform.

Nicholas Menzies is a Justice Reform Specialist at the World Bank, where he works on institutional reform of the justice sector and mainstreaming of justice into development programming. Prior to the World Bank, he worked for indigenous communities in Australia, Cambodia, and Papua New Guinea. He has a bachelor of arts degree and a bachelor of laws degree from the University of Sydney and a master's of public policy degree from the Hertie School of Governance, Berlin.

Patricia Palale is the Deputy Chief Executive Officer, Administration for Millennium Challenge Account, Zambia Limited. Previously, she worked with the World Bank as a Public Sector Management Specialist focusing on Malawi and Zambia. She has 20 years of experience in internal and external audit, public financial management reforms, policy formulation for the public service, and project management.

Carlos Rufin is Associate Professor of International Business at Suffolk University's Sawyer Business School. His research focuses on the relationship between business and the state in developing countries, particularly with regard to private sector initiatives aimed at responding to the needs of the urban poor in these countries.

Miguel Eduardo Sánchez is the Country Economist of the World Bank for the Dominican Republic. He holds a master of science degree in political economy of development from the University of London, School of Oriental and African Studies, and his research interests range from the institutional determinants of foreign direct investment and capital flows to taxation, public expenditure allocation, and public service delivery in countries with a weak social contract.

Roby Senderowitsch, a graduate of Johns Hopkins University, is Program Manager of the Global Partnership for Social Accountability at the World Bank. Previously he served as Country Manager of the World Bank in the Dominican Republic. He focuses on building coalitions for change, anticorruption, and performance-based management of public institutions.

Kavita Sethi is a Senior Transport Economist with the Africa Transport unit at the World Bank, where she manages projects in Ghana and Sierra Leone. She has a particular interest in institutional economics and ways in which infrastructure sectors can be enabled to contribute more effectively to the reduction of poverty.

Vivek Srivastava is a Lead Public Sector Specialist at the World Bank. He is an economist with an interest in institutional reform, decentralization, service delivery, and postconflict countries. Before joining the Bank, he was a civil servant with the Indian Administrative Service for over 20 years. He holds a doctorate in economics from Boston University.

David W. Throup holds a doctorate in African history from Cambridge University. He teaches African politics at the Johns Hopkins School of Advanced International Studies and The George Washington University and serves as Senior Associate at the Center for Strategic and International Studies. He is particularly interested in the politics of Botswana, Ghana, Kenya, Sierra Leone, Tanzania, and Zimbabwe.

Davide Zucchini is a public sector consultant at the World Bank. During the past ten years he has worked in both the public and the private sector on governance issues, political economy, and economic and public financial management. He holds a master's degree in public and social policies from Pompeu Fabra University/Johns Hopkins University.